gospel

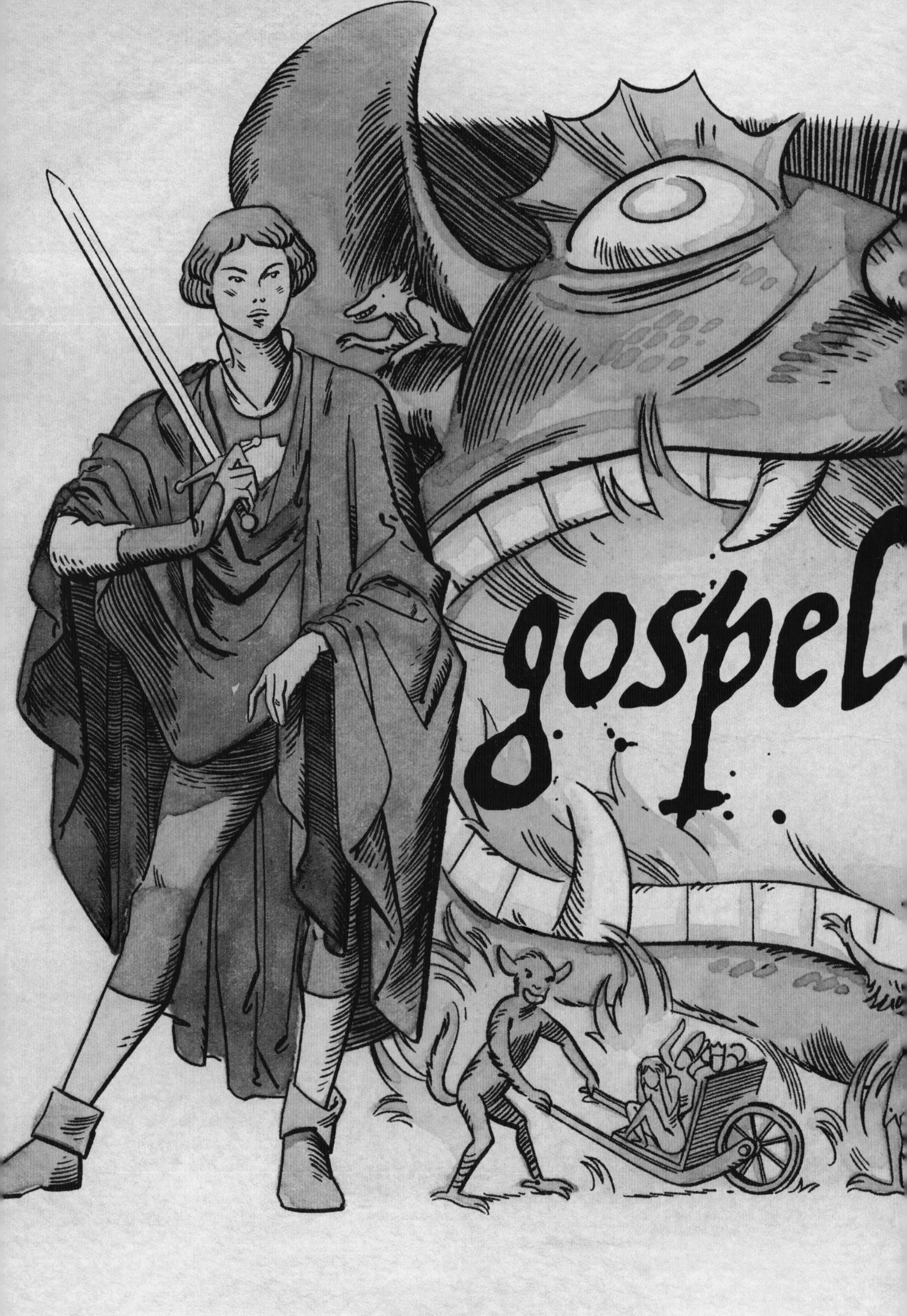
gospel

For Claire

Story & Art
by Will
Morris

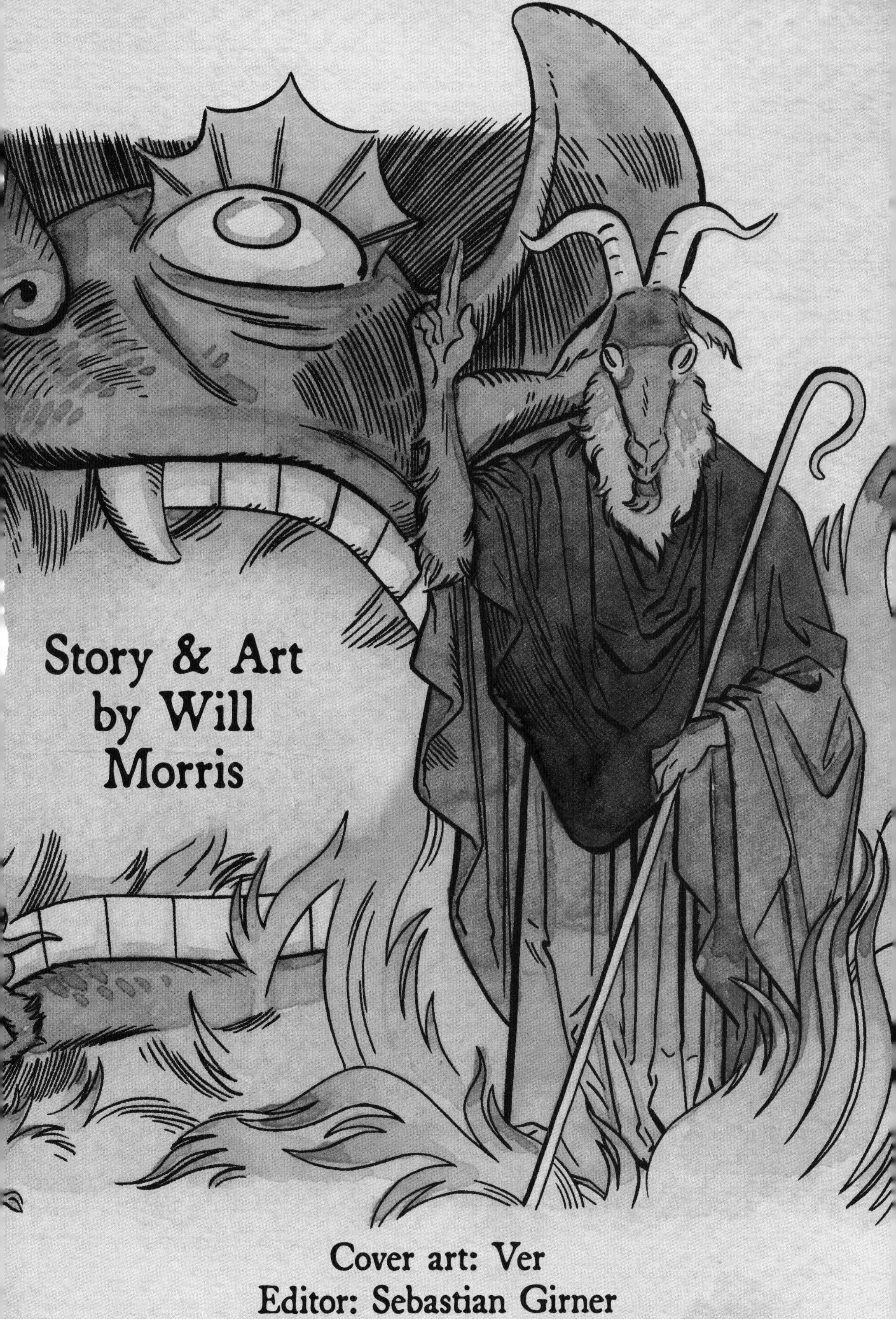

Cover art: Ver
Editor: Sebastian Girner
Colour assist: Holley McKend
Readers: Colette Aburime
and Aimee Lockwood

GOSPEL. First printing. June 2023. Published by Image Comics, Inc. Office of publication: PO BOX 14457, Portland, OR 97293. Printed in the USA. For international rights, contact: foreignlicensing@imagecomics.com. ISBN: 978-1-5343-2599-9.

Chapters two and four of this work contain material taken from *How to Use Your Enemies* by Baltasar Gracián and Jeremy Robbins (translator), used under license from Penguin Books Ltd.

CREATIVE SCOTLAND
ALBA | CHRUTHACHAIL

LOTTERY FUNDED

Chapter 1

England, 1538

It is a period of turmoil. A period of new technology, of progress colliding with old ways, of haves and have-nots, of unbridled ambition and greed.

For over 900 years dynasties have risen and fallen, but one thing has endured: the Church of Rome's power over England's religious life.

Until that is, King Henry VIII wished to remarry.

And the Pope refused him.

The king's advisor, Thomas Cromwell, seized the opportunity. Harbouring ambitions to radically reform the church, he targeted its excesses, corruption and great wealth.

With the Pope's power in England severed, the foundations of daily life and people's hopes beyond it were rocked. Holy mass conducted in Latin and the influence of priests were undermined by bibles printed in English and growing literacy. Saints and purgatory were dismissed. Feast days and festivals scratched from the calendar. Shrines and icons of worship defaced. Holy houses and monasteries plundered.

Unrest followed in Northern and Southwest England. People feared for their souls and the souls of the nation. Many quietly resisted. A few were prepared to act.

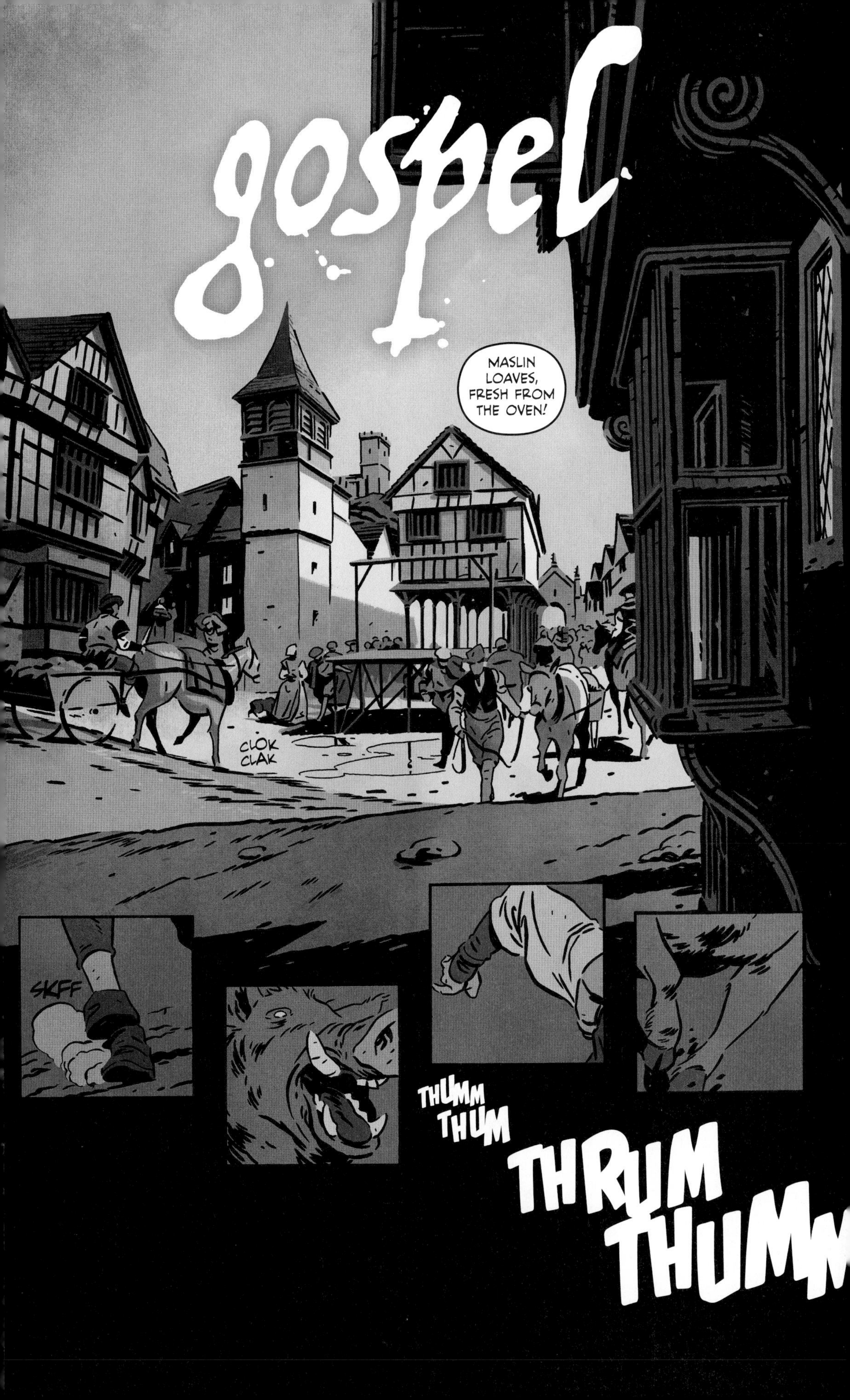
gospel
MASLIN LOAVES, FRESH FROM THE OVEN!
CLOK CLAK
SKFF
THUMM THUM
THRUM THUMM

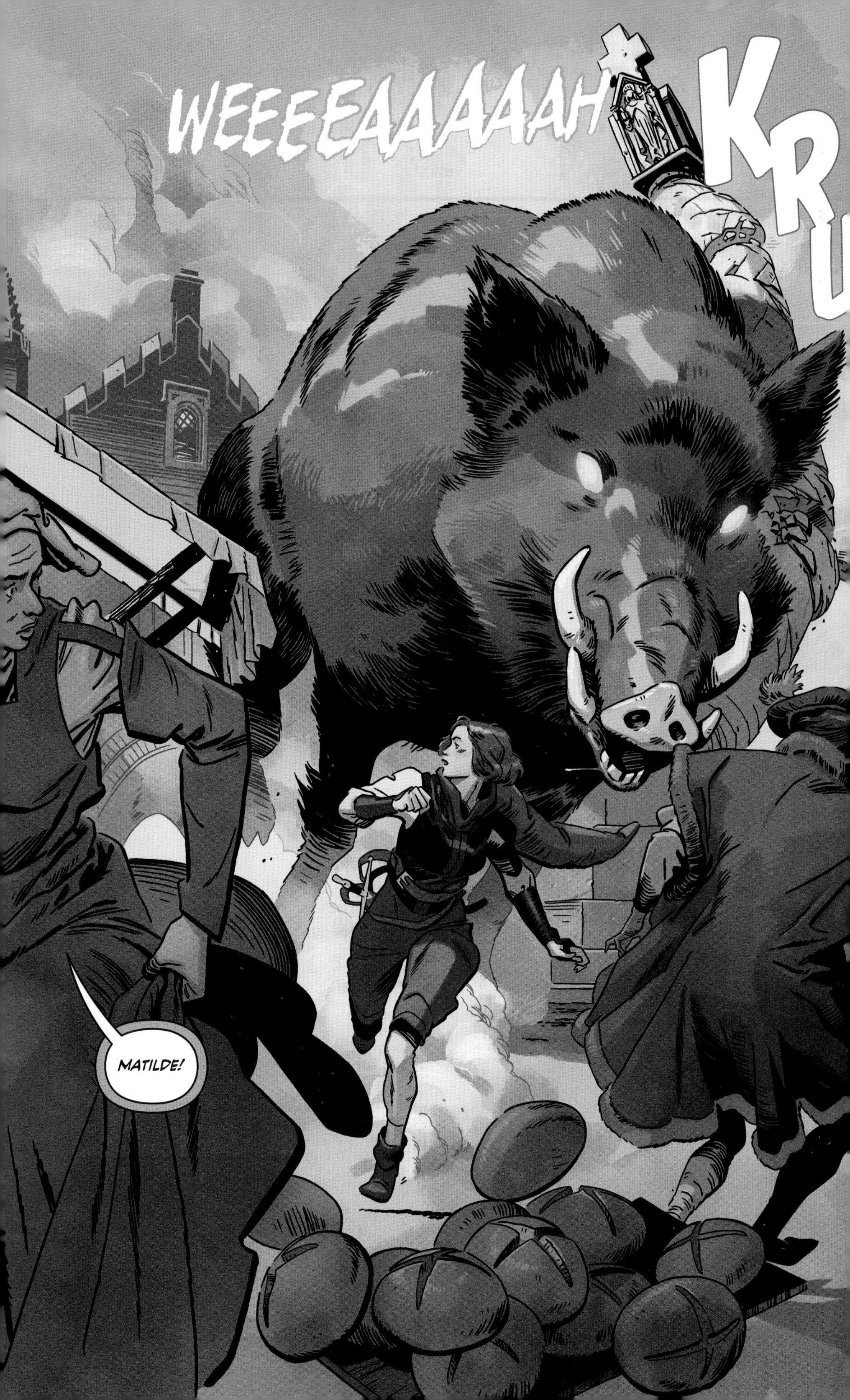
WEEEEAAAAAAH
KRU
MATILDE!

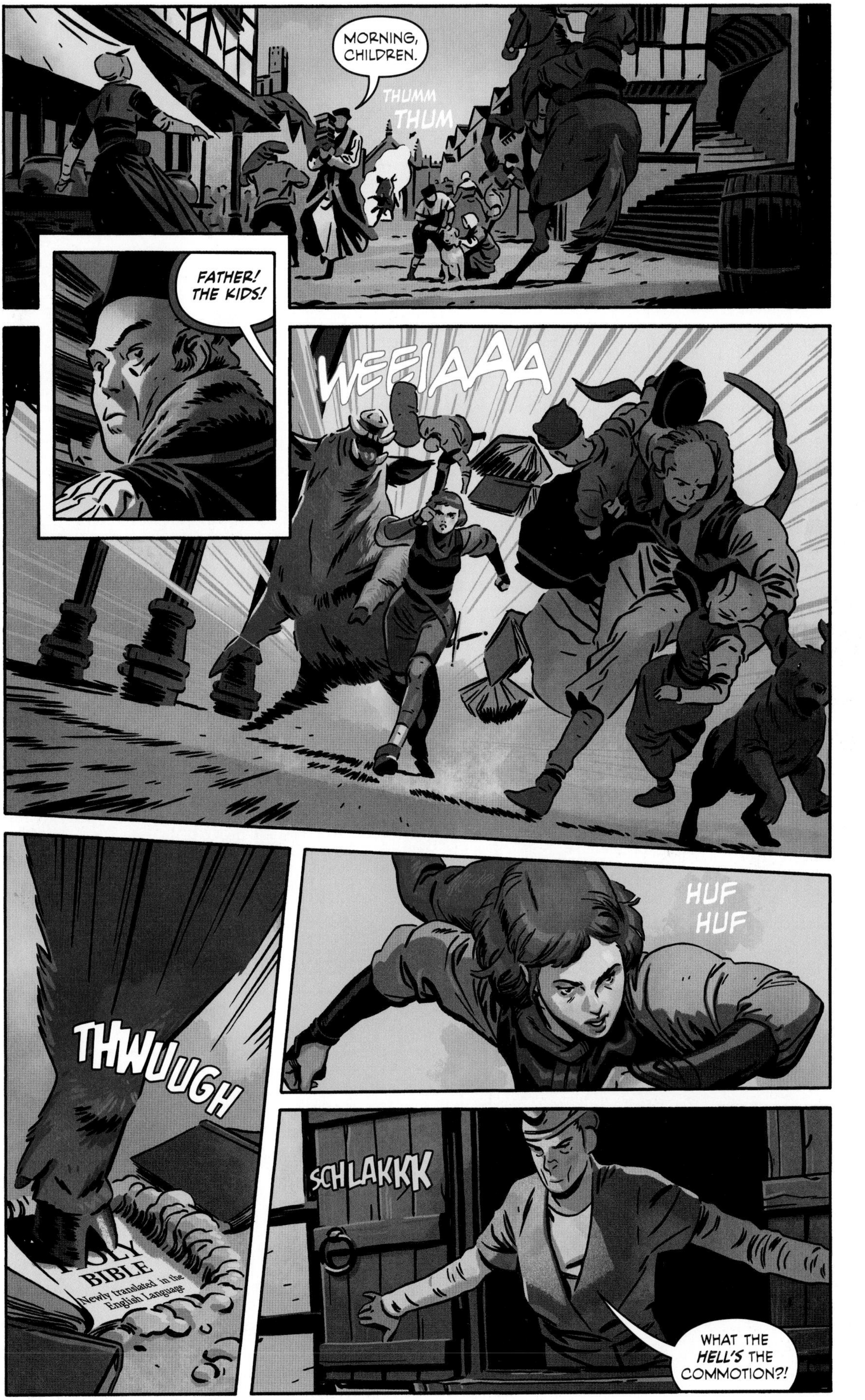
MORNING, CHILDREN.
THUMM THUM
FATHER! THE KIDS!
WEEIAAA
THWUUGH
HOLY BIBLE
Newly translated in the English Language
HUF HUF
SCHLAKKK
WHAT THE HELL'S THE COMMOTION?!

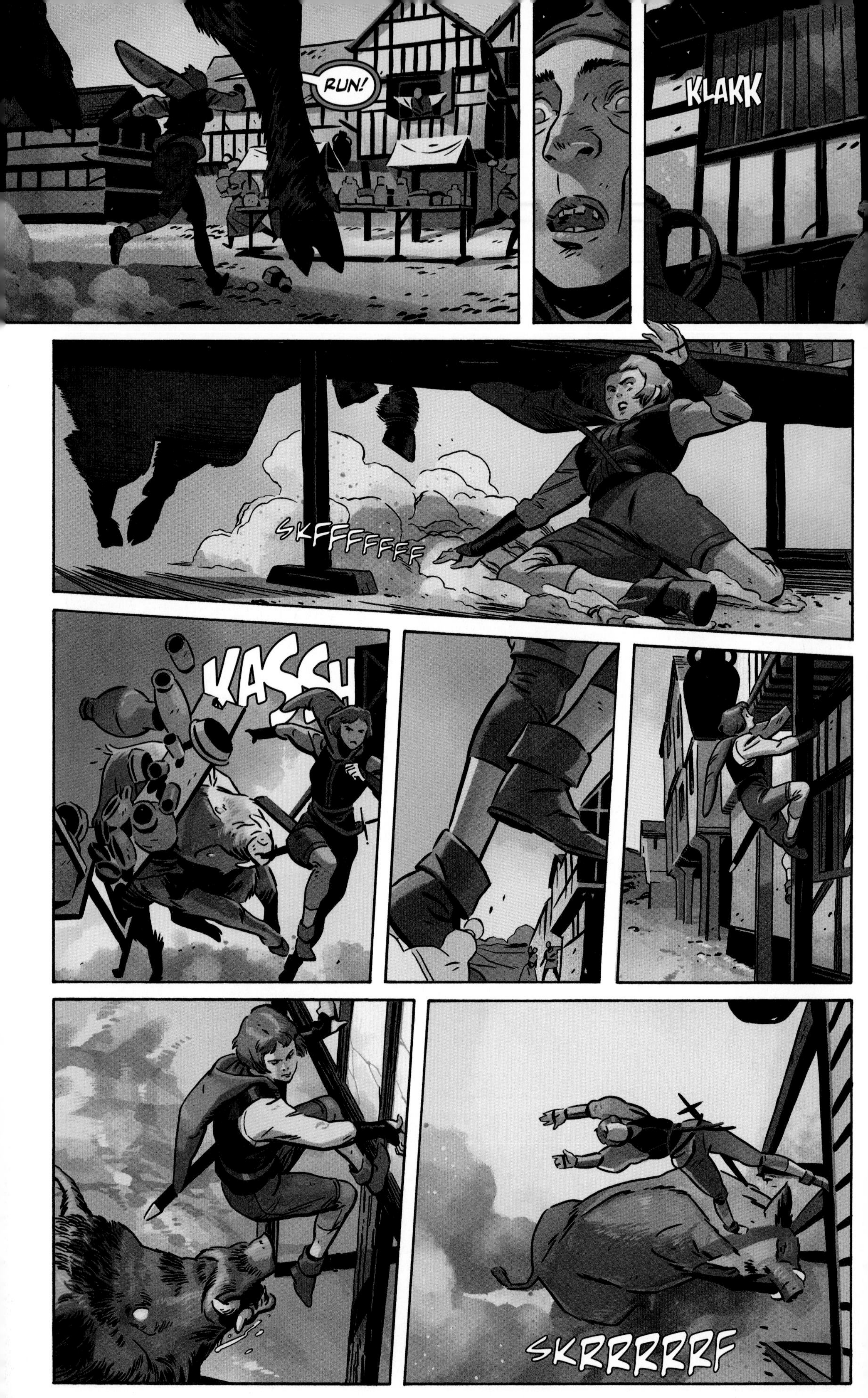
RUN!
KLAKK
SKFFFFFFFF
KASSH
SKRRRRRRF

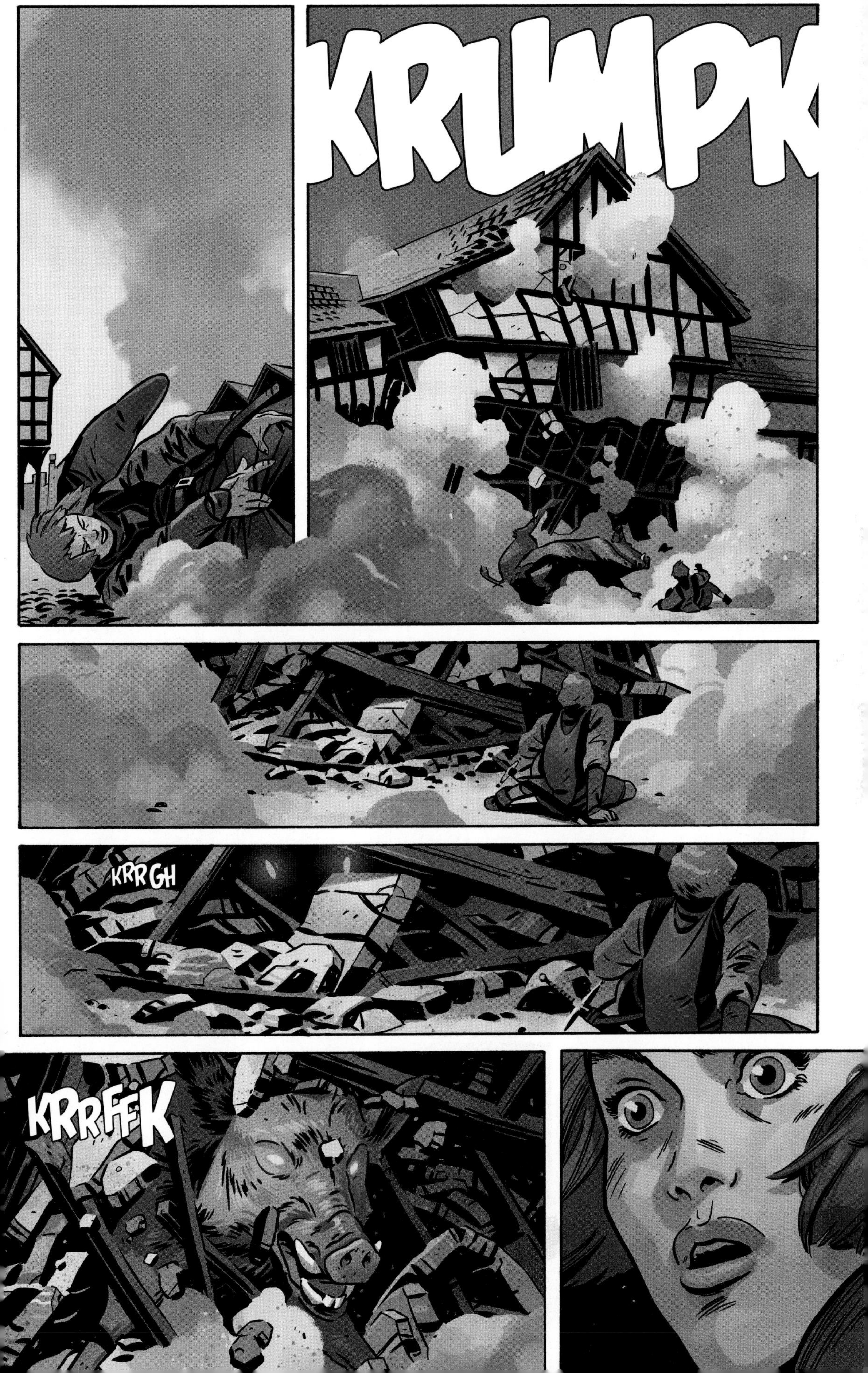
KRUMPK
KRRGH
KRRFFK

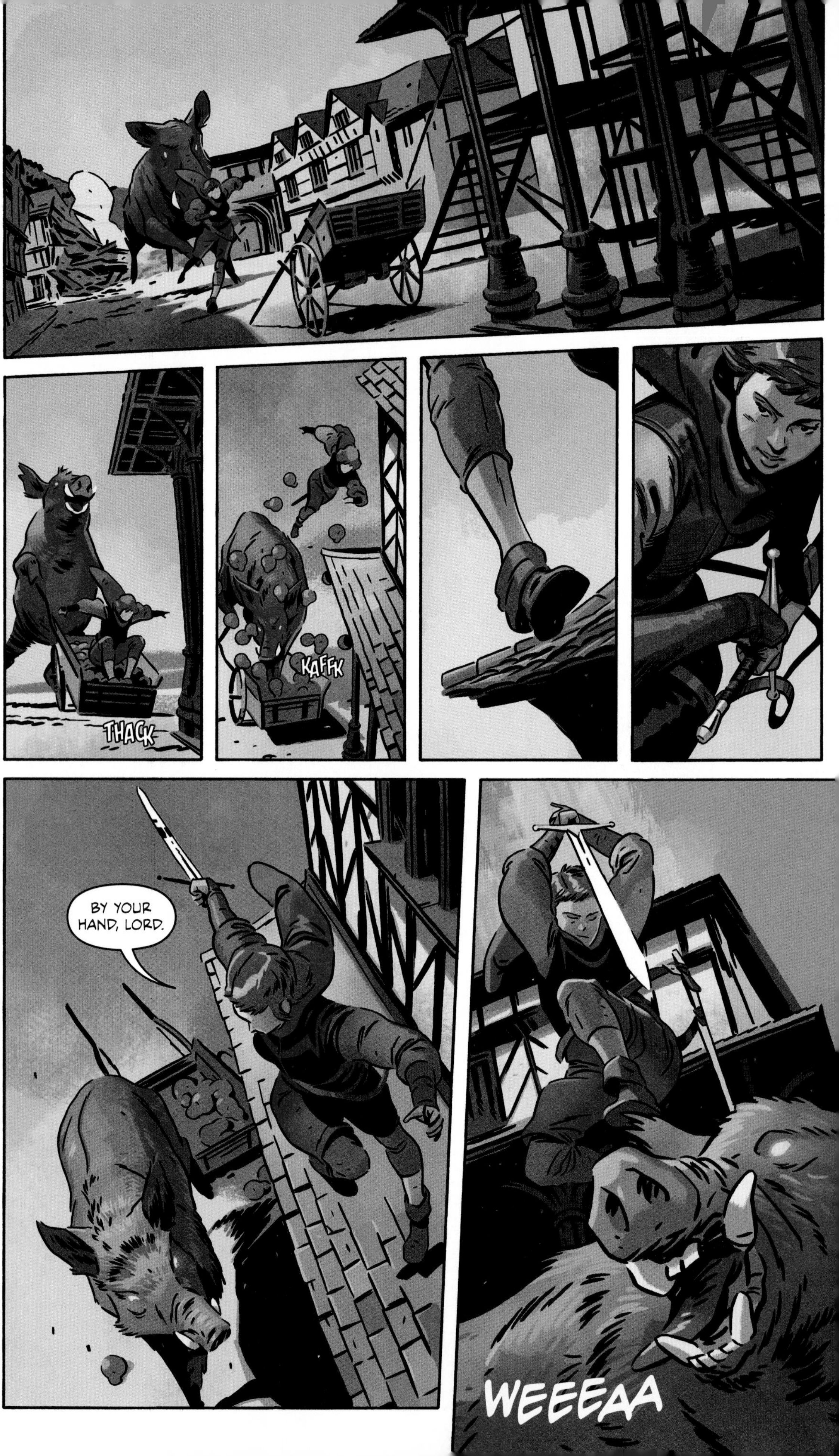
THACK
KAFFK
BY YOUR HAND, LORD.
WEEEAA

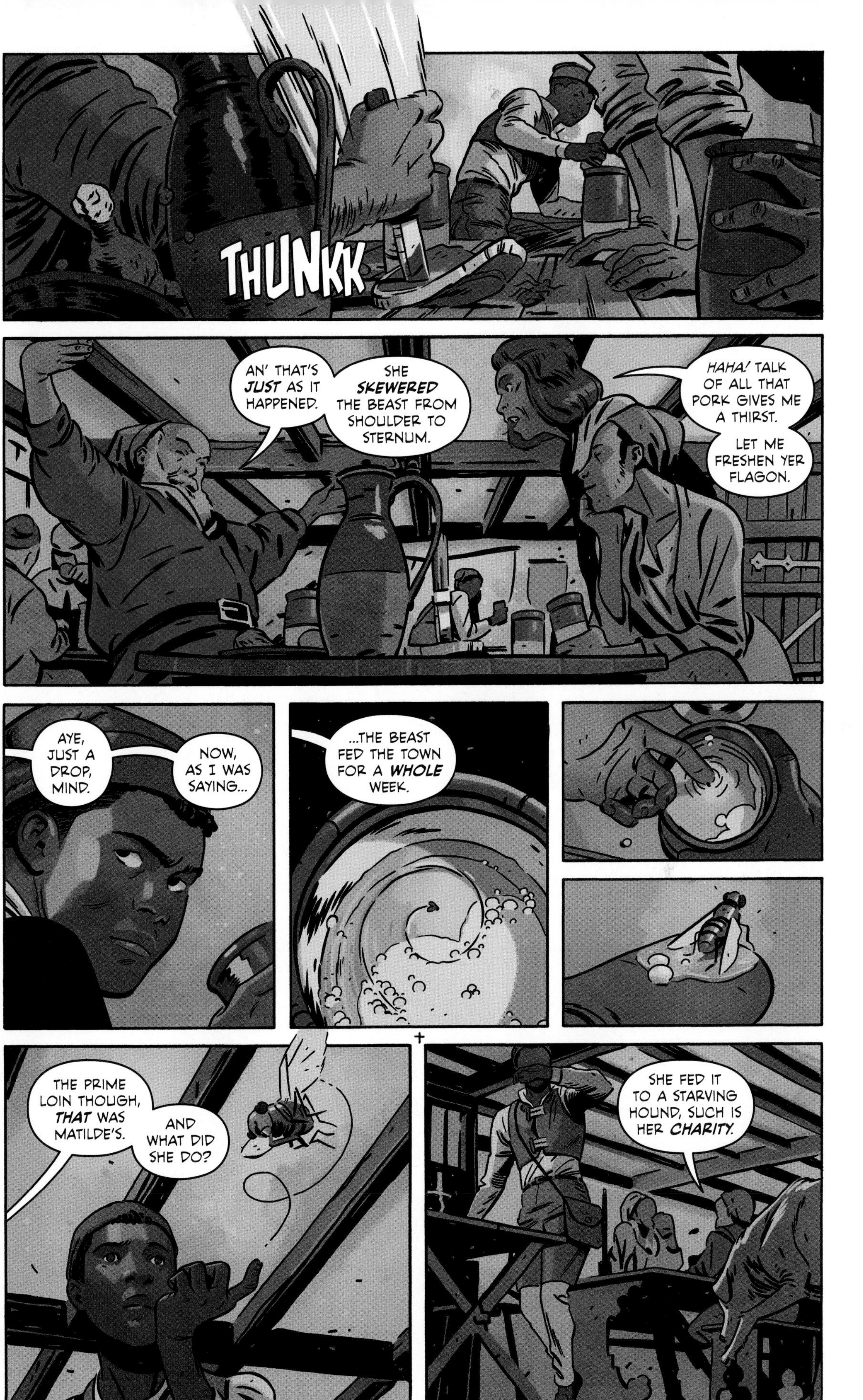
THUNKK
AN' THAT'S JUST AS IT HAPPENED.
SHE SKEWERED THE BEAST FROM SHOULDER TO STERNUM.
HAHA! TALK OF ALL THAT PORK GIVES ME A THIRST.
LET ME FRESHEN YER FLAGON.
AYE, JUST A DROP, MIND.
NOW, AS I WAS SAYING...
...THE BEAST FED THE TOWN FOR A WHOLE WEEK.
THE PRIME LOIN THOUGH, THAT WAS MATILDE'S.
AND WHAT DID SHE DO?
SHE FED IT TO A STARVING HOUND, SUCH IS HER CHARITY.

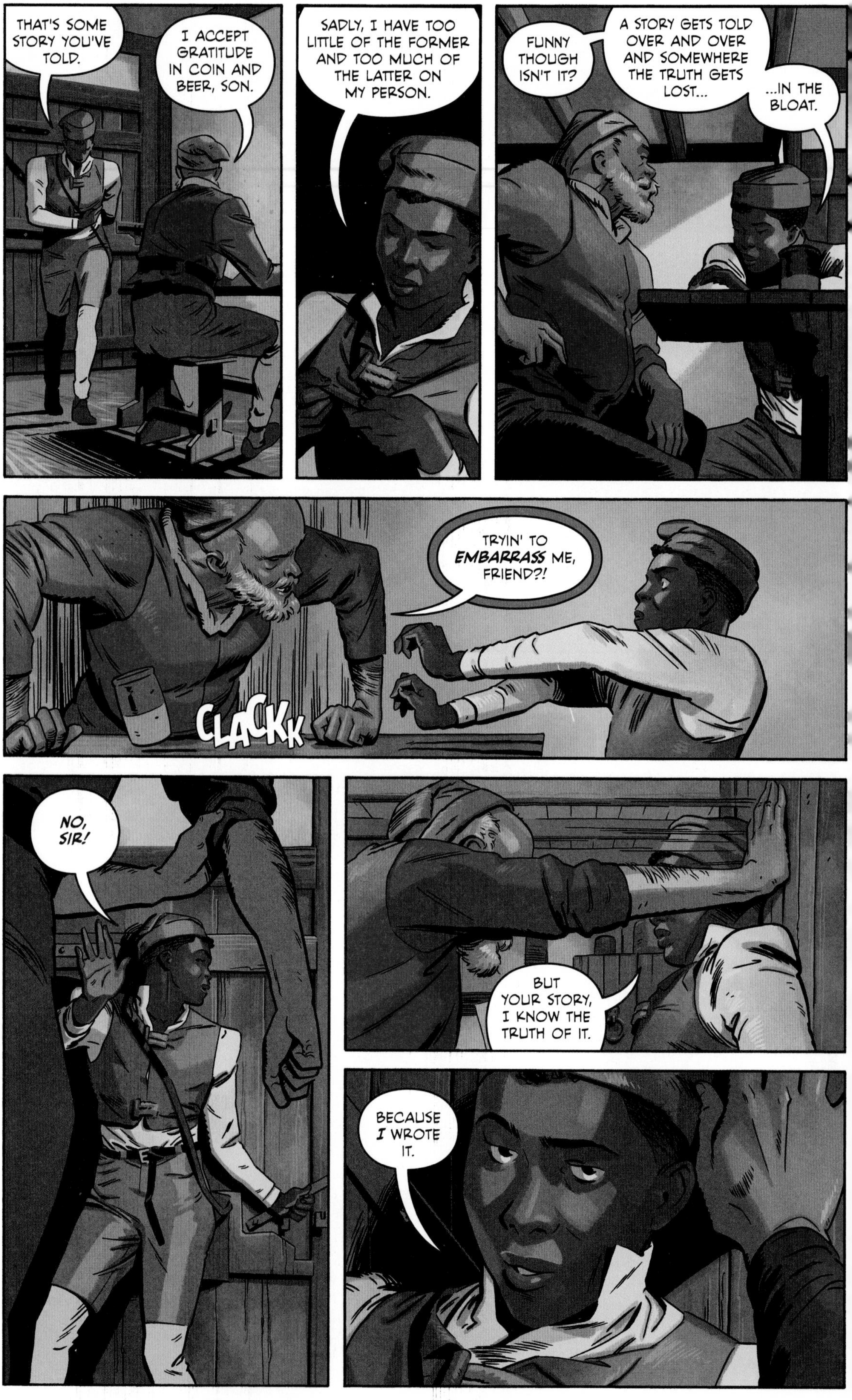
THAT'S SOME STORY YOU'VE TOLD.
I ACCEPT GRATITUDE IN COIN AND BEER, SON.
SADLY, I HAVE TOO LITTLE OF THE FORMER AND TOO MUCH OF THE LATTER ON MY PERSON.
FUNNY THOUGH ISN'T IT?
A STORY GETS TOLD OVER AND OVER AND SOMEWHERE THE TRUTH GETS LOST...
...IN THE BLOAT.
TRYIN' TO EMBARRASS ME, FRIEND?!
CLACKK
NO, SIR!
BUT YOUR STORY, I KNOW THE TRUTH OF IT.
BECAUSE I WROTE IT.

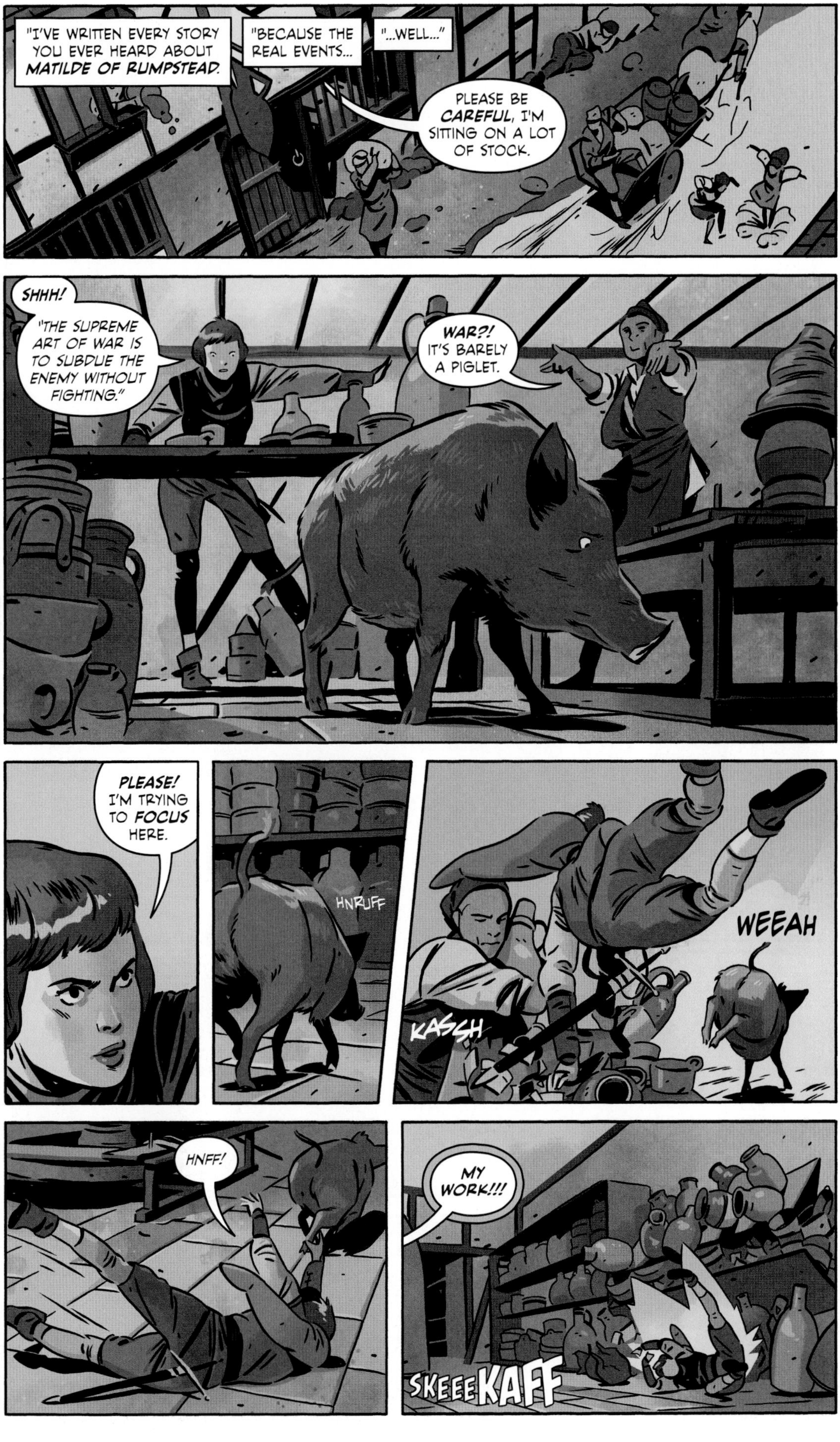
"I'VE WRITTEN EVERY STORY YOU EVER HEARD ABOUT MATILDE OF RUMPSTEAD.
"BECAUSE THE REAL EVENTS...
"...WELL..."
PLEASE BE CAREFUL, I'M SITTING ON A LOT OF STOCK.
SHHH!
"THE SUPREME ART OF WAR IS TO SUBDUE THE ENEMY WITHOUT FIGHTING."
WAR?! IT'S BARELY A PIGLET.
PLEASE! I'M TRYING TO FOCUS HERE.
HNRUFF
WEEAH
KASSH
HNFF!
MY WORK!!!
SKEEEKAFF

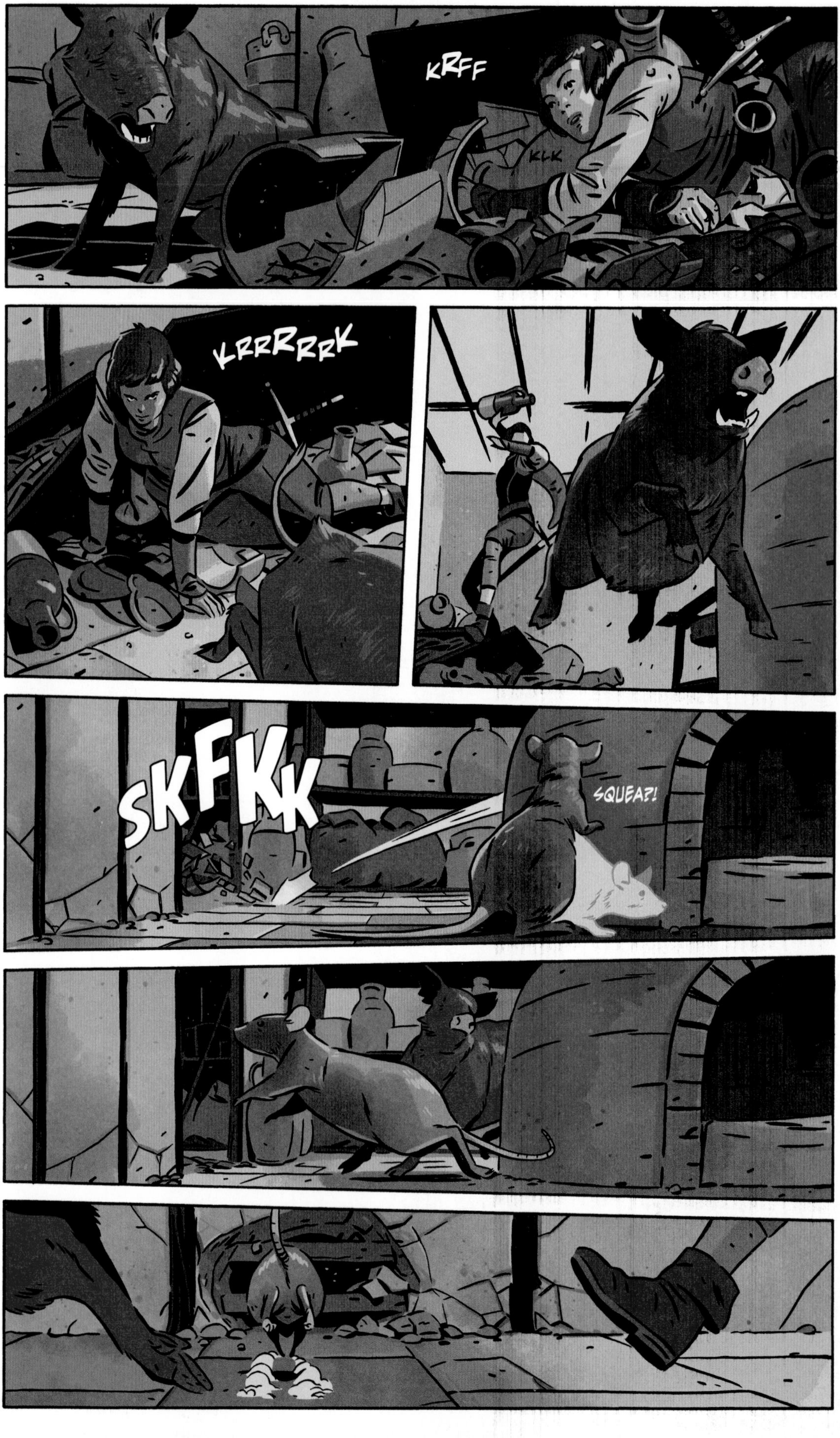
KRFF
KLK
KRRRRRK
SKFKK
SQUEA?!

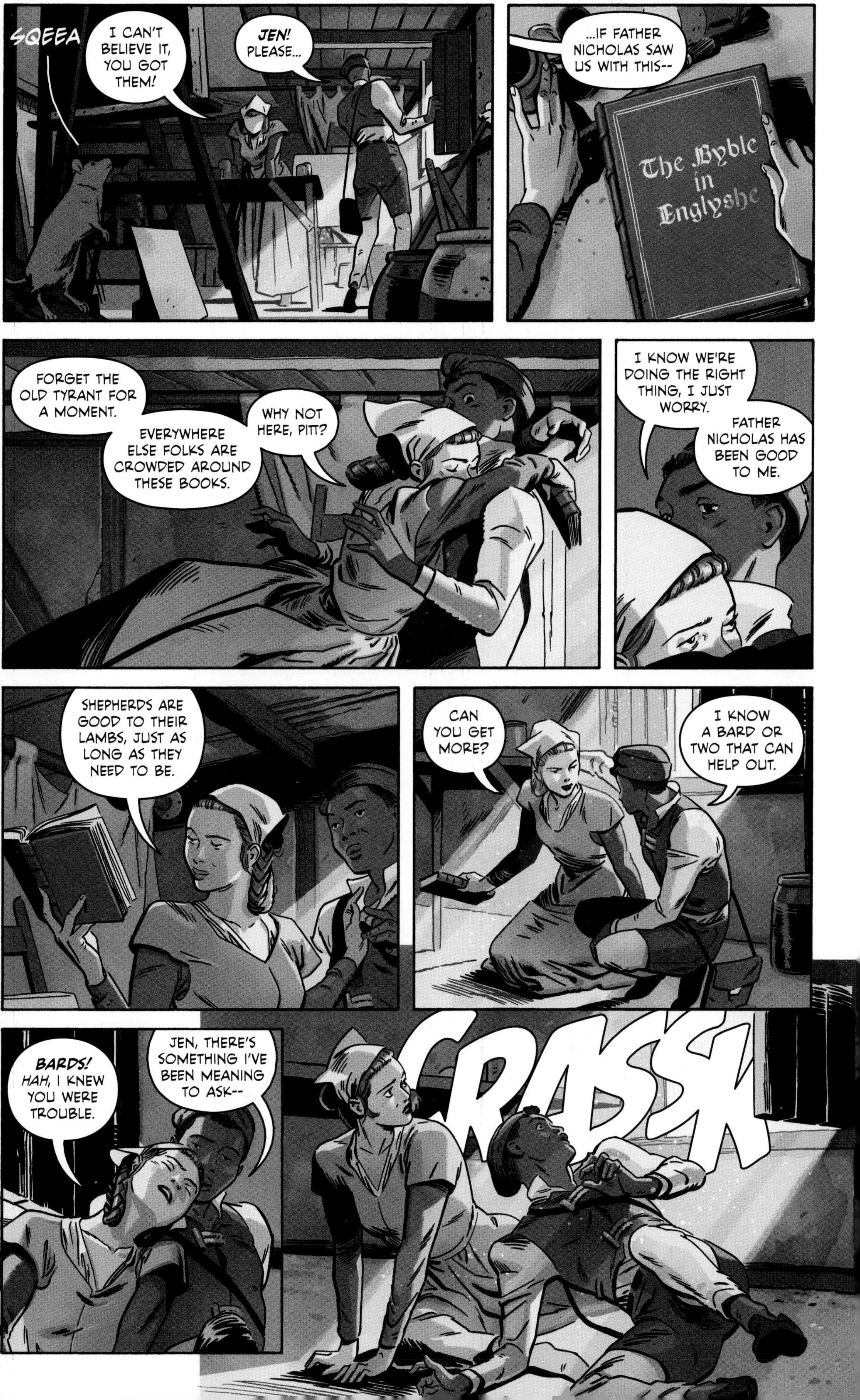
SQEEA
I CAN'T BELIEVE IT, YOU GOT THEM!
JEN! PLEASE...
...IF FATHER NICHOLAS SAW US WITH THIS--
The Byble in Englyshe
FORGET THE OLD TYRANT FOR A MOMENT.
EVERYWHERE ELSE FOLKS ARE CROWDED AROUND THESE BOOKS.
WHY NOT HERE, PITT?
I KNOW WE'RE DOING THE RIGHT THING, I JUST WORRY.
FATHER NICHOLAS HAS BEEN GOOD TO ME.
SHEPHERDS ARE GOOD TO THEIR LAMBS, JUST AS LONG AS THEY NEED TO BE.
CAN YOU GET MORE?
I KNOW A BARD OR TWO THAT CAN HELP OUT.
BARDS! HAH, I KNEW YOU WERE TROUBLE.
JEN, THERE'S SOMETHING I'VE BEEN MEANING TO ASK--
CRASSH

MATILDE!

ARE YOU ALRIGHT?

I'M FINE.

FWEEEEEEEE

PFUDD

SKLASSCHHHH

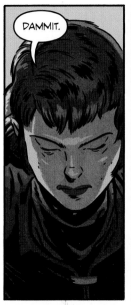

DAMMIT.

ANOTHER "ACT OF GOD," CHILD?

YES, LADY TYRWHIT.

LUCKY I WAS ON HAND.

QUITE.

I'LL TALK WITH THE POTTER.

NO DOUBT HE'LL BE GRATEFUL ONCE HE EMERGES FROM THE *RUBBLE* OF HIS BUSINESS.

FATHER NICHOLAS WILL HELP WITH THAT.

WE JUST COLLECTED A LARGE TITHE OF LIVESTOCK.

I DARESAY HE'D PREFER THE CASH.

RUPERT, YOUR CAPE.

MY GUILD WILL BE IN TOUCH.

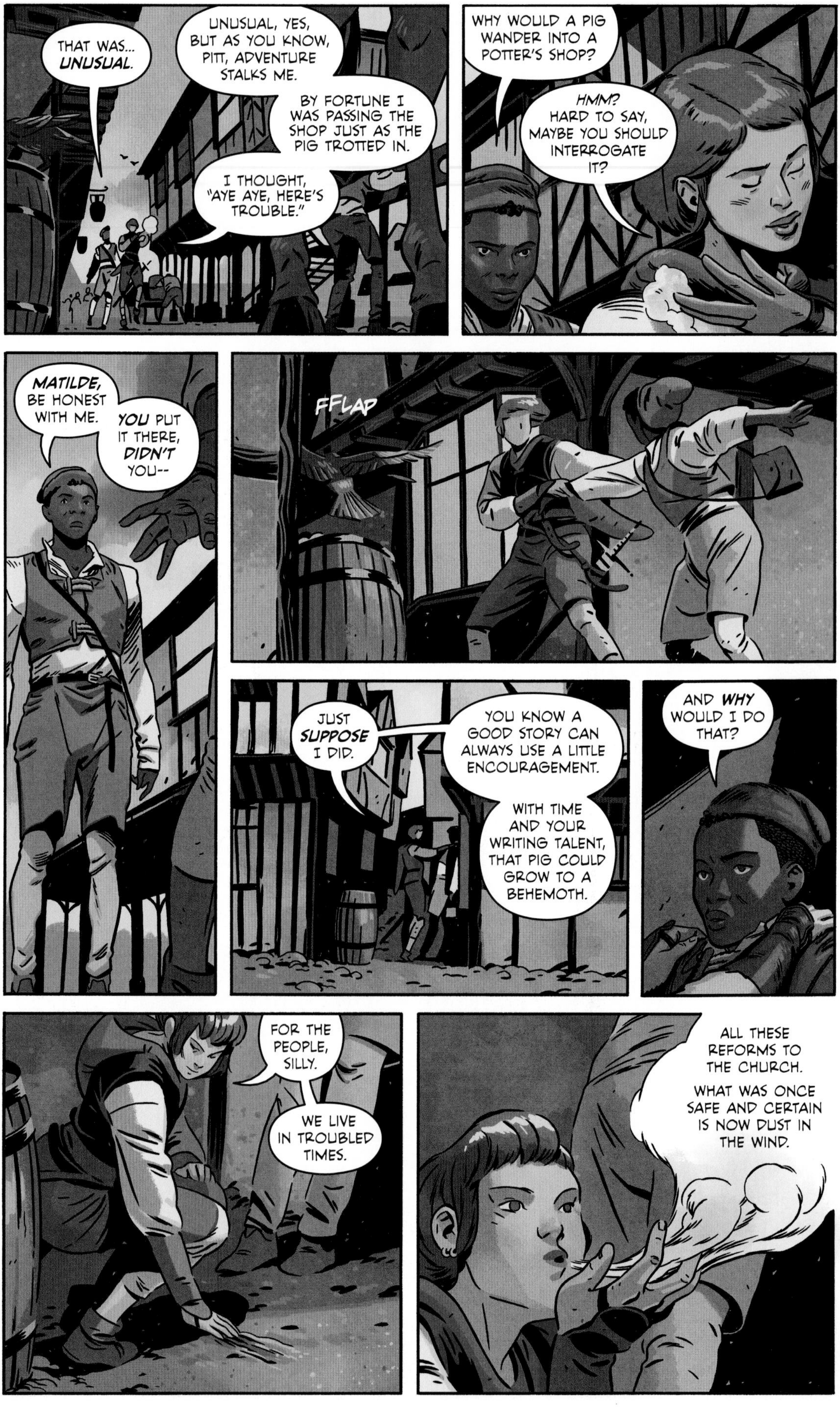

THAT WAS... UNUSUAL.
UNUSUAL, YES, BUT AS YOU KNOW, PITT, ADVENTURE STALKS ME.
BY FORTUNE I WAS PASSING THE SHOP JUST AS THE PIG TROTTED IN.
I THOUGHT, "AYE AYE, HERE'S TROUBLE."
WHY WOULD A PIG WANDER INTO A POTTER'S SHOP?
HMM? HARD TO SAY, MAYBE YOU SHOULD INTERROGATE IT?
MATILDE, BE HONEST WITH ME.
YOU PUT IT THERE, DIDN'T YOU--
FFLAP
JUST SUPPOSE I DID.
YOU KNOW A GOOD STORY CAN ALWAYS USE A LITTLE ENCOURAGEMENT.
WITH TIME AND YOUR WRITING TALENT, THAT PIG COULD GROW TO A BEHEMOTH.
AND WHY WOULD I DO THAT?
FOR THE PEOPLE, SILLY.
WE LIVE IN TROUBLED TIMES.
ALL THESE REFORMS TO THE CHURCH.
WHAT WAS ONCE SAFE AND CERTAIN IS NOW DUST IN THE WIND.

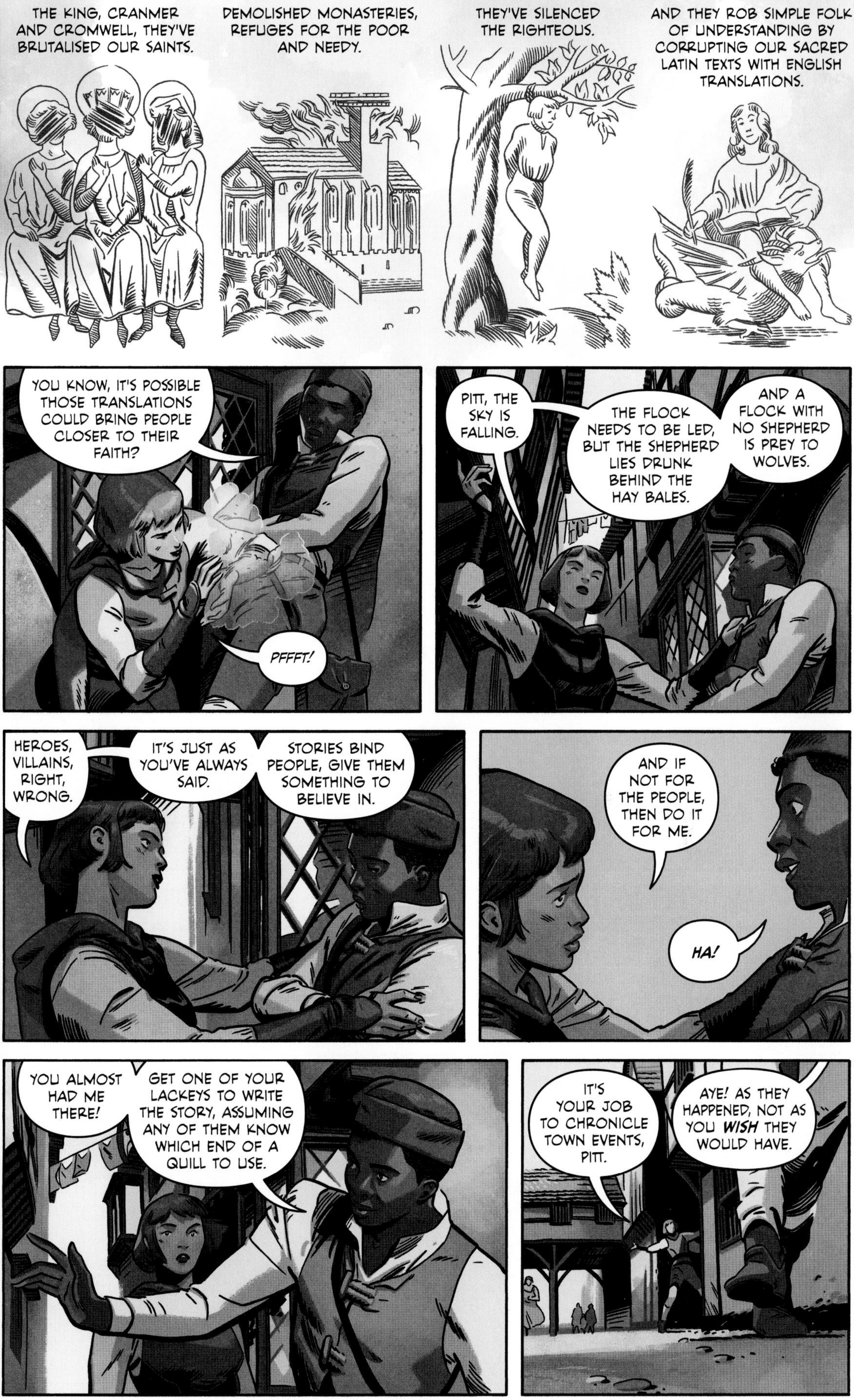
THE KING, CRANMER AND CROMWELL, THEY'VE BRUTALISED OUR SAINTS.
DEMOLISHED MONASTERIES, REFUGES FOR THE POOR AND NEEDY.
THEY'VE SILENCED THE RIGHTEOUS.
AND THEY ROB SIMPLE FOLK OF UNDERSTANDING BY CORRUPTING OUR SACRED LATIN TEXTS WITH ENGLISH TRANSLATIONS.
YOU KNOW, IT'S POSSIBLE THOSE TRANSLATIONS COULD BRING PEOPLE CLOSER TO THEIR FAITH?
PFFFT!
PITT, THE SKY IS FALLING.
THE FLOCK NEEDS TO BE LED, BUT THE SHEPHERD LIES DRUNK BEHIND THE HAY BALES.
AND A FLOCK WITH NO SHEPHERD IS PREY TO WOLVES.
HEROES, VILLAINS, RIGHT, WRONG.
IT'S JUST AS YOU'VE ALWAYS SAID.
STORIES BIND PEOPLE, GIVE THEM SOMETHING TO BELIEVE IN.
AND IF NOT FOR THE PEOPLE, THEN DO IT FOR ME.
HA!
YOU ALMOST HAD ME THERE!
GET ONE OF YOUR LACKEYS TO WRITE THE STORY, ASSUMING ANY OF THEM KNOW WHICH END OF A QUILL TO USE.
IT'S YOUR JOB TO CHRONICLE TOWN EVENTS, PITT.
AYE! AS THEY HAPPENED, NOT AS YOU *WISH* THEY WOULD HAVE.

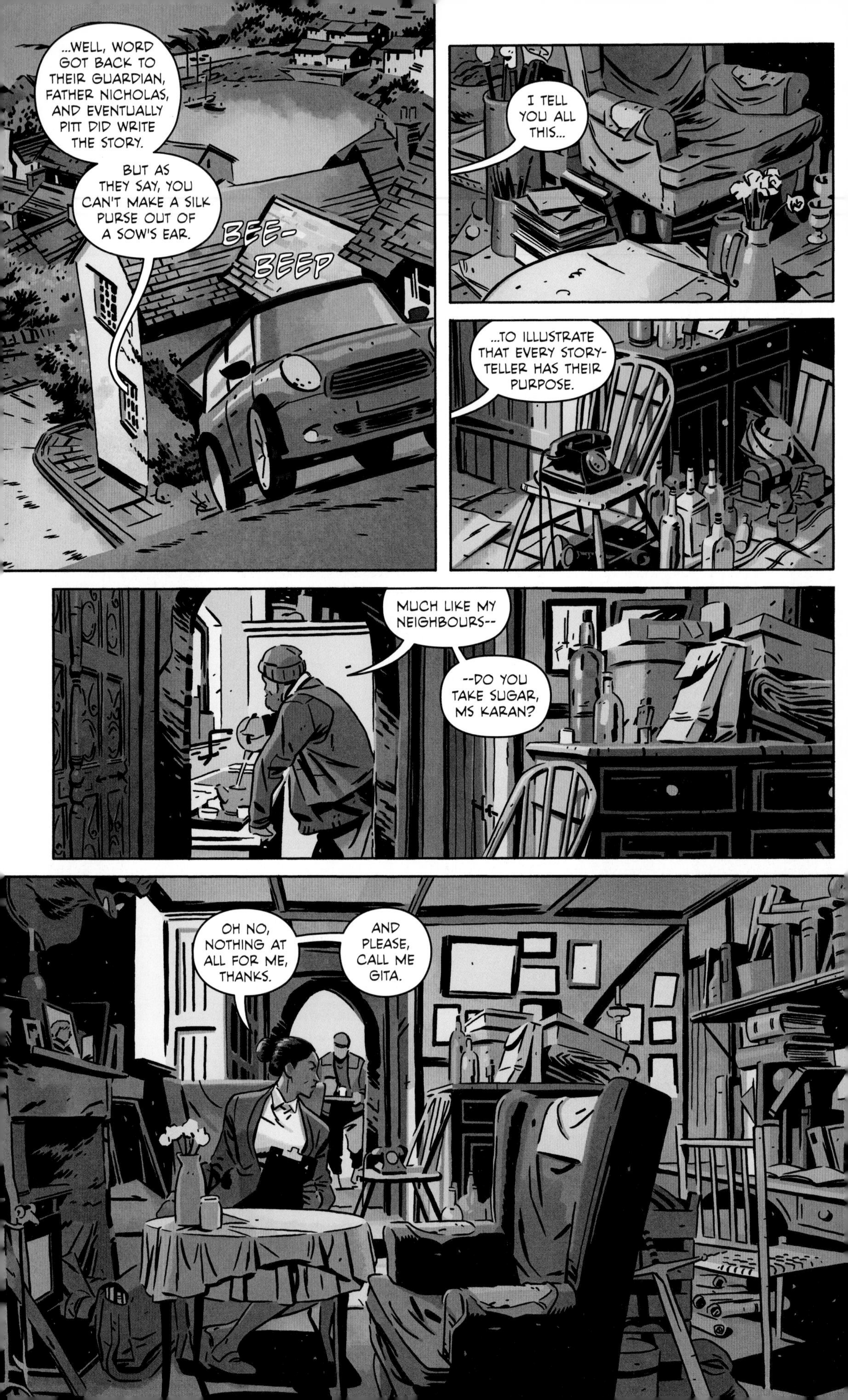
...WELL, WORD GOT BACK TO THEIR GUARDIAN, FATHER NICHOLAS, AND EVENTUALLY PITT DID WRITE THE STORY.
BUT AS THEY SAY, YOU CAN'T MAKE A SILK PURSE OUT OF A SOW'S EAR.
BEE-BEEP
I TELL YOU ALL THIS...
...TO ILLUSTRATE THAT EVERY STORY-TELLER HAS THEIR PURPOSE.
MUCH LIKE MY NEIGHBOURS--
--DO YOU TAKE SUGAR, MS KARAN?
OH NO, NOTHING AT ALL FOR ME, THANKS.
AND PLEASE, CALL ME GITA.

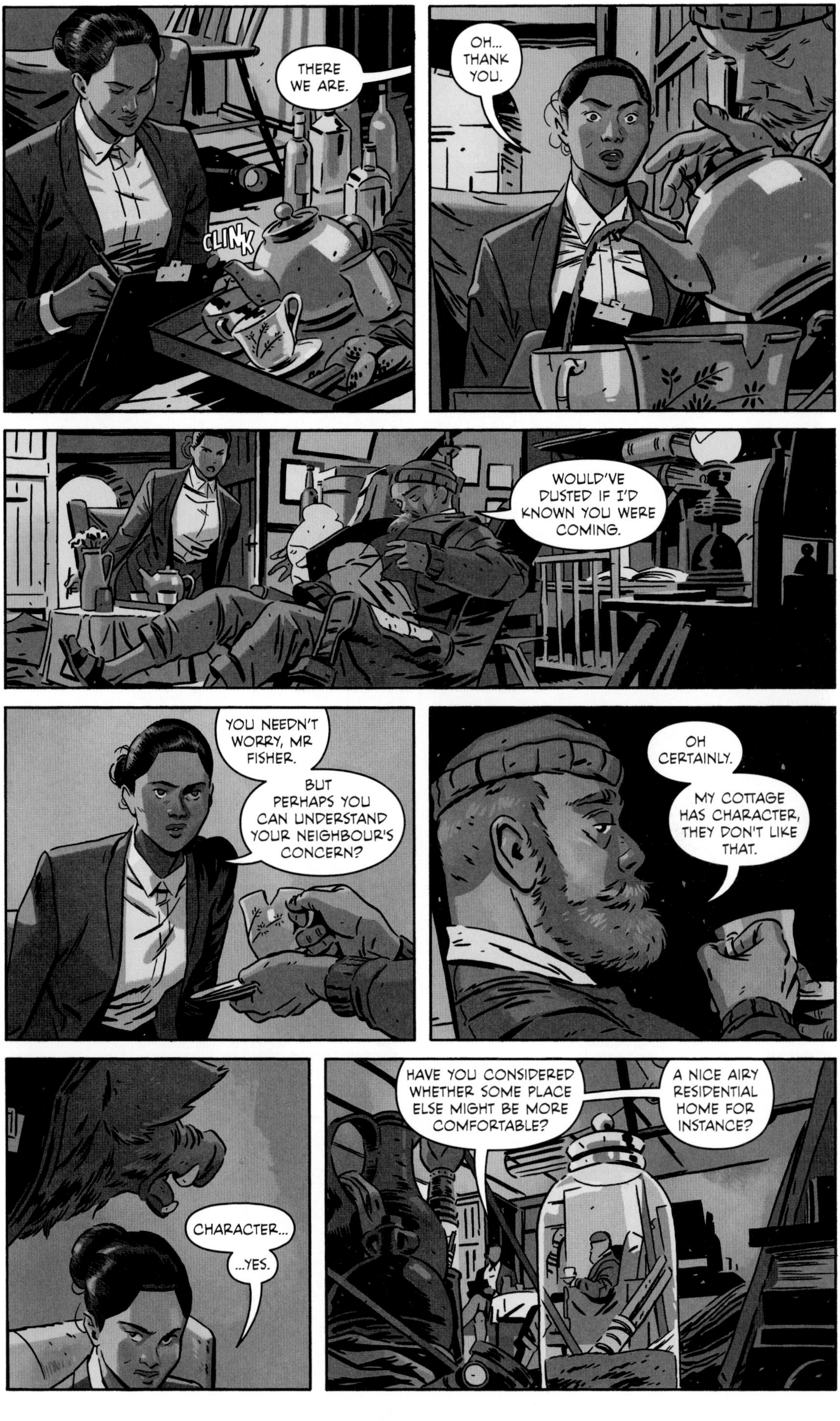
THERE WE ARE.
CLINK
OH... THANK YOU.
WOULD'VE DUSTED IF I'D KNOWN YOU WERE COMING.
YOU NEEDN'T WORRY, MR FISHER.
BUT PERHAPS YOU CAN UNDERSTAND YOUR NEIGHBOUR'S CONCERN?
OH CERTAINLY.
MY COTTAGE HAS CHARACTER, THEY DON'T LIKE THAT.
CHARACTER...
...YES.
HAVE YOU CONSIDERED WHETHER SOME PLACE ELSE MIGHT BE MORE COMFORTABLE?
A NICE AIRY RESIDENTIAL HOME FOR INSTANCE?

OH MY, NO. THIS PLACE IS MY IMAGINATION, MY SOUL, I'D BE LOST WITHOUT IT.

WELL SO FAR YOU'VE NOT GIVEN ME MUCH TO GO ON.

YOU DON'T RECALL A NEXT OF KIN, YOUR DATE OF BIRTH OR EVEN WHEN YOU SETTLED HERE.

Guardianship under Section 7 of the Health Act as amended by the Mental Hea...

be completed by th...

PART I

PERHAPS YOU COULD TELL ME YOUR EARLIEST MEMORY?

OH, A MEMORY'S NOT TO BE RELIED UPON.

"IT MIGHT STAND AS PROUD AS THE CLIFFS THAT LINE THIS COVE.

"BUT THOSE VERY SAME CLIFFS HAVE BEEN ERODED BY TIME AND THE ELEMENTS TO THE POINT WHERE THEY WOULDN'T RECOGNISE THEMSELVES."

WELL MR FISHER, WHAT *CAN* YOU TELL ME?

THE *TRUTH* OF MY SITUATION.

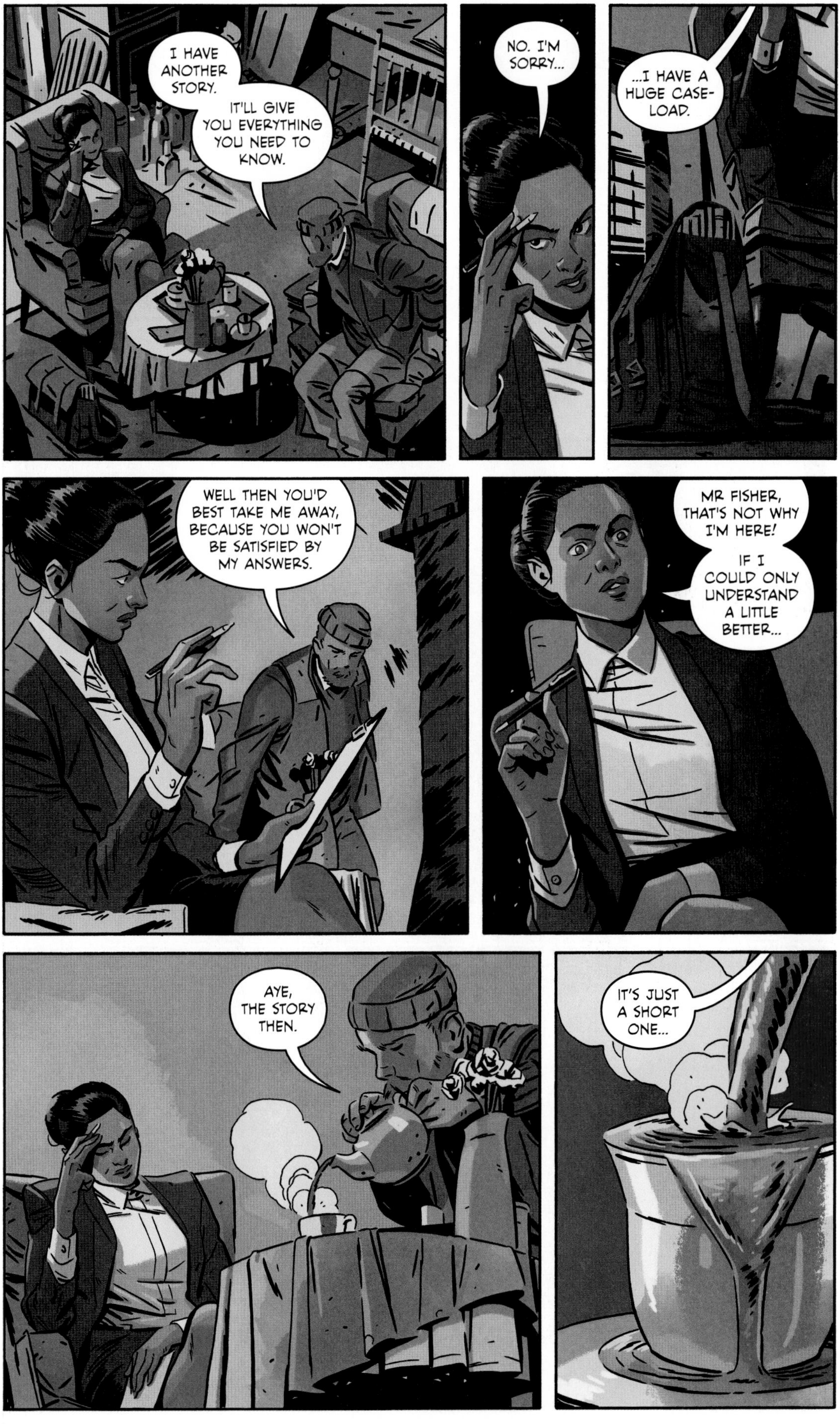
I HAVE ANOTHER STORY.
IT'LL GIVE YOU EVERYTHING YOU NEED TO KNOW.
NO. I'M SORRY...
...I HAVE A HUGE CASE-LOAD.
WELL THEN YOU'D BEST TAKE ME AWAY, BECAUSE YOU WON'T BE SATISFIED BY MY ANSWERS.
MR FISHER, THAT'S NOT WHY I'M HERE!
IF I COULD ONLY UNDERSTAND A LITTLE BETTER...
AYE, THE STORY THEN.
IT'S JUST A SHORT ONE...

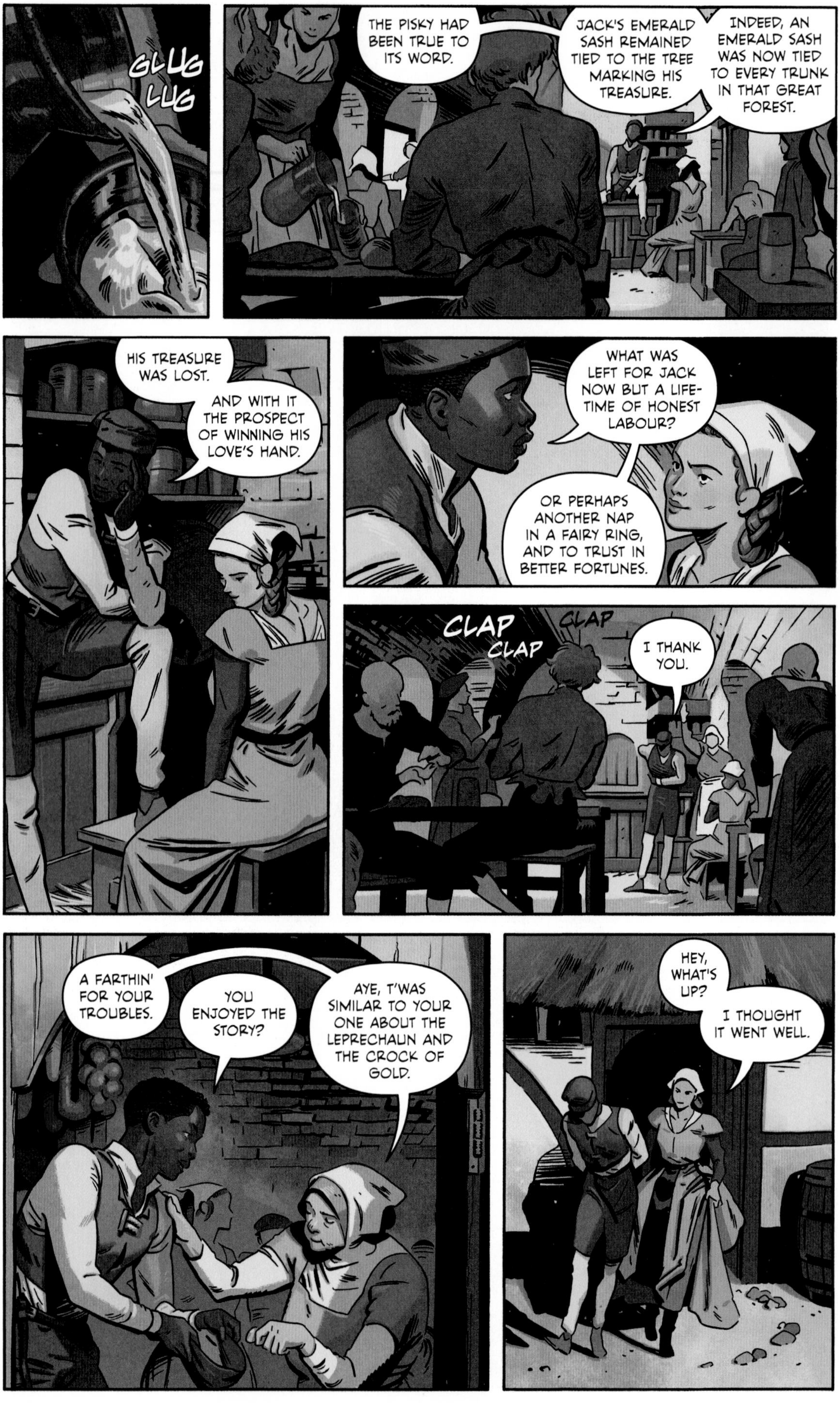
GLUG LUG
THE PISKY HAD BEEN TRUE TO ITS WORD.
JACK'S EMERALD SASH REMAINED TIED TO THE TREE MARKING HIS TREASURE.
INDEED, AN EMERALD SASH WAS NOW TIED TO EVERY TRUNK IN THAT GREAT FOREST.
HIS TREASURE WAS LOST.
AND WITH IT THE PROSPECT OF WINNING HIS LOVE'S HAND.
WHAT WAS LEFT FOR JACK NOW BUT A LIFE-TIME OF HONEST LABOUR?
OR PERHAPS ANOTHER NAP IN A FAIRY RING, AND TO TRUST IN BETTER FORTUNES.
CLAP CLAP CLAP
I THANK YOU.
A FARTHIN' FOR YOUR TROUBLES.
YOU ENJOYED THE STORY?
AYE, T'WAS SIMILAR TO YOUR ONE ABOUT THE LEPRECHAUN AND THE CROCK OF GOLD.
HEY, WHAT'S UP?
I THOUGHT IT WENT WELL.

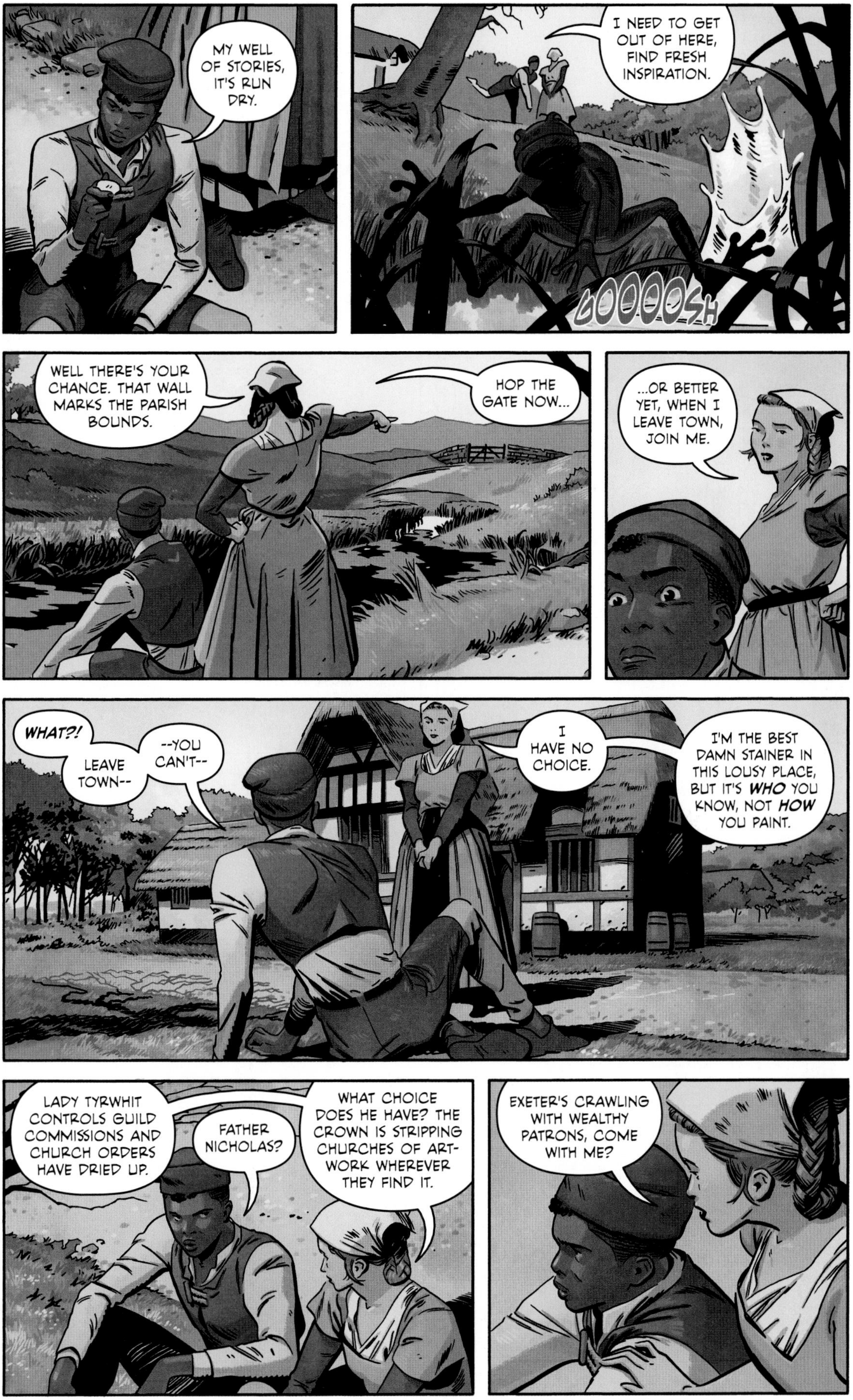
MY WELL OF STORIES, IT'S RUN DRY.
I NEED TO GET OUT OF HERE, FIND FRESH INSPIRATION.
GOOOOSH
WELL THERE'S YOUR CHANCE. THAT WALL MARKS THE PARISH BOUNDS.
HOP THE GATE NOW...
...OR BETTER YET, WHEN I LEAVE TOWN, JOIN ME.
WHAT?!
LEAVE TOWN--
--YOU CAN'T--
I HAVE NO CHOICE.
I'M THE BEST DAMN STAINER IN THIS LOUSY PLACE, BUT IT'S WHO YOU KNOW, NOT HOW YOU PAINT.
LADY TYRWHIT CONTROLS GUILD COMMISSIONS AND CHURCH ORDERS HAVE DRIED UP.
FATHER NICHOLAS?
WHAT CHOICE DOES HE HAVE? THE CROWN IS STRIPPING CHURCHES OF ART-WORK WHEREVER THEY FIND IT.
EXETER'S CRAWLING WITH WEALTHY PATRONS, COME WITH ME?

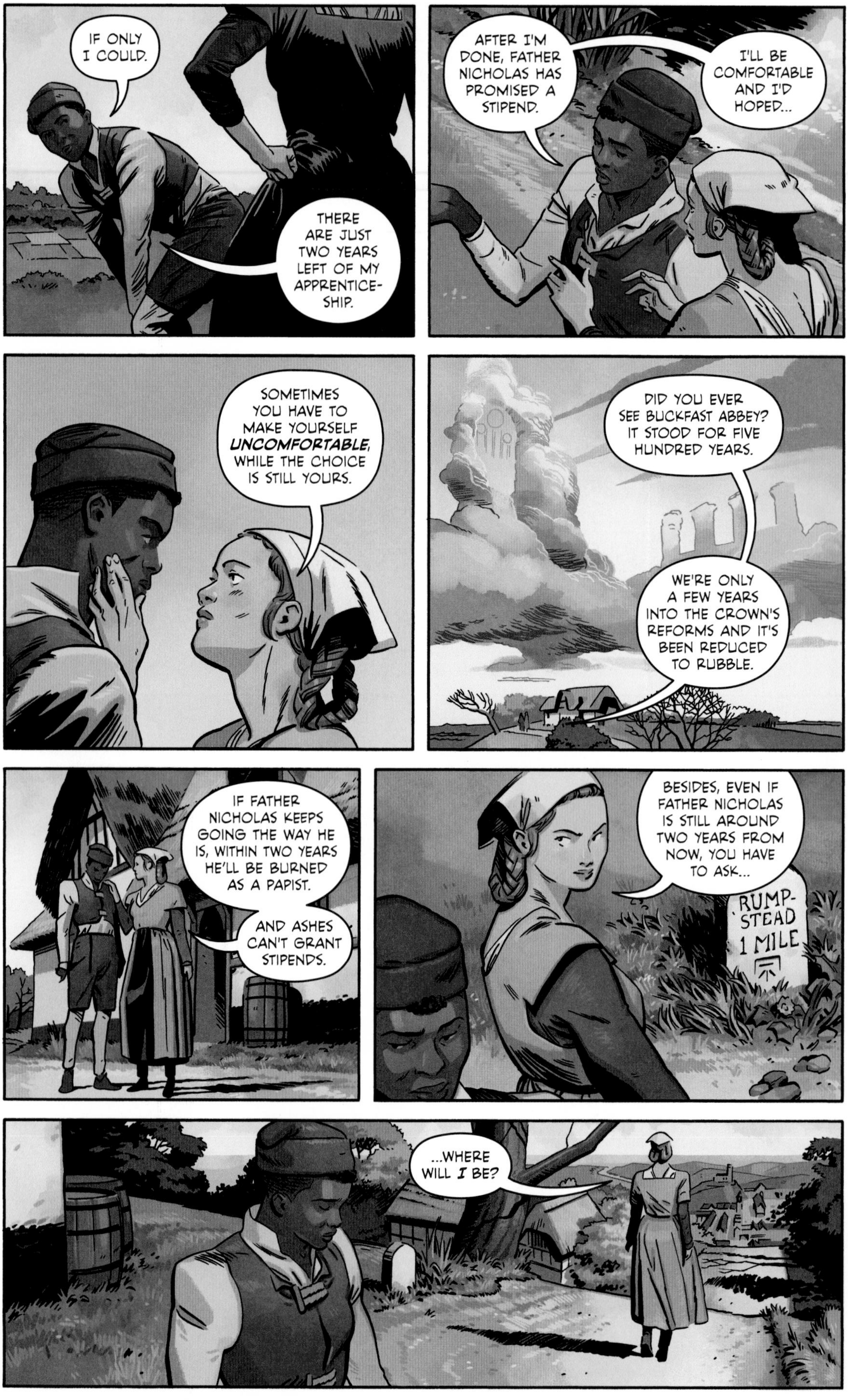
IF ONLY I COULD.
THERE ARE JUST TWO YEARS LEFT OF MY APPRENTICE-SHIP.
AFTER I'M DONE, FATHER NICHOLAS HAS PROMISED A STIPEND.
I'LL BE COMFORTABLE AND I'D HOPED...
SOMETIMES YOU HAVE TO MAKE YOURSELF *UNCOMFORTABLE*, WHILE THE CHOICE IS STILL YOURS.
DID YOU EVER SEE BUCKFAST ABBEY? IT STOOD FOR FIVE HUNDRED YEARS.
WE'RE ONLY A FEW YEARS INTO THE CROWN'S REFORMS AND IT'S BEEN REDUCED TO RUBBLE.
IF FATHER NICHOLAS KEEPS GOING THE WAY HE IS, WITHIN TWO YEARS HE'LL BE BURNED AS A PAPIST.
AND ASHES CAN'T GRANT STIPENDS.
BESIDES, EVEN IF FATHER NICHOLAS IS STILL AROUND TWO YEARS FROM NOW, YOU HAVE TO ASK...
RUMP-STEAD 1 MILE
...WHERE WILL *I* BE?

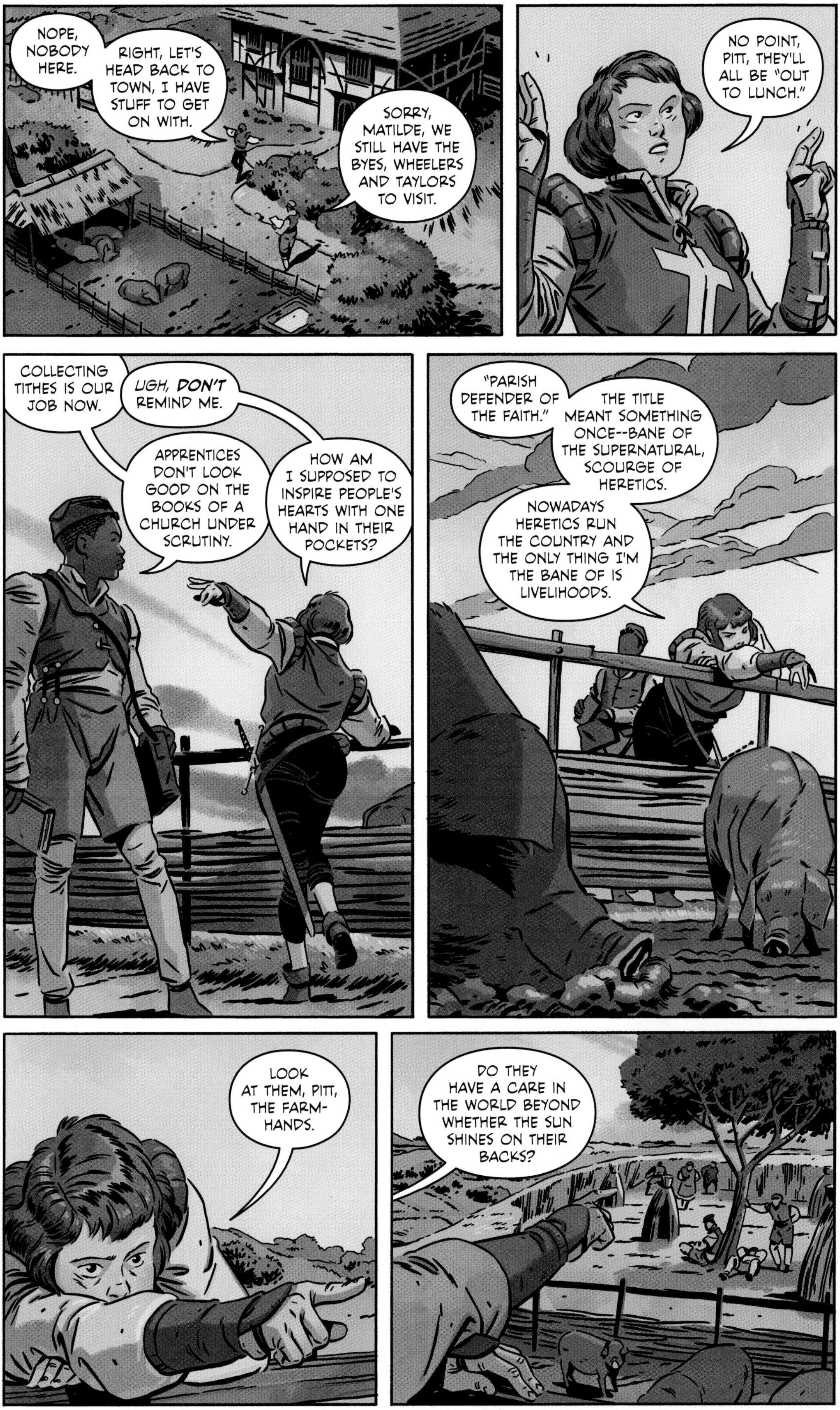
NOPE, NOBODY HERE.
RIGHT, LET'S HEAD BACK TO TOWN, I HAVE STUFF TO GET ON WITH.
SORRY, MATILDE, WE STILL HAVE THE BYES, WHEELERS AND TAYLORS TO VISIT.
NO POINT, PITT, THEY'LL ALL BE "OUT TO LUNCH."
COLLECTING TITHES IS OUR JOB NOW.
UGH, **DON'T** REMIND ME.
APPRENTICES DON'T LOOK GOOD ON THE BOOKS OF A CHURCH UNDER SCRUTINY.
HOW AM I SUPPOSED TO INSPIRE PEOPLE'S HEARTS WITH ONE HAND IN THEIR POCKETS?
"PARISH DEFENDER OF THE FAITH."
THE TITLE MEANT SOMETHING ONCE--BANE OF THE SUPERNATURAL, SCOURGE OF HERETICS.
NOWADAYS HERETICS RUN THE COUNTRY AND THE ONLY THING I'M THE BANE OF IS LIVELIHOODS.
LOOK AT THEM, PITT, THE FARM-HANDS.
DO THEY HAVE A CARE IN THE WORLD BEYOND WHETHER THE SUN SHINES ON THEIR BACKS?

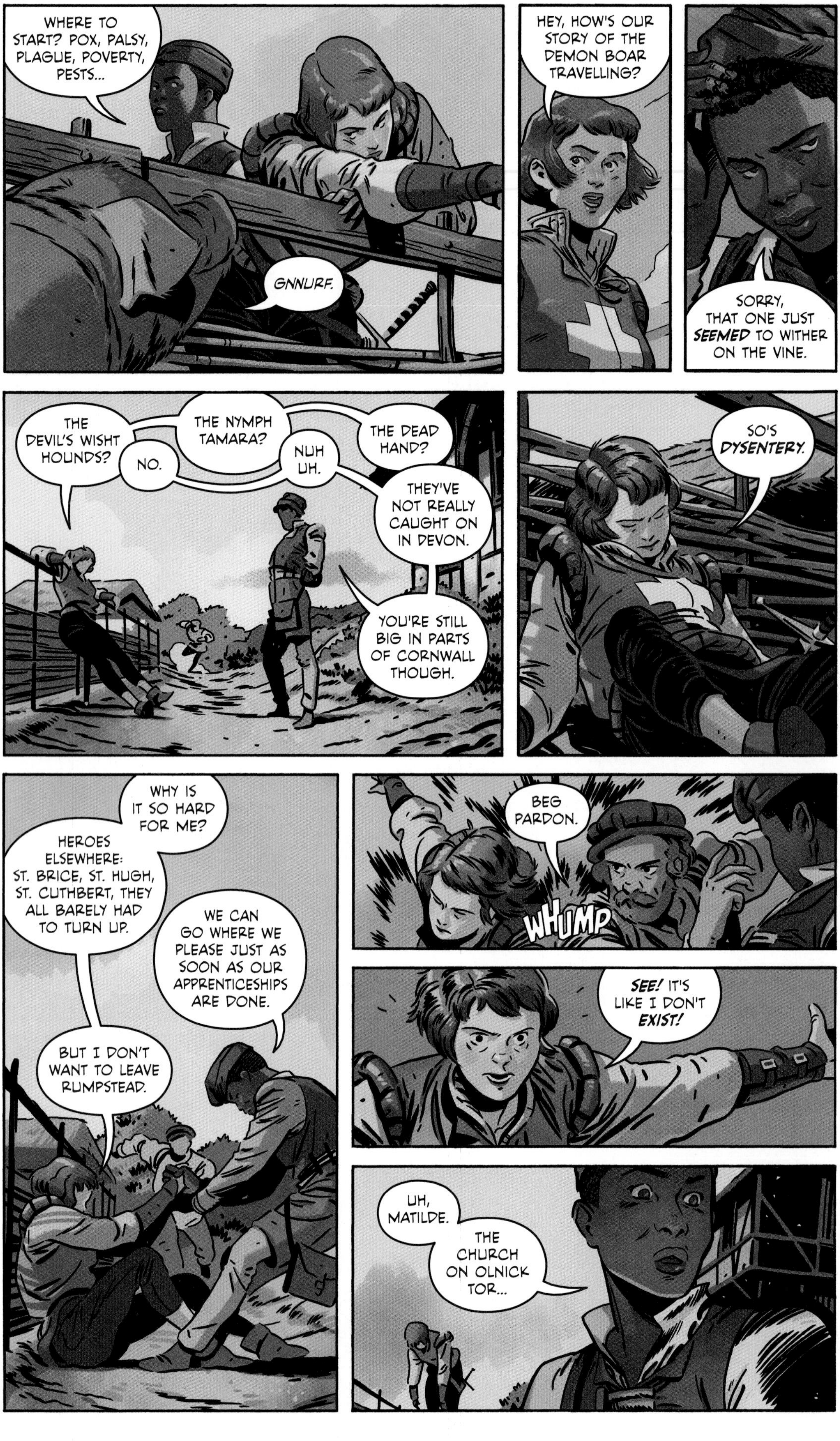
WHERE TO START? POX, PALSY, PLAGUE, POVERTY, PESTS...
GNNURF.
HEY, HOW'S OUR STORY OF THE DEMON BOAR TRAVELLING?
SORRY, THAT ONE JUST SEEMED TO WITHER ON THE VINE.
THE DEVIL'S WISHT HOUNDS?
NO.
THE NYMPH TAMARA?
NUH UH.
THE DEAD HAND?
THEY'VE NOT REALLY CAUGHT ON IN DEVON.
YOU'RE STILL BIG IN PARTS OF CORNWALL THOUGH.
SO'S DYSENTERY.
WHY IS IT SO HARD FOR ME?
HEROES ELSEWHERE: ST. BRICE, ST. HUGH, ST. CUTHBERT, THEY ALL BARELY HAD TO TURN UP.
WE CAN GO WHERE WE PLEASE JUST AS SOON AS OUR APPRENTICESHIPS ARE DONE.
BUT I DON'T WANT TO LEAVE RUMPSTEAD.
BEG PARDON.
WHUMP
SEE! IT'S LIKE I DON'T EXIST!
UH, MATILDE.
THE CHURCH ON OLNICK TOR...

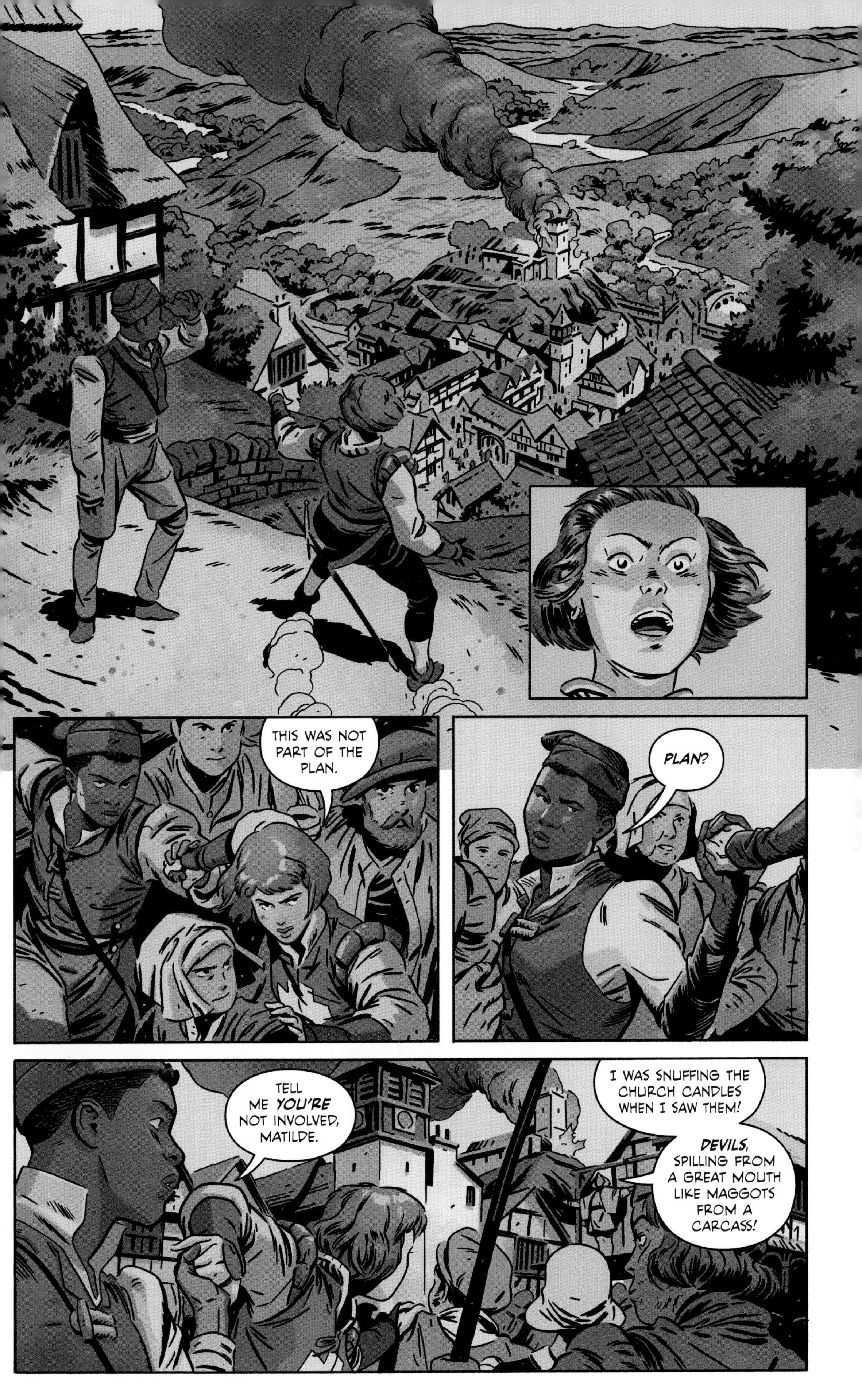
THIS WAS NOT PART OF THE PLAN.
PLAN?
TELL ME YOU'RE NOT INVOLVED, MATILDE.
I WAS SNUFFING THE CHURCH CANDLES WHEN I SAW THEM!
DEVILS, SPILLING FROM A GREAT MOUTH LIKE MAGGOTS FROM A CARCASS!

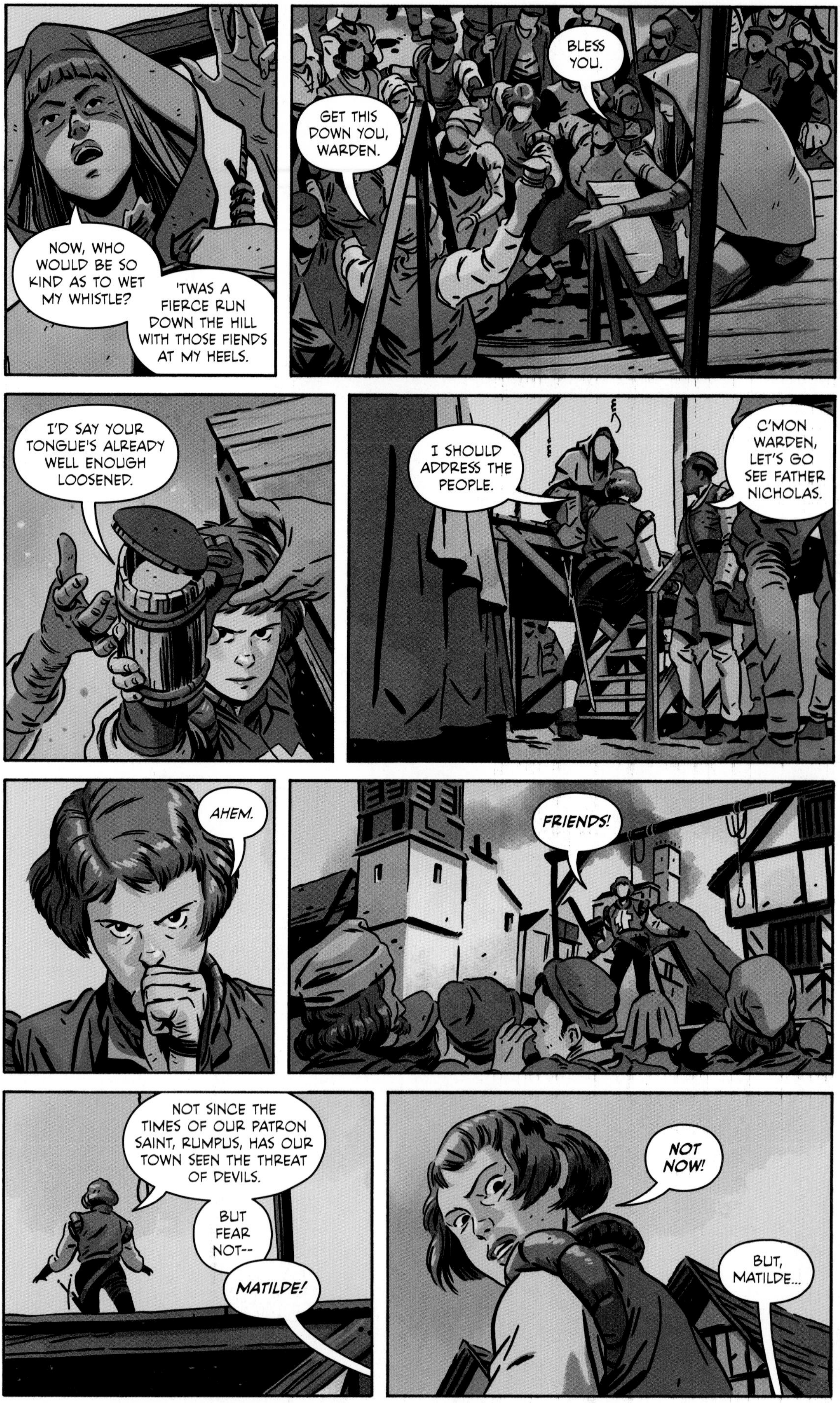
NOW, WHO WOULD BE SO KIND AS TO WET MY WHISTLE?
'TWAS A FIERCE RUN DOWN THE HILL WITH THOSE FIENDS AT MY HEELS.
BLESS YOU.
GET THIS DOWN YOU, WARDEN.
I'D SAY YOUR TONGUE'S ALREADY WELL ENOUGH LOOSENED.
I SHOULD ADDRESS THE PEOPLE.
C'MON WARDEN, LET'S GO SEE FATHER NICHOLAS.
AHEM.
FRIENDS!
NOT SINCE THE TIMES OF OUR PATRON SAINT, RUMPUS, HAS OUR TOWN SEEN THE THREAT OF DEVILS.
BUT FEAR NOT--
MATILDE!
NOT NOW!
BUT, MATILDE...

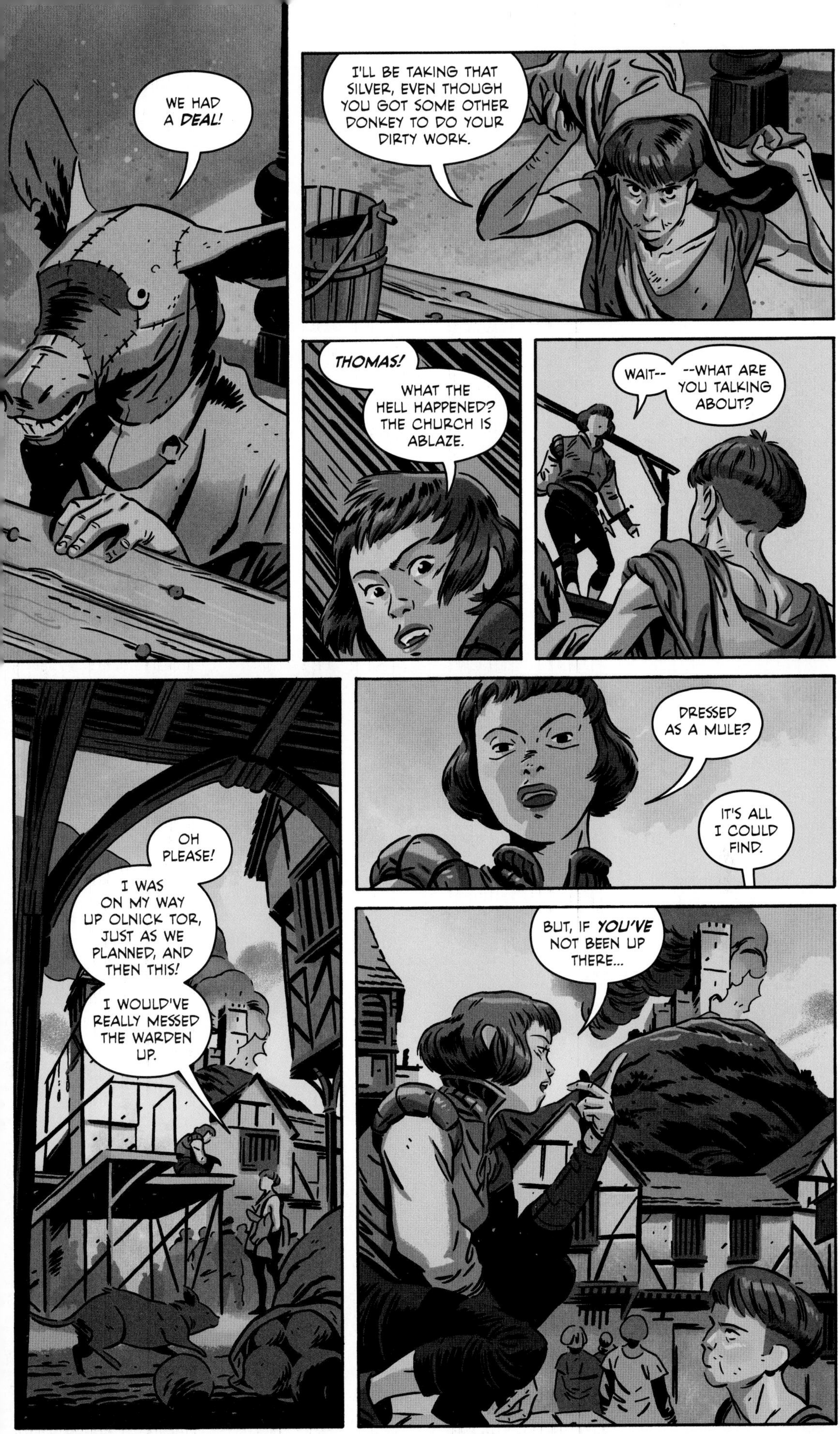
WE HAD A DEAL!
I'LL BE TAKING THAT SILVER, EVEN THOUGH YOU GOT SOME OTHER DONKEY TO DO YOUR DIRTY WORK.
THOMAS!
WHAT THE HELL HAPPENED? THE CHURCH IS ABLAZE.
WAIT--
--WHAT ARE YOU TALKING ABOUT?
OH PLEASE!
I WAS ON MY WAY UP OLNICK TOR, JUST AS WE PLANNED, AND THEN THIS!
I WOULD'VE REALLY MESSED THE WARDEN UP.
DRESSED AS A MULE?
IT'S ALL I COULD FIND.
BUT, IF YOU'VE NOT BEEN UP THERE...

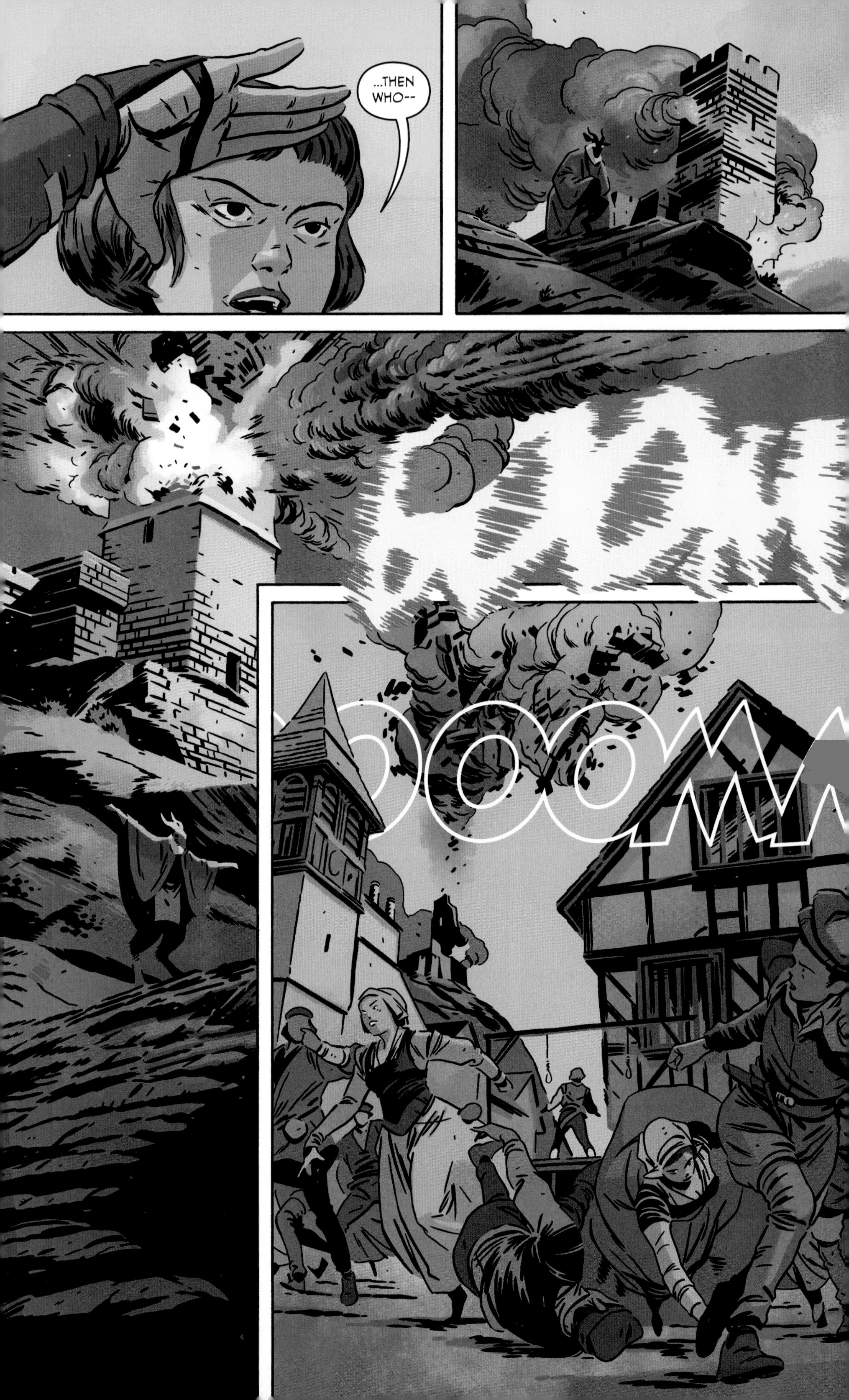
...THEN
WHO--
OOOM

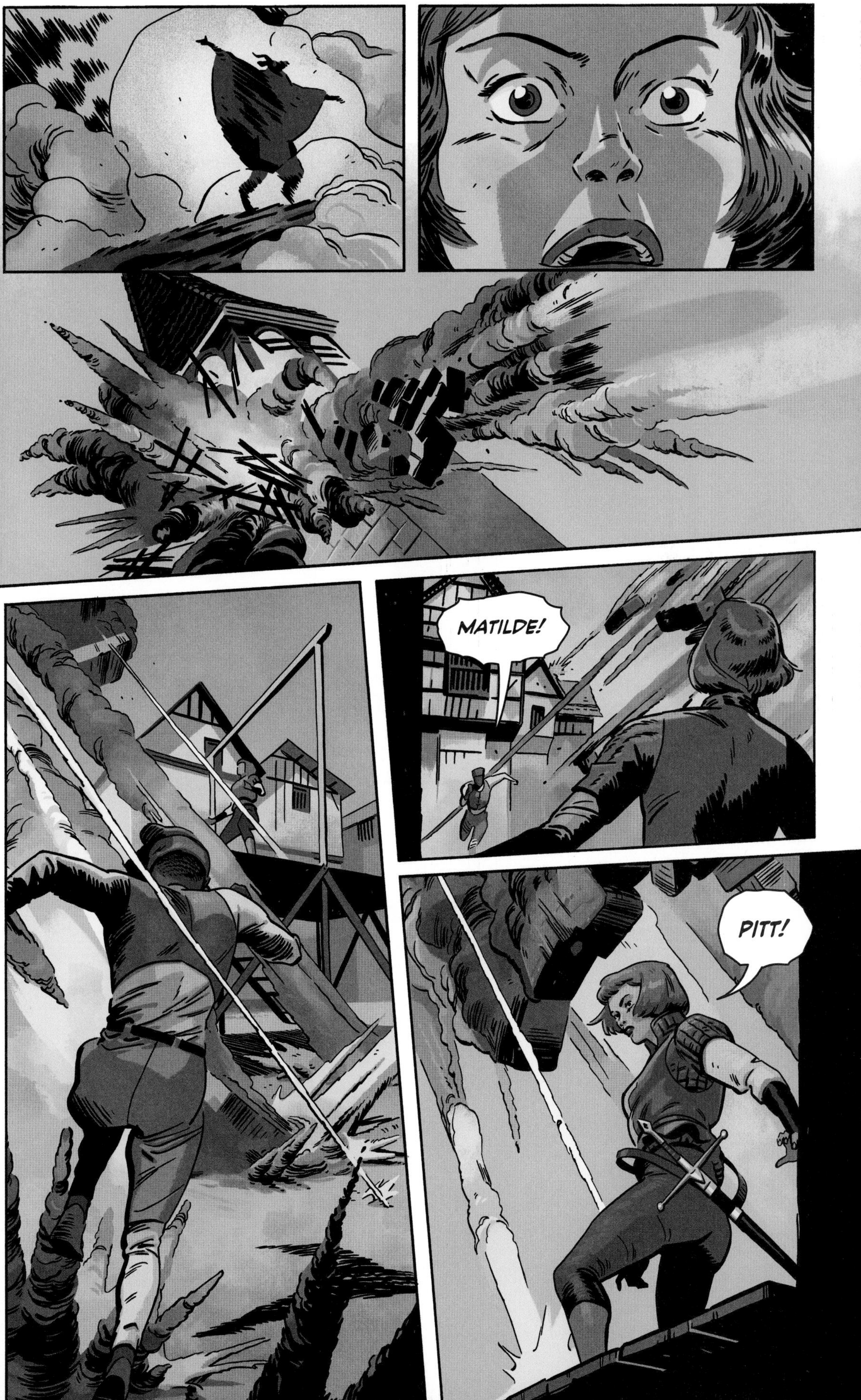
MATILDE!
PITT!

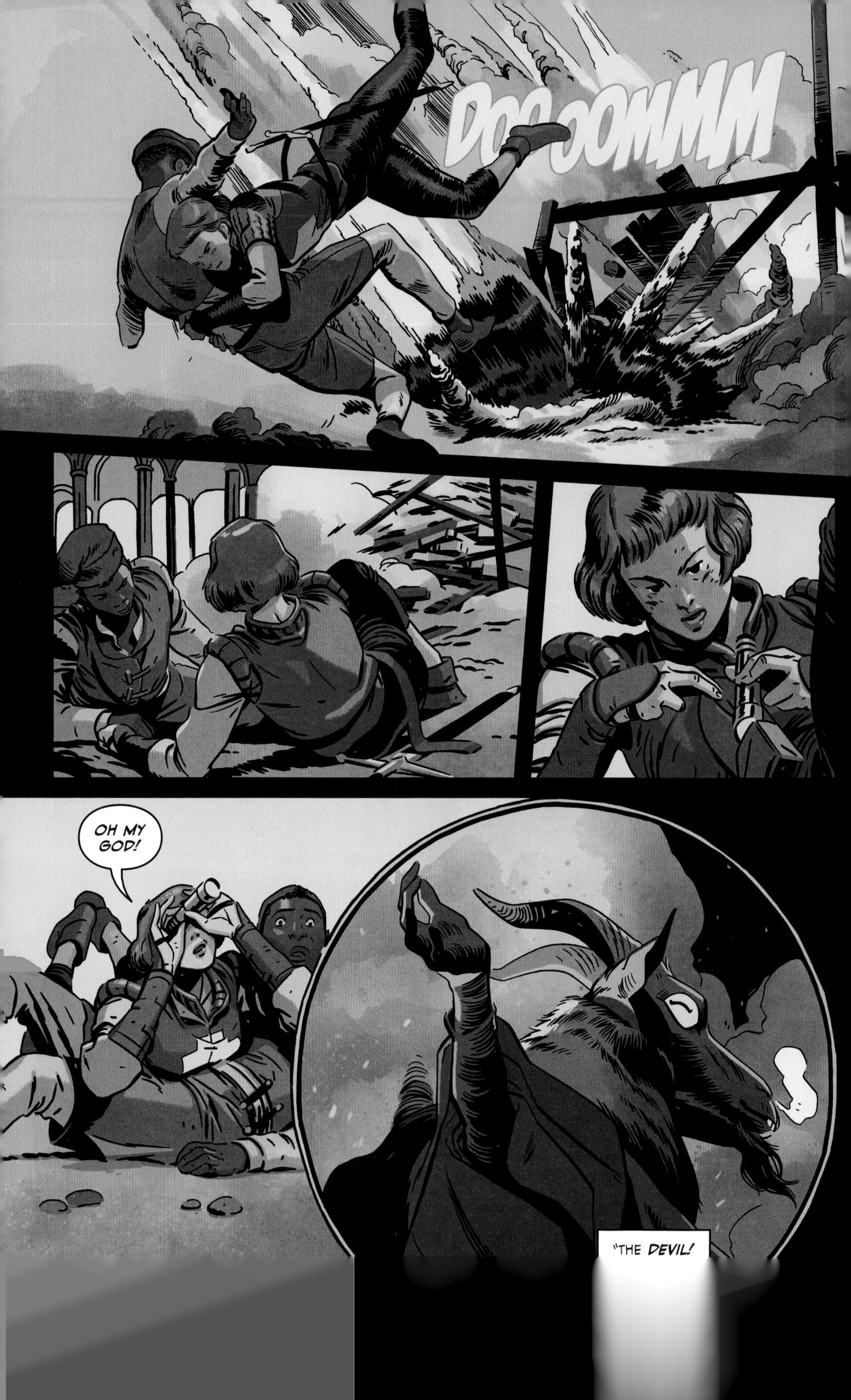
DOOOOMMMM
OH MY GOD!
"THE DEVIL!

Chapter 2

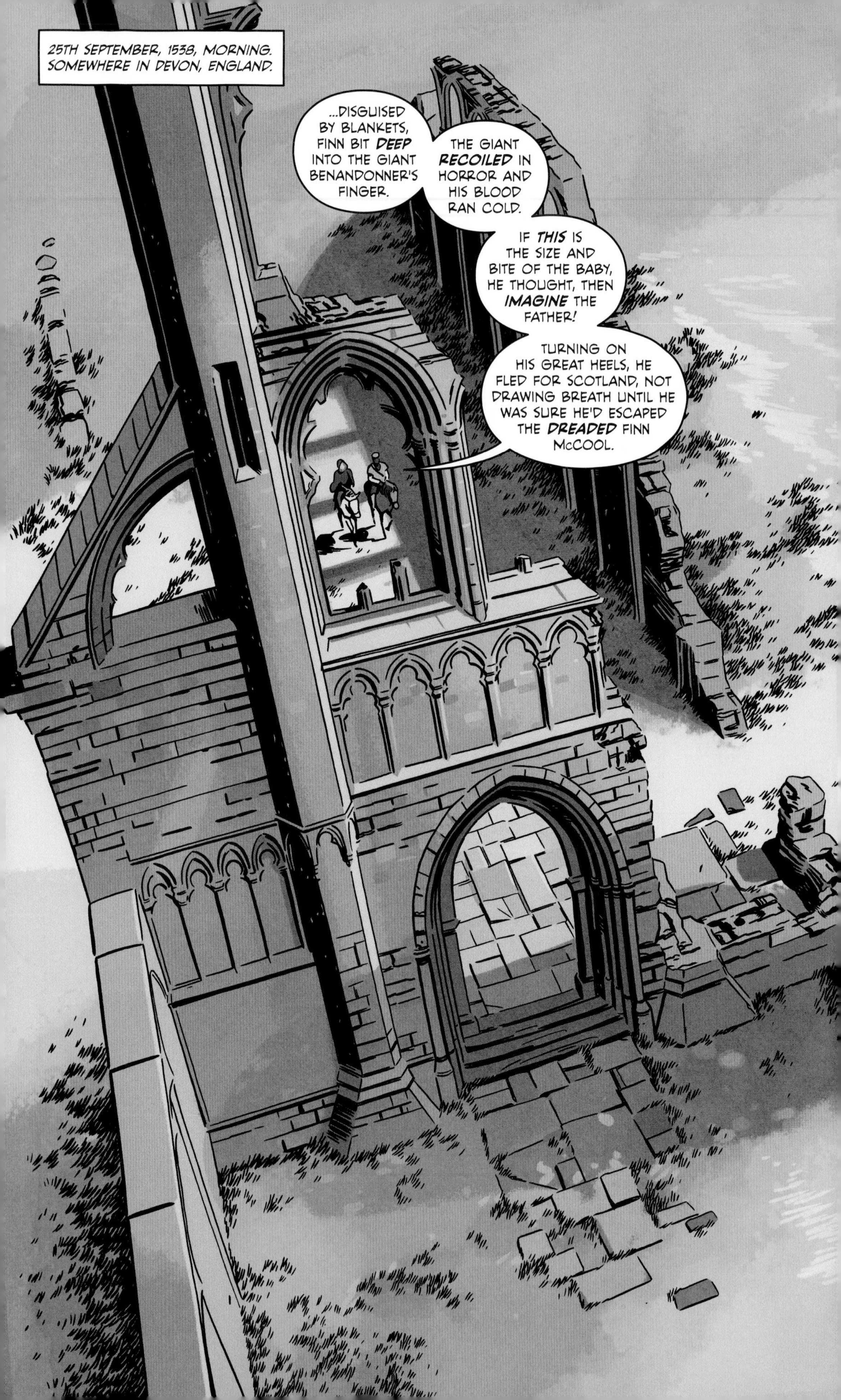

25TH SEPTEMBER, 1538, MORNING. SOMEWHERE IN DEVON, ENGLAND.
...DISGUISED BY BLANKETS, FINN BIT DEEP INTO THE GIANT BENANDONNER'S FINGER.
THE GIANT RECOILED IN HORROR AND HIS BLOOD RAN COLD.
IF THIS IS THE SIZE AND BITE OF THE BABY, HE THOUGHT, THEN IMAGINE THE FATHER!
TURNING ON HIS GREAT HEELS, HE FLED FOR SCOTLAND, NOT DRAWING BREATH UNTIL HE WAS SURE HE'D ESCAPED THE DREADED FINN McCOOL.

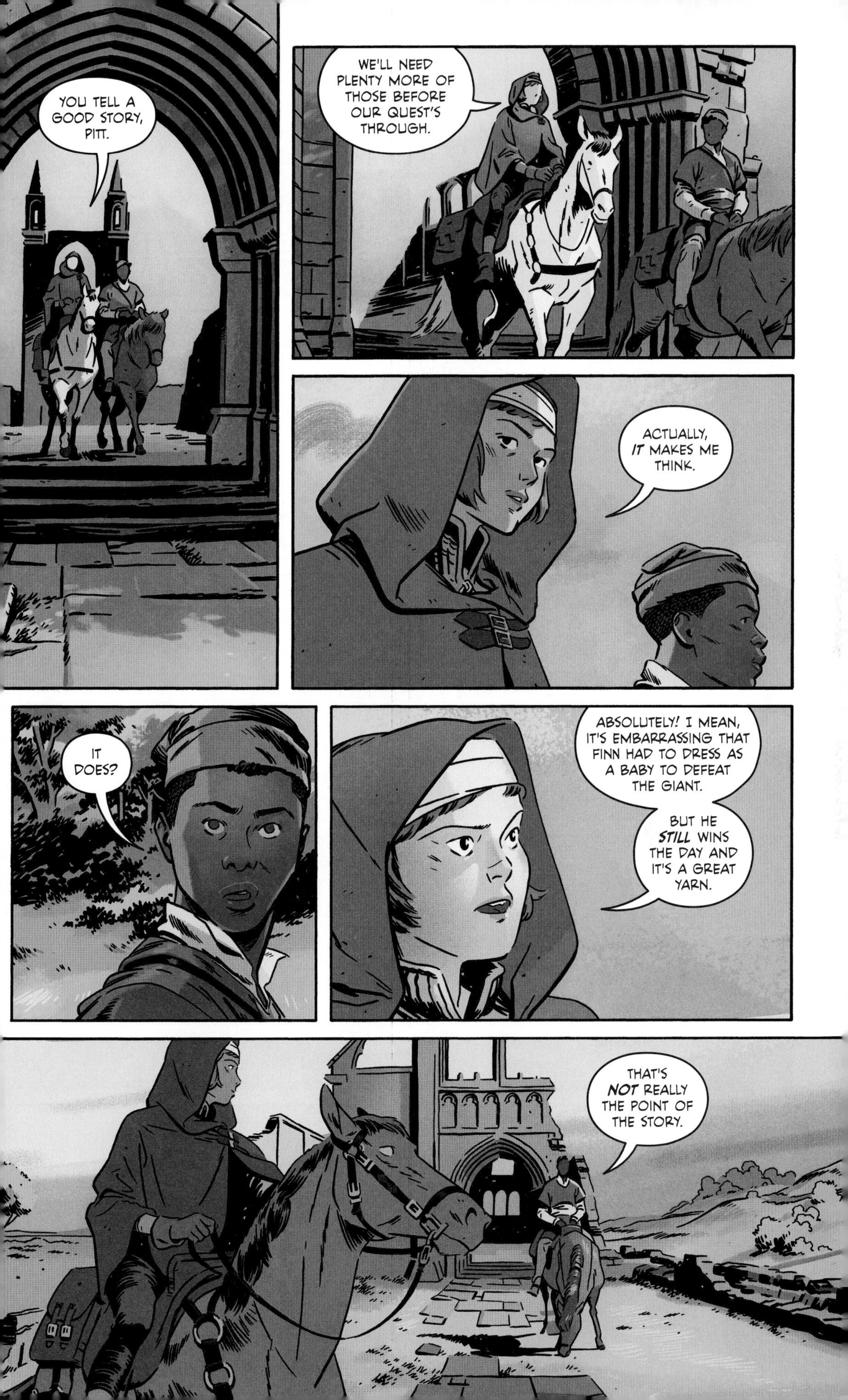
YOU TELL A GOOD STORY, PITT.
WE'LL NEED PLENTY MORE OF THOSE BEFORE OUR QUEST'S THROUGH.
ACTUALLY, *IT* MAKES ME THINK.
IT DOES?
ABSOLUTELY! I MEAN, IT'S EMBARRASSING THAT FINN HAD TO DRESS AS A BABY TO DEFEAT THE GIANT.
BUT HE ***STILL*** WINS THE DAY AND IT'S A GREAT YARN.
THAT'S ***NOT*** REALLY THE POINT OF THE STORY.

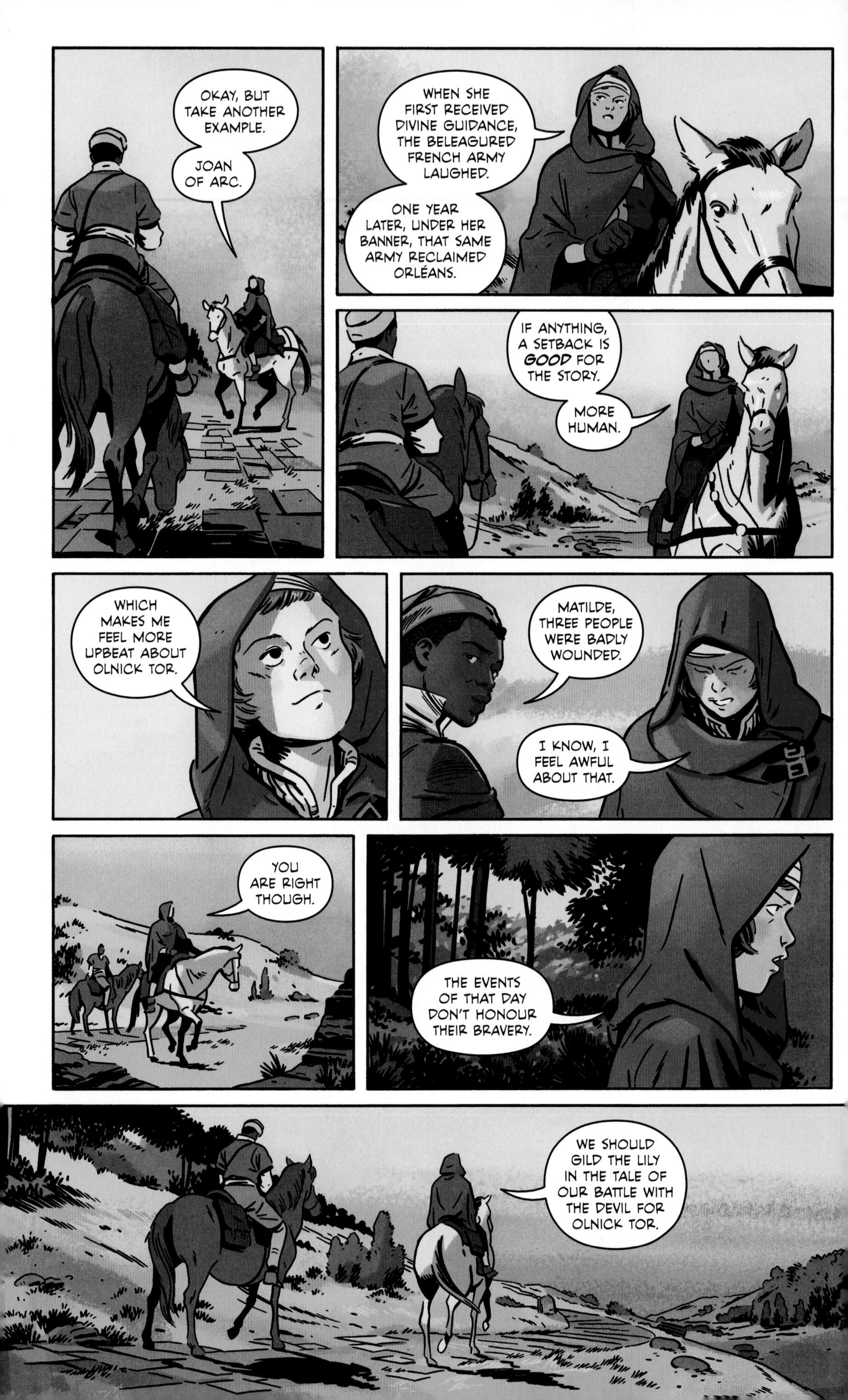
OKAY, BUT TAKE ANOTHER EXAMPLE.
JOAN OF ARC.
WHEN SHE FIRST RECEIVED DIVINE GUIDANCE, THE BELEAGURED FRENCH ARMY LAUGHED.
ONE YEAR LATER, UNDER HER BANNER, THAT SAME ARMY RECLAIMED ORLÉANS.
IF ANYTHING, A SETBACK IS GOOD FOR THE STORY.
MORE HUMAN.
WHICH MAKES ME FEEL MORE UPBEAT ABOUT OLNICK TOR.
MATILDE, THREE PEOPLE WERE BADLY WOUNDED.
I KNOW, I FEEL AWFUL ABOUT THAT.
YOU ARE RIGHT THOUGH.
THE EVENTS OF THAT DAY DON'T HONOUR THEIR BRAVERY.
WE SHOULD GILD THE LILY IN THE TALE OF OUR BATTLE WITH THE DEVIL FOR OLNICK TOR.

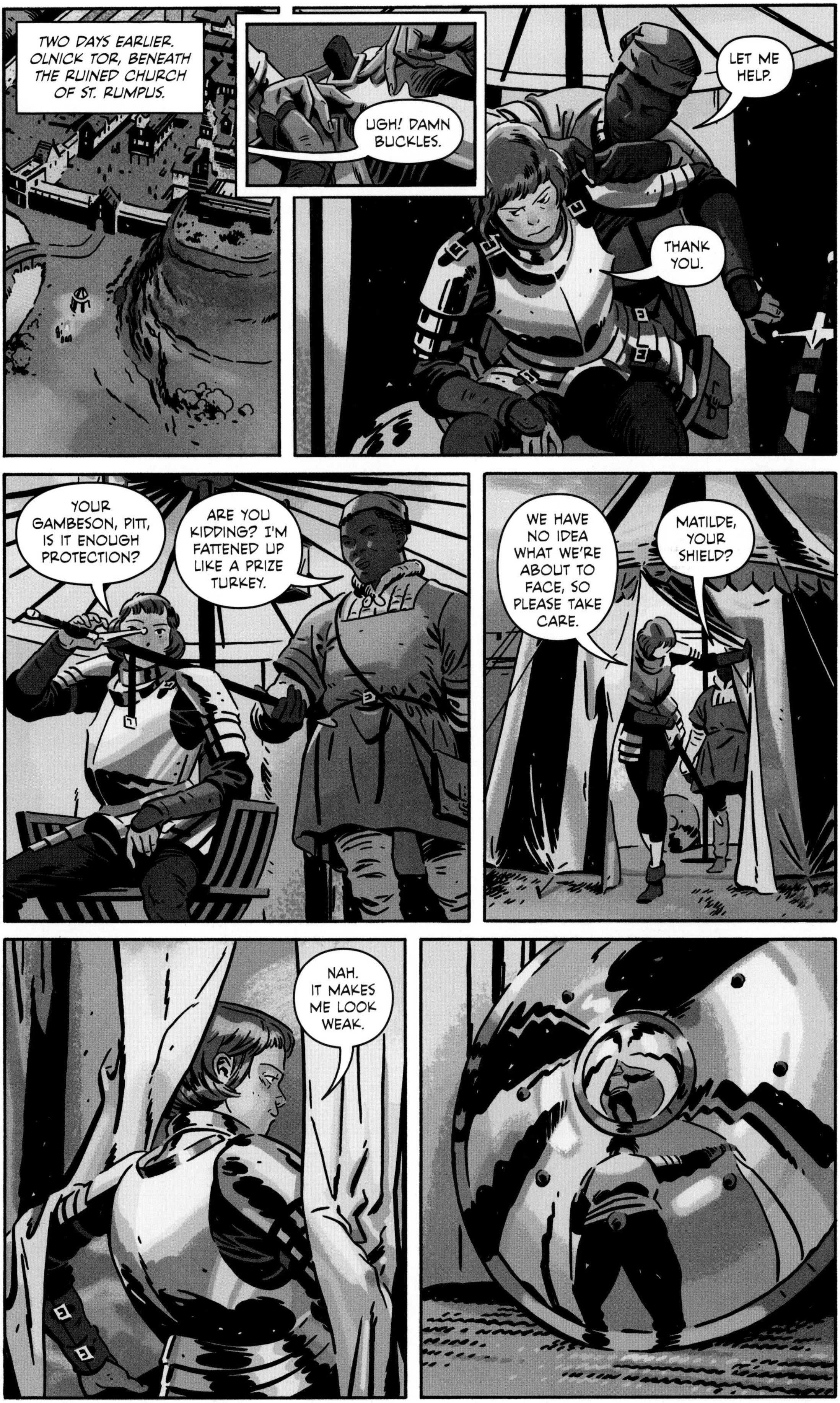

TWO DAYS EARLIER. OLNICK TOR, BENEATH THE RUINED CHURCH OF ST. RUMPUS.
UGH! DAMN BUCKLES.
LET ME HELP.
THANK YOU.
YOUR GAMBESON, PITT, IS IT ENOUGH PROTECTION?
ARE YOU KIDDING? I'M FATTENED UP LIKE A PRIZE TURKEY.
WE HAVE NO IDEA WHAT WE'RE ABOUT TO FACE, SO PLEASE TAKE CARE.
MATILDE, YOUR SHIELD?
NAH. IT MAKES ME LOOK WEAK.

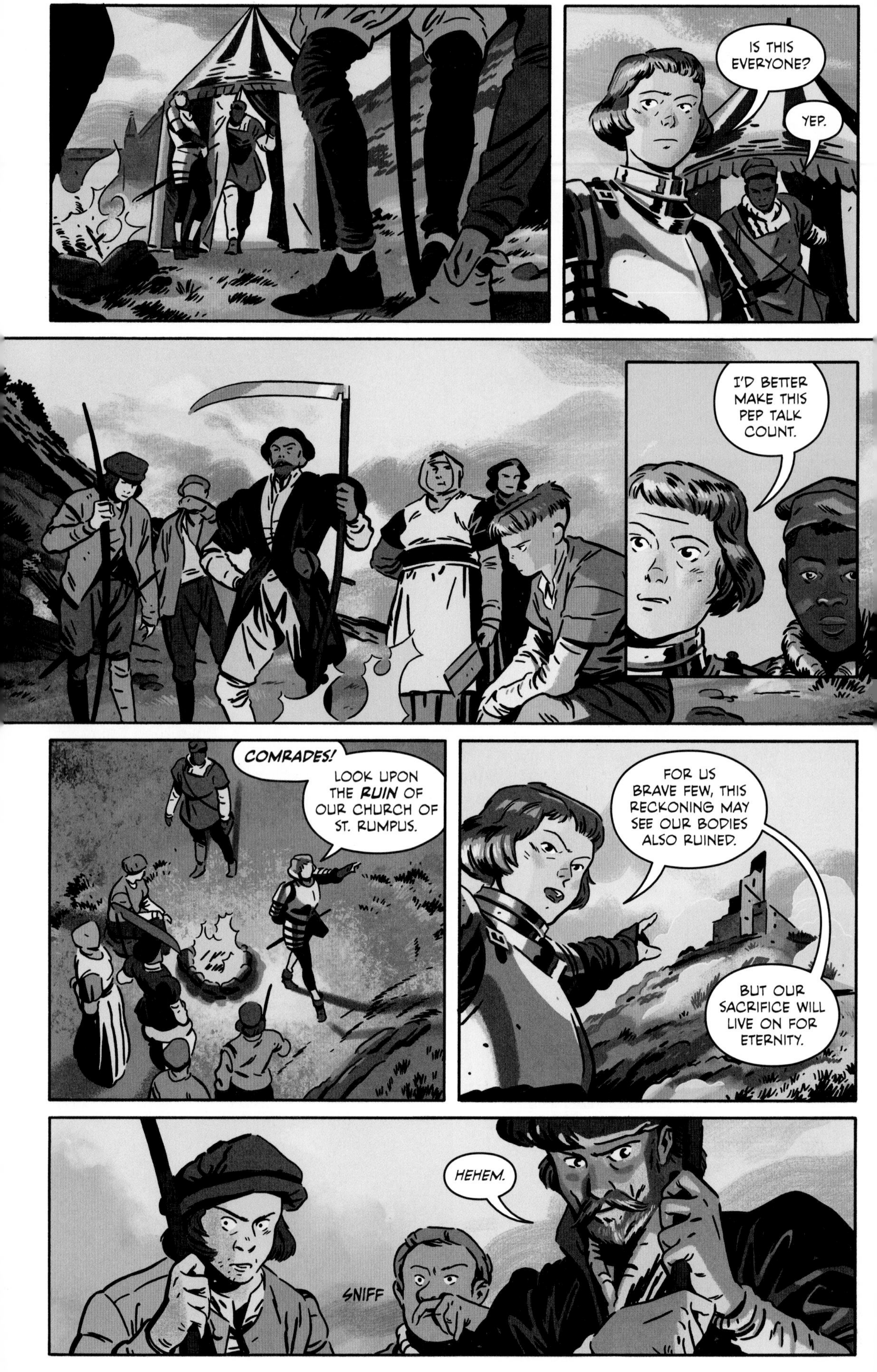
IS THIS EVERYONE?
YEP.
I'D BETTER MAKE THIS PEP TALK COUNT.
COMRADES!
LOOK UPON THE RUIN OF OUR CHURCH OF ST. RUMPUS.
FOR US BRAVE FEW, THIS RECKONING MAY SEE OUR BODIES ALSO RUINED.
BUT OUR SACRIFICE WILL LIVE ON FOR ETERNITY.
HEHEM.
SNIFF

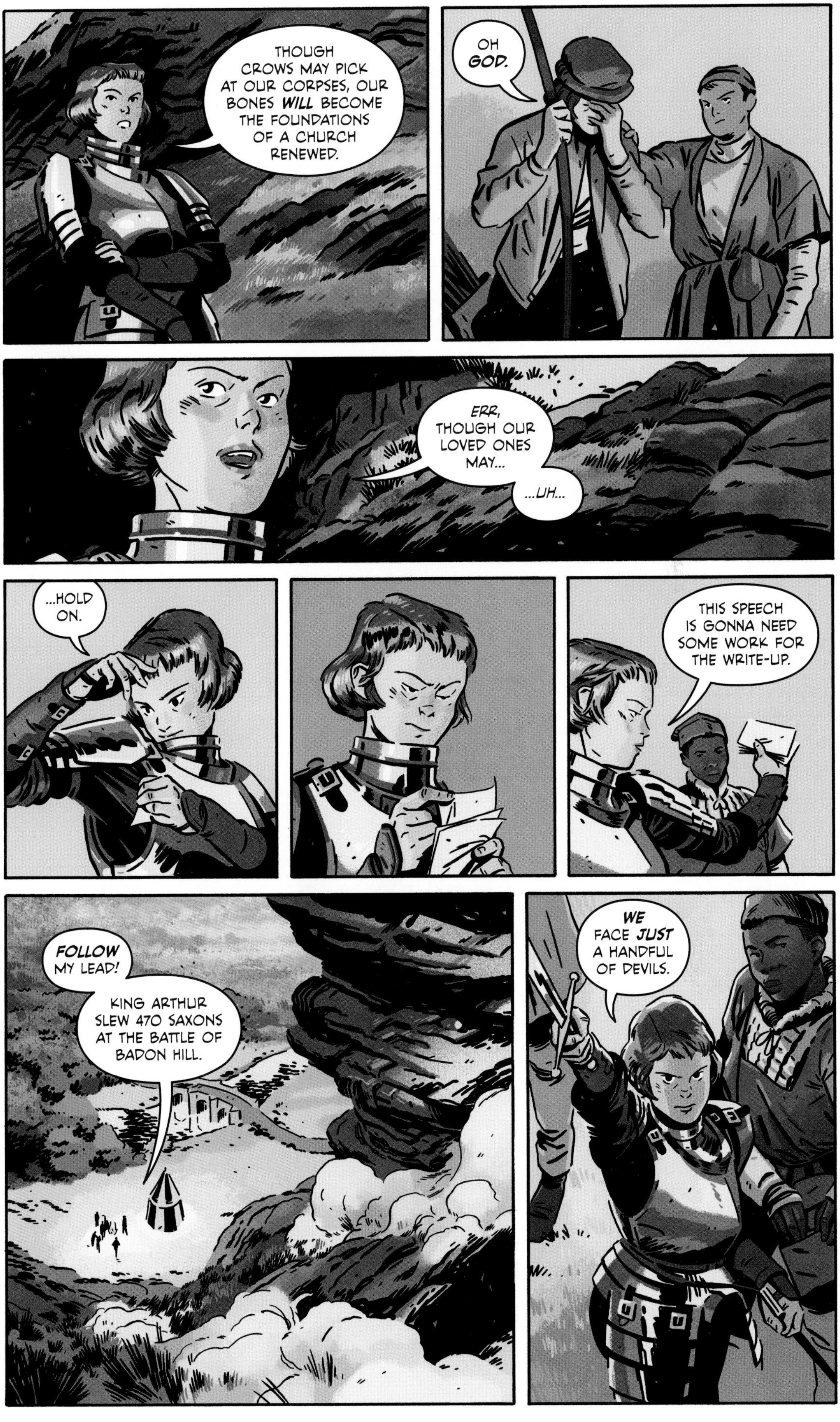
THOUGH CROWS MAY PICK AT OUR CORPSES, OUR BONES WILL BECOME THE FOUNDATIONS OF A CHURCH RENEWED.
OH GOD.
ERR, THOUGH OUR LOVED ONES MAY...
...UH...
...HOLD ON.
THIS SPEECH IS GONNA NEED SOME WORK FOR THE WRITE-UP.
FOLLOW MY LEAD!
KING ARTHUR SLEW 470 SAXONS AT THE BATTLE OF BADON HILL.
WE FACE JUST A HANDFUL OF DEVILS.

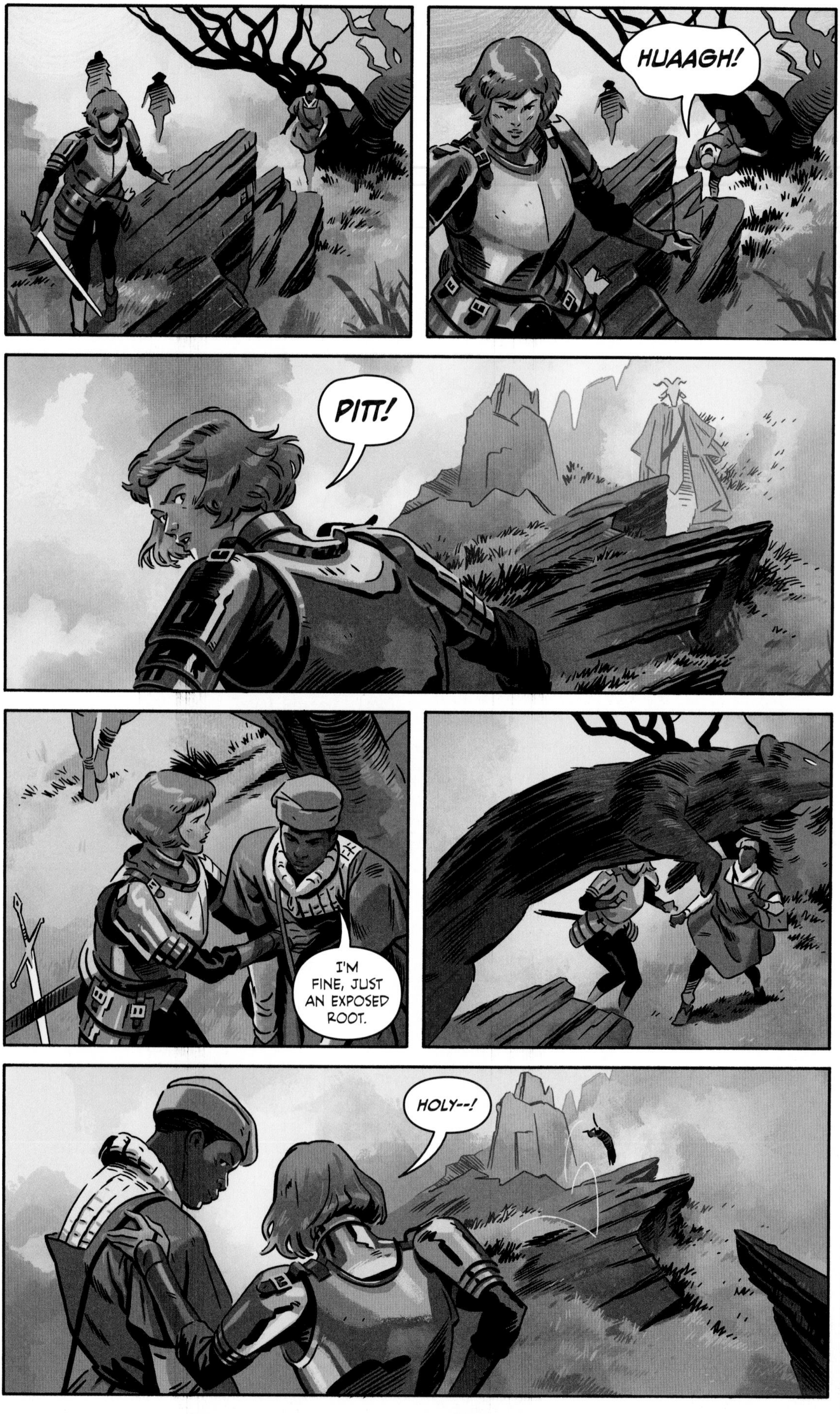
HUAAGH!
PITT!
I'M FINE, JUST AN EXPOSED ROOT.
HOLY--!

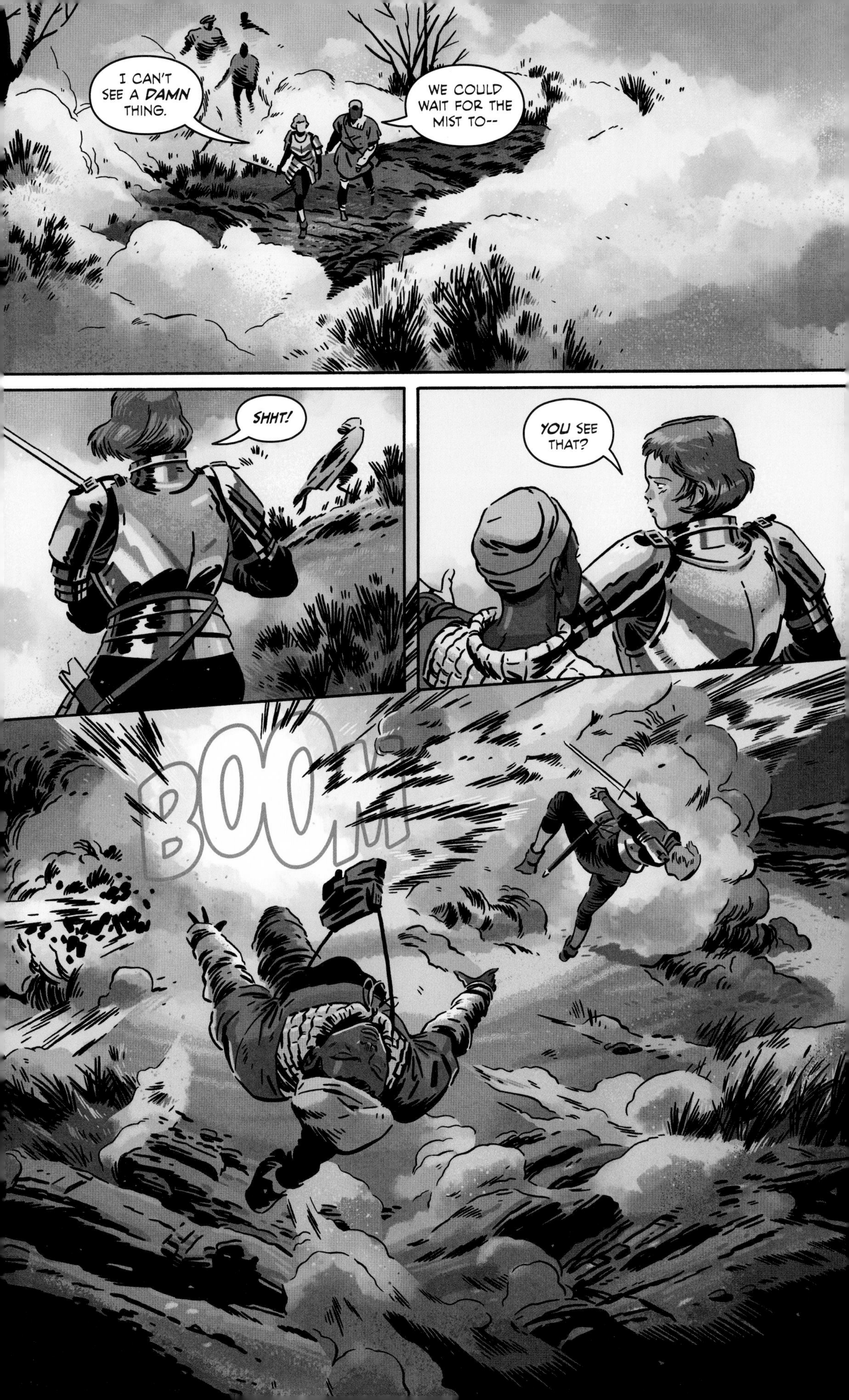
I CAN'T SEE A DAMN THING.
WE COULD WAIT FOR THE MIST TO--
SHHT!
YOU SEE THAT?
BOOM

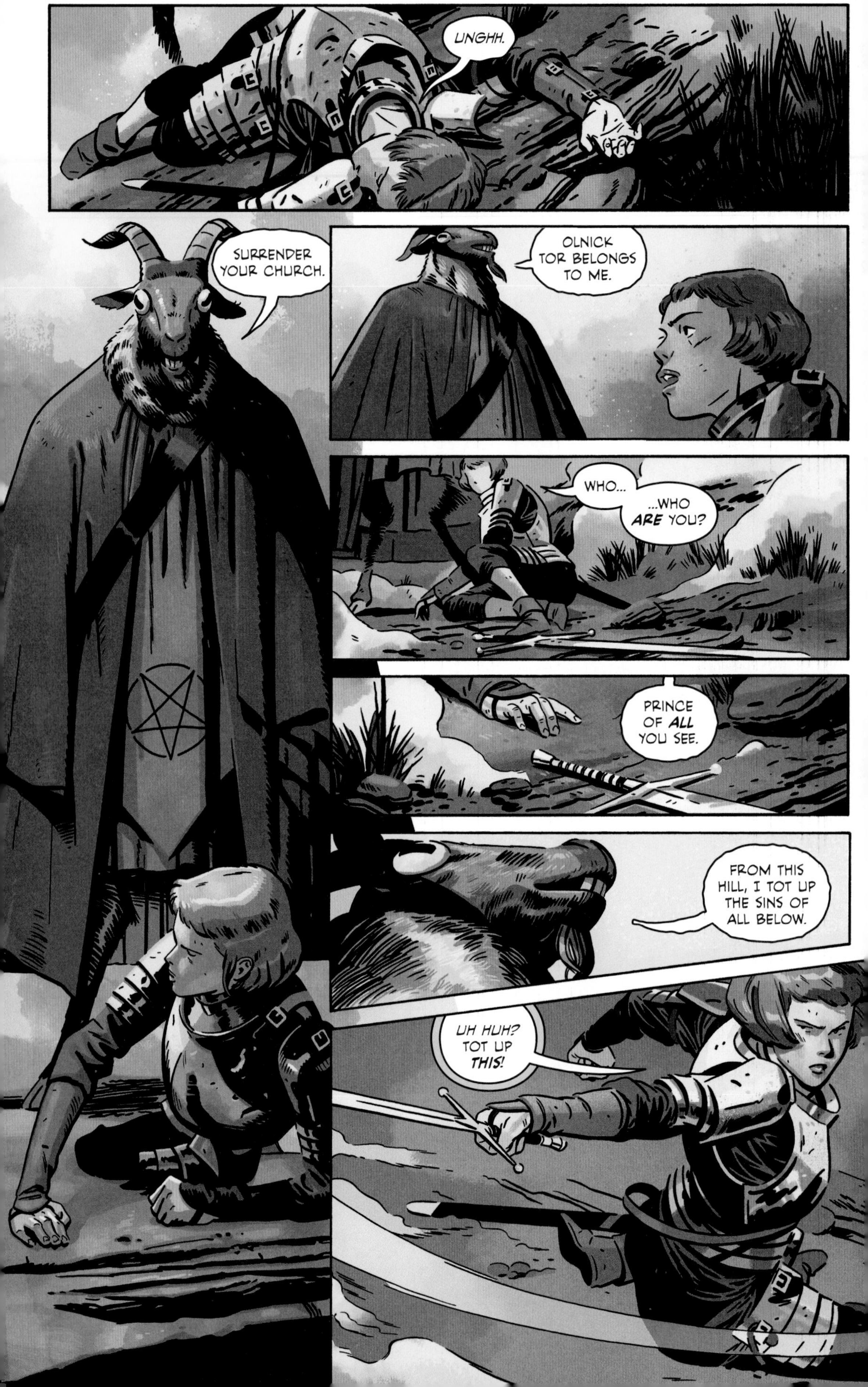

UNGHH.
SURRENDER YOUR CHURCH.
OLNICK TOR BELONGS TO ME.
WHO...
...WHO ARE YOU?
PRINCE OF ALL YOU SEE.
FROM THIS HILL, I TOT UP THE SINS OF ALL BELOW.
UH HUH? TOT UP THIS!

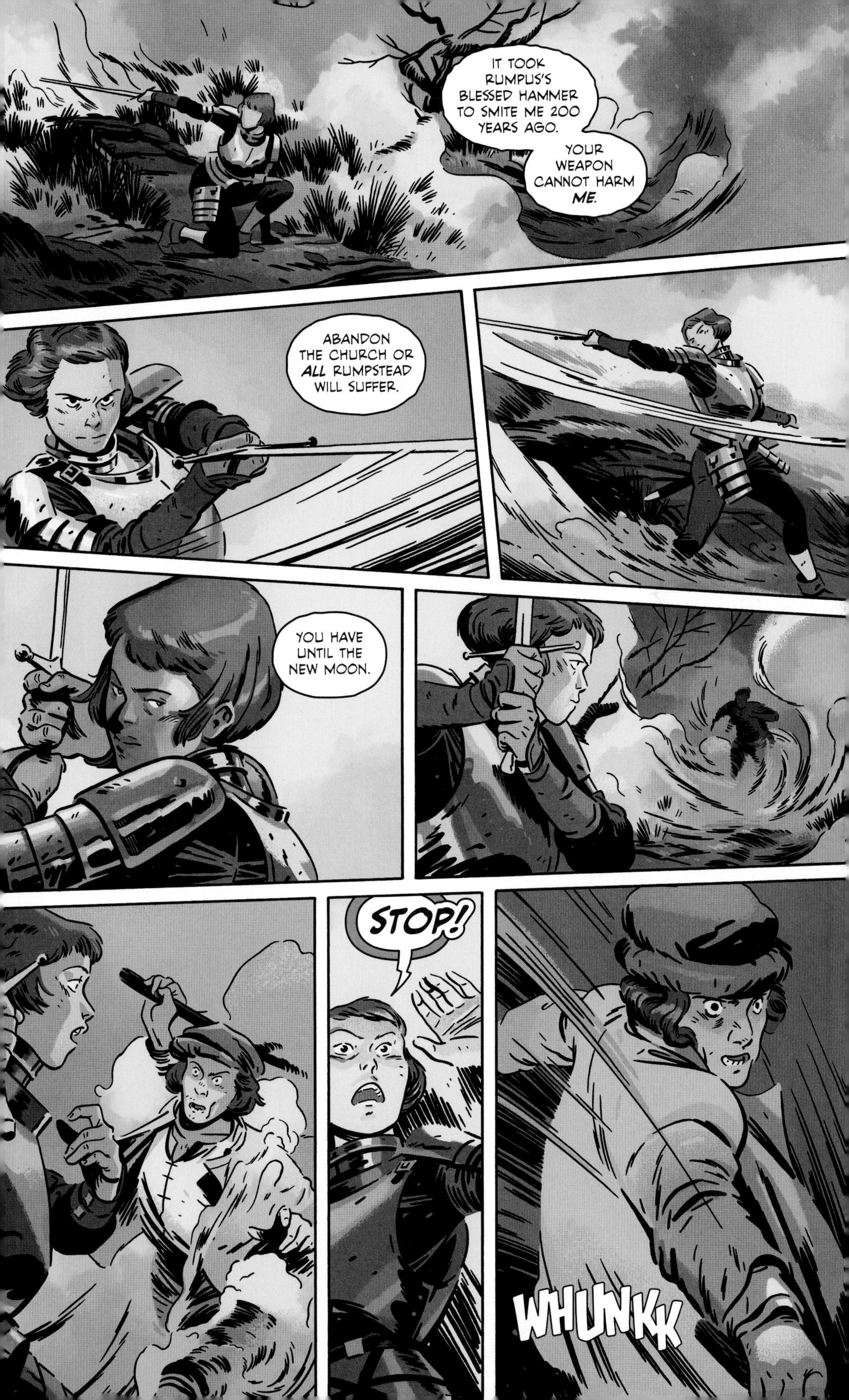
IT TOOK RUMPUS'S BLESSED HAMMER TO SMITE ME 200 YEARS AGO.
YOUR WEAPON CANNOT HARM *ME*.
ABANDON THE CHURCH OR *ALL* RUMPSTEAD WILL SUFFER.
YOU HAVE UNTIL THE NEW MOON.
STOP!
WHUNKK

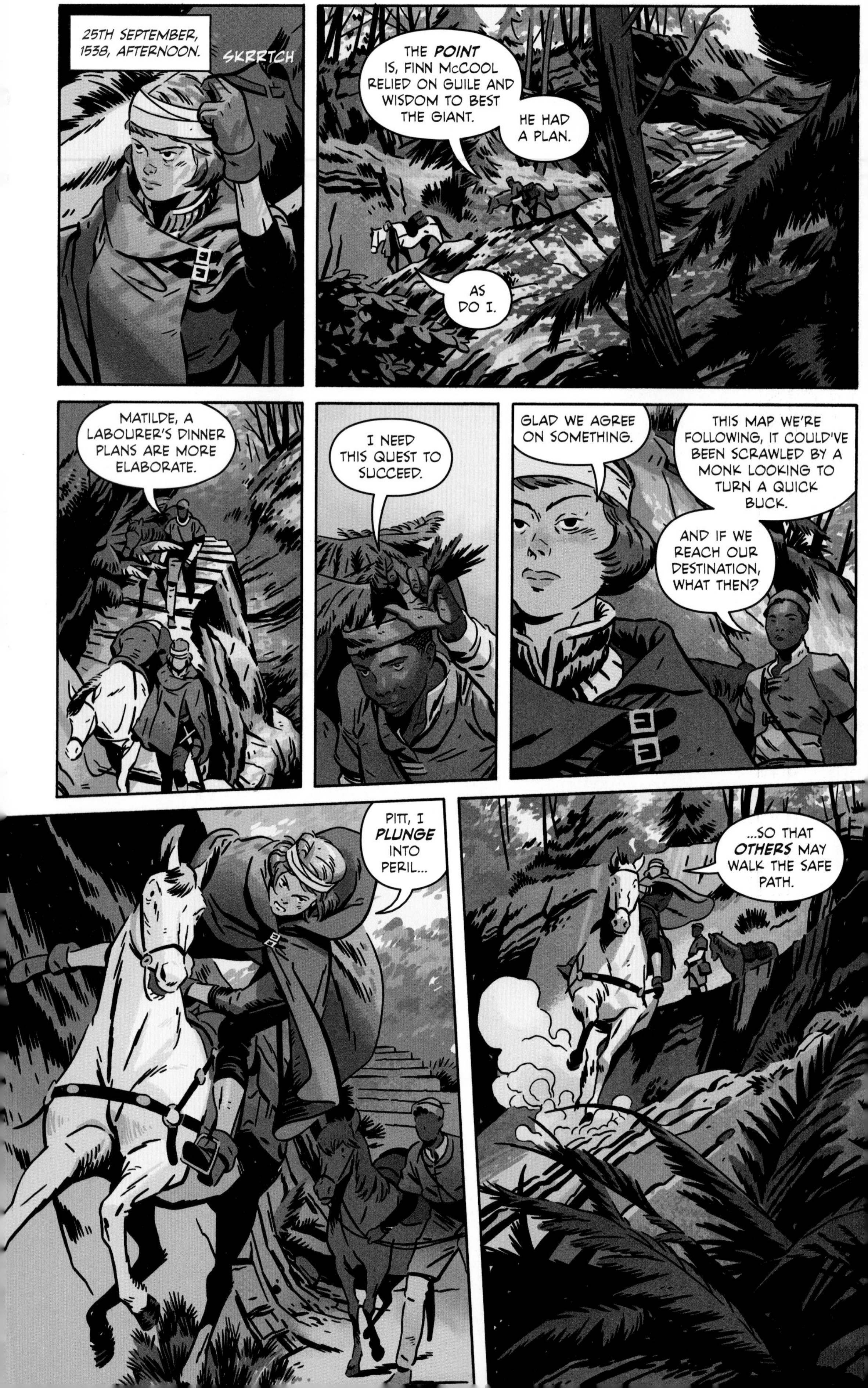
25TH SEPTEMBER, 1538, AFTERNOON.
SKRRTCH
THE POINT IS, FINN McCOOL RELIED ON GUILE AND WISDOM TO BEST THE GIANT.
HE HAD A PLAN.
AS DO I.
MATILDE, A LABOURER'S DINNER PLANS ARE MORE ELABORATE.
I NEED THIS QUEST TO SUCCEED.
GLAD WE AGREE ON SOMETHING.
THIS MAP WE'RE FOLLOWING, IT COULD'VE BEEN SCRAWLED BY A MONK LOOKING TO TURN A QUICK BUCK.
AND IF WE REACH OUR DESTINATION, WHAT THEN?
PITT, I PLUNGE INTO PERIL...
...SO THAT OTHERS MAY WALK THE SAFE PATH.

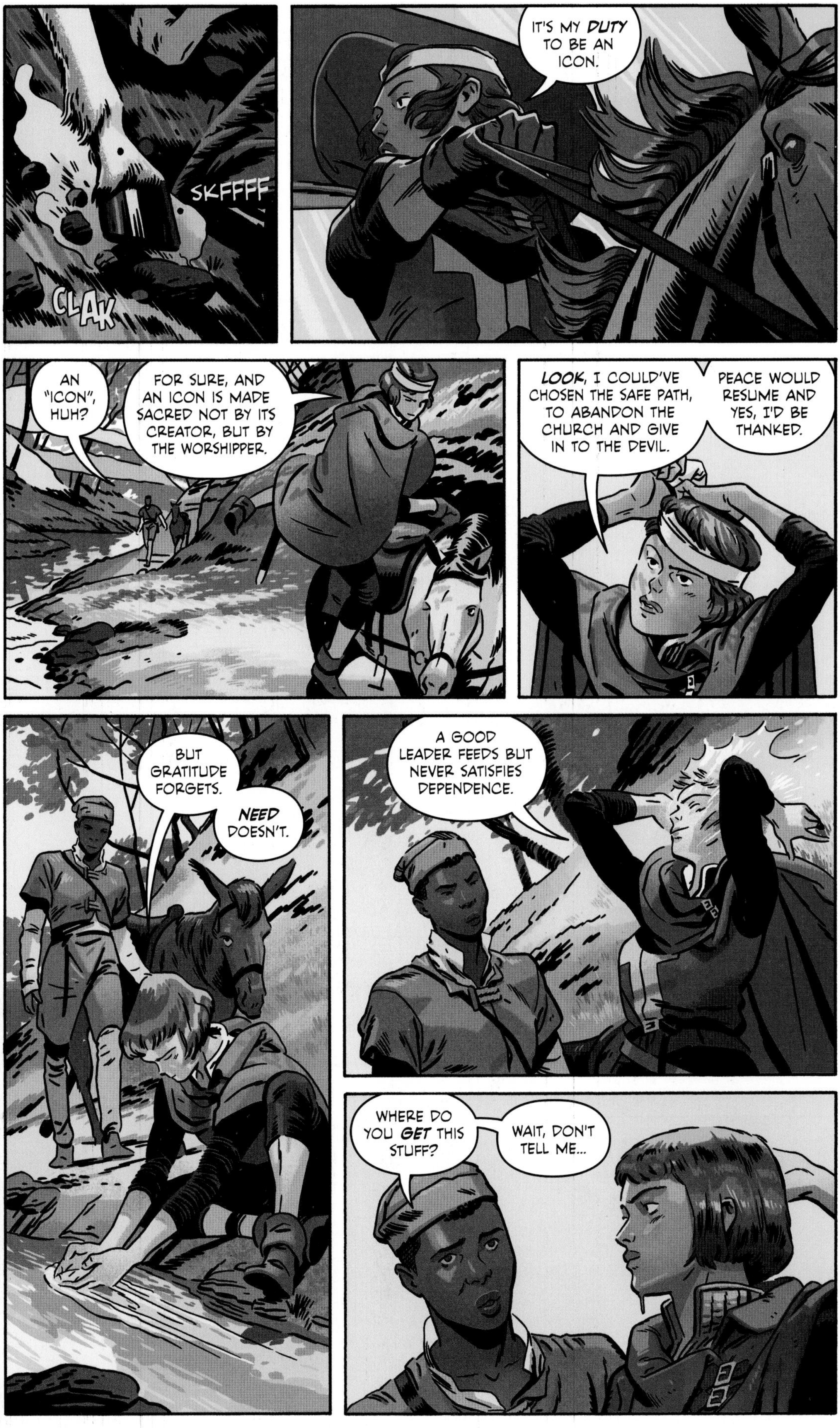
SKFFFF
CLAK
IT'S MY DUTY TO BE AN ICON.
AN "ICON", HUH?
FOR SURE, AND AN ICON IS MADE SACRED NOT BY ITS CREATOR, BUT BY THE WORSHIPPER.
LOOK, I COULD'VE CHOSEN THE SAFE PATH, TO ABANDON THE CHURCH AND GIVE IN TO THE DEVIL.
PEACE WOULD RESUME AND YES, I'D BE THANKED.
BUT GRATITUDE FORGETS.
NEED DOESN'T.
A GOOD LEADER FEEDS BUT NEVER SATISFIES DEPENDENCE.
WHERE DO YOU GET THIS STUFF?
WAIT, DON'T TELL ME...

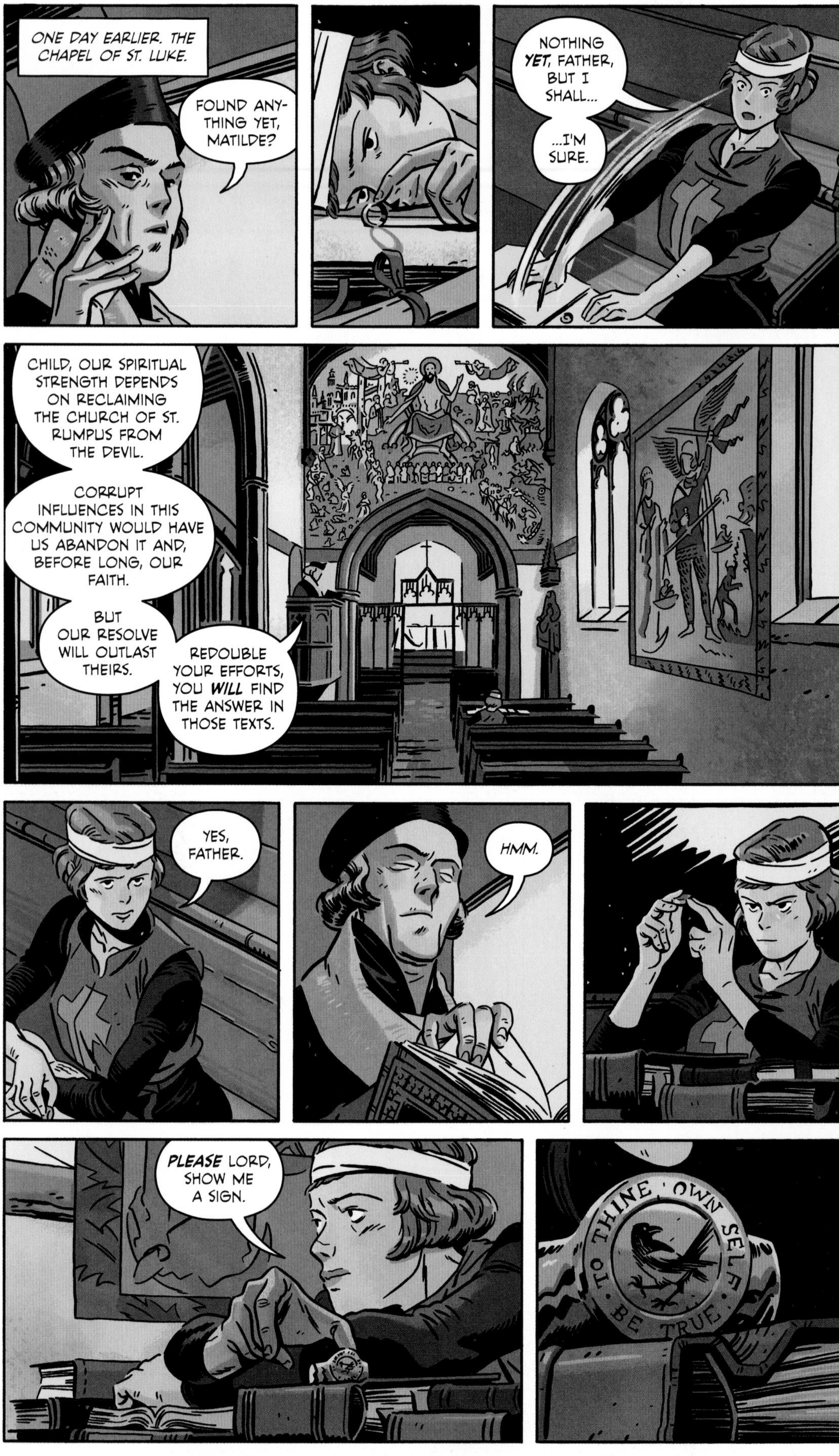

ONE DAY EARLIER. THE CHAPEL OF ST. LUKE.
FOUND ANYTHING YET, MATILDE?
NOTHING *YET*, FATHER, BUT I SHALL...
...I'M SURE.
CHILD, OUR SPIRITUAL STRENGTH DEPENDS ON RECLAIMING THE CHURCH OF ST. RUMPUS FROM THE DEVIL.
CORRUPT INFLUENCES IN THIS COMMUNITY WOULD HAVE US ABANDON IT AND, BEFORE LONG, OUR FAITH.
BUT OUR RESOLVE WILL OUTLAST THEIRS.
REDOUBLE YOUR EFFORTS, YOU *WILL* FIND THE ANSWER IN THOSE TEXTS.
YES, FATHER.
HMM.
PLEASE LORD, SHOW ME A SIGN.
TO THINE OWN SELF BE TRUE

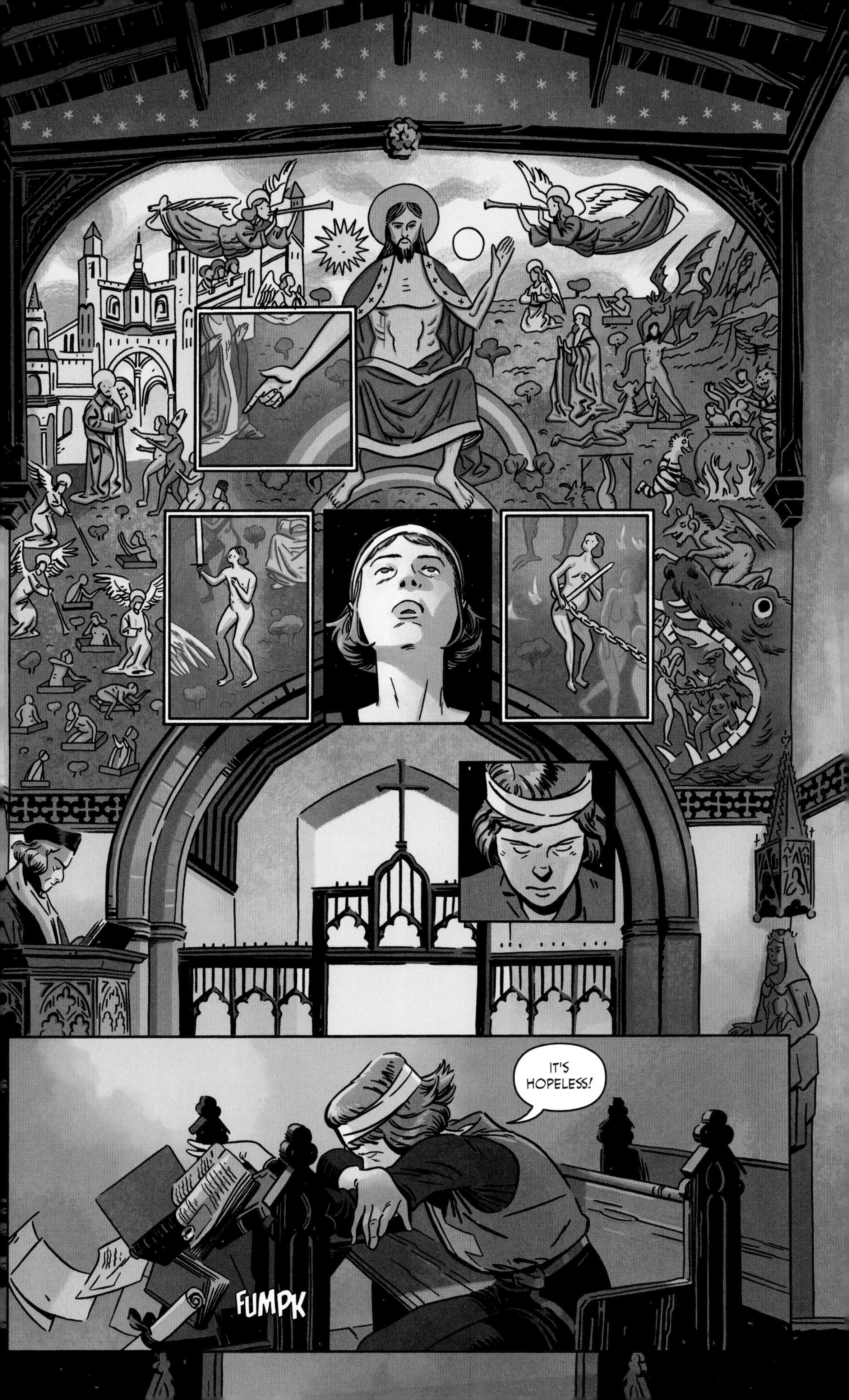
IT'S HOPELESS!
FUMPK

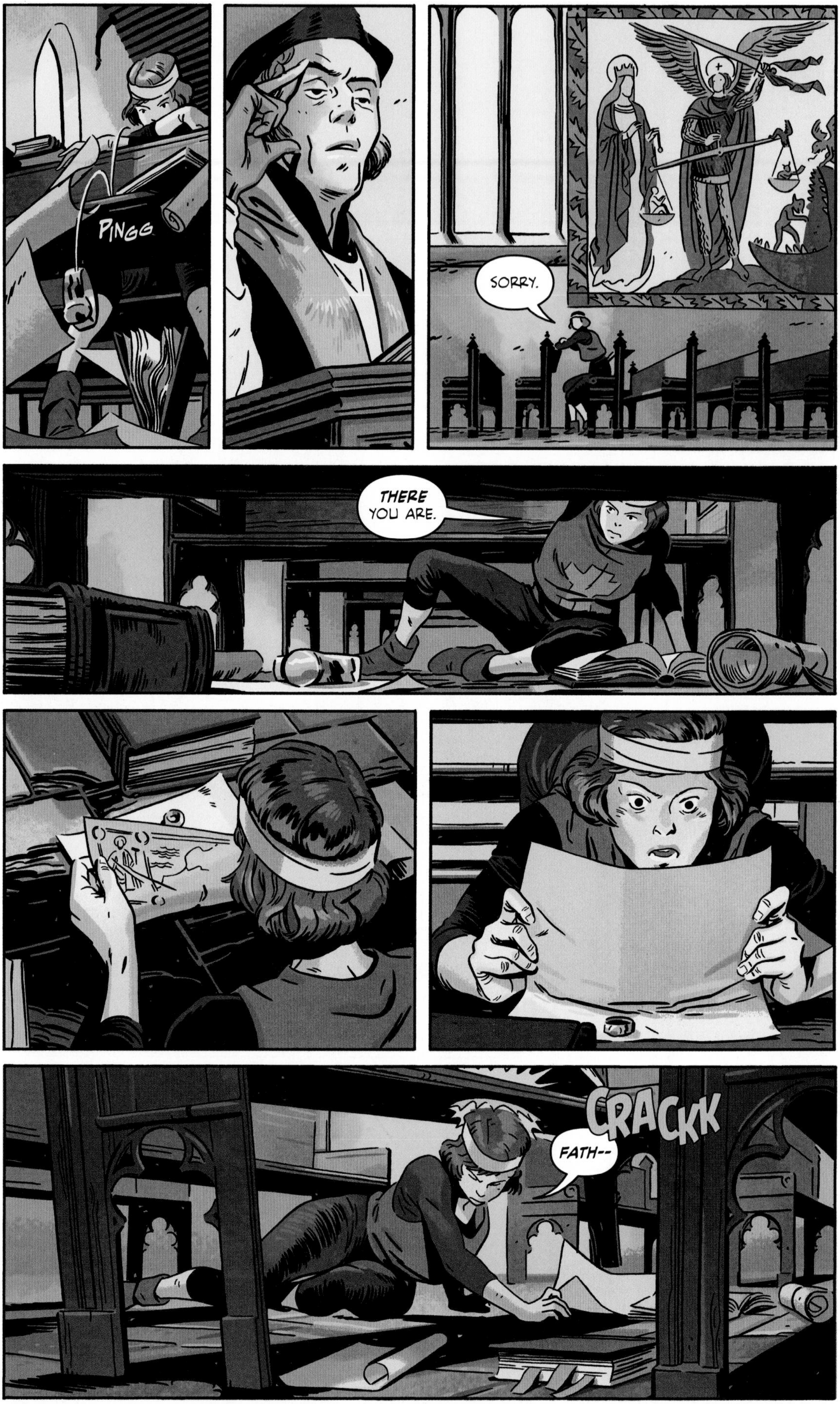
PINGG
..
SORRY.
THERE YOU ARE.
CRACKK
FATH--

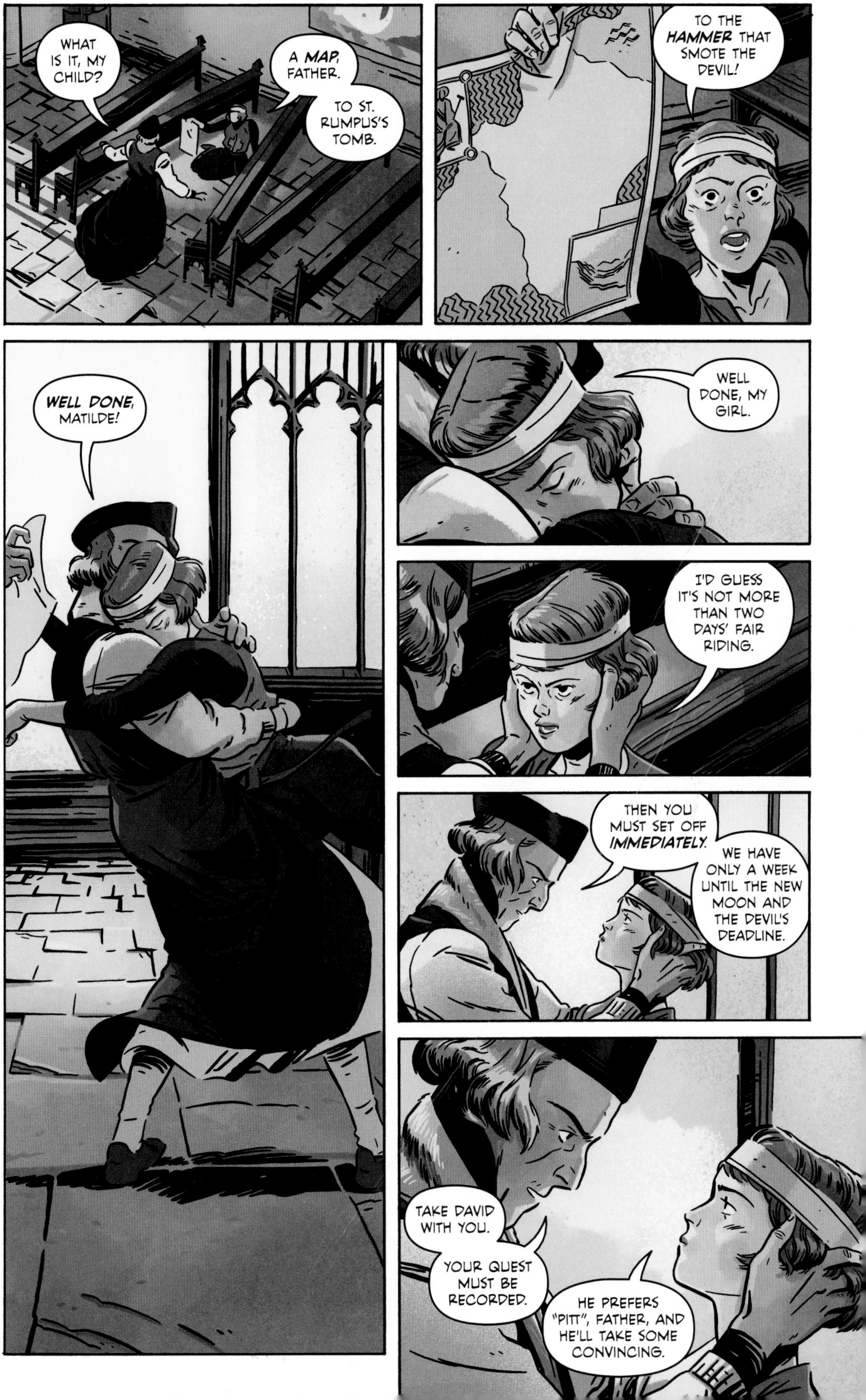
WHAT IS IT, MY CHILD?
A MAP, FATHER.
TO ST. RUMPUS'S TOMB.
TO THE HAMMER THAT SMOTE THE DEVIL!
WELL DONE, MATILDE!
WELL DONE, MY GIRL.
I'D GUESS IT'S NOT MORE THAN TWO DAYS' FAIR RIDING.
THEN YOU MUST SET OFF IMMEDIATELY.
WE HAVE ONLY A WEEK UNTIL THE NEW MOON AND THE DEVIL'S DEADLINE.
TAKE DAVID WITH YOU.
YOUR QUEST MUST BE RECORDED.
HE PREFERS "PITT", FATHER, AND HE'LL TAKE SOME CONVINCING.

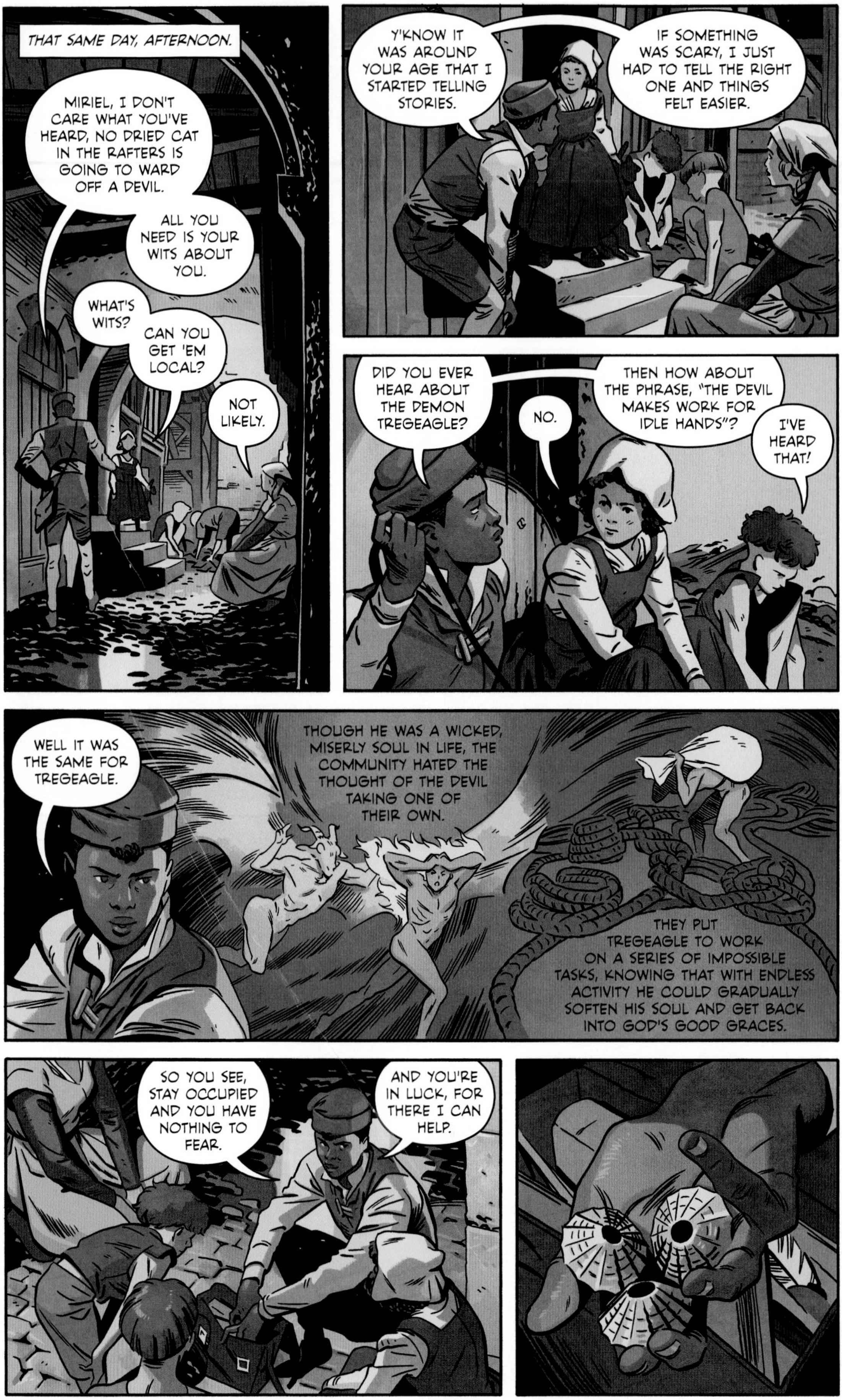
THAT SAME DAY, AFTERNOON.
MIRIEL, I DON'T CARE WHAT YOU'VE HEARD, NO DRIED CAT IN THE RAFTERS IS GOING TO WARD OFF A DEVIL.
ALL YOU NEED IS YOUR WITS ABOUT YOU.
WHAT'S WITS?
CAN YOU GET 'EM LOCAL?
NOT LIKELY.
Y'KNOW IT WAS AROUND YOUR AGE THAT I STARTED TELLING STORIES.
IF SOMETHING WAS SCARY, I JUST HAD TO TELL THE RIGHT ONE AND THINGS FELT EASIER.
DID YOU EVER HEAR ABOUT THE DEMON TREGEAGLE?
NO.
THEN HOW ABOUT THE PHRASE, "THE DEVIL MAKES WORK FOR IDLE HANDS"?
I'VE HEARD THAT!
WELL IT WAS THE SAME FOR TREGEAGLE.
THOUGH HE WAS A WICKED, MISERLY SOUL IN LIFE, THE COMMUNITY HATED THE THOUGHT OF THE DEVIL TAKING ONE OF THEIR OWN.
THEY PUT TREGEAGLE TO WORK ON A SERIES OF IMPOSSIBLE TASKS, KNOWING THAT WITH ENDLESS ACTIVITY HE COULD GRADUALLY SOFTEN HIS SOUL AND GET BACK INTO GOD'S GOOD GRACES.
SO YOU SEE, STAY OCCUPIED AND YOU HAVE NOTHING TO FEAR.
AND YOU'RE IN LUCK, FOR THERE I CAN HELP.

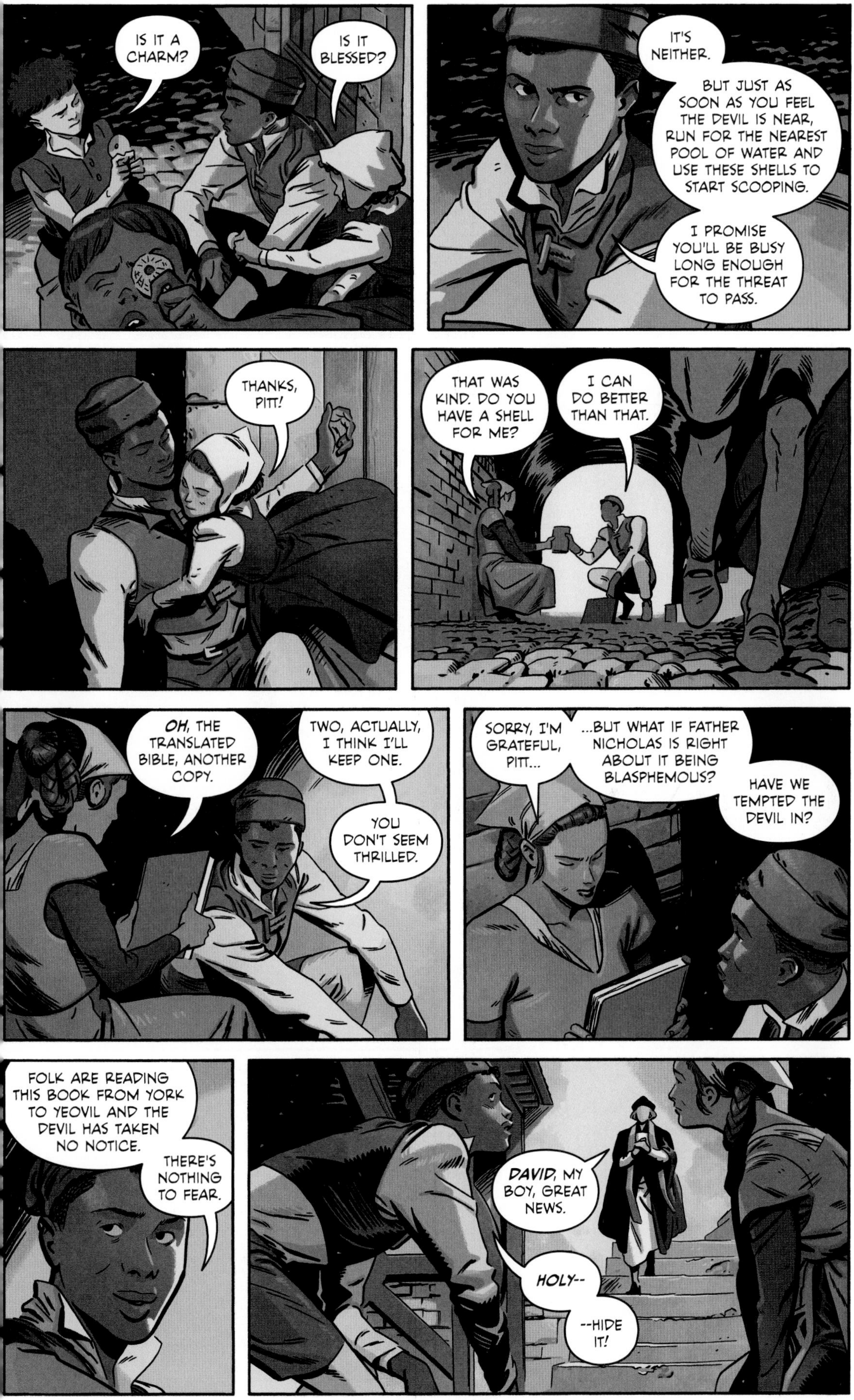
IS IT A CHARM?
IS IT BLESSED?
IT'S NEITHER.
BUT JUST AS SOON AS YOU FEEL THE DEVIL IS NEAR, RUN FOR THE NEAREST POOL OF WATER AND USE THESE SHELLS TO START SCOOPING.
I PROMISE YOU'LL BE BUSY LONG ENOUGH FOR THE THREAT TO PASS.
THANKS, PITT!
THAT WAS KIND. DO YOU HAVE A SHELL FOR ME?
I CAN DO BETTER THAN THAT.
OH, THE TRANSLATED BIBLE, ANOTHER COPY.
TWO, ACTUALLY, I THINK I'LL KEEP ONE.
YOU DON'T SEEM THRILLED.
SORRY, I'M GRATEFUL, PITT...
...BUT WHAT IF FATHER NICHOLAS IS RIGHT ABOUT IT BEING BLASPHEMOUS?
HAVE WE TEMPTED THE DEVIL IN?
FOLK ARE READING THIS BOOK FROM YORK TO YEOVIL AND THE DEVIL HAS TAKEN NO NOTICE.
THERE'S NOTHING TO FEAR.
DAVID, MY BOY, GREAT NEWS.
HOLY--
--HIDE IT!

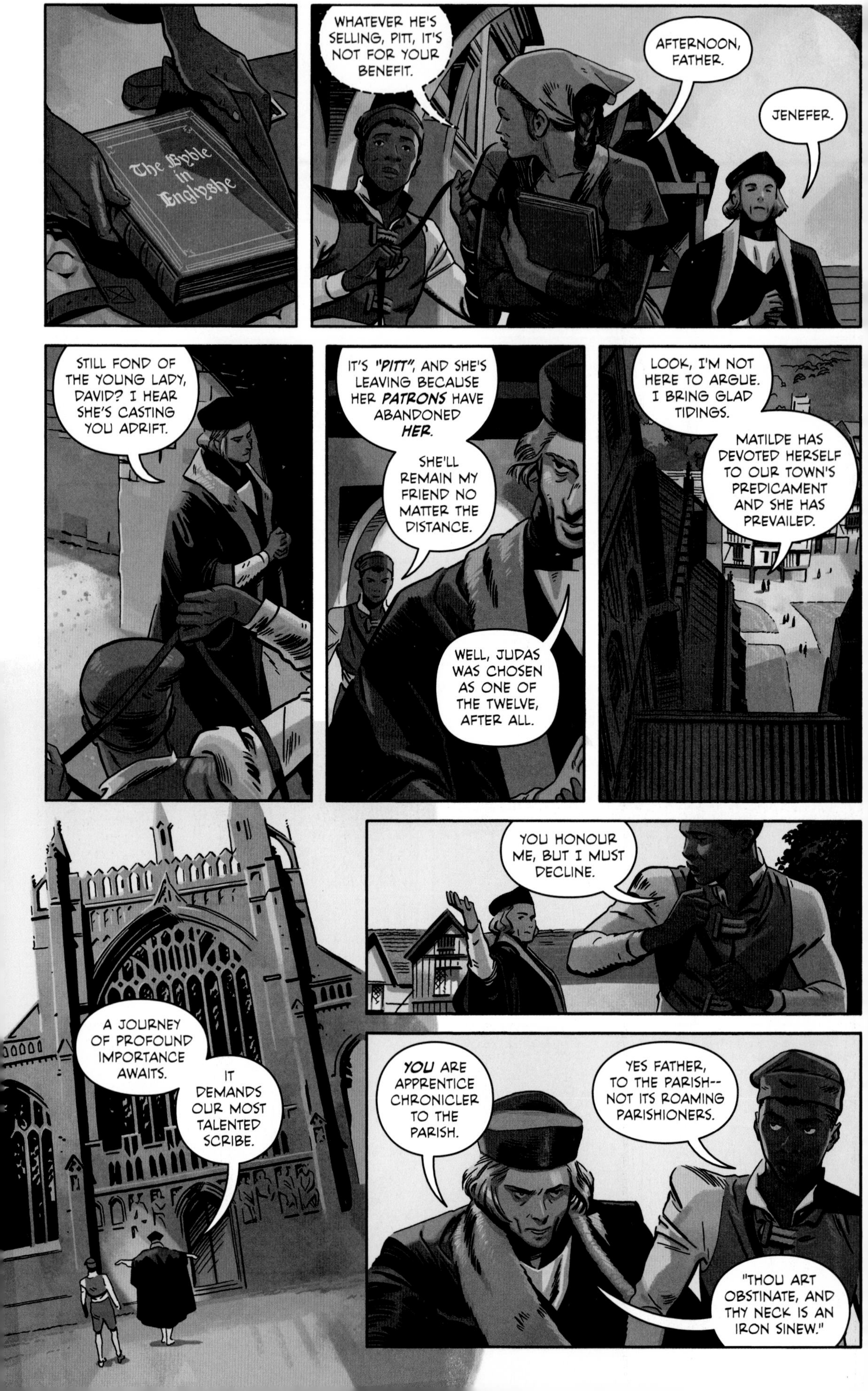
The Byble in Englyshe
WHATEVER HE'S SELLING, PITT, IT'S NOT FOR YOUR BENEFIT.
AFTERNOON, FATHER.
JENEFER.
STILL FOND OF THE YOUNG LADY, DAVID? I HEAR SHE'S CASTING YOU ADRIFT.
IT'S "PITT", AND SHE'S LEAVING BECAUSE HER PATRONS HAVE ABANDONED HER.
SHE'LL REMAIN MY FRIEND NO MATTER THE DISTANCE.
WELL, JUDAS WAS CHOSEN AS ONE OF THE TWELVE, AFTER ALL.
LOOK, I'M NOT HERE TO ARGUE. I BRING GLAD TIDINGS.
MATILDE HAS DEVOTED HERSELF TO OUR TOWN'S PREDICAMENT AND SHE HAS PREVAILED.
A JOURNEY OF PROFOUND IMPORTANCE AWAITS.
IT DEMANDS OUR MOST TALENTED SCRIBE.
YOU HONOUR ME, BUT I MUST DECLINE.
YOU ARE APPRENTICE CHRONICLER TO THE PARISH.
YES FATHER, TO THE PARISH-- NOT ITS ROAMING PARISHIONERS.
"THOU ART OBSTINATE, AND THY NECK IS AN IRON SINEW."

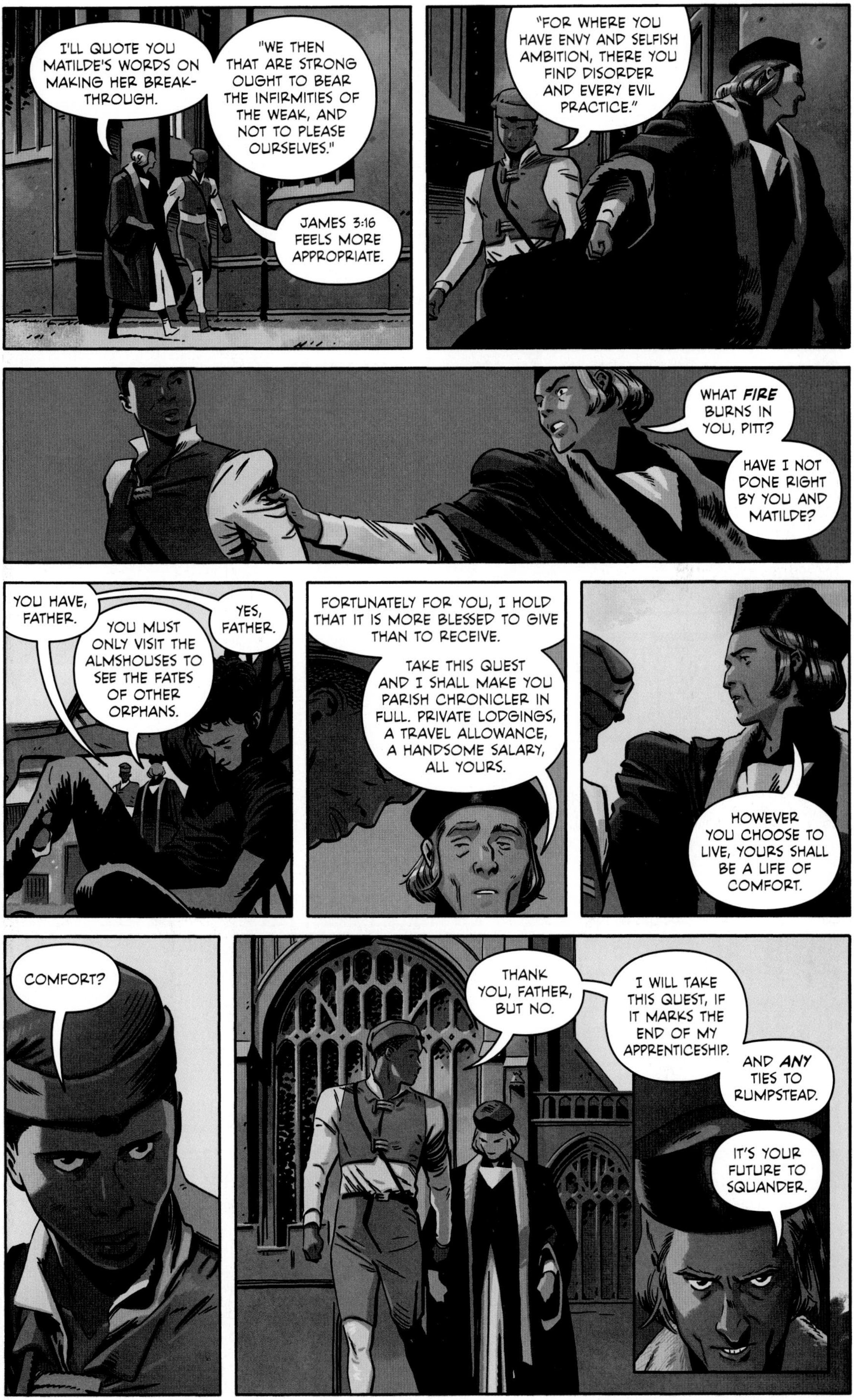
I'LL QUOTE YOU MATILDE'S WORDS ON MAKING HER BREAK-THROUGH.
"WE THEN THAT ARE STRONG OUGHT TO BEAR THE INFIRMITIES OF THE WEAK, AND NOT TO PLEASE OURSELVES."
JAMES 3:16 FEELS MORE APPROPRIATE.
"FOR WHERE YOU HAVE ENVY AND SELFISH AMBITION, THERE YOU FIND DISORDER AND EVERY EVIL PRACTICE."
WHAT FIRE BURNS IN YOU, PITT?
HAVE I NOT DONE RIGHT BY YOU AND MATILDE?
YOU HAVE, FATHER.
YOU MUST ONLY VISIT THE ALMSHOUSES TO SEE THE FATES OF OTHER ORPHANS.
YES, FATHER.
FORTUNATELY FOR YOU, I HOLD THAT IT IS MORE BLESSED TO GIVE THAN TO RECEIVE.
TAKE THIS QUEST AND I SHALL MAKE YOU PARISH CHRONICLER IN FULL. PRIVATE LODGINGS, A TRAVEL ALLOWANCE, A HANDSOME SALARY, ALL YOURS.
HOWEVER YOU CHOOSE TO LIVE, YOURS SHALL BE A LIFE OF COMFORT.
COMFORT?
THANK YOU, FATHER, BUT NO.
I WILL TAKE THIS QUEST, IF IT MARKS THE END OF MY APPRENTICESHIP.
AND ANY TIES TO RUMPSTEAD.
IT'S YOUR FUTURE TO SQUANDER.

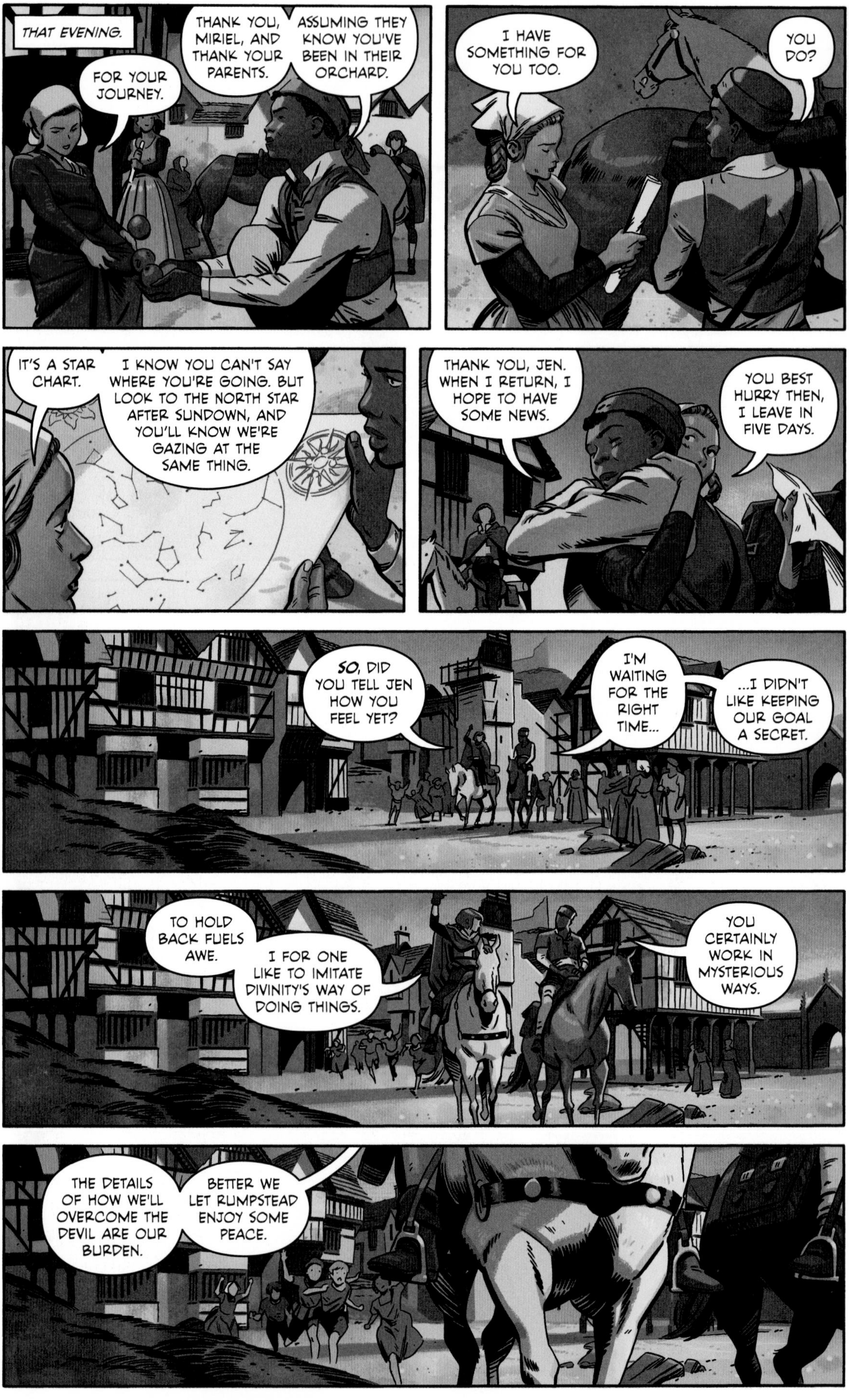
THAT EVENING.
FOR YOUR JOURNEY.
THANK YOU, MIRIEL, AND THANK YOUR PARENTS.
ASSUMING THEY KNOW YOU'VE BEEN IN THEIR ORCHARD.
I HAVE SOMETHING FOR YOU TOO.
YOU DO?
IT'S A STAR CHART.
I KNOW YOU CAN'T SAY WHERE YOU'RE GOING. BUT LOOK TO THE NORTH STAR AFTER SUNDOWN, AND YOU'LL KNOW WE'RE GAZING AT THE SAME THING.
THANK YOU, JEN. WHEN I RETURN, I HOPE TO HAVE SOME NEWS.
YOU BEST HURRY THEN, I LEAVE IN FIVE DAYS.
SO, DID YOU TELL JEN HOW YOU FEEL YET?
I'M WAITING FOR THE RIGHT TIME...
...I DIDN'T LIKE KEEPING OUR GOAL A SECRET.
TO HOLD BACK FUELS AWE.
I FOR ONE LIKE TO IMITATE DIVINITY'S WAY OF DOING THINGS.
YOU CERTAINLY WORK IN MYSTERIOUS WAYS.
THE DETAILS OF HOW WE'LL OVERCOME THE DEVIL ARE OUR BURDEN.
BETTER WE LET RUMPSTEAD ENJOY SOME PEACE.

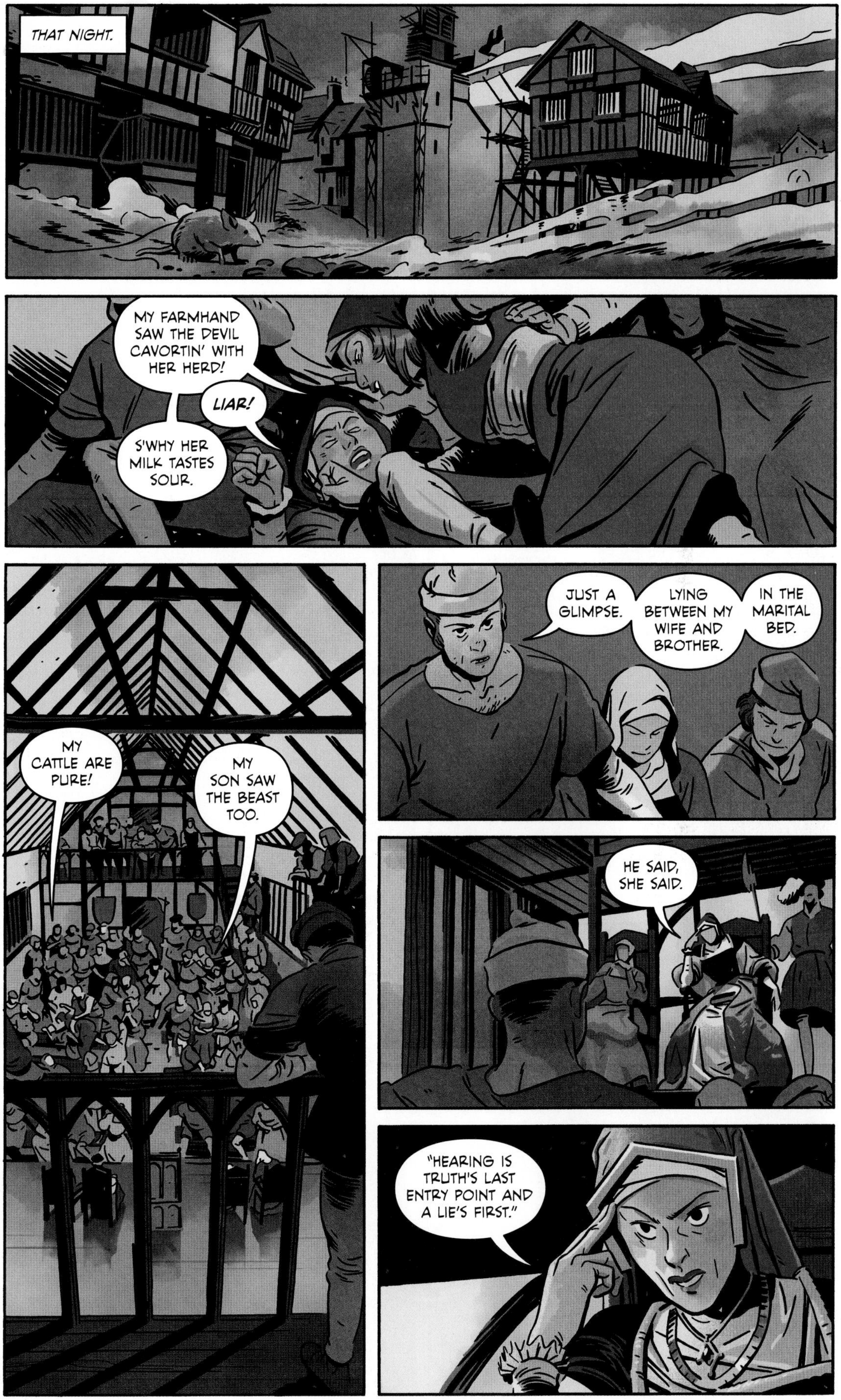
THAT NIGHT.
MY FARMHAND SAW THE DEVIL CAVORTIN' WITH HER HERD!
LIAR!
S'WHY HER MILK TASTES SOUR.
MY CATTLE ARE PURE!
MY SON SAW THE BEAST TOO.
JUST A GLIMPSE.
LYING BETWEEN MY WIFE AND BROTHER.
IN THE MARITAL BED.
HE SAID, SHE SAID.
"HEARING IS TRUTH'S LAST ENTRY POINT AND A LIE'S FIRST."

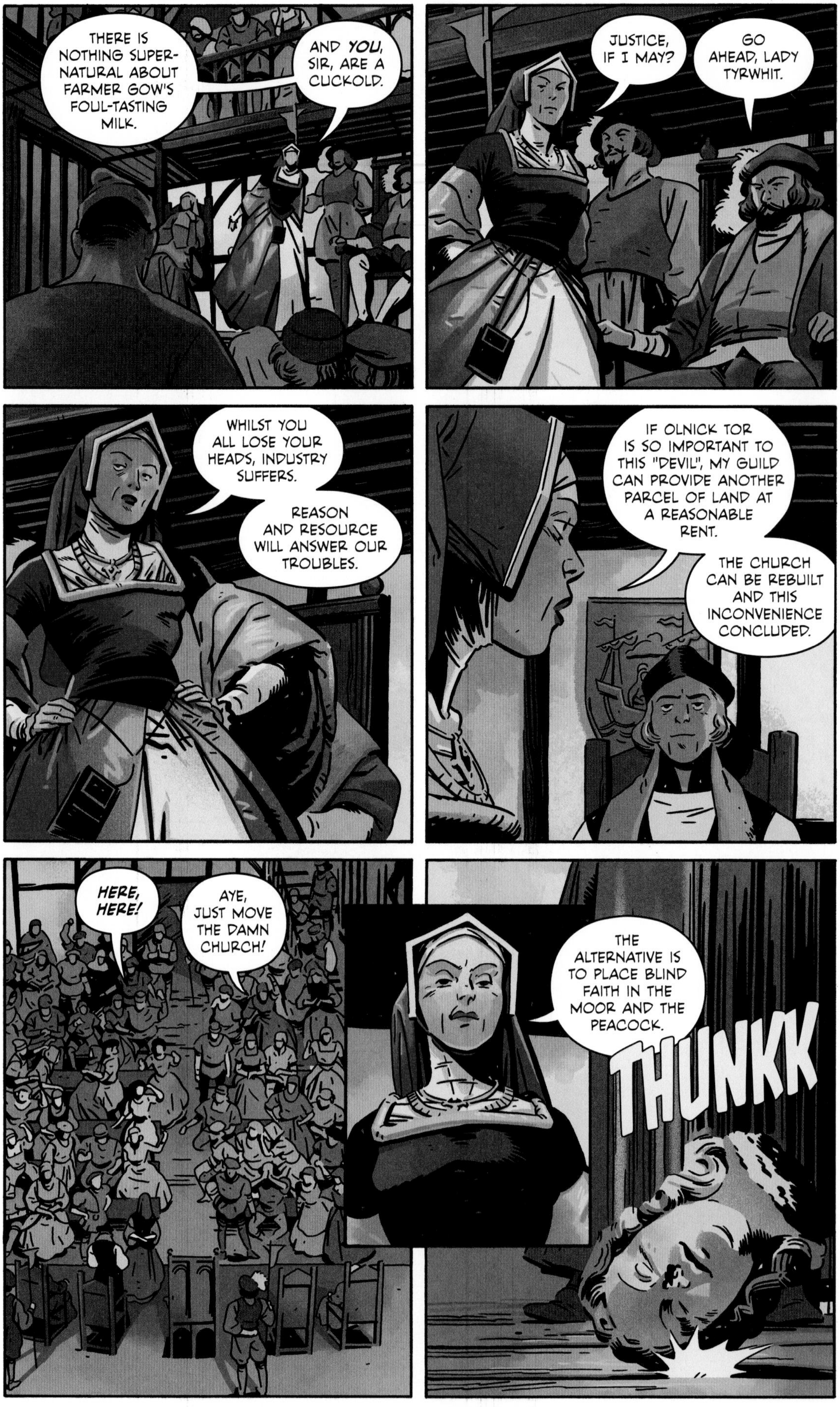

THERE IS NOTHING SUPER-NATURAL ABOUT FARMER GOW'S FOUL-TASTING MILK.
AND *YOU*, SIR, ARE A CUCKOLD.
JUSTICE, IF I MAY?
GO AHEAD, LADY TYRWHIT.
WHILST YOU ALL LOSE YOUR HEADS, INDUSTRY SUFFERS.
REASON AND RESOURCE WILL ANSWER OUR TROUBLES.
IF OLNICK TOR IS SO IMPORTANT TO THIS "DEVIL", MY GUILD CAN PROVIDE ANOTHER PARCEL OF LAND AT A REASONABLE RENT.
THE CHURCH CAN BE REBUILT AND THIS INCONVENIENCE CONCLUDED.
HERE, HERE!
AYE, JUST MOVE THE DAMN CHURCH!
THE ALTERNATIVE IS TO PLACE BLIND FAITH IN THE MOOR AND THE PEACOCK.
THUNKK

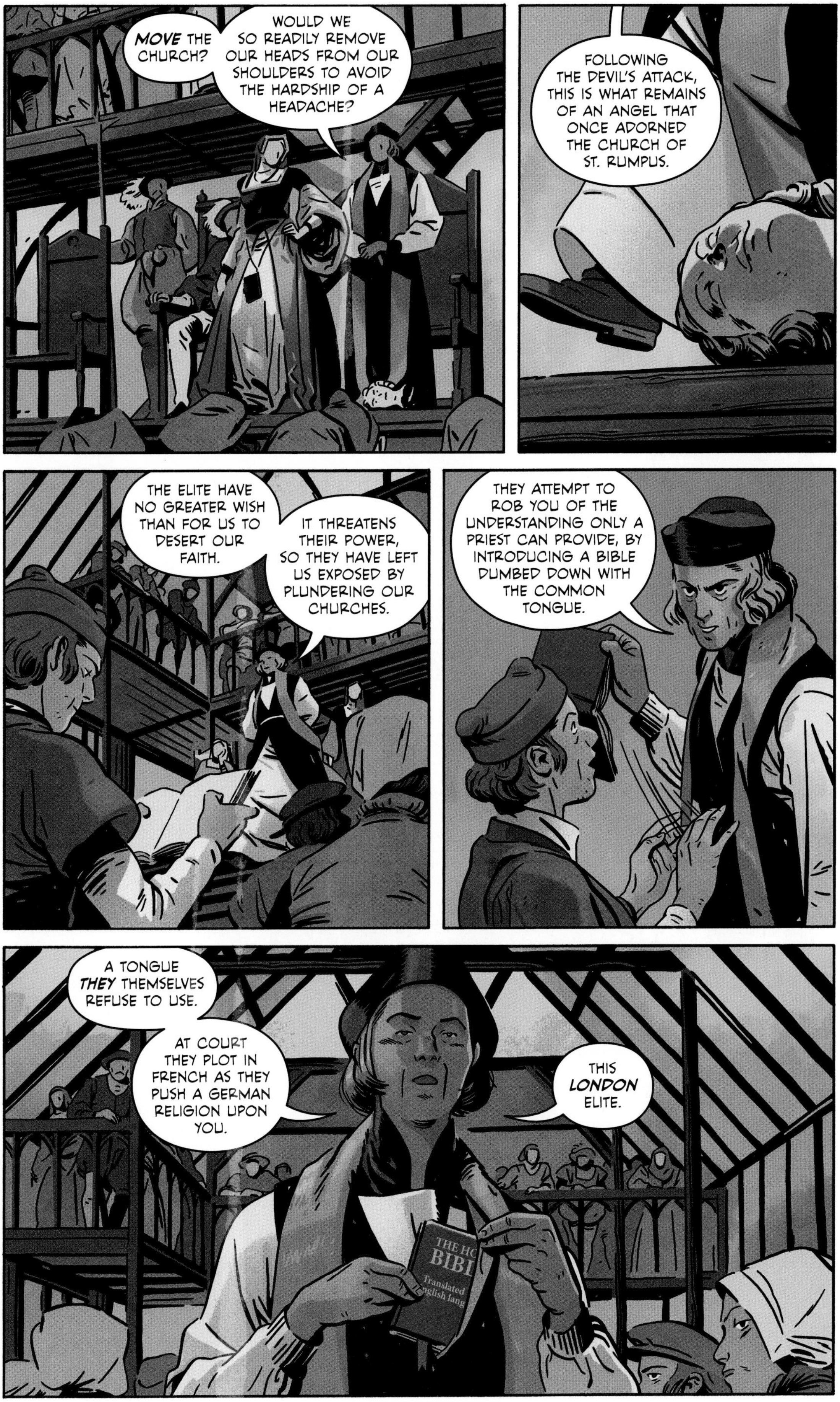
MOVE THE CHURCH?
WOULD WE SO READILY REMOVE OUR HEADS FROM OUR SHOULDERS TO AVOID THE HARDSHIP OF A HEADACHE?
FOLLOWING THE DEVIL'S ATTACK, THIS IS WHAT REMAINS OF AN ANGEL THAT ONCE ADORNED THE CHURCH OF ST. RUMPUS.
THE ELITE HAVE NO GREATER WISH THAN FOR US TO DESERT OUR FAITH.
IT THREATENS THEIR POWER, SO THEY HAVE LEFT US EXPOSED BY PLUNDERING OUR CHURCHES.
THEY ATTEMPT TO ROB YOU OF THE UNDERSTANDING ONLY A PRIEST CAN PROVIDE, BY INTRODUCING A BIBLE DUMBED DOWN WITH THE COMMON TONGUE.
A TONGUE THEY THEMSELVES REFUSE TO USE.
AT COURT THEY PLOT IN FRENCH AS THEY PUSH A GERMAN RELIGION UPON YOU.
THIS LONDON ELITE.

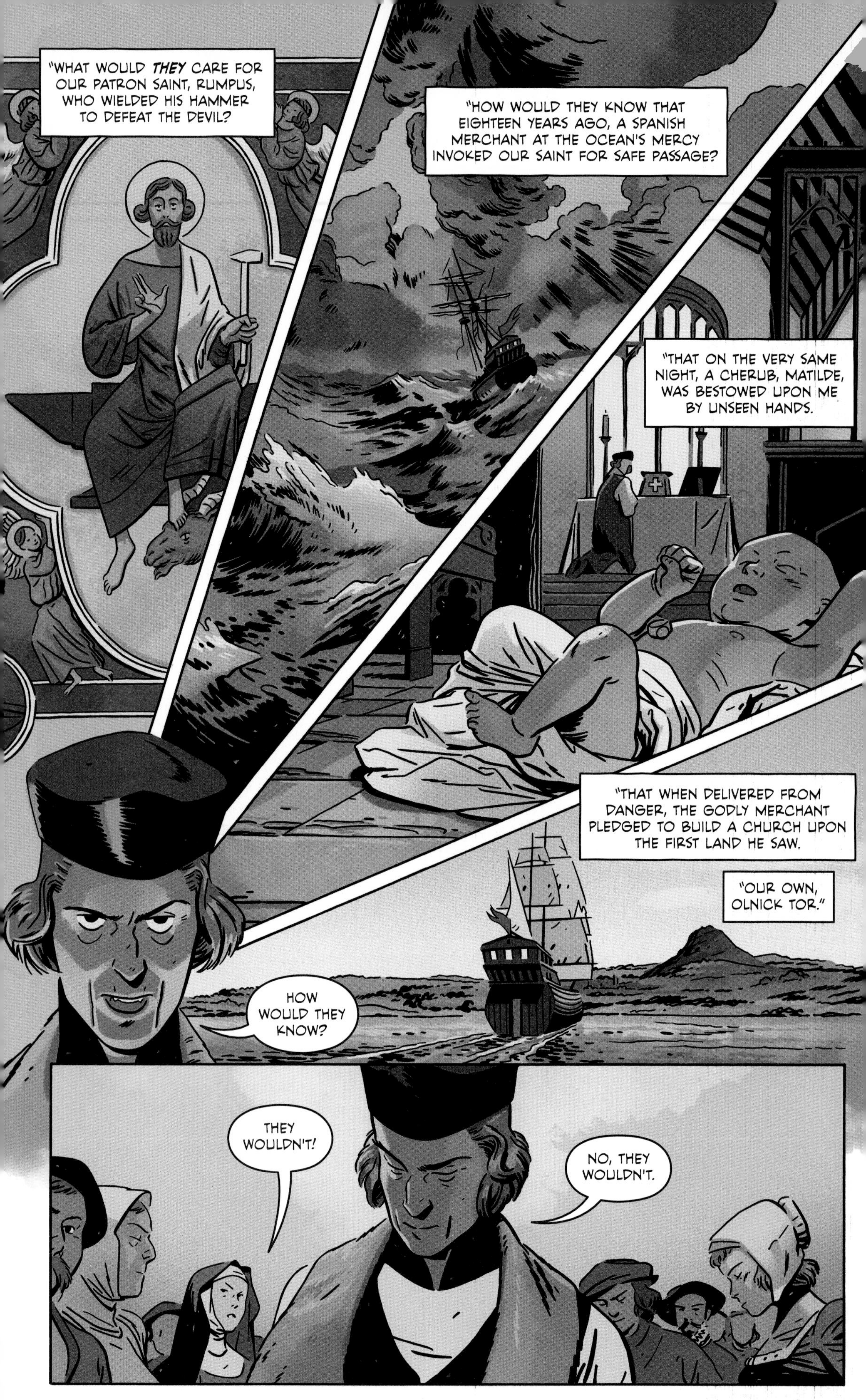
"WHAT WOULD THEY CARE FOR OUR PATRON SAINT, RUMPUS, WHO WIELDED HIS HAMMER TO DEFEAT THE DEVIL?
"HOW WOULD THEY KNOW THAT EIGHTEEN YEARS AGO, A SPANISH MERCHANT AT THE OCEAN'S MERCY INVOKED OUR SAINT FOR SAFE PASSAGE?
"THAT ON THE VERY SAME NIGHT, A CHERUB, MATILDE, WAS BESTOWED UPON ME BY UNSEEN HANDS.
"THAT WHEN DELIVERED FROM DANGER, THE GODLY MERCHANT PLEDGED TO BUILD A CHURCH UPON THE FIRST LAND HE SAW.
"OUR OWN, OLNICK TOR."
HOW WOULD THEY KNOW?
THEY WOULDN'T!
NO, THEY WOULDN'T.

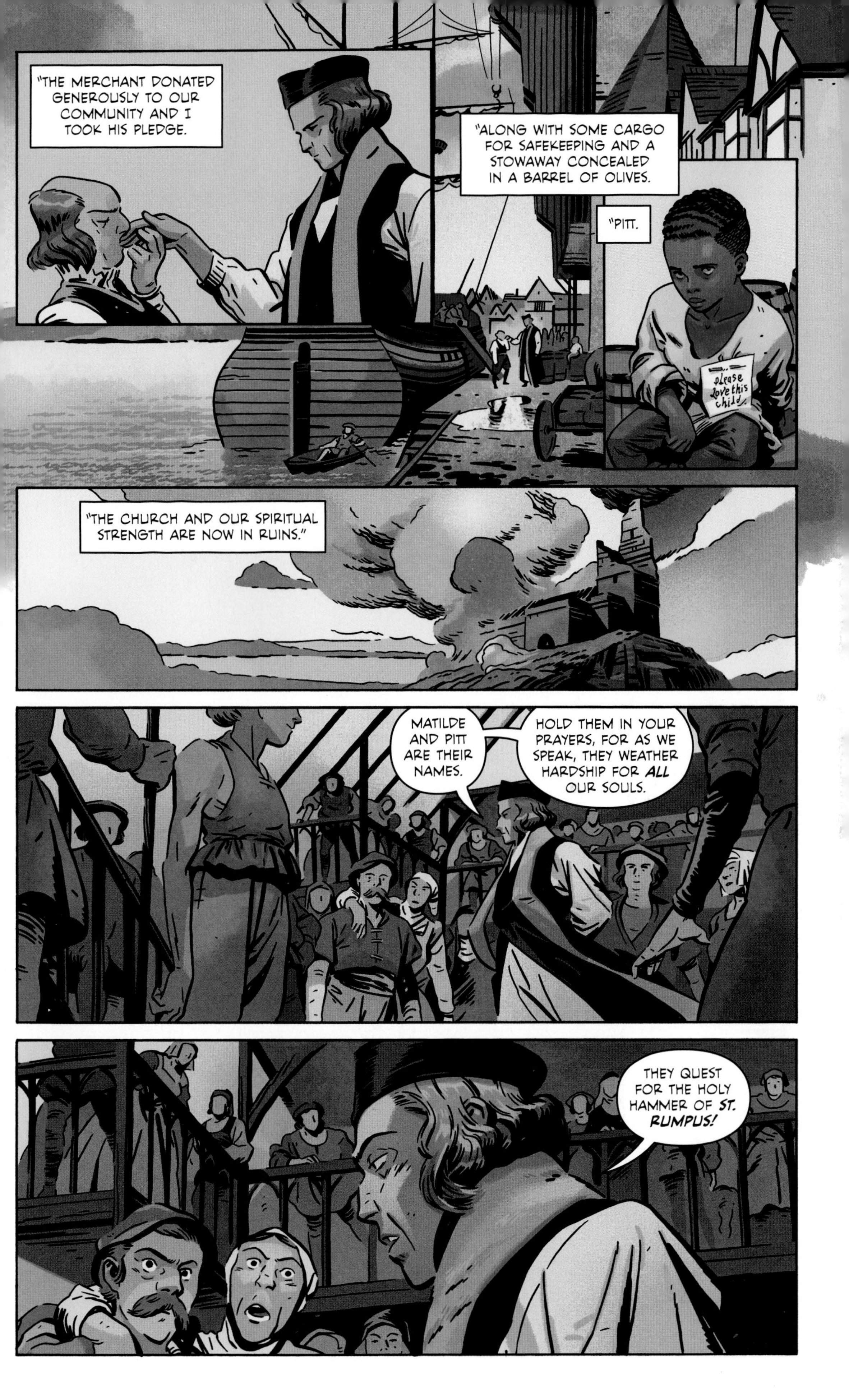

"THE MERCHANT DONATED GENEROUSLY TO OUR COMMUNITY AND I TOOK HIS PLEDGE.
"ALONG WITH SOME CARGO FOR SAFEKEEPING AND A STOWAWAY CONCEALED IN A BARREL OF OLIVES.
"PITT.
please love this child
"THE CHURCH AND OUR SPIRITUAL STRENGTH ARE NOW IN RUINS."
MATILDE AND PITT ARE THEIR NAMES.
HOLD THEM IN YOUR PRAYERS, FOR AS WE SPEAK, THEY WEATHER HARDSHIP FOR ALL OUR SOULS.
THEY QUEST FOR THE HOLY HAMMER OF ST. RUMPUS!

THE HAMMER OF ST. RUMPUS?!

'TIS BUT A *STORY*.

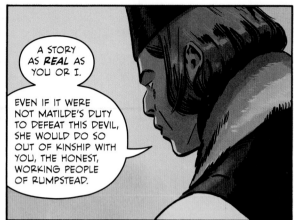

A STORY AS *REAL* AS YOU OR I.

EVEN IF IT WERE NOT MATILDE'S DUTY TO DEFEAT THIS DEVIL, SHE WOULD DO SO OUT OF KINSHIP WITH YOU, THE HONEST, WORKING PEOPLE OF RUMPSTEAD.

AND WE CAN HELP HER BY NOT BOWING TO EVIL OR TO THE ELITE.

BY RESTORING OUR CHURCH!

HURRAH!

CLAP CLAP HERE, HERE

CLAP

CLAP

JUSTICE!

HALT THIS *NONSENSE*.

THE HILL IS CHURCH LAND, M'LADY. THIS IS THEIR JURISDICTION.

BESIDES, IT SEEMS THE TOWN HAS SPOKEN.

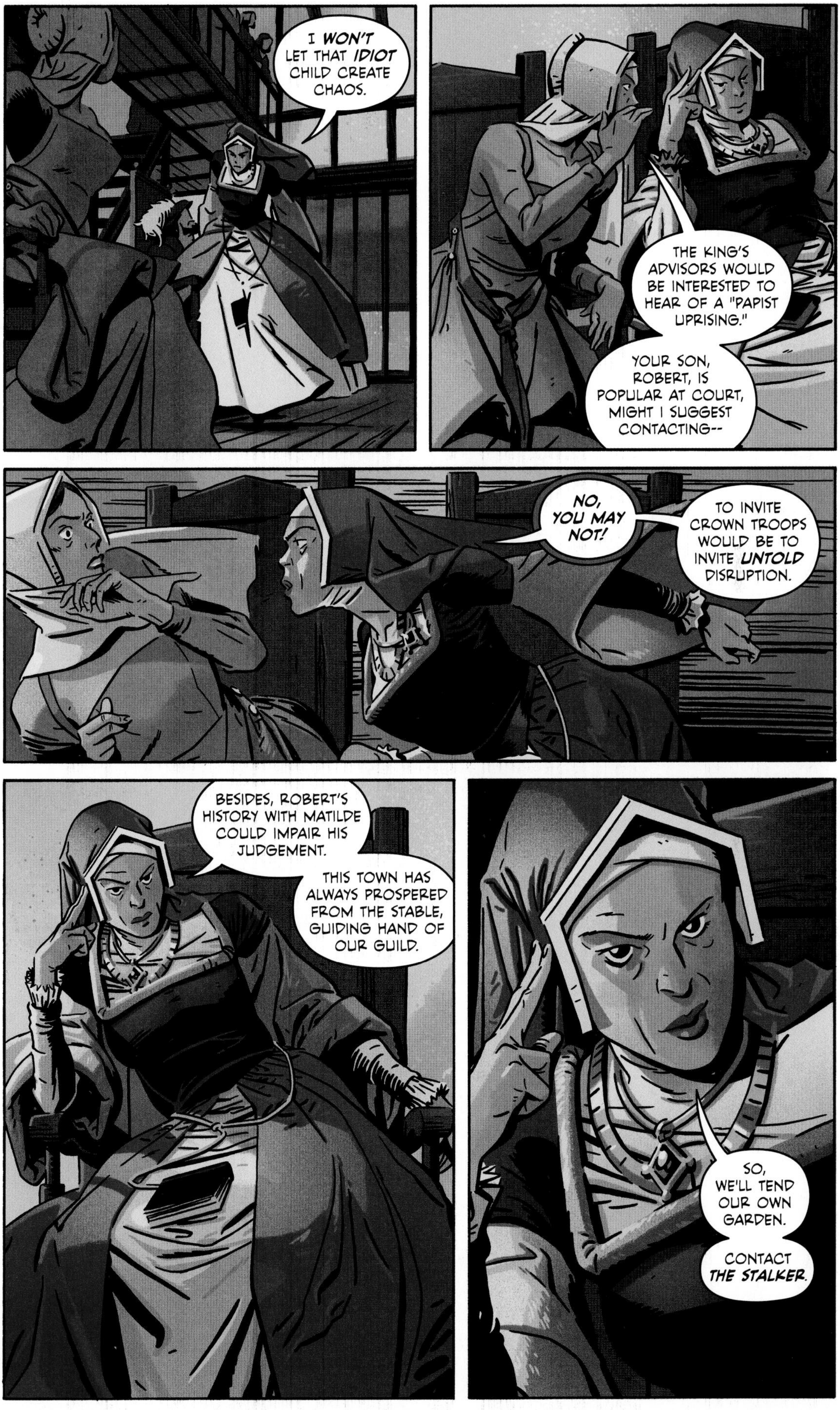
I *WON'T* LET THAT *IDIOT* CHILD CREATE CHAOS.
THE KING'S ADVISORS WOULD BE INTERESTED TO HEAR OF A "PAPIST UPRISING."
YOUR SON, ROBERT, IS POPULAR AT COURT, MIGHT I SUGGEST CONTACTING--
NO, YOU MAY NOT!
TO INVITE CROWN TROOPS WOULD BE TO INVITE *UNTOLD* DISRUPTION.
BESIDES, ROBERT'S HISTORY WITH MATILDE COULD IMPAIR HIS JUDGEMENT.
THIS TOWN HAS ALWAYS PROSPERED FROM THE STABLE, GUIDING HAND OF OUR GUILD.
SO, WE'LL TEND OUR OWN GARDEN.
CONTACT *THE STALKER.*

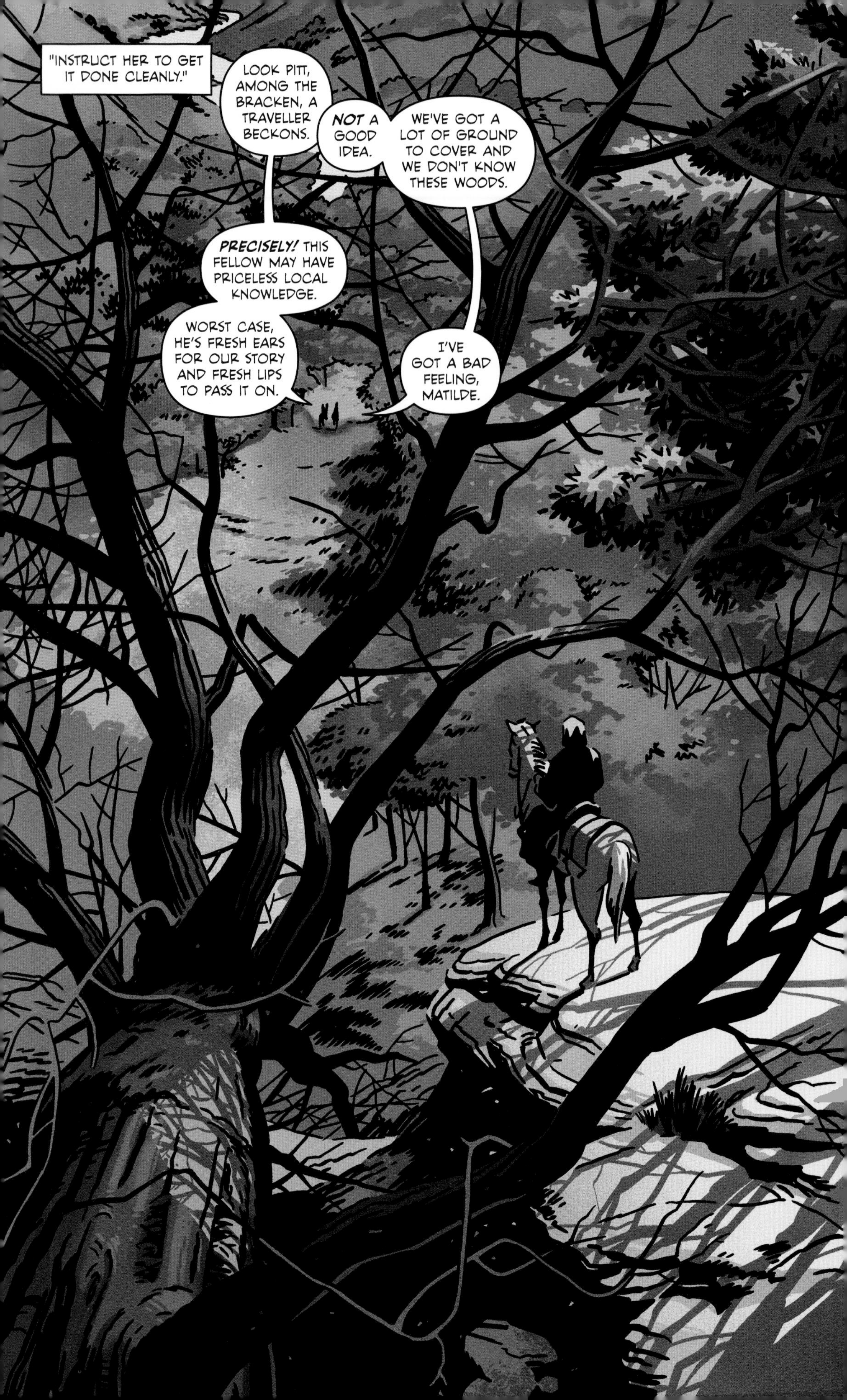
"INSTRUCT HER TO GET IT DONE CLEANLY."
LOOK PITT, AMONG THE BRACKEN, A TRAVELLER BECKONS.
NOT A GOOD IDEA.
WE'VE GOT A LOT OF GROUND TO COVER AND WE DON'T KNOW THESE WOODS.
PRECISELY! THIS FELLOW MAY HAVE PRICELESS LOCAL KNOWLEDGE.
WORST CASE, HE'S FRESH EARS FOR OUR STORY AND FRESH LIPS TO PASS IT ON.
I'VE GOT A BAD FEELING, MATILDE.

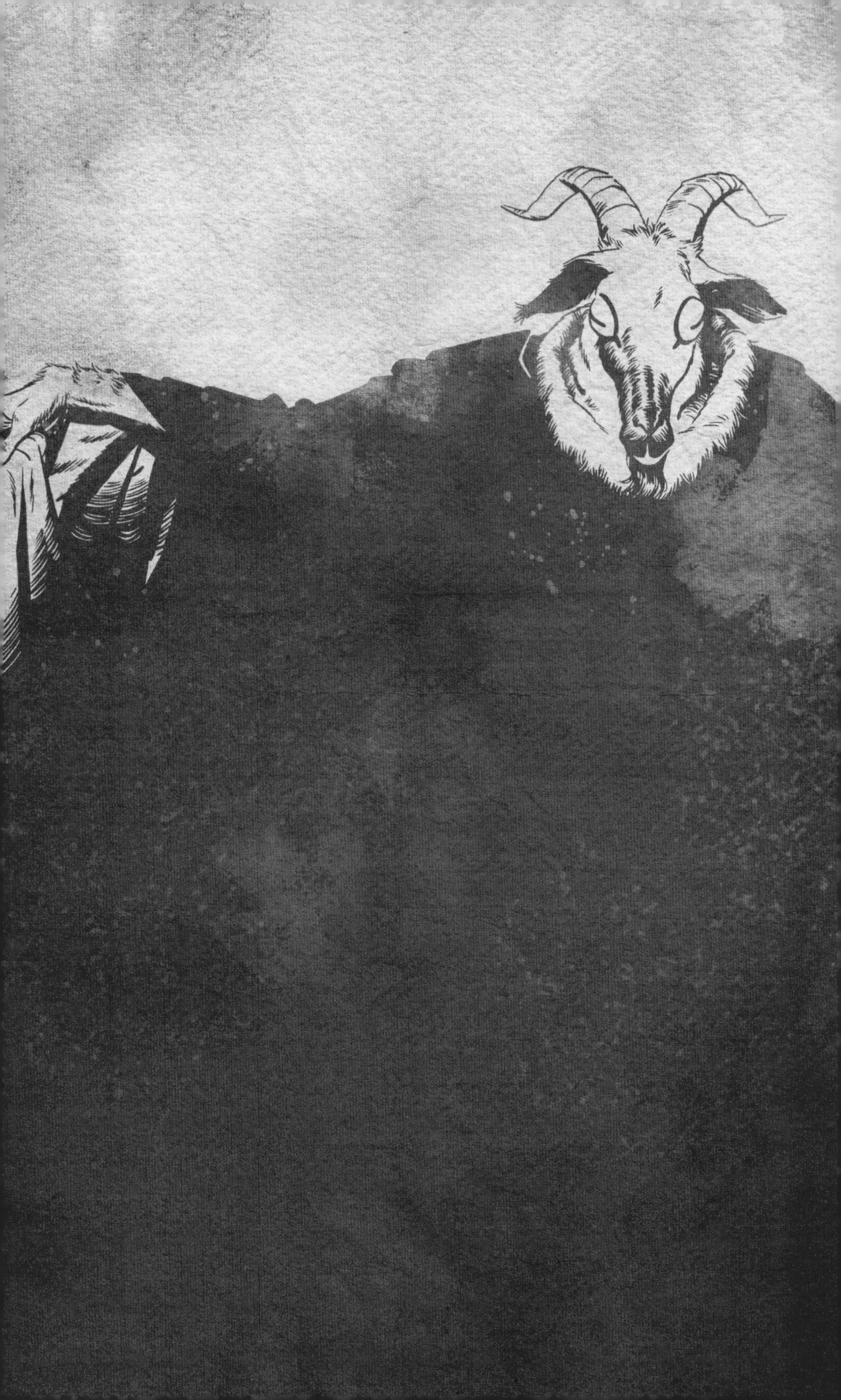

Chapter 3

Five days until the devil's deadline

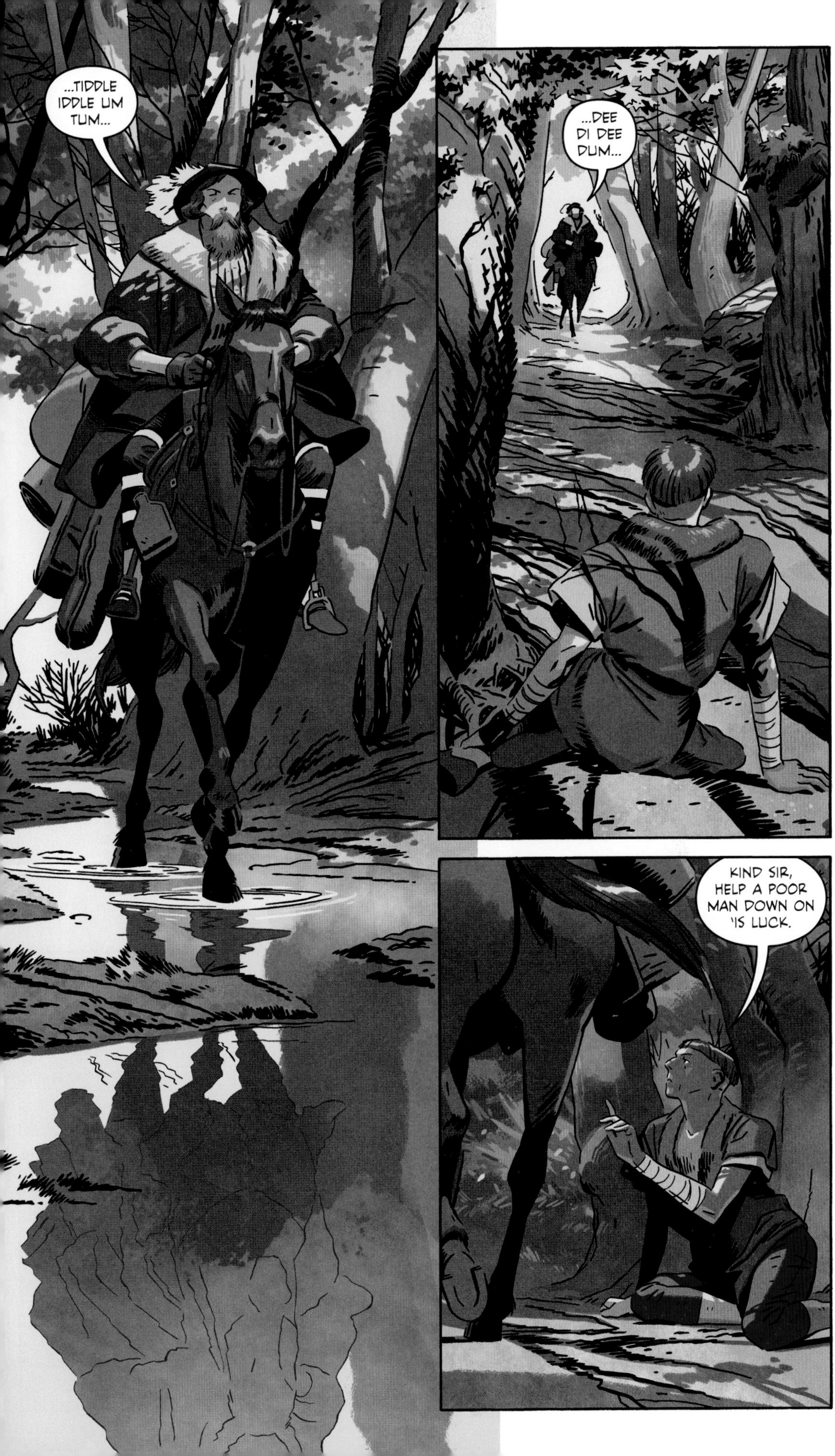
...TIDDLE IDDLE UM TUM...
...DEE DI DEE DUM...
KIND SIR, HELP A POOR MAN DOWN ON 'IS LUCK.

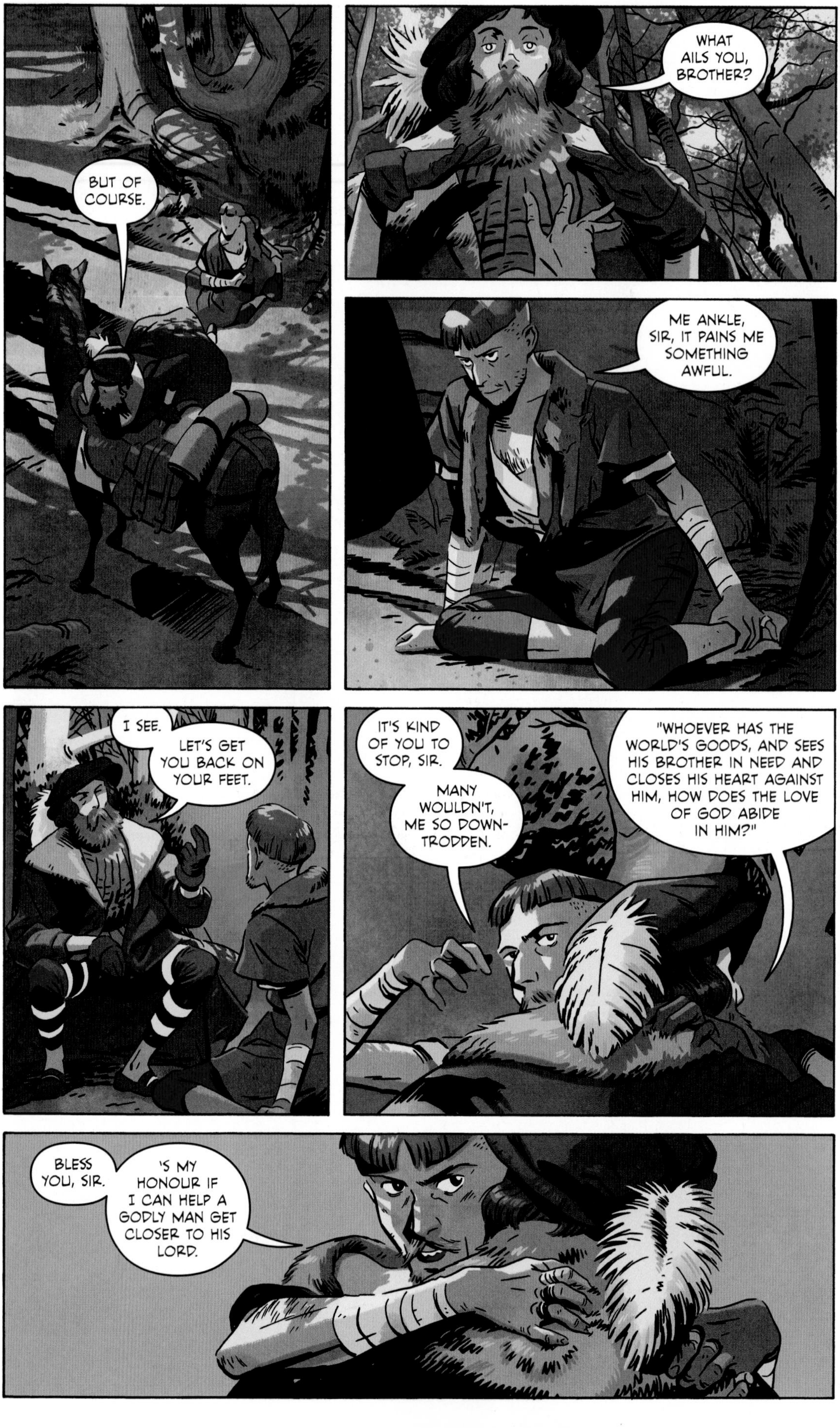

BUT OF COURSE.
WHAT AILS YOU, BROTHER?
ME ANKLE, SIR, IT PAINS ME SOMETHING AWFUL.
I SEE.
LET'S GET YOU BACK ON YOUR FEET.
IT'S KIND OF YOU TO STOP, SIR.
MANY WOULDN'T, ME SO DOWN-TRODDEN.
"WHOEVER HAS THE WORLD'S GOODS, AND SEES HIS BROTHER IN NEED AND CLOSES HIS HEART AGAINST HIM, HOW DOES THE LOVE OF GOD ABIDE IN HIM?"
BLESS YOU, SIR.
'S MY HONOUR IF I CAN HELP A GODLY MAN GET CLOSER TO HIS LORD.

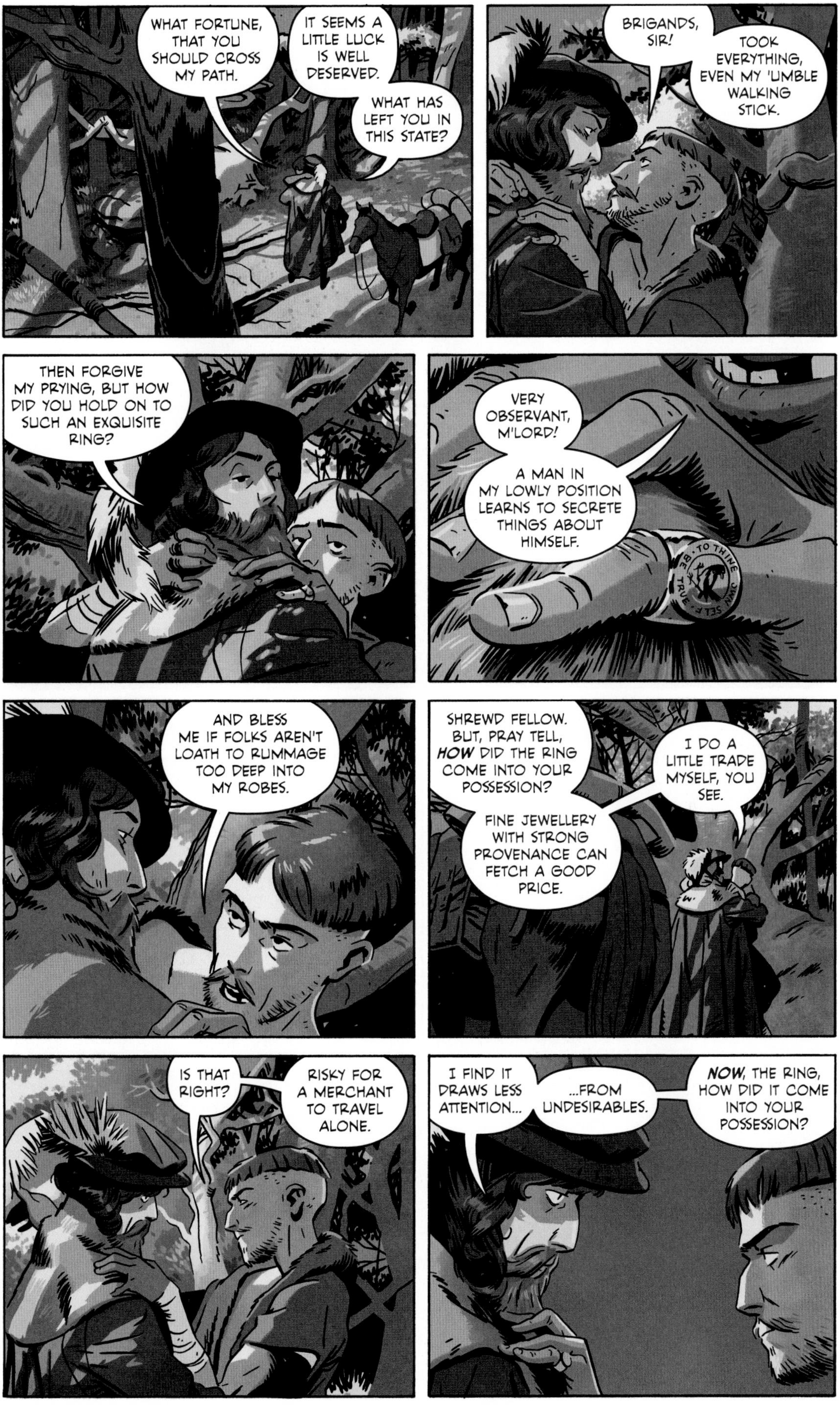
WHAT FORTUNE, THAT YOU SHOULD CROSS MY PATH.
IT SEEMS A LITTLE LUCK IS WELL DESERVED.
WHAT HAS LEFT YOU IN THIS STATE?
BRIGANDS, SIR!
TOOK EVERYTHING, EVEN MY 'UMBLE WALKING STICK.
THEN FORGIVE MY PRYING, BUT HOW DID YOU HOLD ON TO SUCH AN EXQUISITE RING?
VERY OBSERVANT, M'LORD!
A MAN IN MY LOWLY POSITION LEARNS TO SECRETE THINGS ABOUT HIMSELF.
TO THINE OWN SELF BE TRUE
AND BLESS ME IF FOLKS AREN'T LOATH TO RUMMAGE TOO DEEP INTO MY ROBES.
SHREWD FELLOW. BUT, PRAY TELL, ***HOW*** DID THE RING COME INTO YOUR POSSESSION?
I DO A LITTLE TRADE MYSELF, YOU SEE.
FINE JEWELLERY WITH STRONG PROVENANCE CAN FETCH A GOOD PRICE.
IS THAT RIGHT?
RISKY FOR A MERCHANT TO TRAVEL ALONE.
I FIND IT DRAWS LESS ATTENTION...
...FROM UNDESIRABLES.
NOW, THE RING, HOW DID IT COME INTO YOUR POSSESSION?

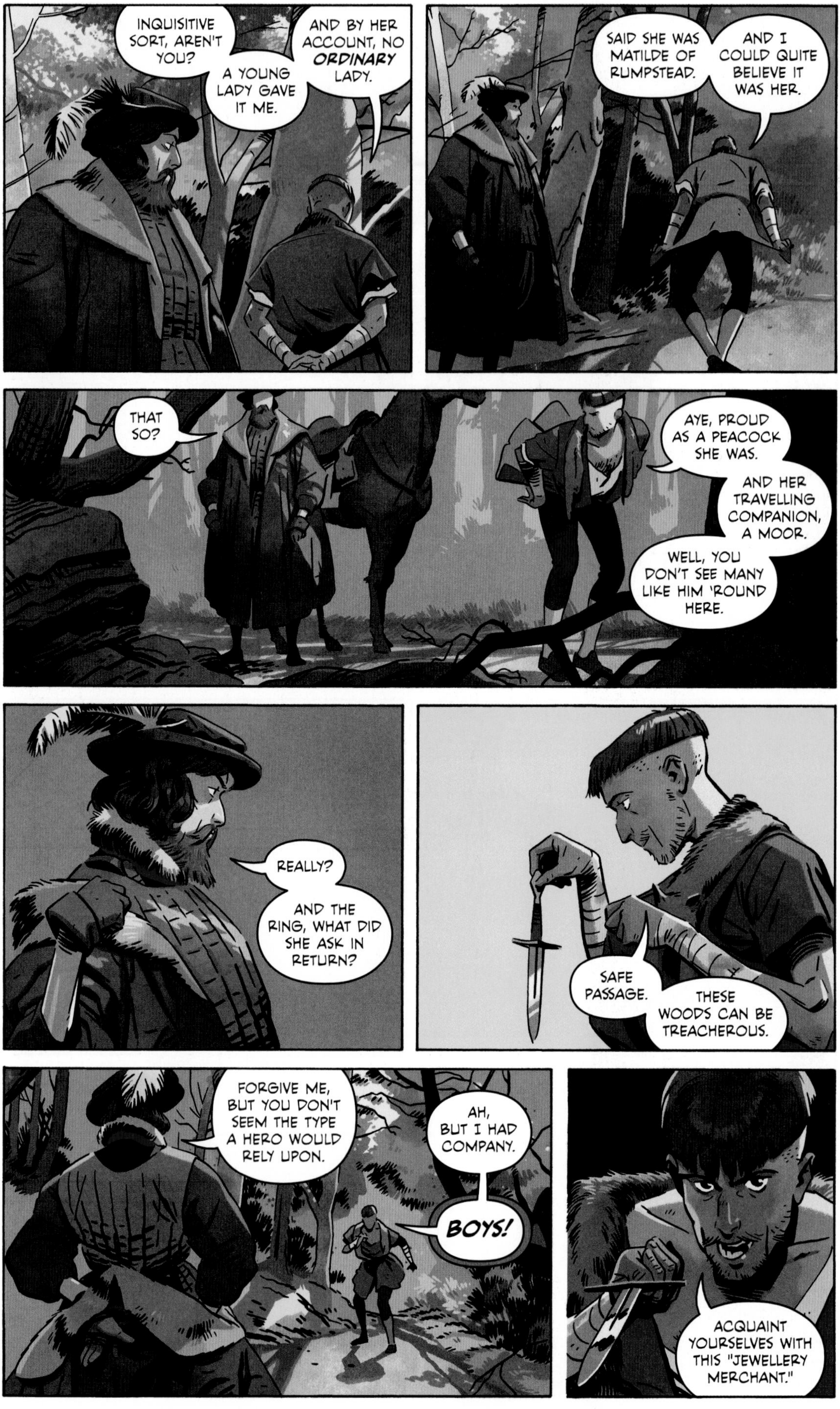
INQUISITIVE SORT, AREN'T YOU?
A YOUNG LADY GAVE IT ME.
AND BY HER ACCOUNT, NO ORDINARY LADY.
SAID SHE WAS MATILDE OF RUMPSTEAD.
AND I COULD QUITE BELIEVE IT WAS HER.
THAT SO?
AYE, PROUD AS A PEACOCK SHE WAS.
AND HER TRAVELLING COMPANION, A MOOR.
WELL, YOU DON'T SEE MANY LIKE HIM 'ROUND HERE.
REALLY?
AND THE RING, WHAT DID SHE ASK IN RETURN?
SAFE PASSAGE.
THESE WOODS CAN BE TREACHEROUS.
FORGIVE ME, BUT YOU DON'T SEEM THE TYPE A HERO WOULD RELY UPON.
AH, BUT I HAD COMPANY.
BOYS!
ACQUAINT YOURSELVES WITH THIS "JEWELLERY MERCHANT."

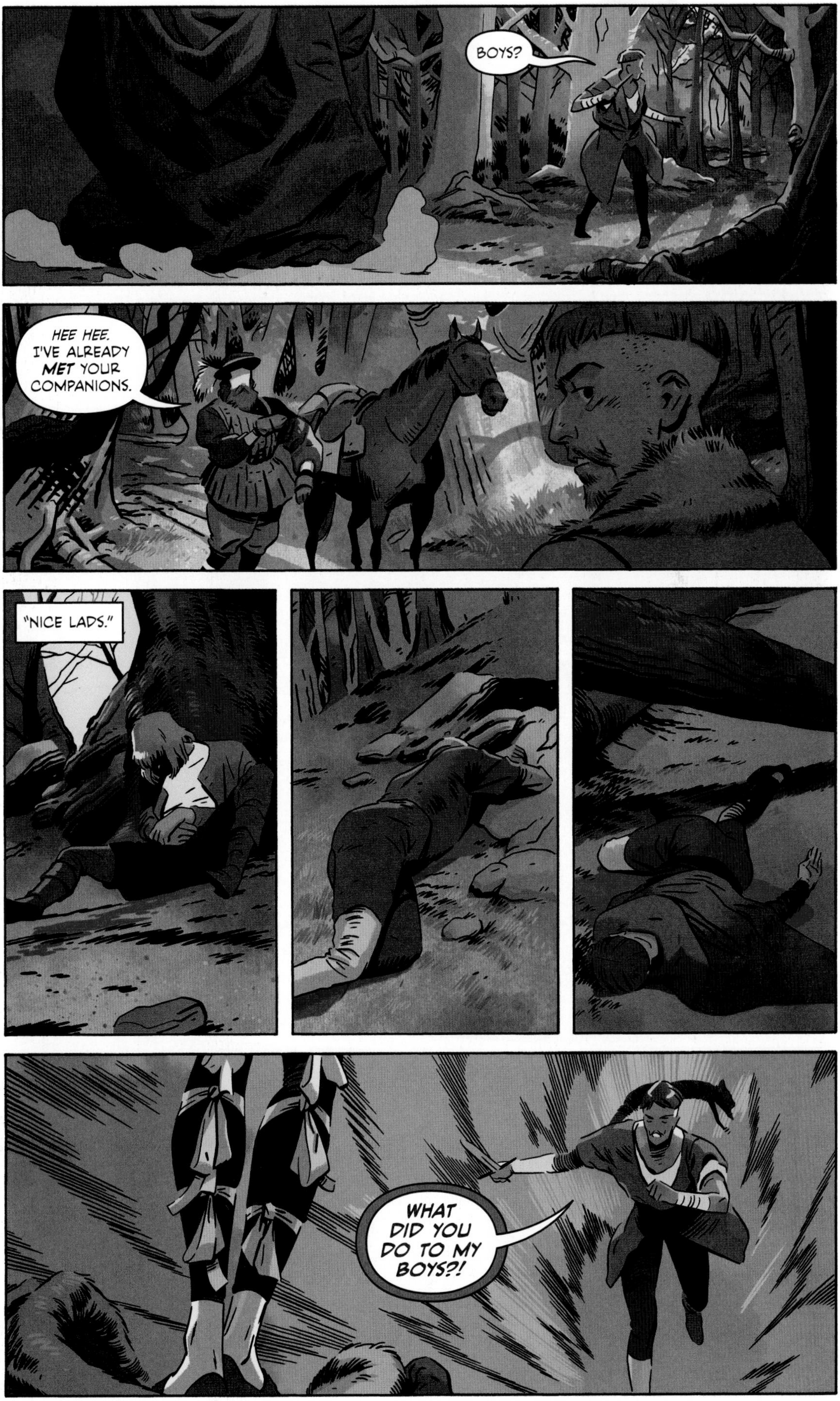
BOYS?
HEE HEE. I'VE ALREADY MET YOUR COMPANIONS.
"NICE LADS."
WHAT DID YOU DO TO MY BOYS?!

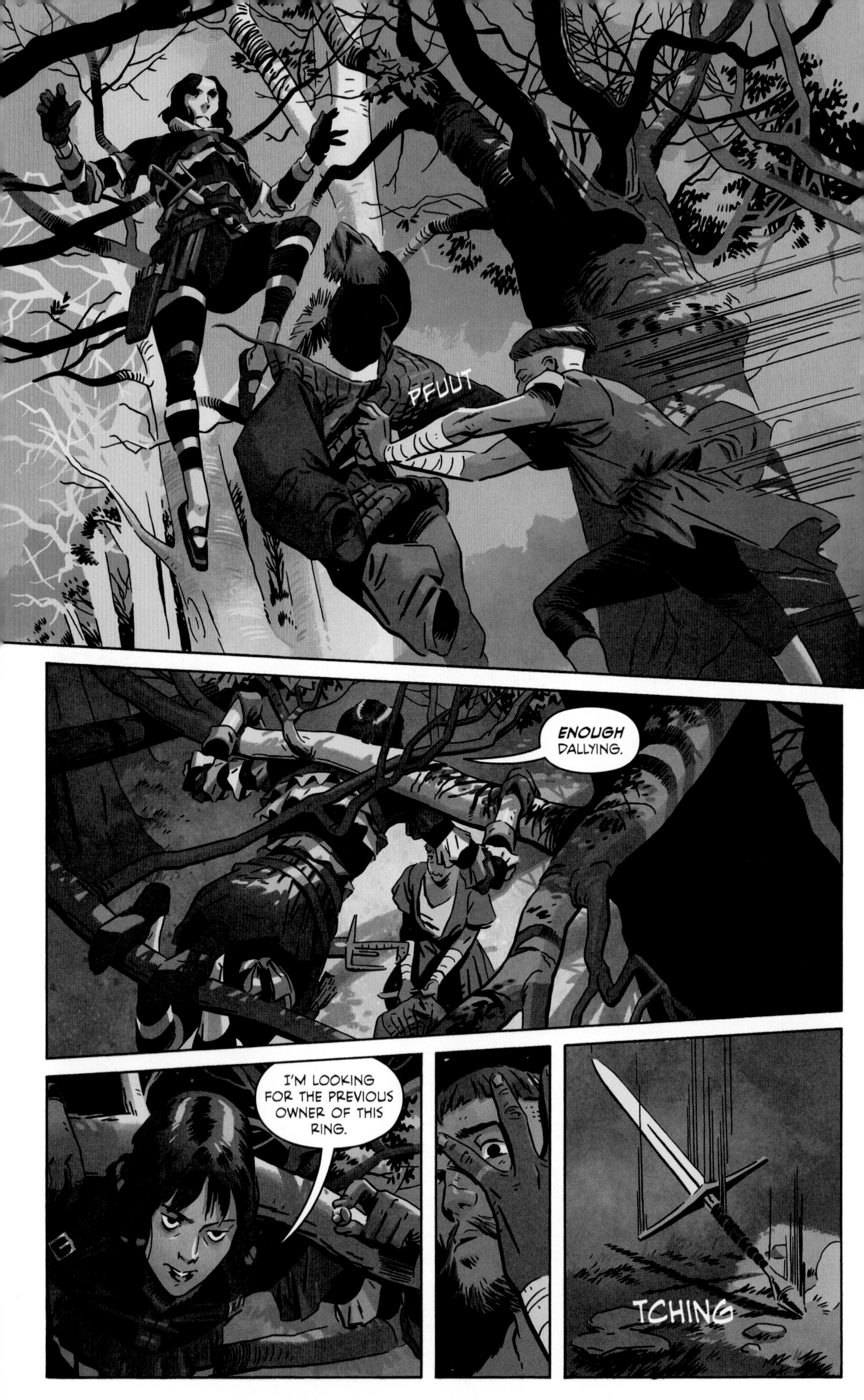
PFUUT
ENOUGH DALLYING.
I'M LOOKING FOR THE PREVIOUS OWNER OF THIS RING.
TCHING

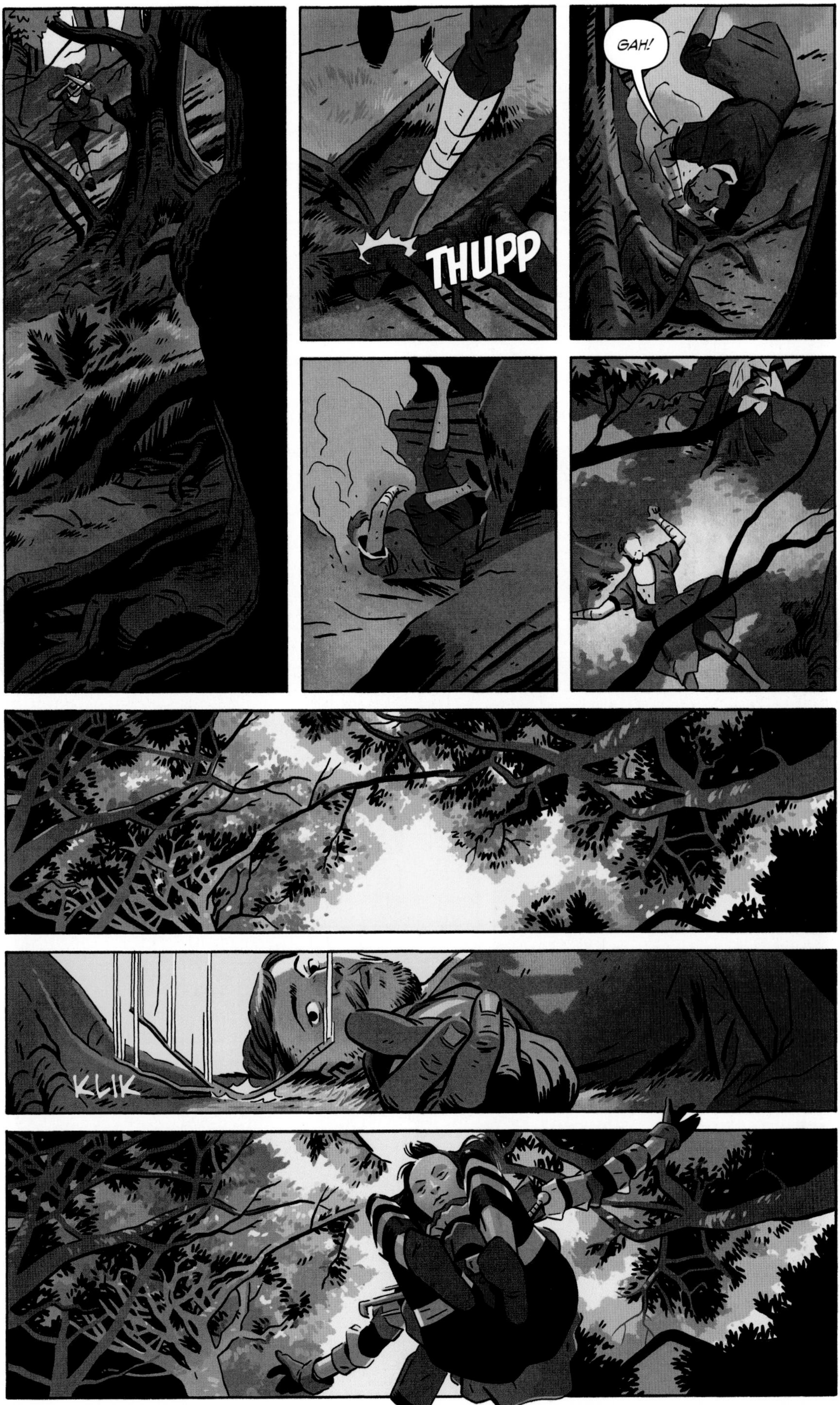
THUPP
GAH!
KLIK

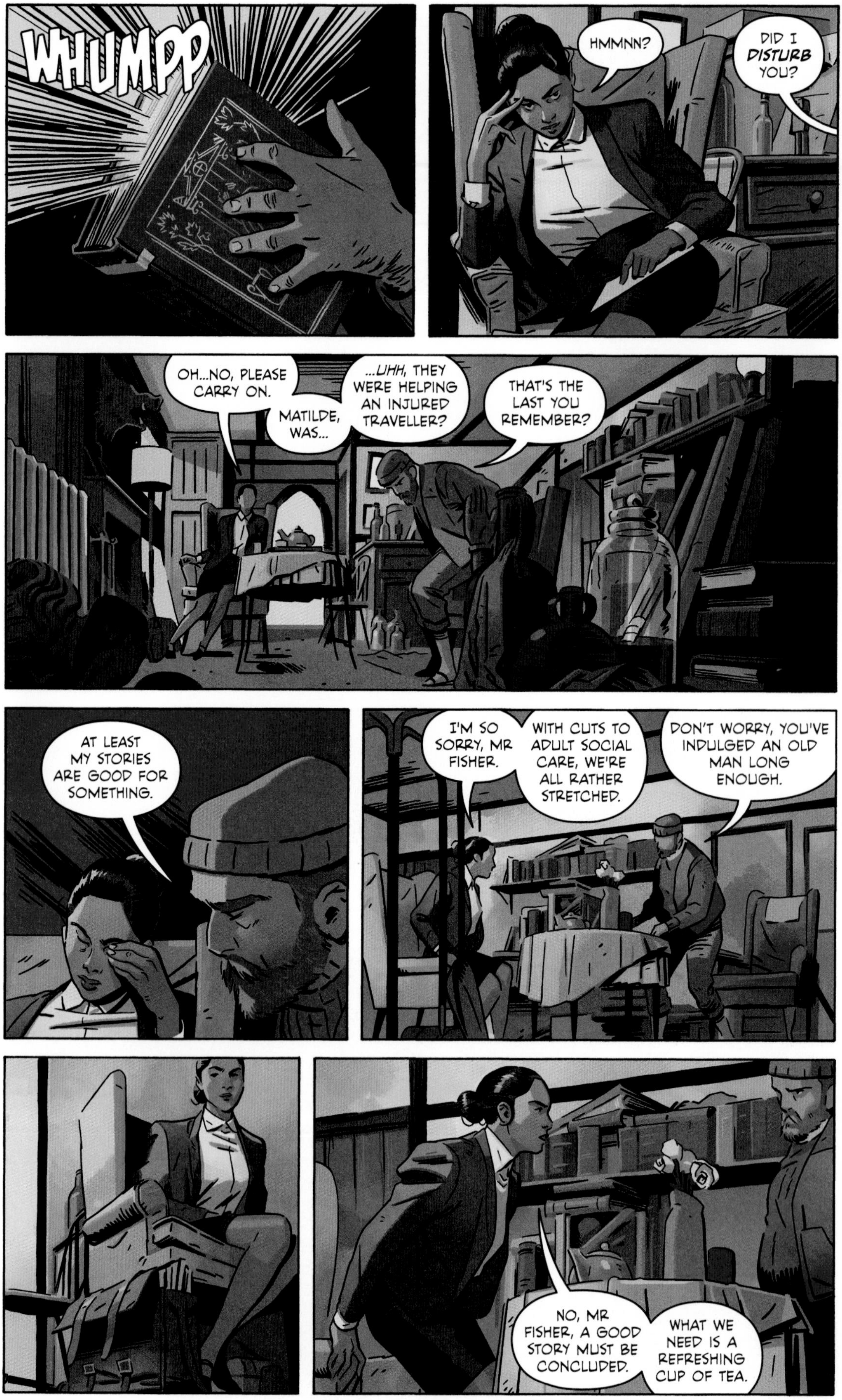
WHUMPP
HMMNN?
DID I *DISTURB* YOU?
OH...NO, PLEASE CARRY ON.
MATILDE, WAS...
...*UHH*, THEY WERE HELPING AN INJURED TRAVELLER?
THAT'S THE LAST YOU REMEMBER?
AT LEAST MY STORIES ARE GOOD FOR SOMETHING.
I'M SO SORRY, MR FISHER.
WITH CUTS TO ADULT SOCIAL CARE, WE'RE ALL RATHER STRETCHED.
DON'T WORRY, YOU'VE INDULGED AN OLD MAN LONG ENOUGH.
NO, MR FISHER, A GOOD STORY MUST BE CONCLUDED.
WHAT WE NEED IS A REFRESHING CUP OF TEA.

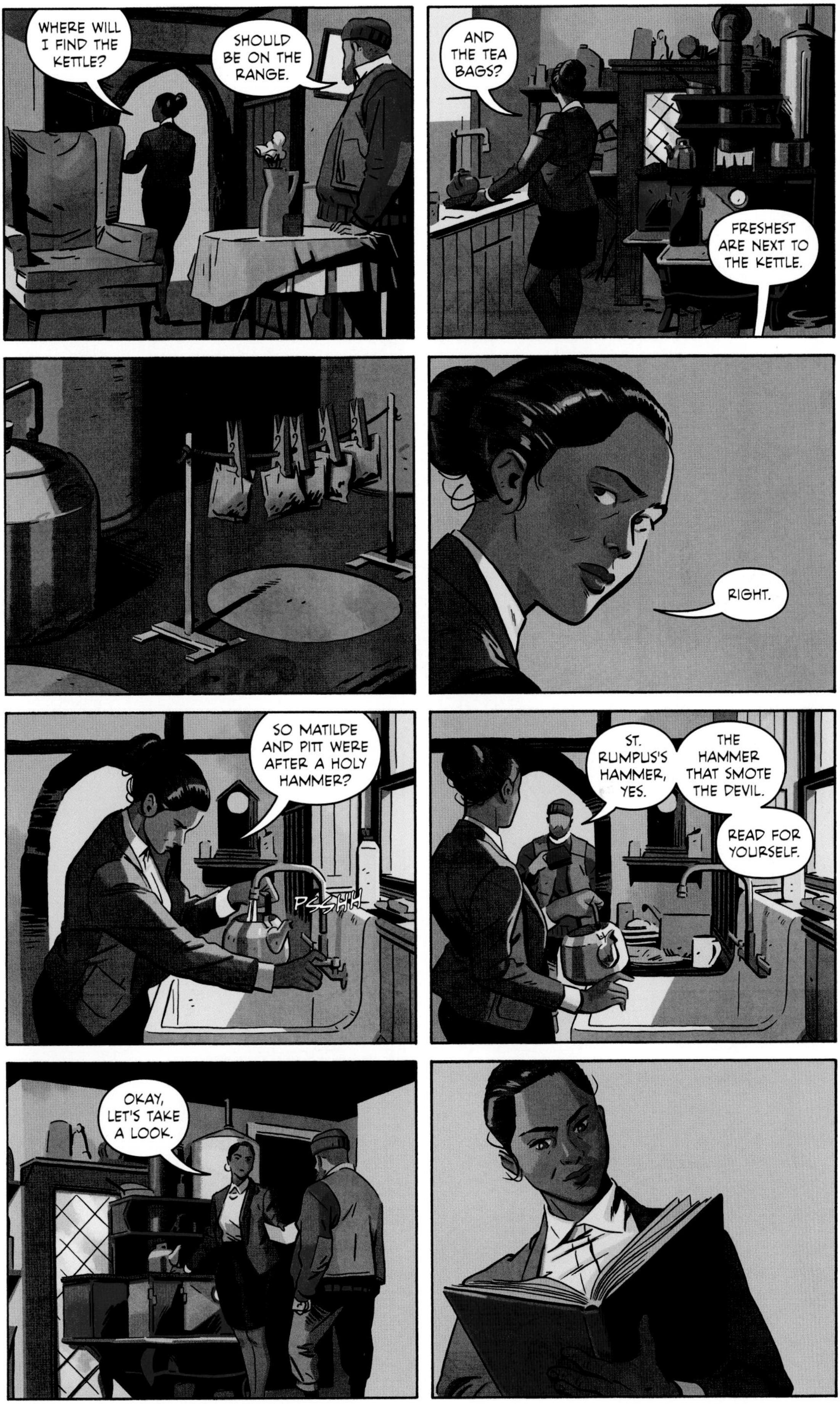
WHERE WILL I FIND THE KETTLE?
SHOULD BE ON THE RANGE.
AND THE TEA BAGS?
FRESHEST ARE NEXT TO THE KETTLE.
RIGHT.
SO MATILDE AND PITT WERE AFTER A HOLY HAMMER?
PSSHH
ST. RUMPUS'S HAMMER, YES.
THE HAMMER THAT SMOTE THE DEVIL.
READ FOR YOURSELF.
OKAY, LET'S TAKE A LOOK.

Popular Tales from the West of England

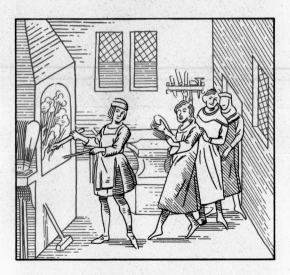

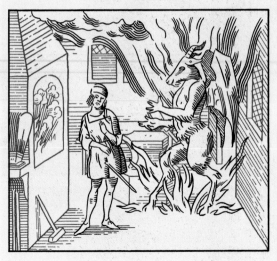

To Rumpus we turn, a smith of renown,
A talent well loved through his humble town.
"What sickles! What hoes!" The layfolk enthused,
And smiles clad his face, while inward he mused
To cheers I grow deaf, to compliments numb
An everyman's praise is easily won.

New patrons they came with titles and thrones,
Yet still their applause, it sank like a stone.
Till word of his craft, told far, wide and deep,
Drew two cloven hooves, not of goat, nor of sheep.
This princely patron made clear his desires,
For such a poker as could stoke his fires.

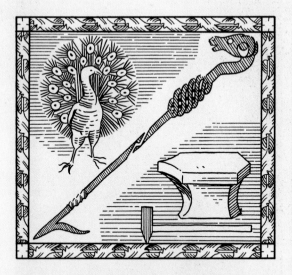

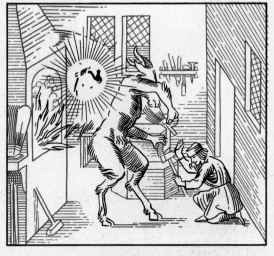

Rumpus assented, great wealth was assured,
Though proof of his skill was his true reward.
With this tool, he schemed, the fiend I'll deceive,
Creating a flaw, no man could perceive,
To withstand all fires however they glow,
Save for the fires of inferno below.

Rumpus hailed the beast, "My work is done,
I present a poker, rivalled by none."
The smith urged a test, "My hearth burns fierce."
"Nay," came the devil, "your furnace I'll pierce."
That belly of heat hellish in its rage,
Shattered the poker, like hopes on the stage.

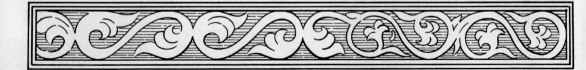

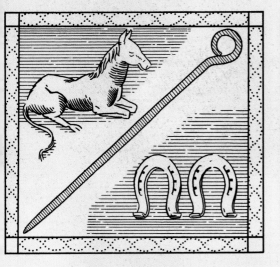

Peacock!" spat the fiend, "this poker make fit,
Or not only riches your soul be forfeit."
Pride punctured, the smith returned to his forge,
To fashion a tool of splendor disgorged.
Raw in appearance, ripe to its duty,
Its lusterless iron reflected beauty.

In front of the brute, Rumpus's trembling stool,
Belied his calm hand, which plunged the tool
Deep into the fire and long though it stayed
No glimmer of light nor red hue betrayed
The skill of the smith, who sat head hung low
In spite of the cheers of his fawning foe.

The beast snatched the iron to enjoy a stint,
When Rumpus's eye caught his hammer's glint.
Gathering the tool, though hope was remote,
The smith hauled it up and fiercely he smote
The fiend who was by the furnace consumed,
Returning to fire, thereafter entombed.

Humility earned, peace was not the yield,
As pilgrims abuzz swarmed from far afield.
Unable to work or think, Rumpus fled,
To where is unknown, though Cornwall it's said.
Herding their flocks, shepherds' stories impart,
The beat of a hammer, proud as a heart.

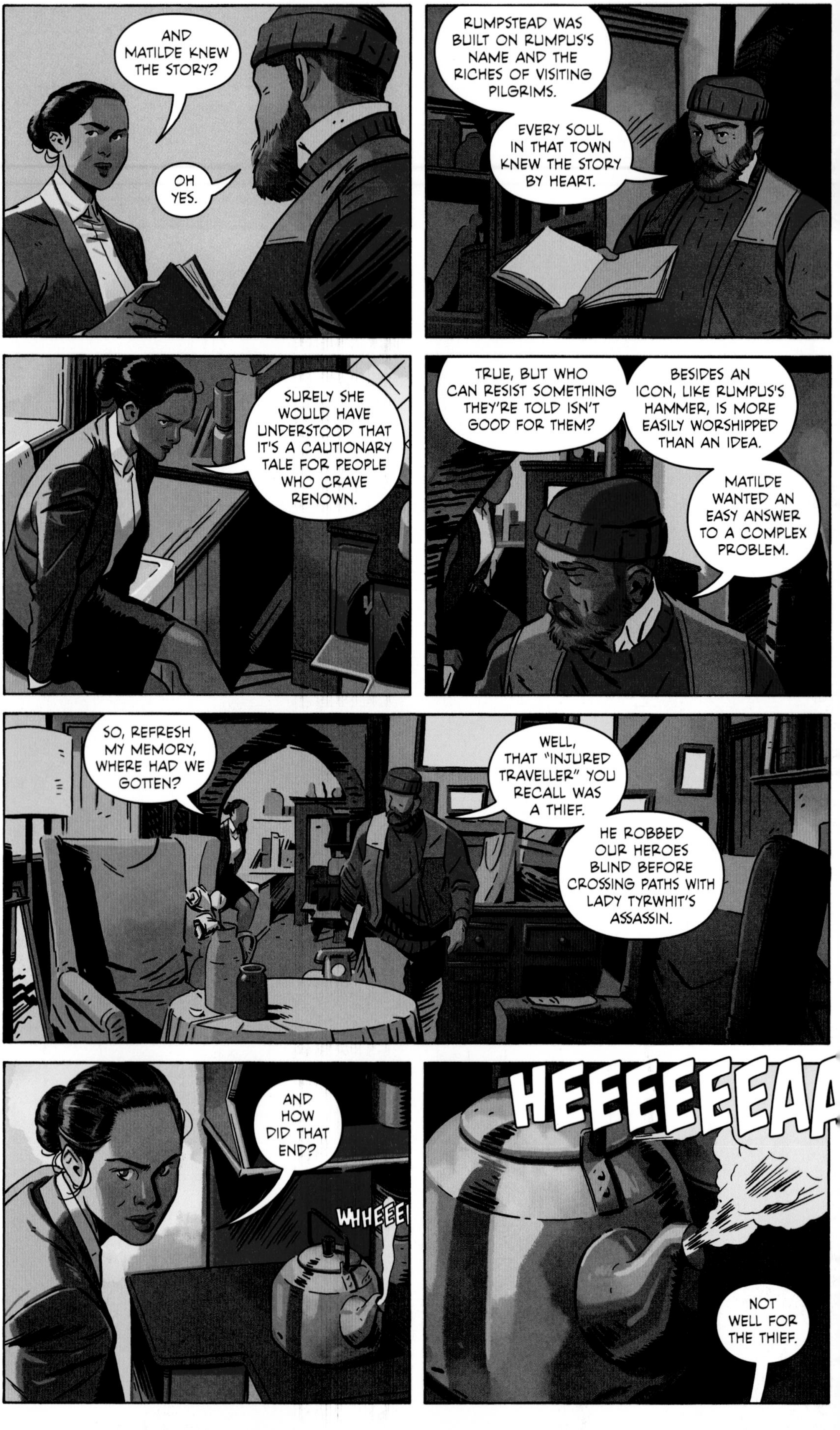
AND MATILDE KNEW THE STORY?
OH YES.
RUMPSTEAD WAS BUILT ON RUMPUS'S NAME AND THE RICHES OF VISITING PILGRIMS.
EVERY SOUL IN THAT TOWN KNEW THE STORY BY HEART.
SURELY SHE WOULD HAVE UNDERSTOOD THAT IT'S A CAUTIONARY TALE FOR PEOPLE WHO CRAVE RENOWN.
TRUE, BUT WHO CAN RESIST SOMETHING THEY'RE TOLD ISN'T GOOD FOR THEM?
BESIDES AN ICON, LIKE RUMPUS'S HAMMER, IS MORE EASILY WORSHIPPED THAN AN IDEA.
MATILDE WANTED AN EASY ANSWER TO A COMPLEX PROBLEM.
SO, REFRESH MY MEMORY, WHERE HAD WE GOTTEN?
WELL, THAT "INJURED TRAVELLER" YOU RECALL WAS A THIEF.
HE ROBBED OUR HEROES BLIND BEFORE CROSSING PATHS WITH LADY TYRWHIT'S ASSASSIN.
AND HOW DID THAT END?
WHHEEE
HEEEEEEAA
NOT WELL FOR THE THIEF.

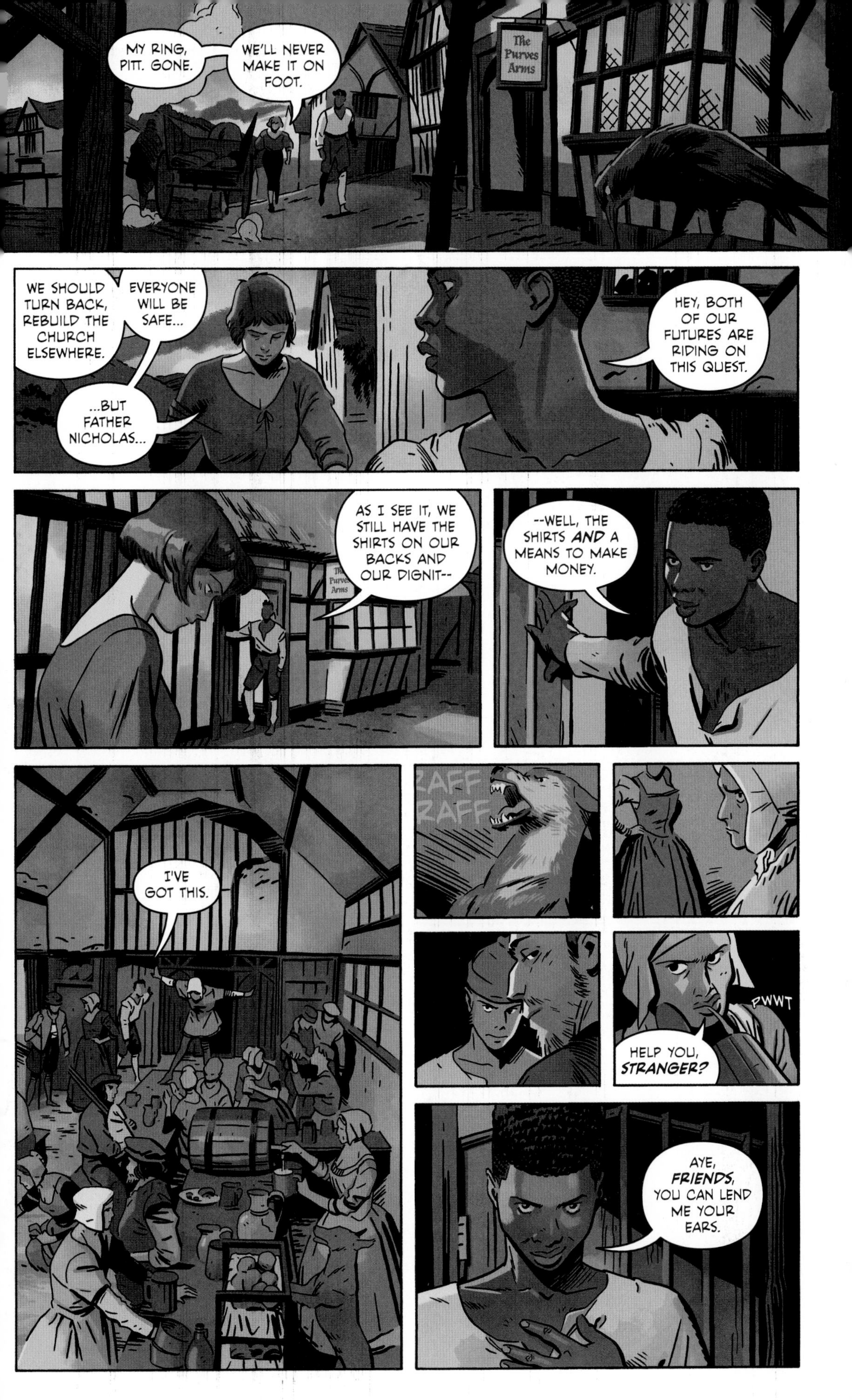
MY RING, PITT. GONE.
WE'LL NEVER MAKE IT ON FOOT.
The Purves Arms
WE SHOULD TURN BACK, REBUILD THE CHURCH ELSEWHERE.
EVERYONE WILL BE SAFE...
...BUT FATHER NICHOLAS...
HEY, BOTH OF OUR FUTURES ARE RIDING ON THIS QUEST.
AS I SEE IT, WE STILL HAVE THE SHIRTS ON OUR BACKS AND OUR DIGNIT--
--WELL, THE SHIRTS AND A MEANS TO MAKE MONEY.
I'VE GOT THIS.
PWWT
HELP YOU, STRANGER?
AYE, FRIENDS, YOU CAN LEND ME YOUR EARS.

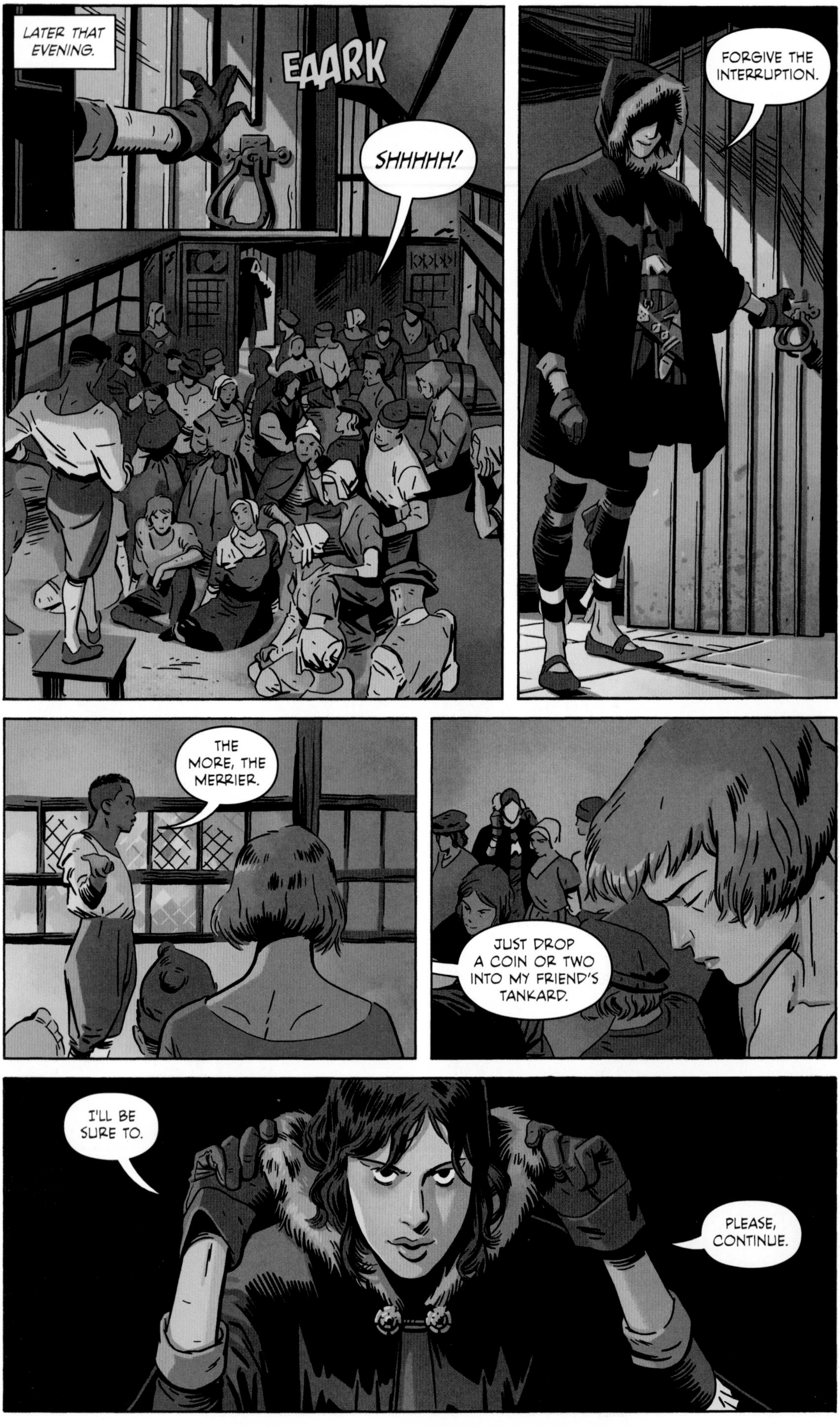
LATER THAT EVENING.
EAARK
SHHHHH!
FORGIVE THE INTERRUPTION.
THE MORE, THE MERRIER.
JUST DROP A COIN OR TWO INTO MY FRIEND'S TANKARD.
I'LL BE SURE TO.
PLEASE, CONTINUE.

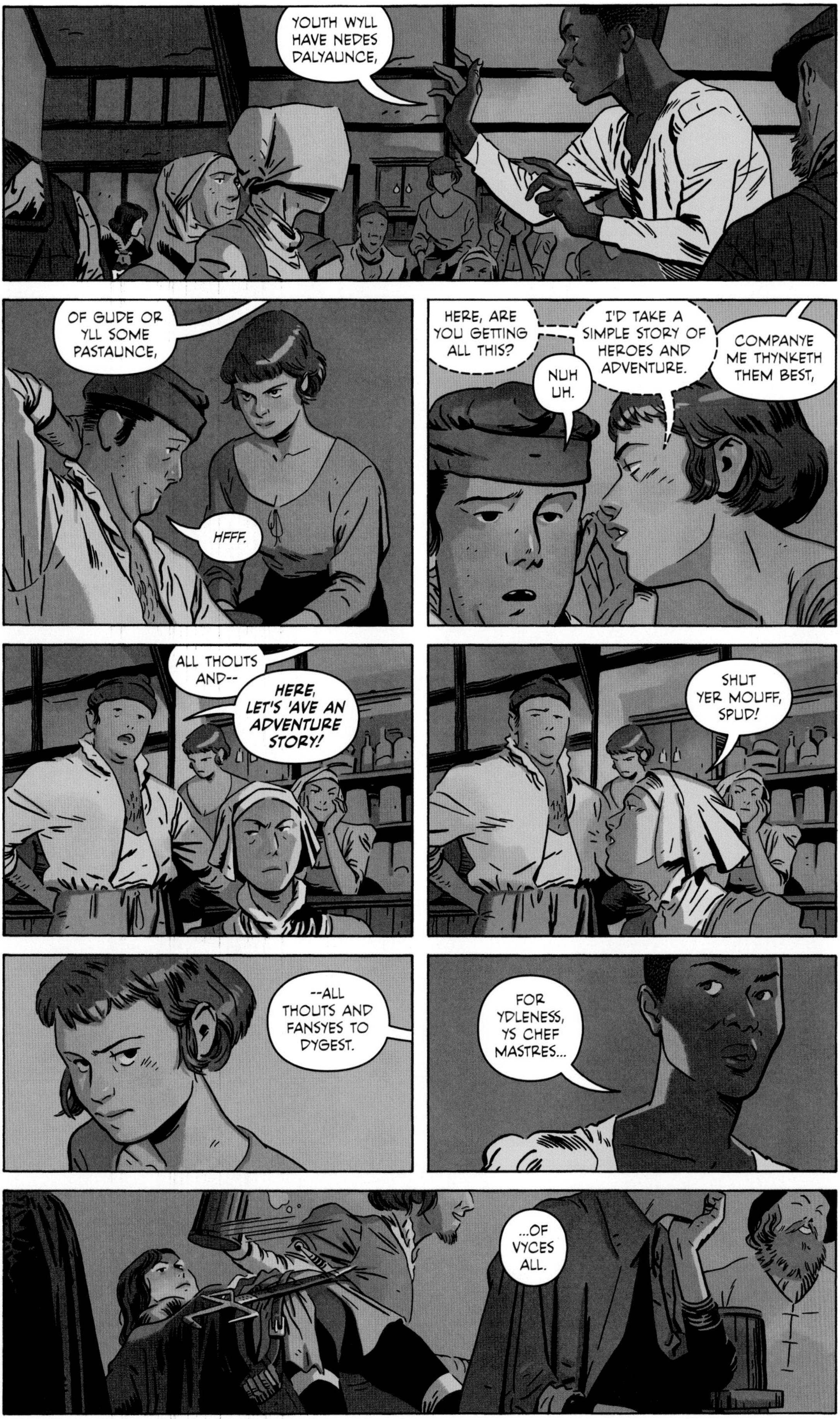
YOUTH WYLL HAVE NEDES DALYAUNCE,
OF GUDE OR YLL SOME PASTAUNCE,
HFFF.
HERE, ARE YOU GETTING ALL THIS?
I'D TAKE A SIMPLE STORY OF HEROES AND ADVENTURE.
NUH UH.
COMPANYE ME THYNKETH THEM BEST,
ALL THOUTS AND--
HERE, LET'S 'AVE AN ADVENTURE STORY!
SHUT YER MOUFF, SPUD!
--ALL THOUTS AND FANSYES TO DYGEST.
FOR YDLENESS, YS CHEF MASTRES...
...OF VYCES ALL.

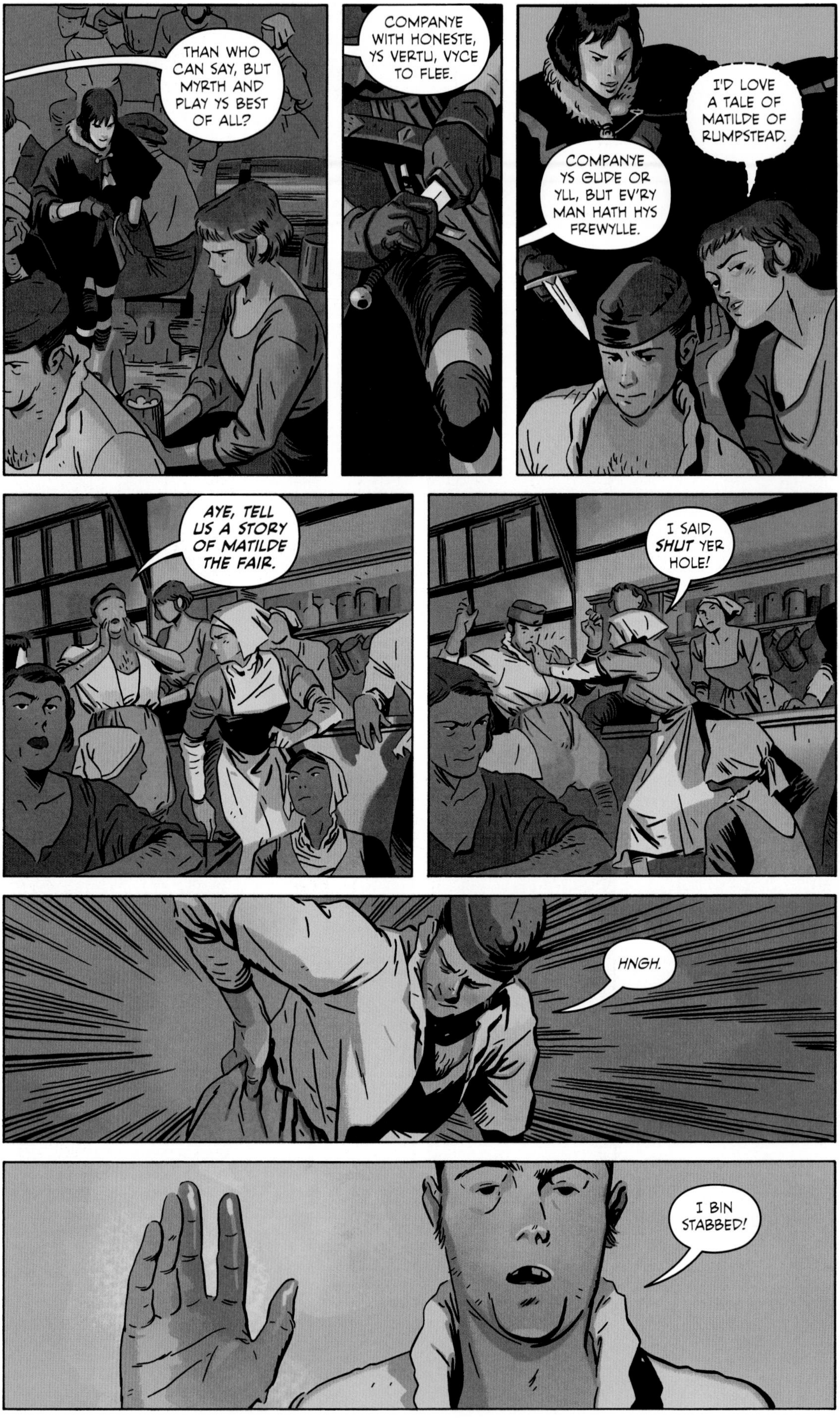
THAN WHO CAN SAY, BUT MYRTH AND PLAY YS BEST OF ALL?
COMPANYE WITH HONESTE, YS VERTU, VYCE TO FLEE.
I'D LOVE A TALE OF MATILDE OF RUMPSTEAD.
COMPANYE YS GUDE OR YLL, BUT EV'RY MAN HATH HYS FREWYLLE.
AYE, TELL US A STORY OF MATILDE THE FAIR.
I SAID, SHUT YER HOLE!
HNGH.
I BIN STABBED!

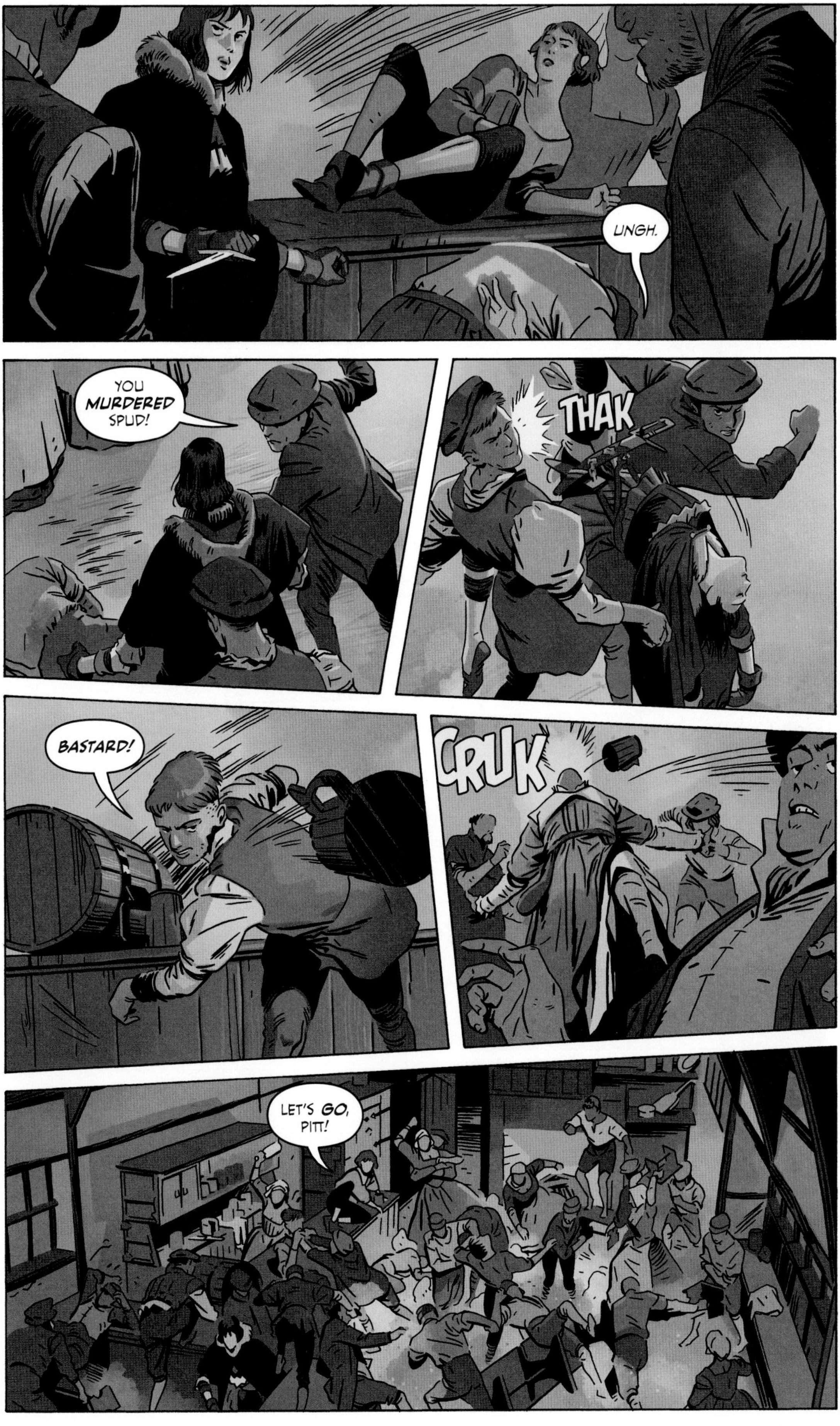
UNGH.
YOU MURDERED SPUD!
THAK
BASTARD!
CRUK
LET'S GO, PITT!

TING

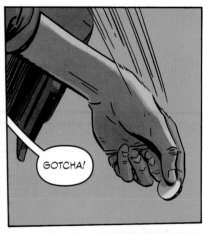

GOTCHA!

MATILDE, HELP!

KAFF

PITT!

HOLD ON!

CLING

TING

TING

SKFF

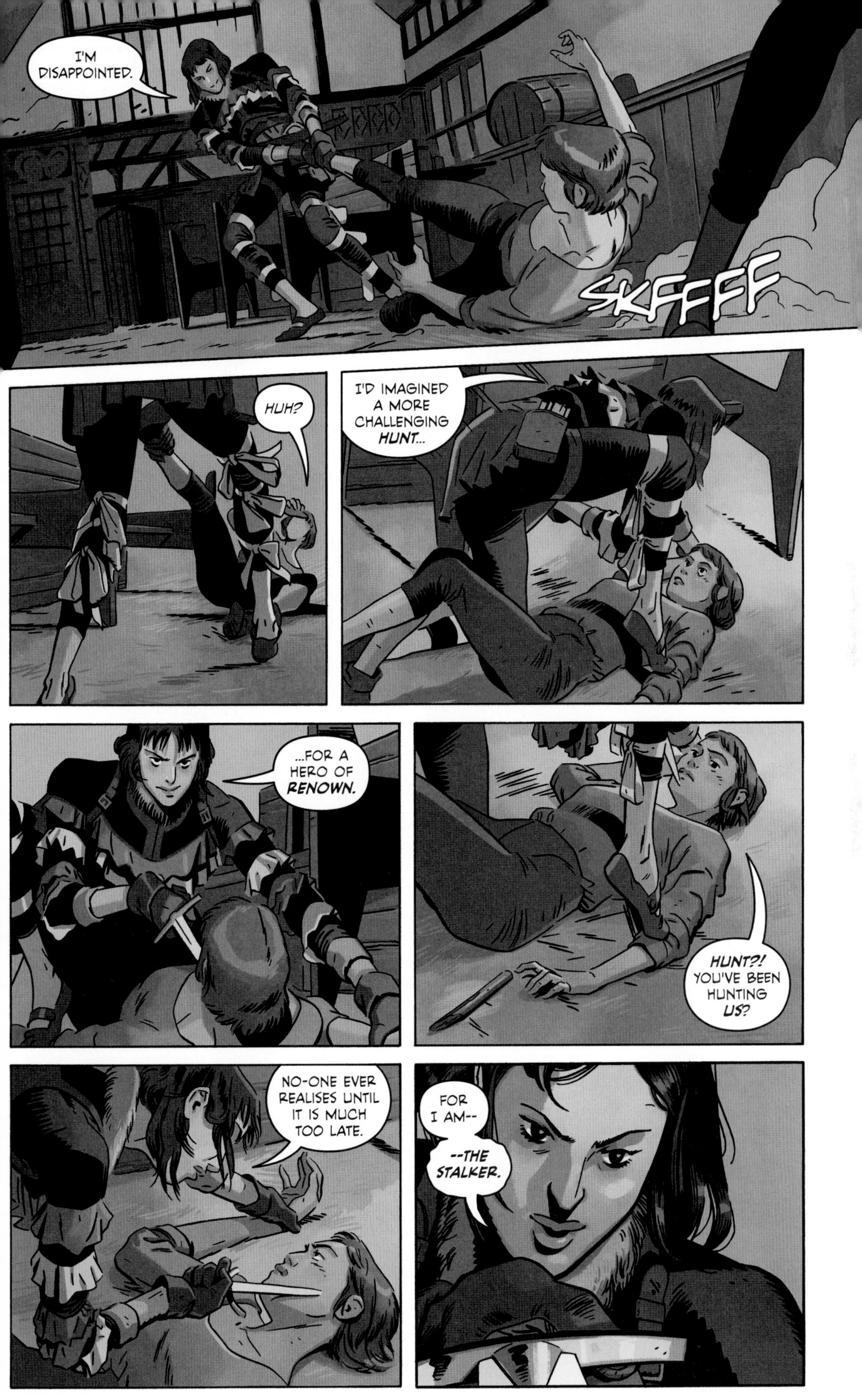
I'M DISAPPOINTED.
SKFFFF
HUH?
I'D IMAGINED A MORE CHALLENGING HUNT...
...FOR A HERO OF RENOWN.
HUNT?! YOU'VE BEEN HUNTING US?
NO-ONE EVER REALISES UNTIL IT IS MUCH TOO LATE.
FOR I AM--
--THE STALKER.

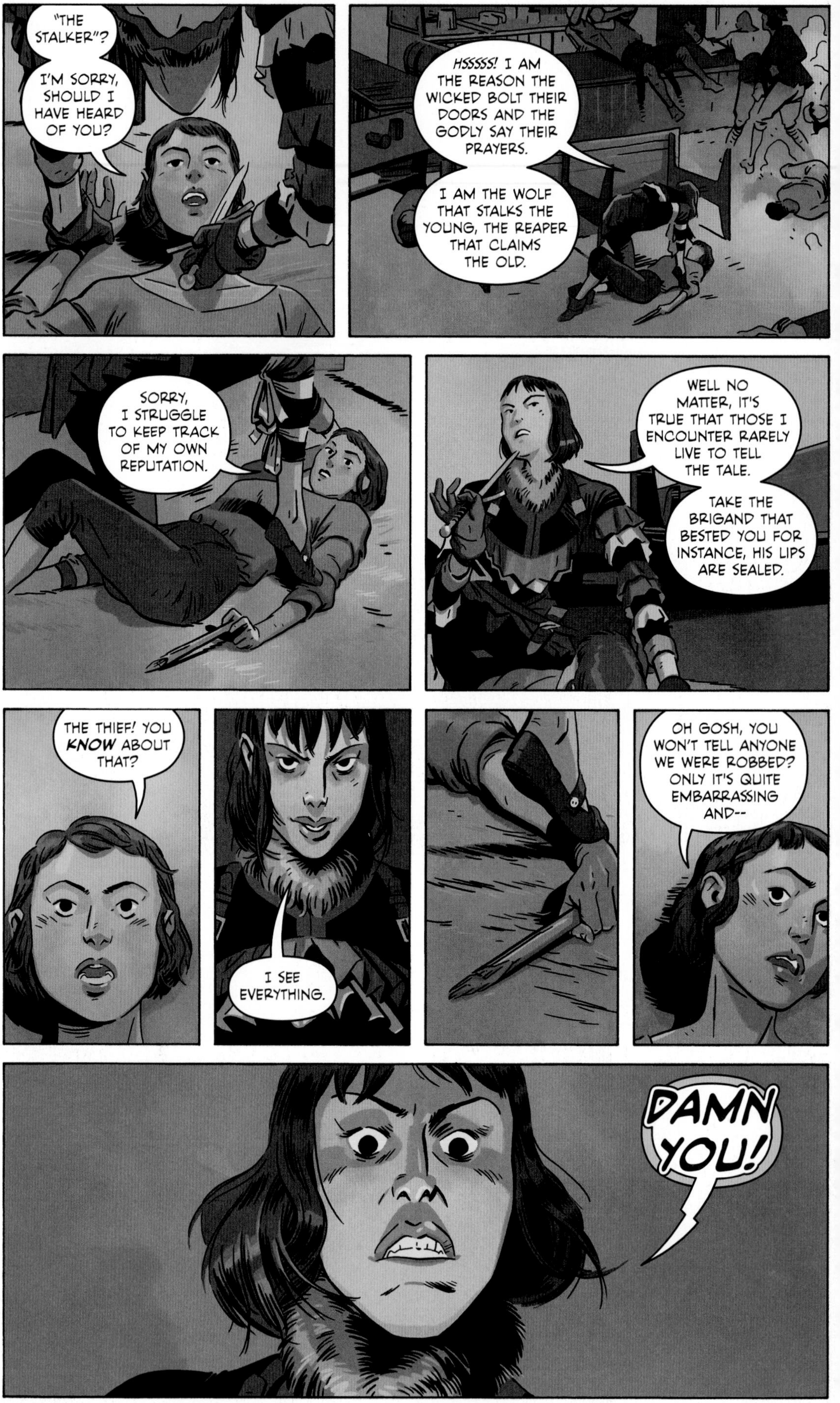

"THE STALKER"?
I'M SORRY, SHOULD I HAVE HEARD OF YOU?
HSSSSS! I AM THE REASON THE WICKED BOLT THEIR DOORS AND THE GODLY SAY THEIR PRAYERS.
I AM THE WOLF THAT STALKS THE YOUNG, THE REAPER THAT CLAIMS THE OLD.
SORRY, I STRUGGLE TO KEEP TRACK OF MY OWN REPUTATION.
WELL NO MATTER, IT'S TRUE THAT THOSE I ENCOUNTER RARELY LIVE TO TELL THE TALE.
TAKE THE BRIGAND THAT BESTED YOU FOR INSTANCE, HIS LIPS ARE SEALED.
THE THIEF! YOU *KNOW* ABOUT THAT?
I SEE EVERYTHING.
OH GOSH, YOU WON'T TELL ANYONE WE WERE ROBBED? ONLY IT'S QUITE EMBARRASSING AND--
DAMN YOU!

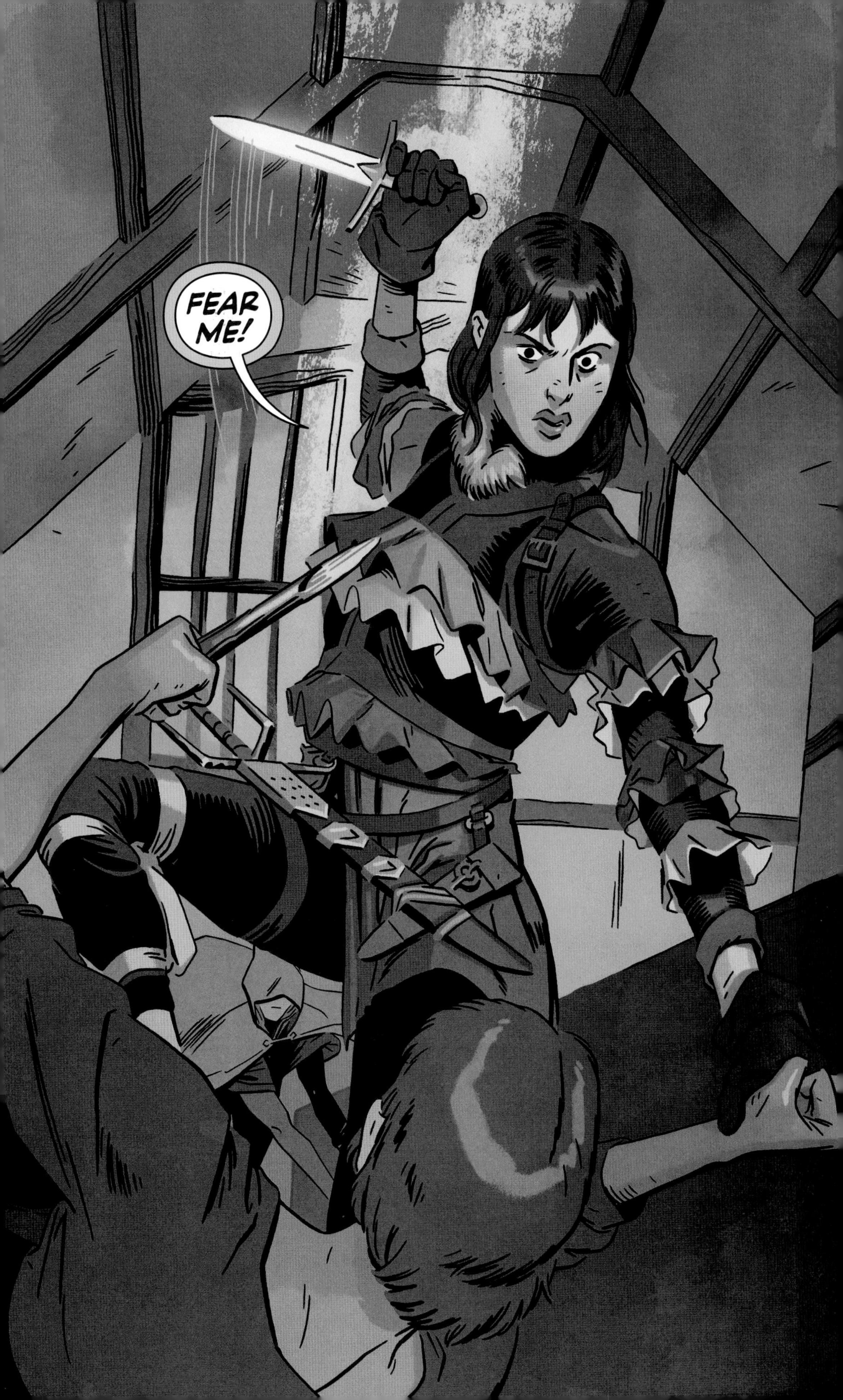
FEAR ME!

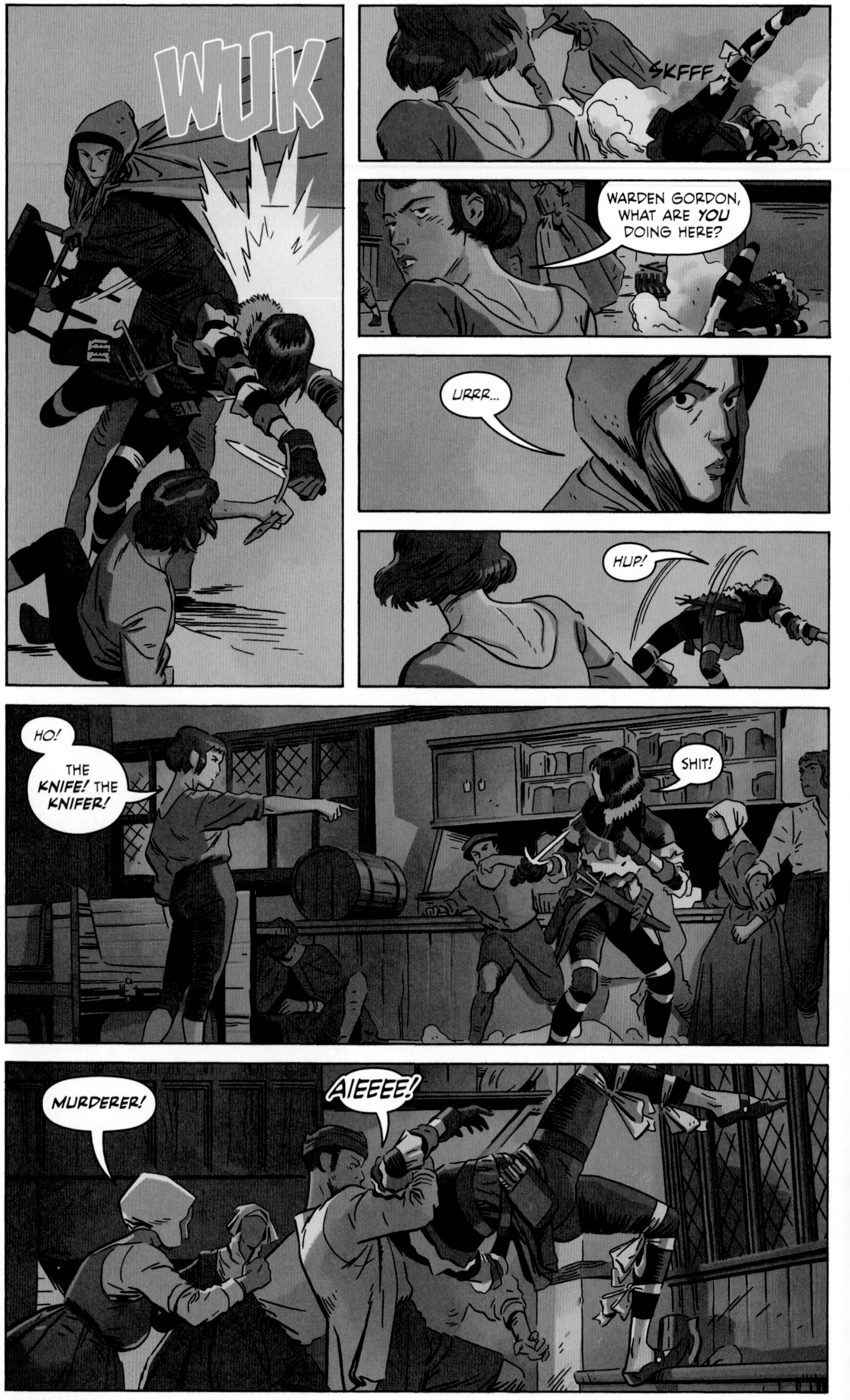
WUK
SKFFF
WARDEN GORDON, WHAT ARE YOU DOING HERE?
URRR...
HUP!
HO!
THE KNIFE! THE KNIFER!
SHIT!
MURDERER!
AIEEEE!

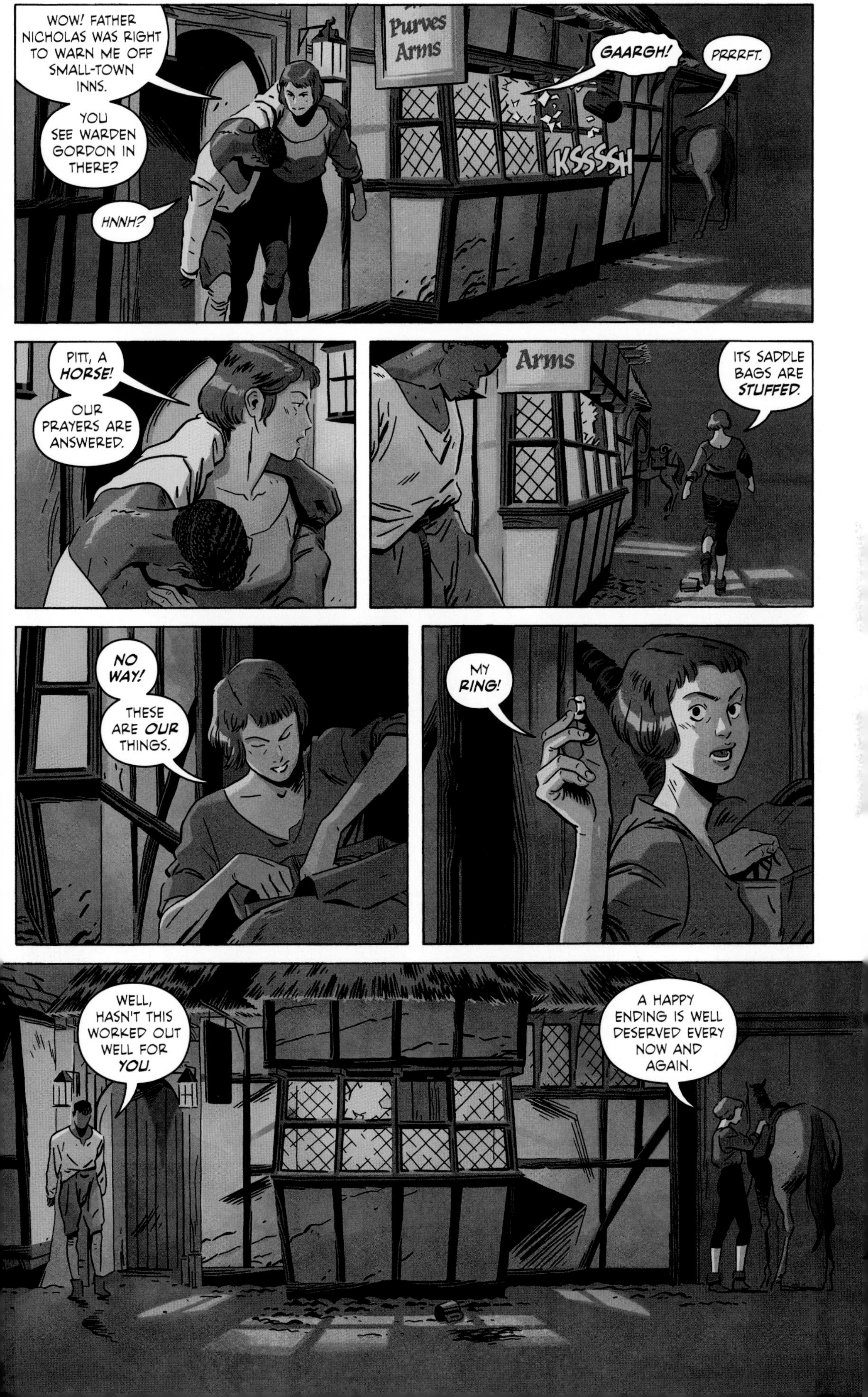

WOW! FATHER NICHOLAS WAS RIGHT TO WARN ME OFF SMALL-TOWN INNS.
YOU SEE WARDEN GORDON IN THERE?
HNNH?
Purves Arms
GAARGH!
KSSSSH
PRRRFT.
PITT, A HORSE!
OUR PRAYERS ARE ANSWERED.
Arms
ITS SADDLE BAGS ARE STUFFED.
NO WAY!
THESE ARE OUR THINGS.
MY RING!
WELL, HASN'T THIS WORKED OUT WELL FOR YOU.
A HAPPY ENDING IS WELL DESERVED EVERY NOW AND AGAIN.

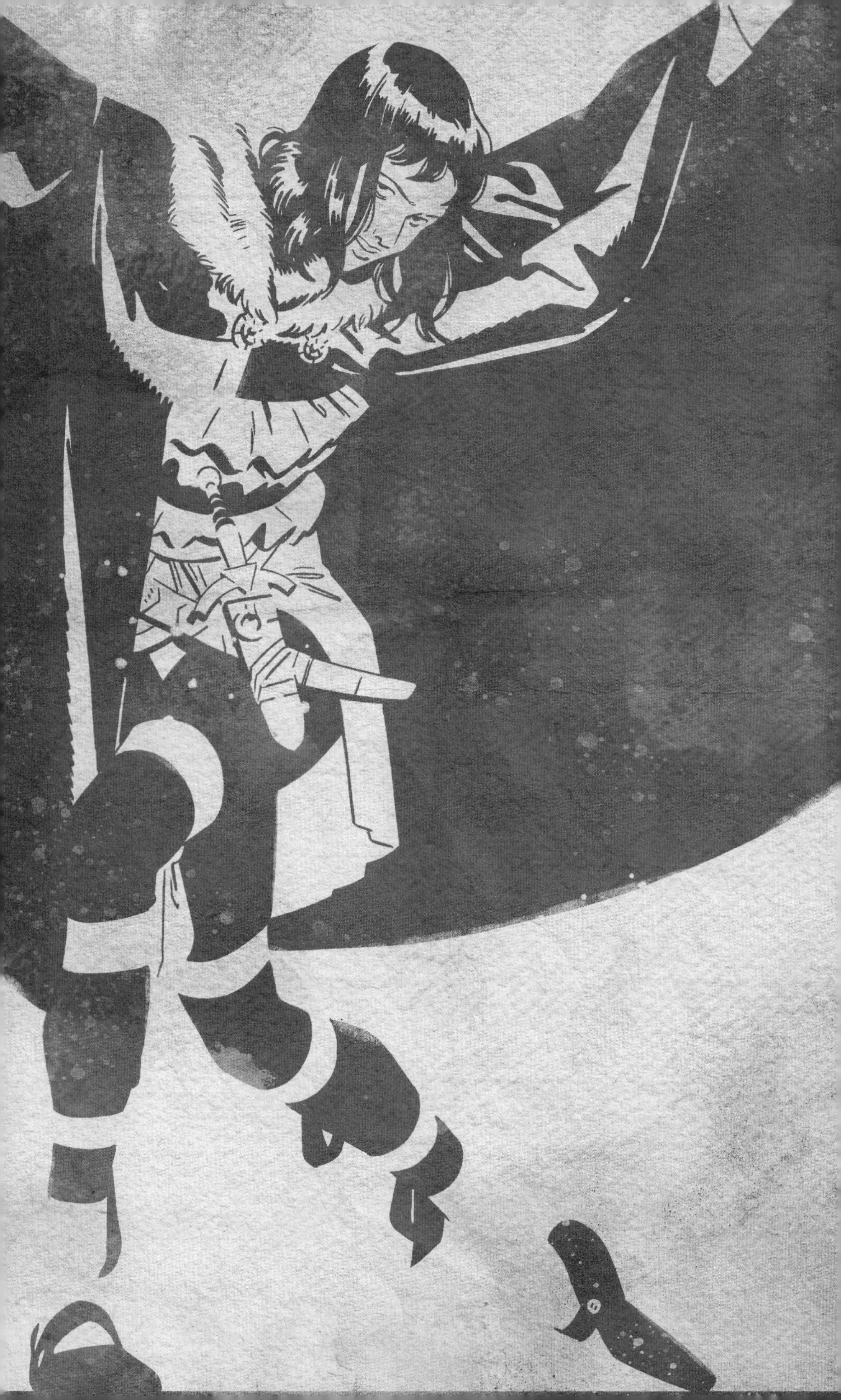

Chapter 4

Four days until the devil's deadline

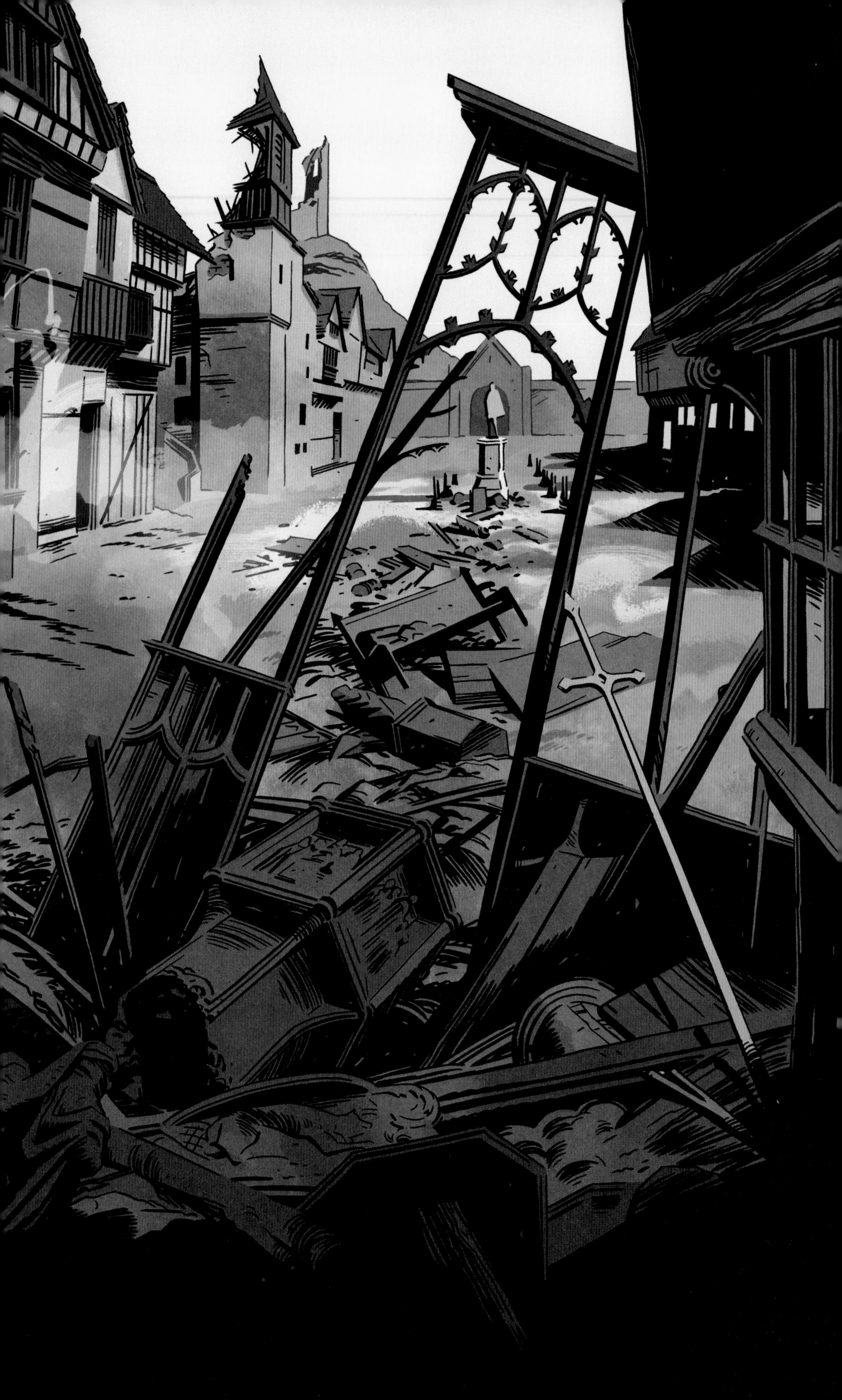

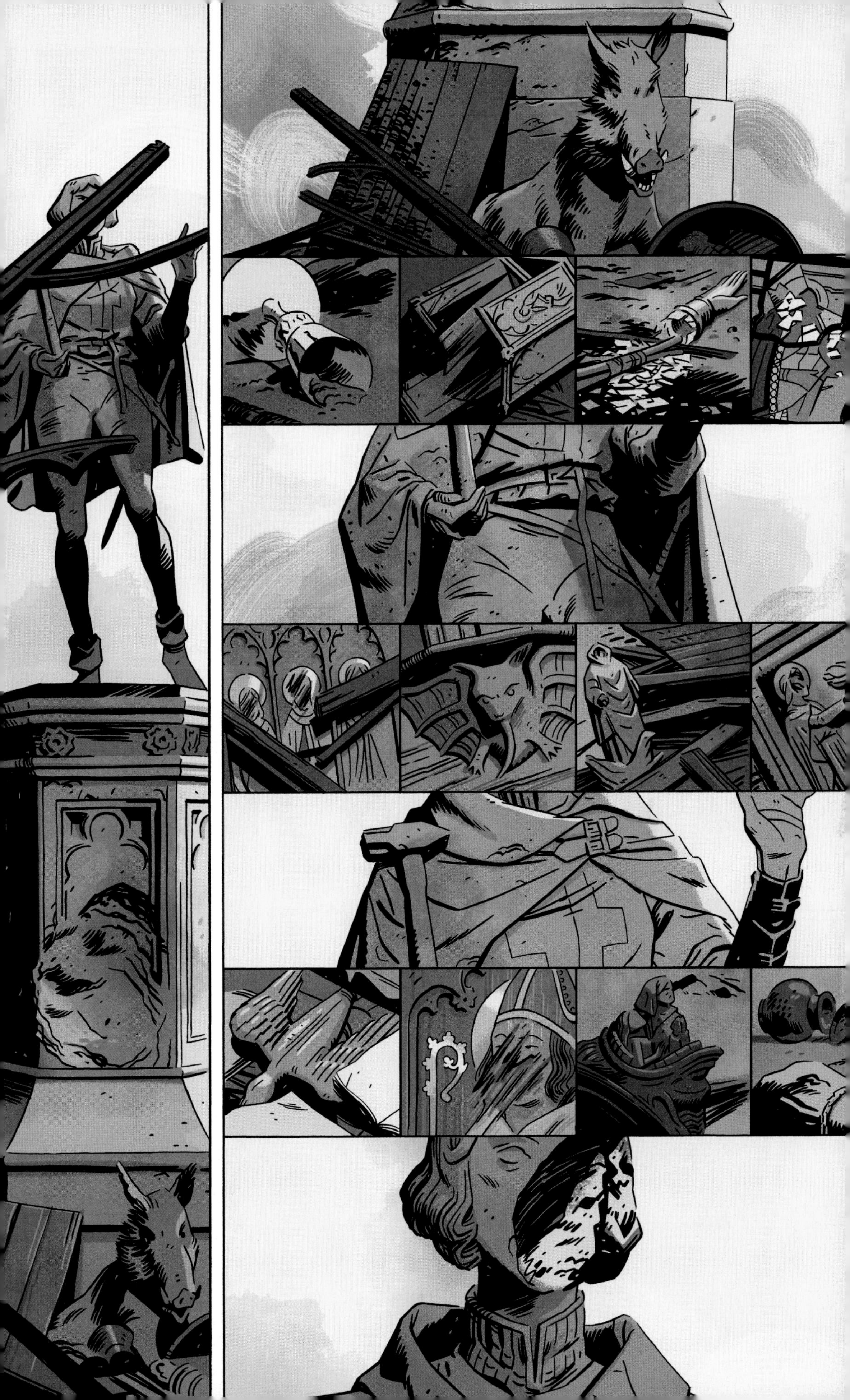

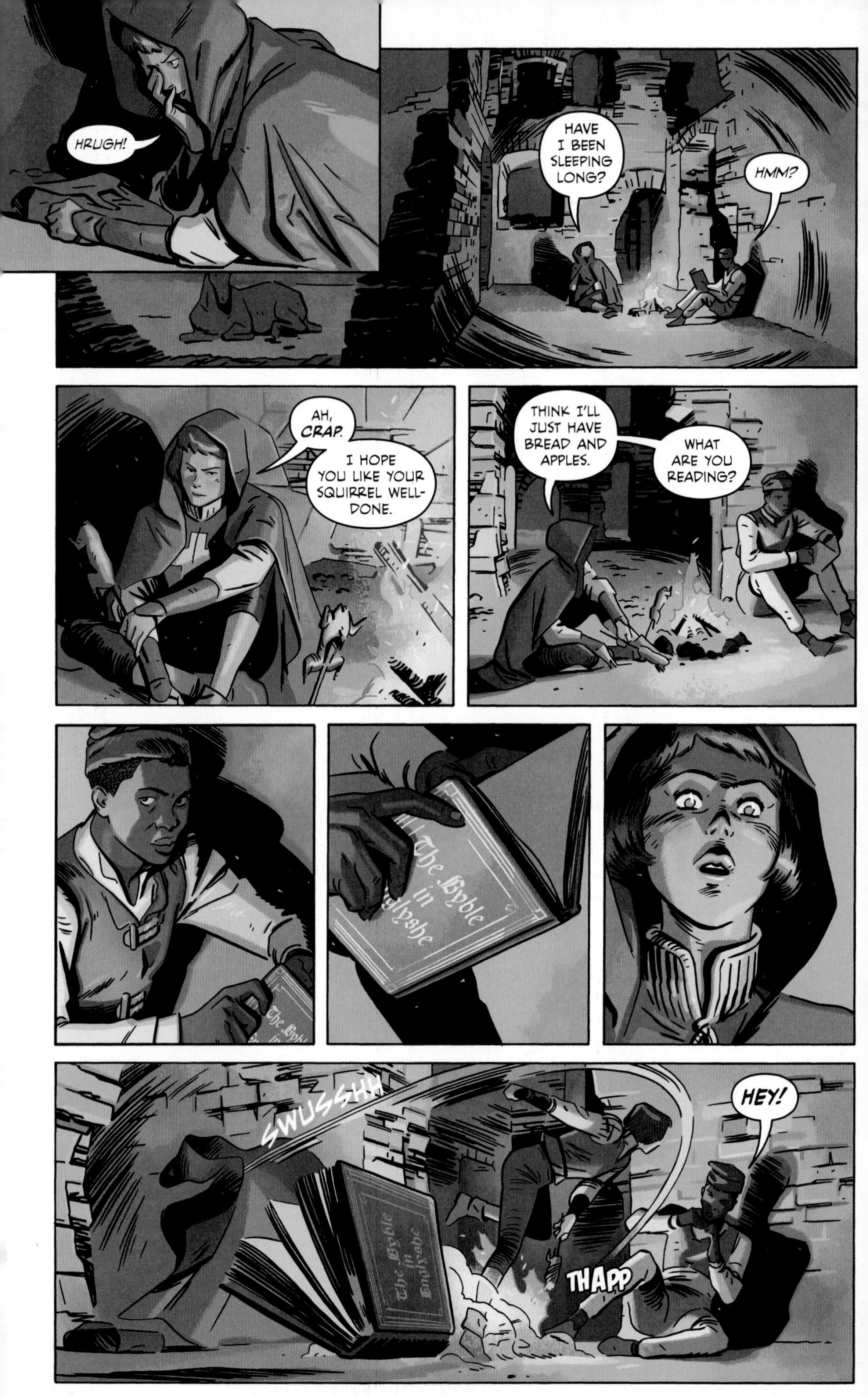
HRUGH!
HAVE I BEEN SLEEPING LONG?
HMM?
AH, CRAP.
I HOPE YOU LIKE YOUR SQUIRREL WELL-DONE.
THINK I'LL JUST HAVE BREAD AND APPLES.
WHAT ARE YOU READING?
The Byble in Englyshe
SWUSSHH
The Byble in Englyshe
THAPP
HEY!

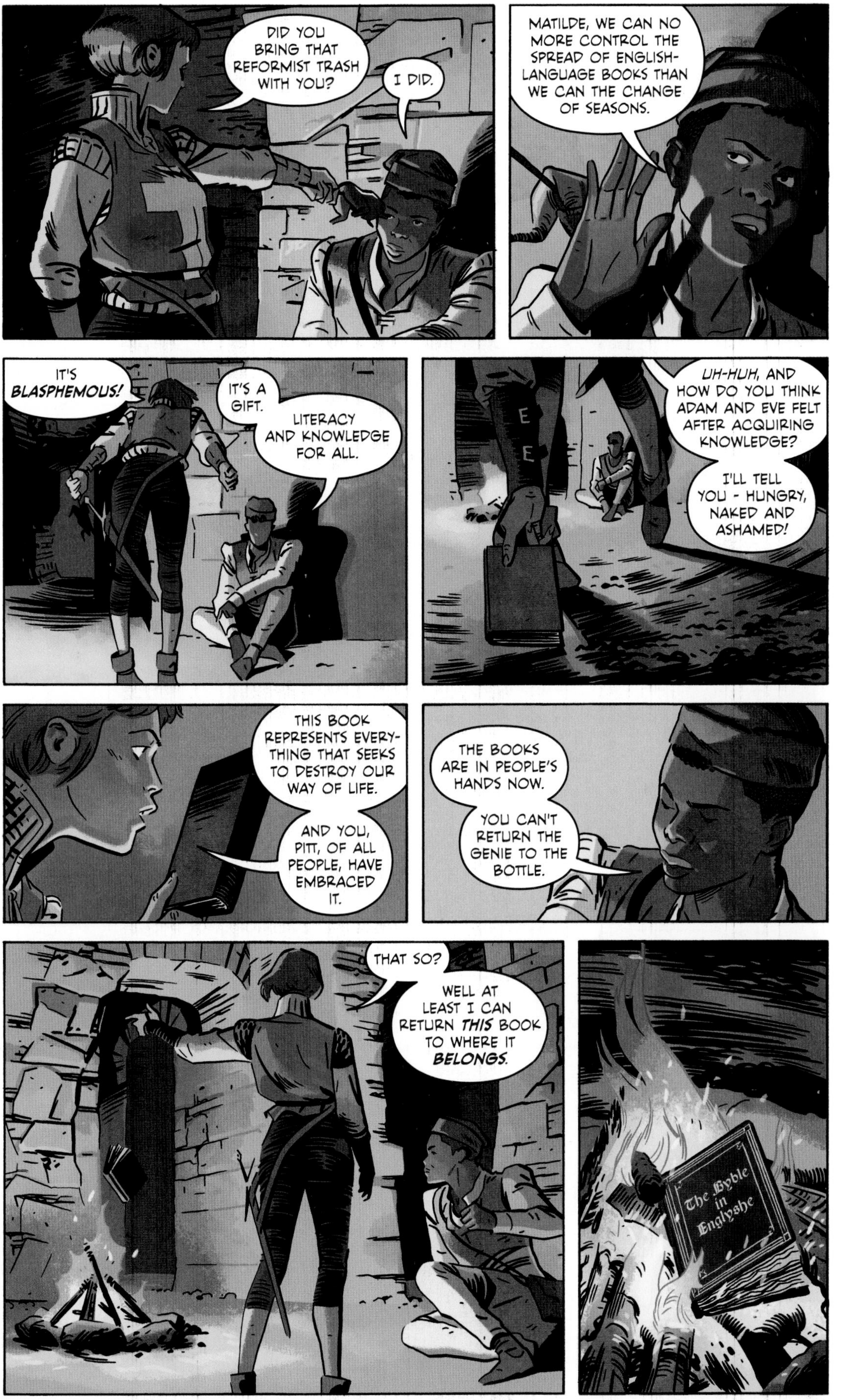
DID YOU BRING THAT REFORMIST TRASH WITH YOU?
I DID.
MATILDE, WE CAN NO MORE CONTROL THE SPREAD OF ENGLISH-LANGUAGE BOOKS THAN WE CAN THE CHANGE OF SEASONS.
IT'S *BLASPHEMOUS!*
IT'S A GIFT.
LITERACY AND KNOWLEDGE FOR ALL.
UH-HUH, AND HOW DO YOU THINK ADAM AND EVE FELT AFTER ACQUIRING KNOWLEDGE?
I'LL TELL YOU - HUNGRY, NAKED AND ASHAMED!
THIS BOOK REPRESENTS EVERYTHING THAT SEEKS TO DESTROY OUR WAY OF LIFE.
AND YOU, PITT, OF ALL PEOPLE, HAVE EMBRACED IT.
THE BOOKS ARE IN PEOPLE'S HANDS NOW.
YOU CAN'T RETURN THE GENIE TO THE BOTTLE.
THAT SO?
WELL AT LEAST I CAN RETURN ***THIS*** BOOK TO WHERE IT ***BELONGS***.
The Byble in Englyshe

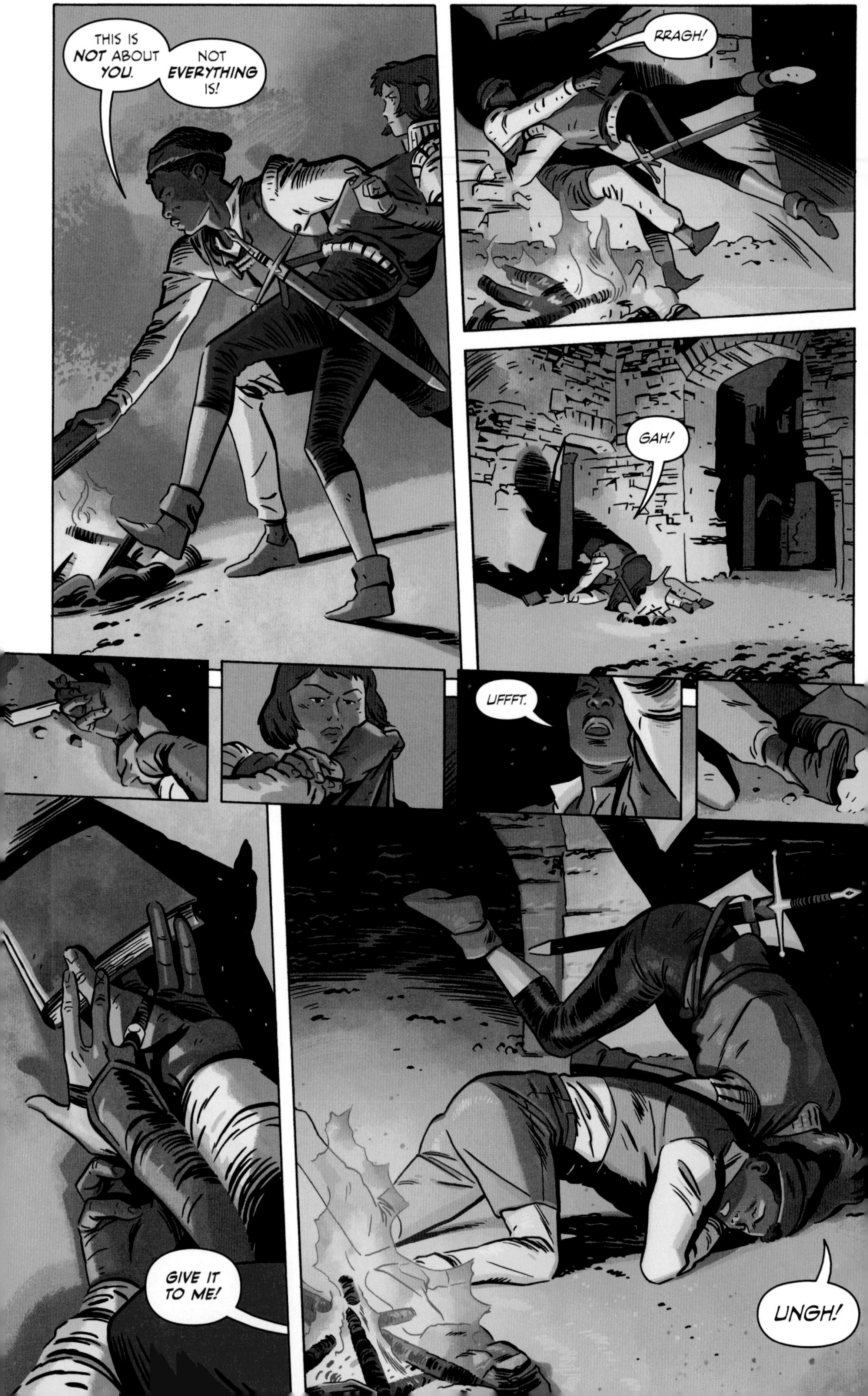
THIS IS NOT ABOUT YOU.
NOT EVERYTHING IS!
RRAGH!
GAH!
UFFFT.
GIVE IT TO ME!
UNGH!

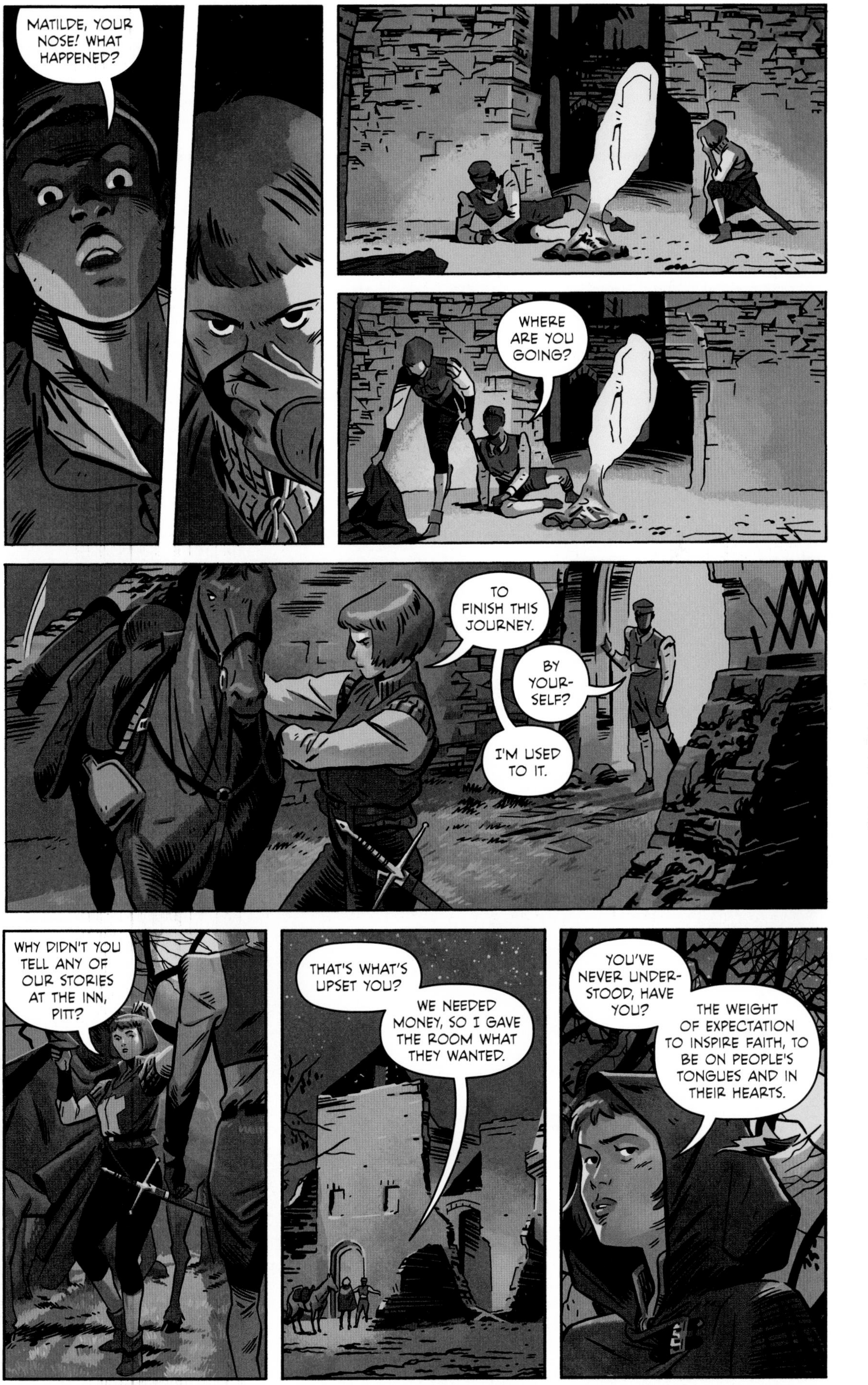
MATILDE, YOUR NOSE! WHAT HAPPENED?
WHERE ARE YOU GOING?
TO FINISH THIS JOURNEY.
BY YOURSELF?
I'M USED TO IT.
WHY DIDN'T YOU TELL ANY OF OUR STORIES AT THE INN, PITT?
THAT'S WHAT'S UPSET YOU?
WE NEEDED MONEY, SO I GAVE THE ROOM WHAT THEY WANTED.
YOU'VE NEVER UNDERSTOOD, HAVE YOU?
THE WEIGHT OF EXPECTATION TO INSPIRE FAITH, TO BE ON PEOPLE'S TONGUES AND IN THEIR HEARTS.

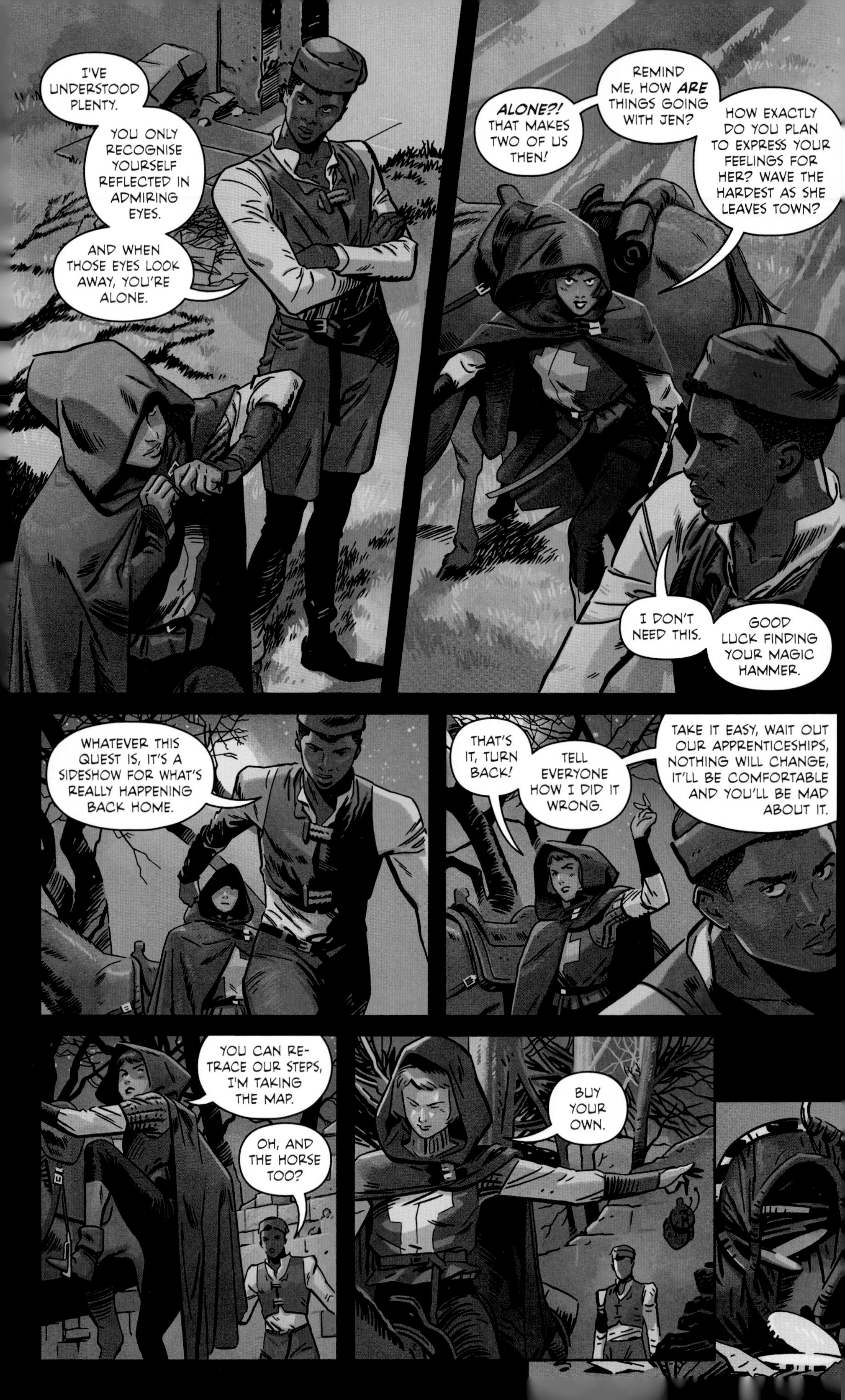

I'VE UNDERSTOOD PLENTY.
YOU ONLY RECOGNISE YOURSELF REFLECTED IN ADMIRING EYES.
AND WHEN THOSE EYES LOOK AWAY, YOU'RE ALONE.
ALONE?! THAT MAKES TWO OF US THEN!
REMIND ME, HOW ARE THINGS GOING WITH JEN?
HOW EXACTLY DO YOU PLAN TO EXPRESS YOUR FEELINGS FOR HER? WAVE THE HARDEST AS SHE LEAVES TOWN?
I DON'T NEED THIS.
GOOD LUCK FINDING YOUR MAGIC HAMMER.
WHATEVER THIS QUEST IS, IT'S A SIDESHOW FOR WHAT'S REALLY HAPPENING BACK HOME.
THAT'S IT, TURN BACK!
TELL EVERYONE HOW I DID IT WRONG.
TAKE IT EASY, WAIT OUT OUR APPRENTICESHIPS, NOTHING WILL CHANGE, IT'LL BE COMFORTABLE AND YOU'LL BE MAD ABOUT IT.
YOU CAN RE-TRACE OUR STEPS, I'M TAKING THE MAP.
OH, AND THE HORSE TOO?
BUY YOUR OWN.

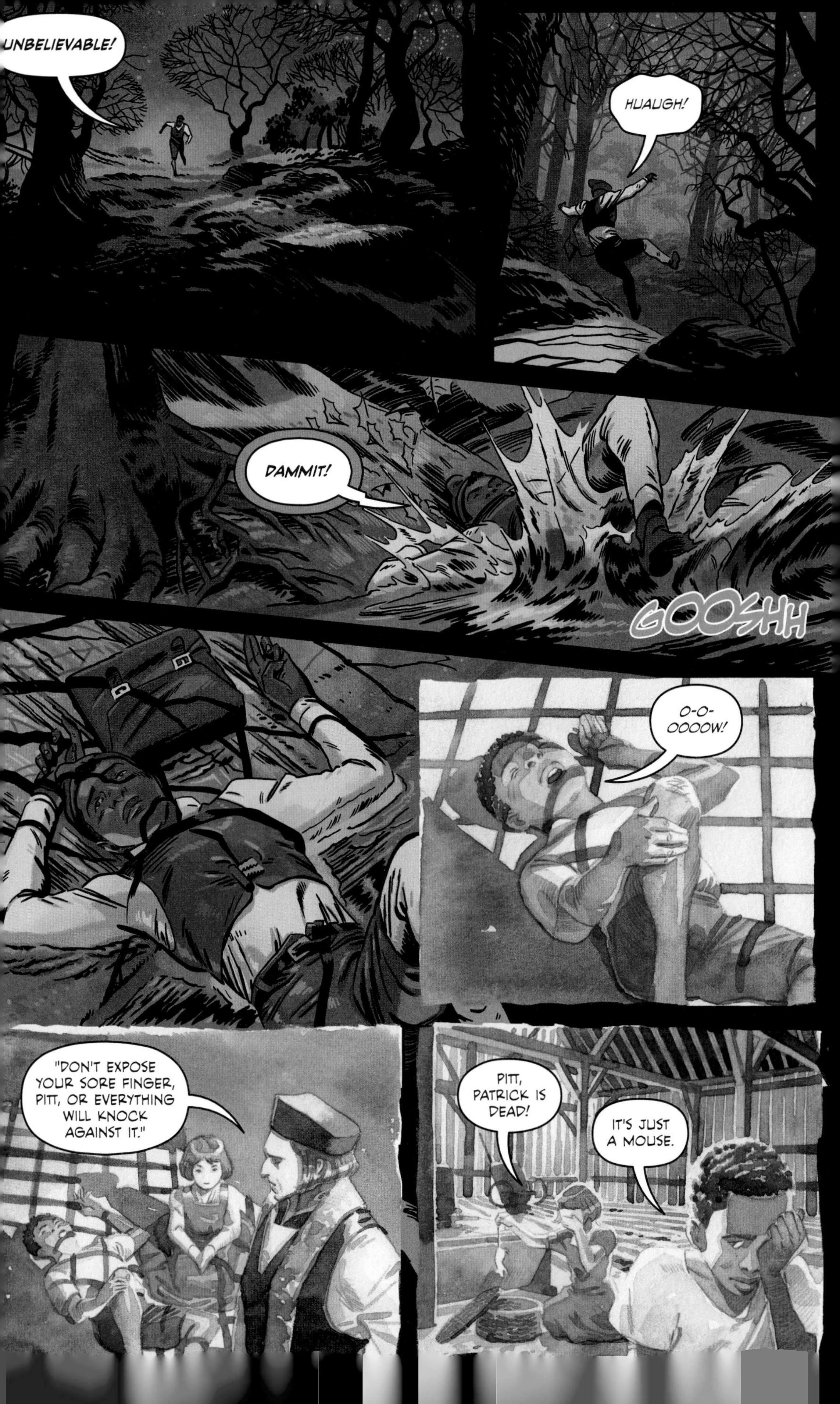
UNBELIEVABLE!
HUAUGH!
DAMMIT!
GOOSHH
O-O-OOOOW!
"DON'T EXPOSE YOUR SORE FINGER, PITT, OR EVERYTHING WILL KNOCK AGAINST IT."
PITT, PATRICK IS DEAD!
IT'S JUST A MOUSE.

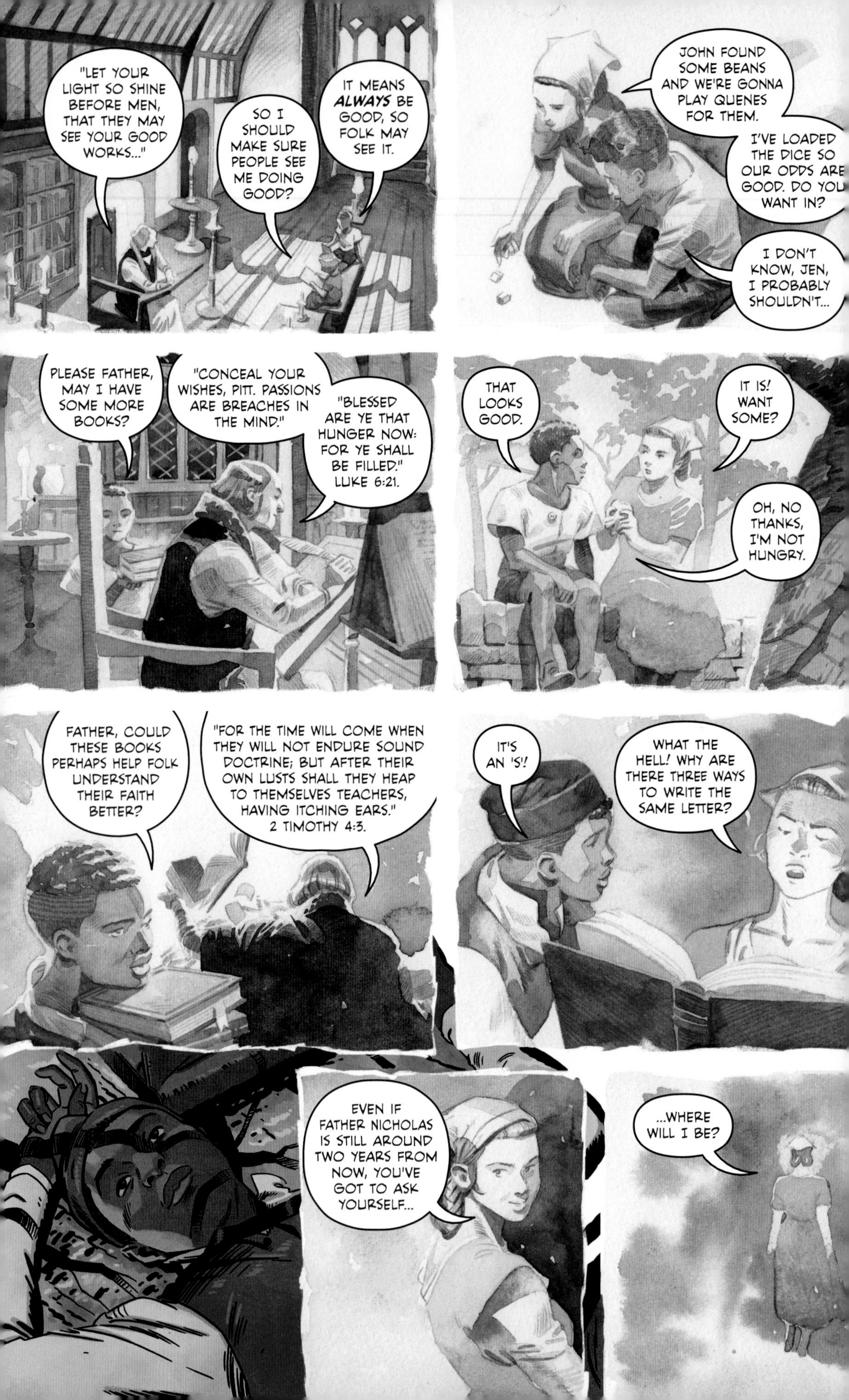
"LET YOUR LIGHT SO SHINE BEFORE MEN, THAT THEY MAY SEE YOUR GOOD WORKS..."
SO I SHOULD MAKE SURE PEOPLE SEE ME DOING GOOD?
IT MEANS *ALWAYS* BE GOOD, SO FOLK MAY SEE IT.
JOHN FOUND SOME BEANS AND WE'RE GONNA PLAY QUENES FOR THEM.
I'VE LOADED THE DICE SO OUR ODDS ARE GOOD. DO YOU WANT IN?
I DON'T KNOW, JEN, I PROBABLY SHOULDN'T...
PLEASE FATHER, MAY I HAVE SOME MORE BOOKS?
"CONCEAL YOUR WISHES, PITT. PASSIONS ARE BREACHES IN THE MIND."
"BLESSED ARE YE THAT HUNGER NOW: FOR YE SHALL BE FILLED." LUKE 6:21.
THAT LOOKS GOOD.
IT IS! WANT SOME?
OH, NO THANKS, I'M NOT HUNGRY.
FATHER, COULD THESE BOOKS PERHAPS HELP FOLK UNDERSTAND THEIR FAITH BETTER?
"FOR THE TIME WILL COME WHEN THEY WILL NOT ENDURE SOUND DOCTRINE; BUT AFTER THEIR OWN LUSTS SHALL THEY HEAP TO THEMSELVES TEACHERS, HAVING ITCHING EARS." 2 TIMOTHY 4:3.
IT'S AN 'S'!
WHAT THE HELL! WHY ARE THERE THREE WAYS TO WRITE THE SAME LETTER?
EVEN IF FATHER NICHOLAS IS STILL AROUND TWO YEARS FROM NOW, YOU'VE GOT TO ASK YOURSELF...
...WHERE WILL I BE?

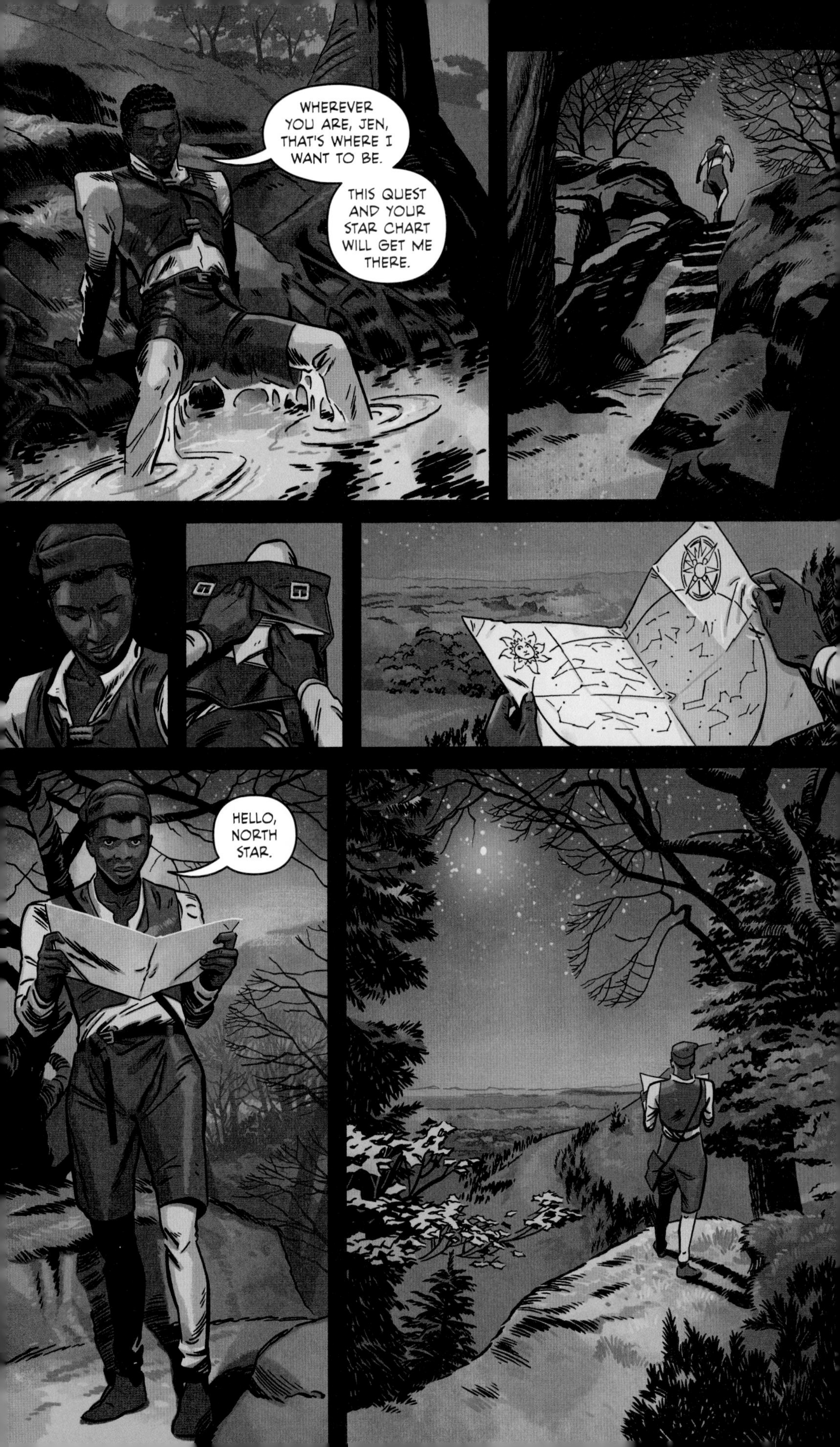
WHEREVER YOU ARE, JEN, THAT'S WHERE I WANT TO BE.
THIS QUEST AND YOUR STAR CHART WILL GET ME THERE.
HELLO, NORTH STAR.

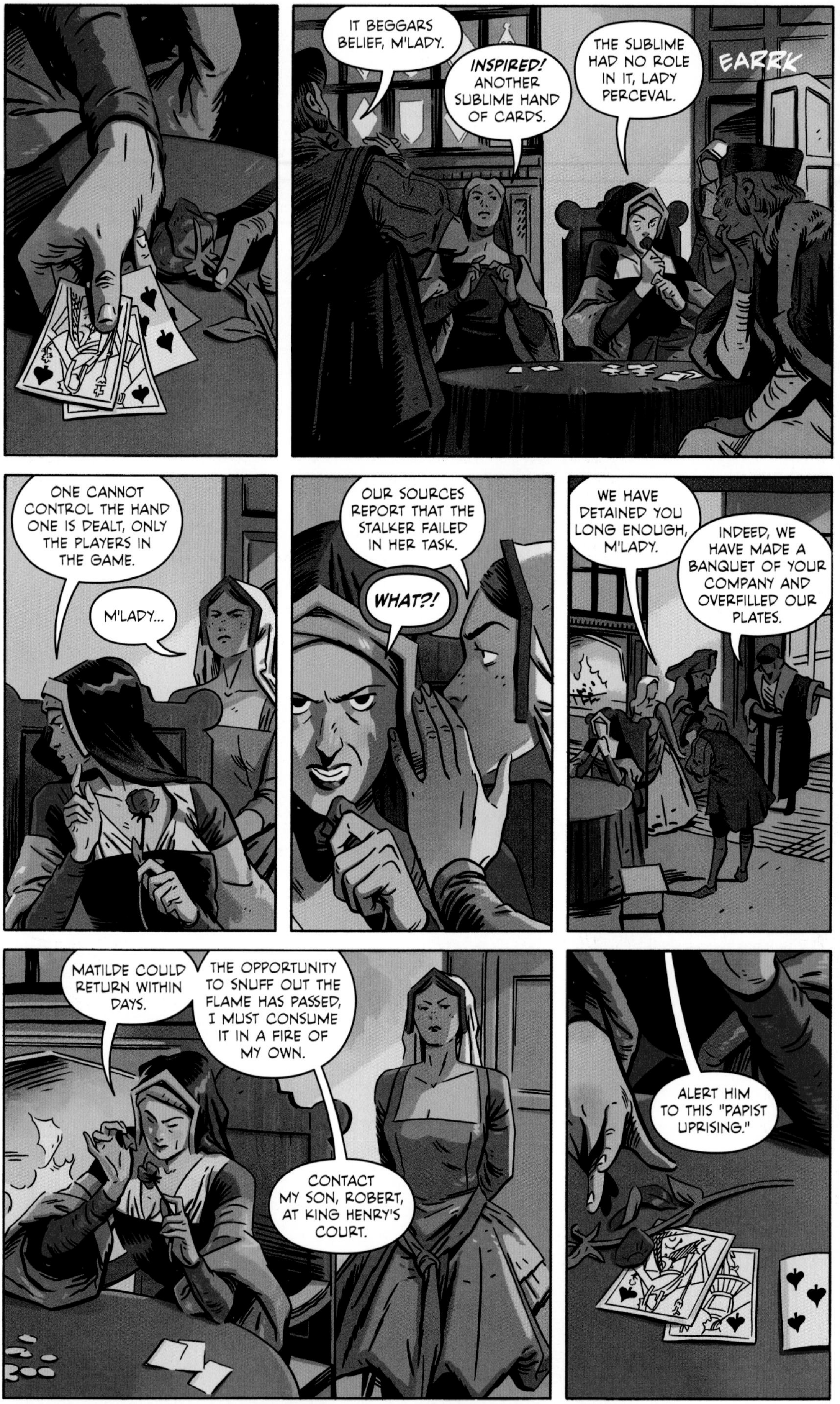
IT BEGGARS BELIEF, M'LADY.
INSPIRED! ANOTHER SUBLIME HAND OF CARDS.
THE SUBLIME HAD NO ROLE IN IT, LADY PERCEVAL.
EARRK
ONE CANNOT CONTROL THE HAND ONE IS DEALT, ONLY THE PLAYERS IN THE GAME.
M'LADY...
OUR SOURCES REPORT THAT THE STALKER FAILED IN HER TASK.
WHAT?!
WE HAVE DETAINED YOU LONG ENOUGH, M'LADY.
INDEED, WE HAVE MADE A BANQUET OF YOUR COMPANY AND OVERFILLED OUR PLATES.
MATILDE COULD RETURN WITHIN DAYS.
THE OPPORTUNITY TO SNUFF OUT THE FLAME HAS PASSED, I MUST CONSUME IT IN A FIRE OF MY OWN.
CONTACT MY SON, ROBERT, AT KING HENRY'S COURT.
ALERT HIM TO THIS "PAPIST UPRISING."

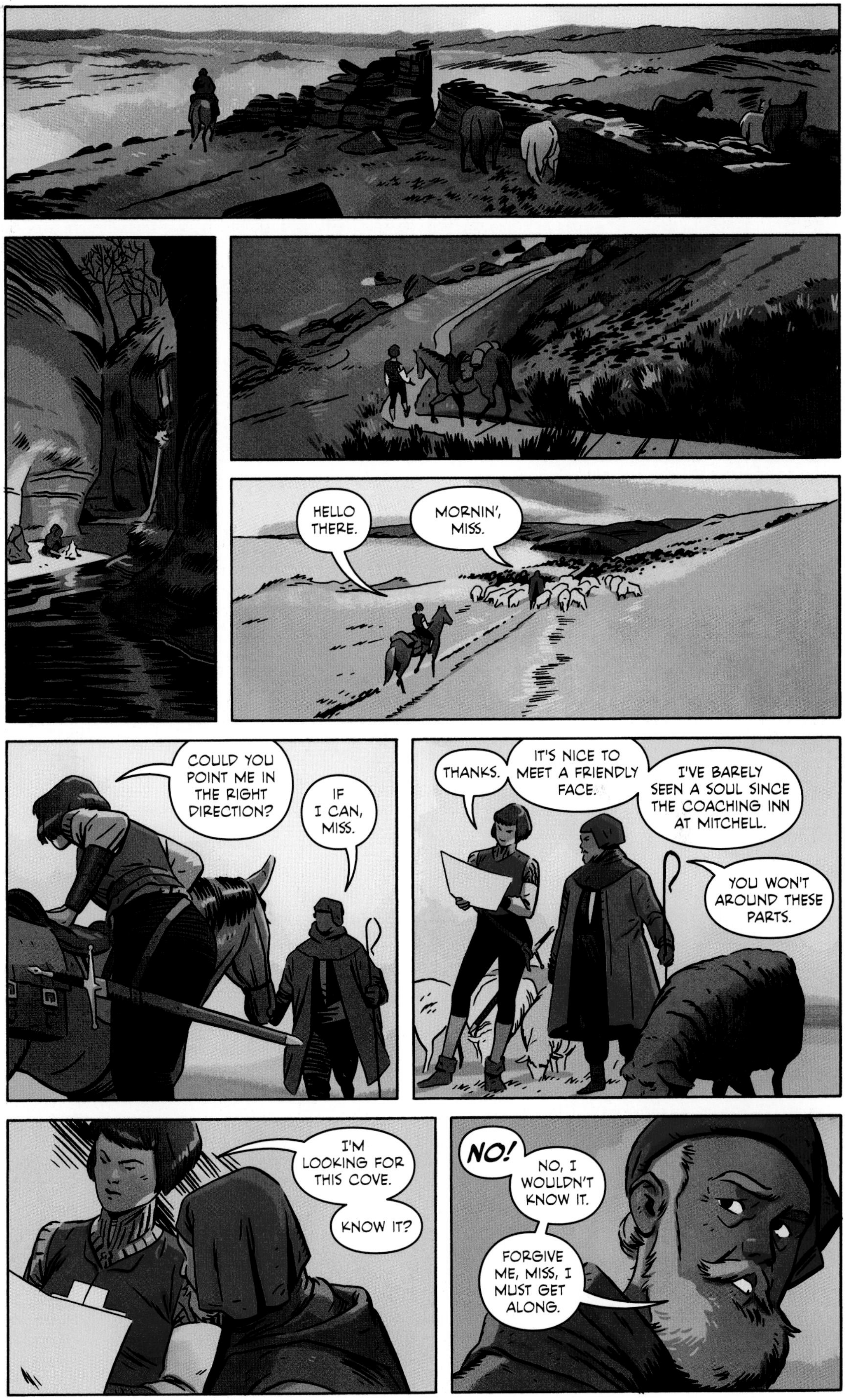
HELLO THERE.
MORNIN', MISS.
COULD YOU POINT ME IN THE RIGHT DIRECTION?
IF I CAN, MISS.
THANKS.
IT'S NICE TO MEET A FRIENDLY FACE.
I'VE BARELY SEEN A SOUL SINCE THE COACHING INN AT MITCHELL.
YOU WON'T AROUND THESE PARTS.
I'M LOOKING FOR THIS COVE.
KNOW IT?
NO!
NO, I WOULDN'T KNOW IT.
FORGIVE ME, MISS, I MUST GET ALONG.

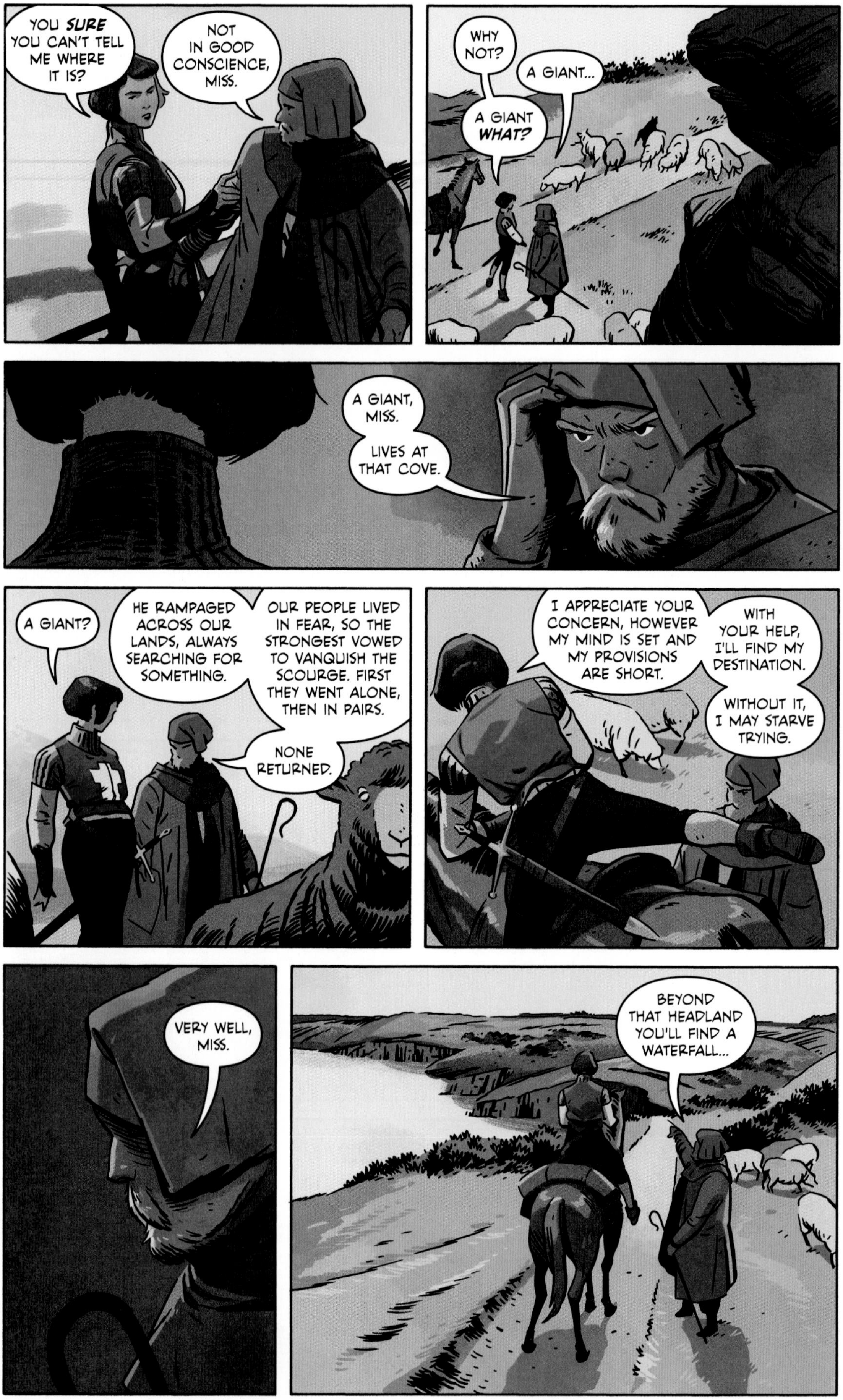

YOU **SURE** YOU CAN'T TELL ME WHERE IT IS?
NOT IN GOOD CONSCIENCE, MISS.
WHY NOT?
A GIANT...
A GIANT **WHAT?**
A GIANT, MISS.
LIVES AT THAT COVE.
A GIANT?
HE RAMPAGED ACROSS OUR LANDS, ALWAYS SEARCHING FOR SOMETHING.
OUR PEOPLE LIVED IN FEAR, SO THE STRONGEST VOWED TO VANQUISH THE SCOURGE. FIRST THEY WENT ALONE, THEN IN PAIRS.
NONE RETURNED.
I APPRECIATE YOUR CONCERN, HOWEVER MY MIND IS SET AND MY PROVISIONS ARE SHORT.
WITH YOUR HELP, I'LL FIND MY DESTINATION.
WITHOUT IT, I MAY STARVE TRYING.
VERY WELL, MISS.
BEYOND THAT HEADLAND YOU'LL FIND A WATERFALL...

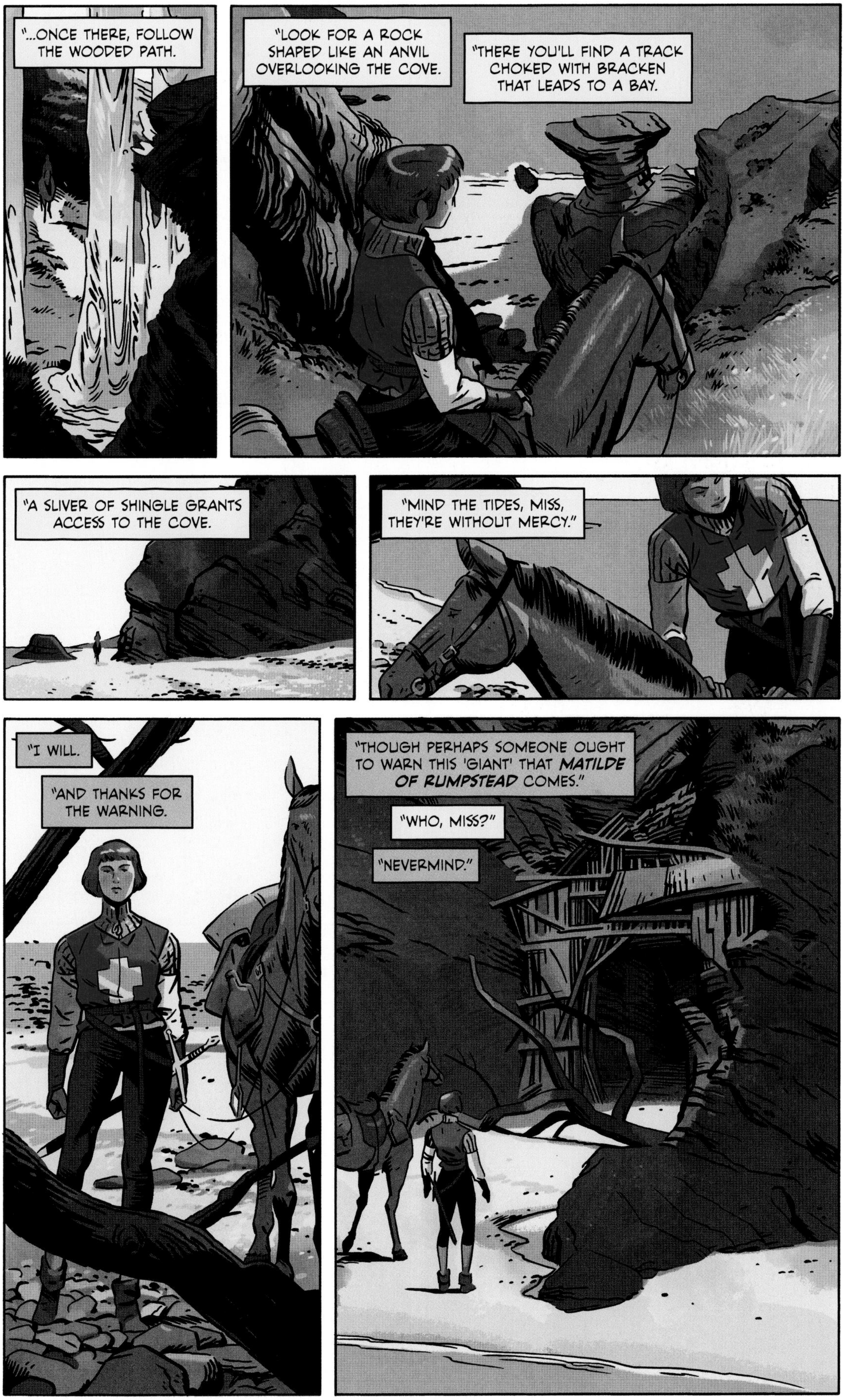
"...ONCE THERE, FOLLOW THE WOODED PATH.
"LOOK FOR A ROCK SHAPED LIKE AN ANVIL OVERLOOKING THE COVE.
"THERE YOU'LL FIND A TRACK CHOKED WITH BRACKEN THAT LEADS TO A BAY.
"A SLIVER OF SHINGLE GRANTS ACCESS TO THE COVE.
"MIND THE TIDES, MISS, THEY'RE WITHOUT MERCY."
"I WILL.
"AND THANKS FOR THE WARNING.
"THOUGH PERHAPS SOMEONE OUGHT TO WARN THIS 'GIANT' THAT MATILDE OF RUMPSTEAD COMES."
"WHO, MISS?"
"NEVERMIND."

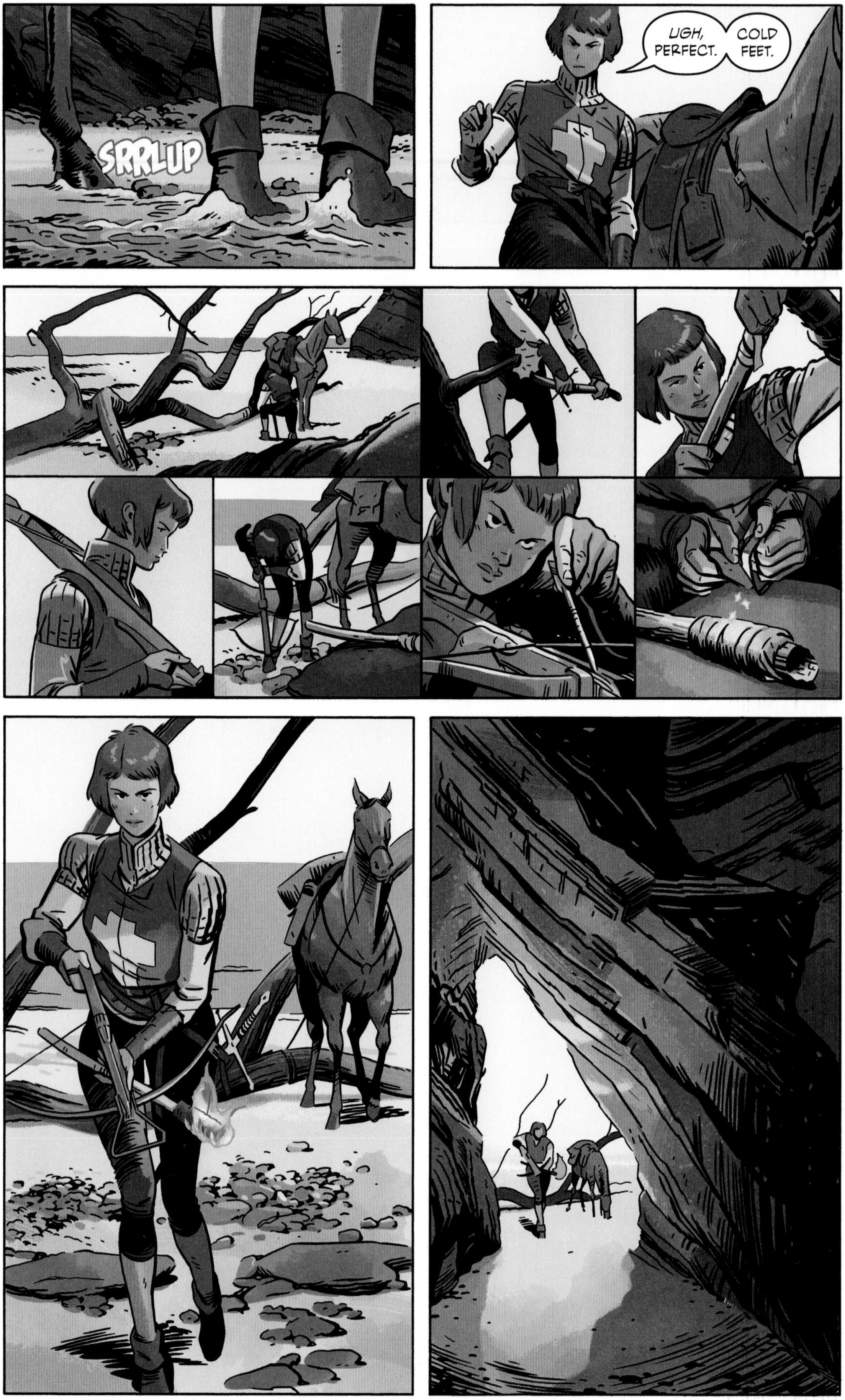
SRRLUP
UGH, PERFECT.
COLD FEET.

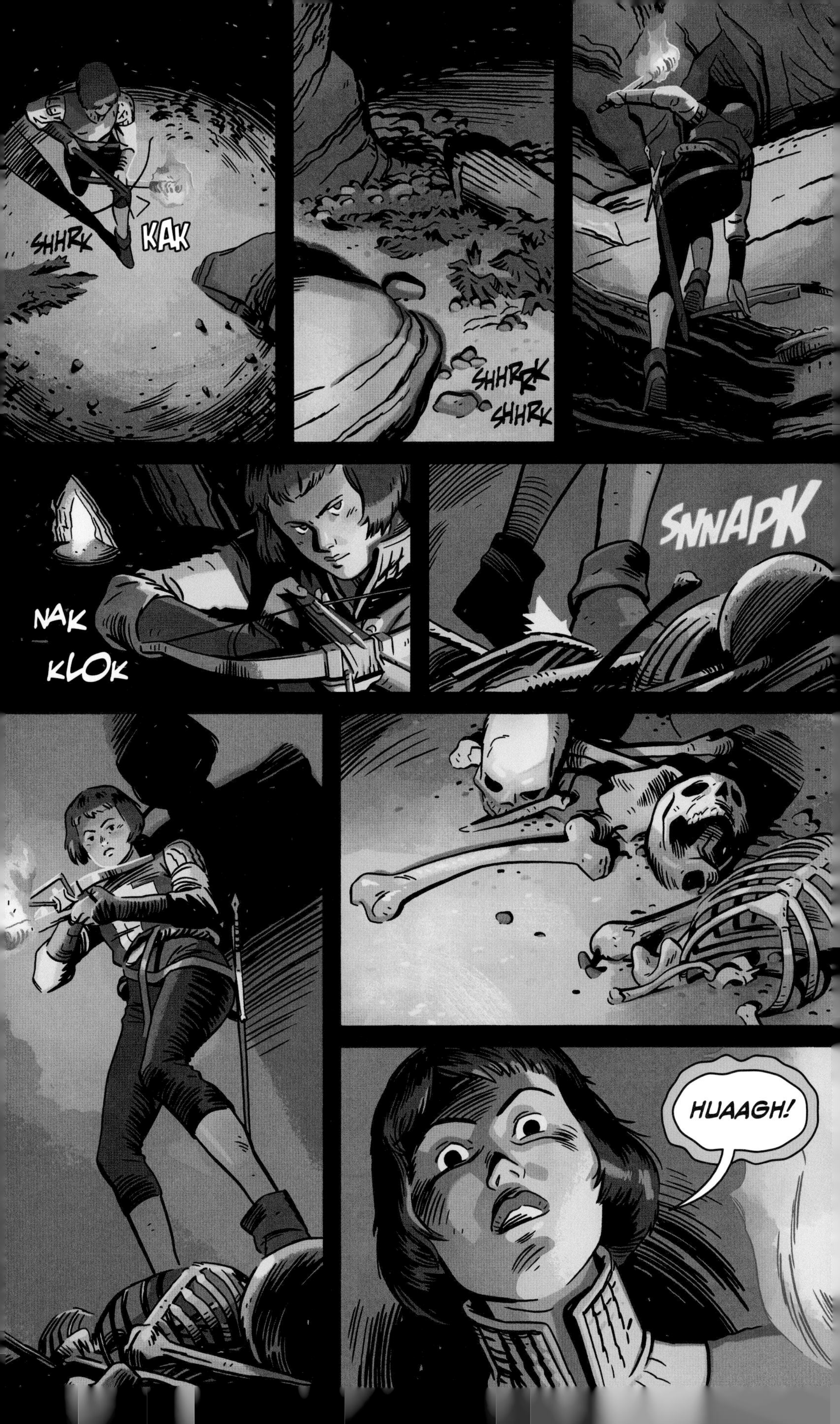
SHHRK
KAK
SHHRK
SHHRK
NAK
KLOK
SNNAPK
HUAAGH!

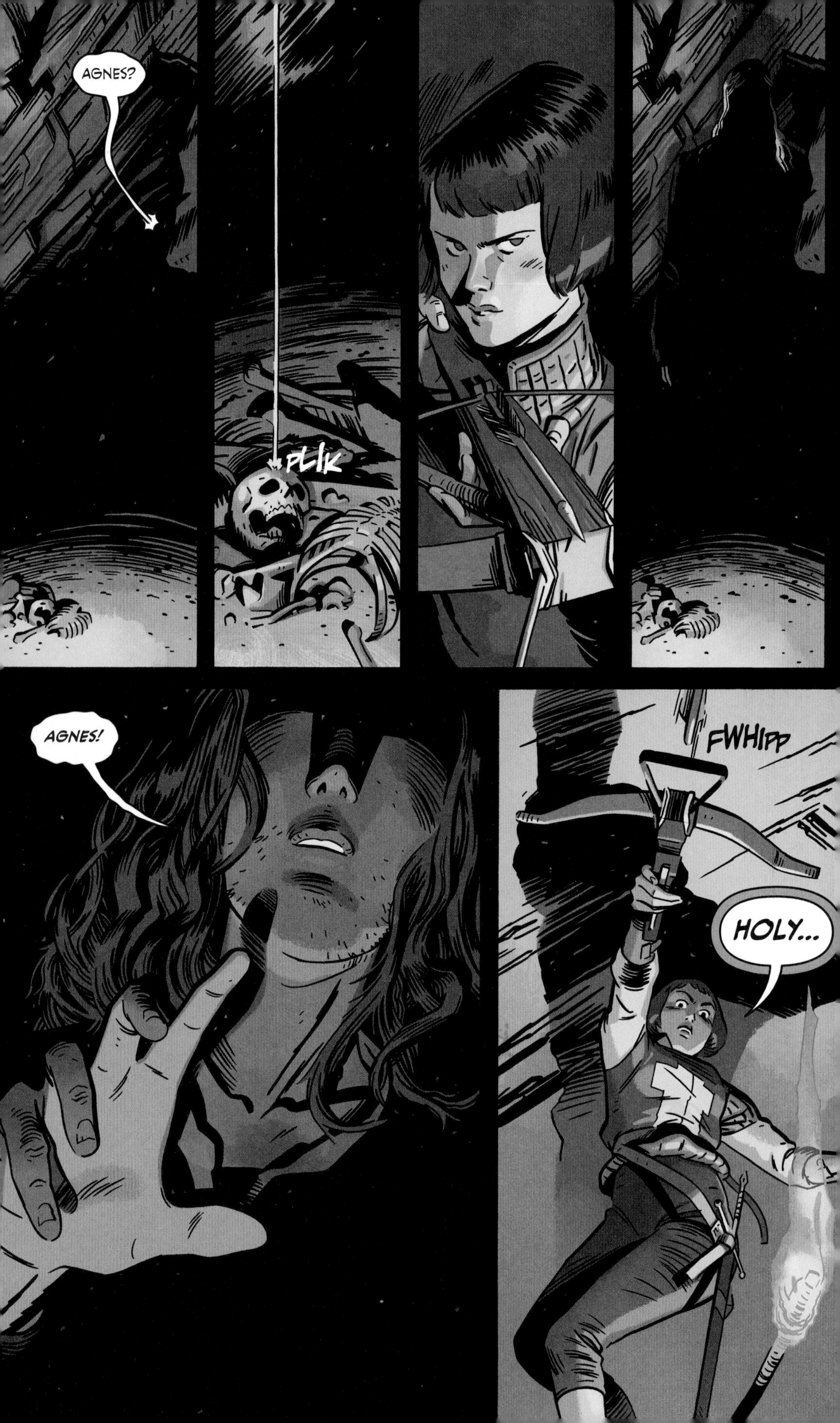
AGNES?
PLIK
AGNES!
FWHIPP
HOLY...

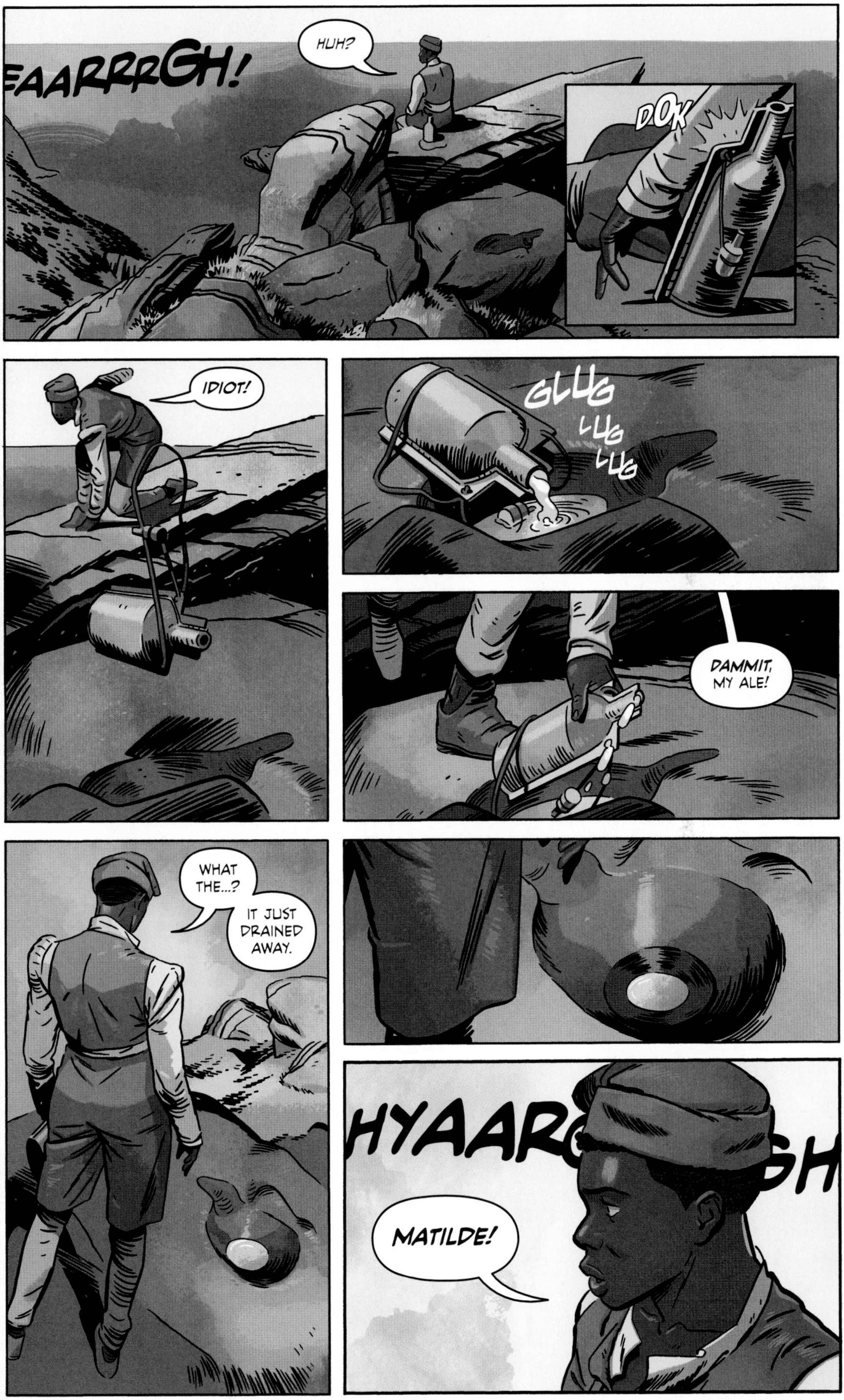
EAARRRGH!
HUH?
DOK
IDIOT!
GLUG
LUG
LUG
DAMMIT, MY ALE!
WHAT THE...?
IT JUST DRAINED AWAY.
HYAARG
GH
MATILDE!

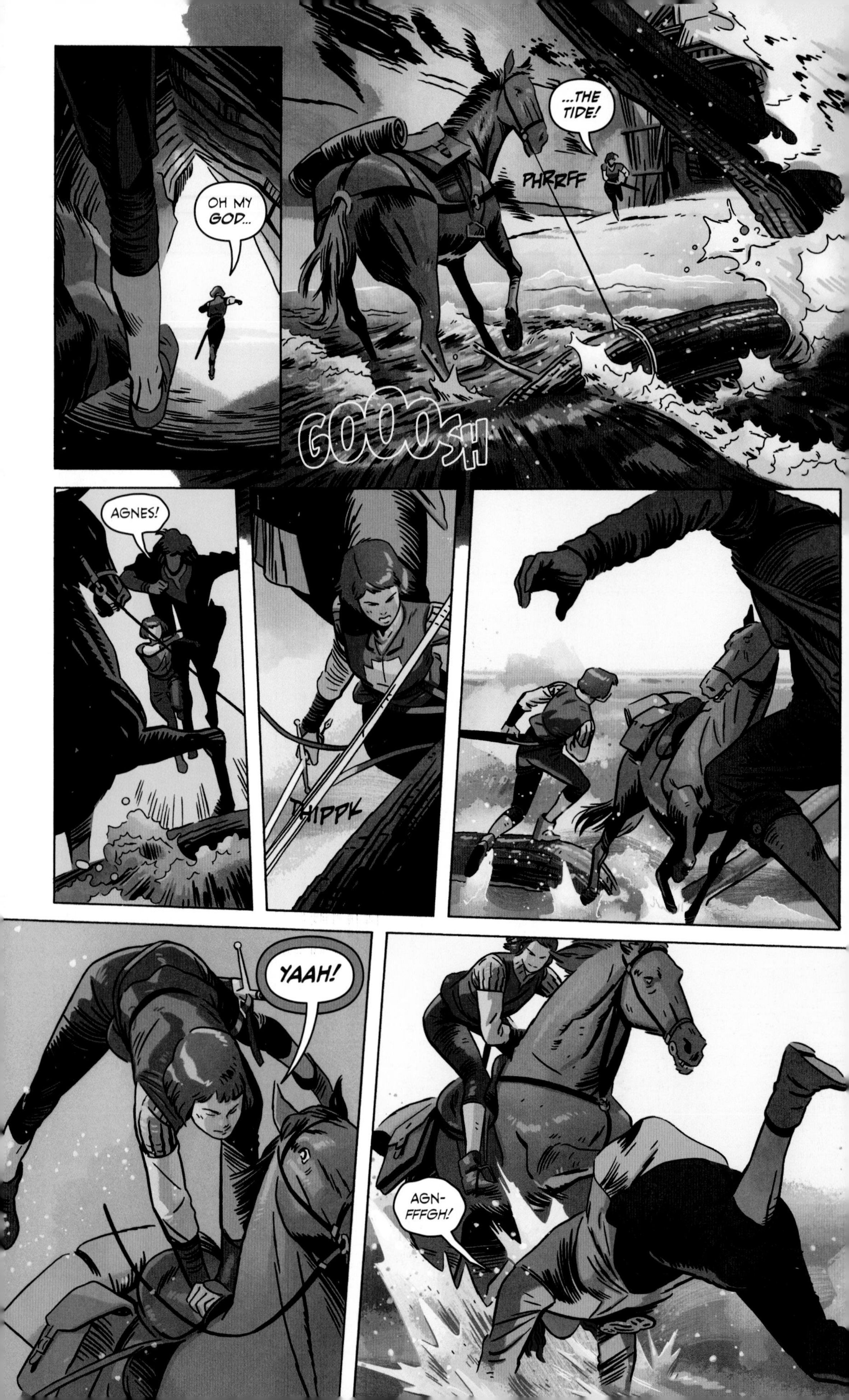
OH MY GOD...
...THE TIDE!
PHRRFF
GOOOSH
AGNES!
THIPPK
YAAH!
AGN-FFFGH!

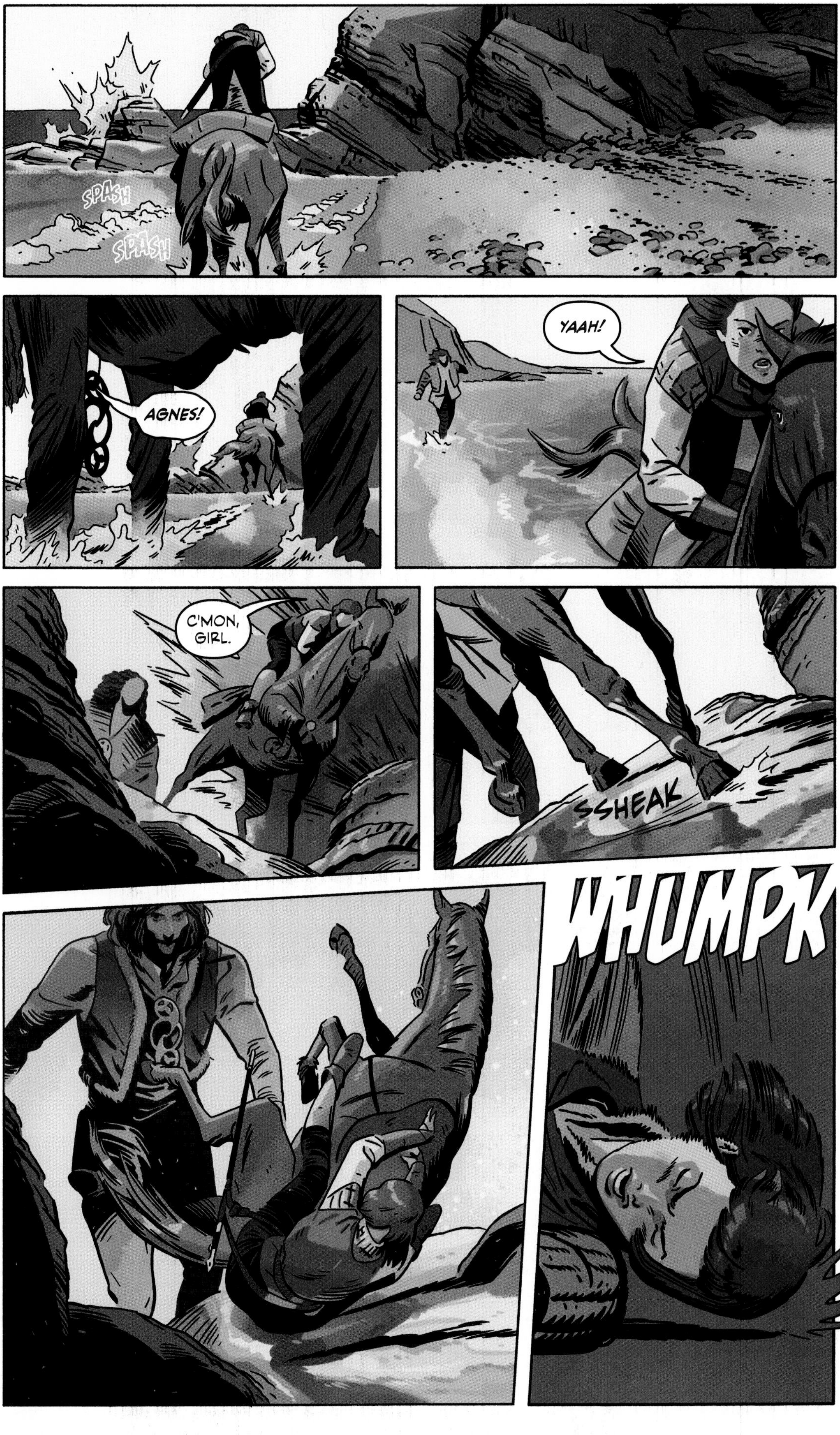
SPASH
SPASH
AGNES!
YAAH!
C'MON, GIRL.
SSHEAK
WHUMPK

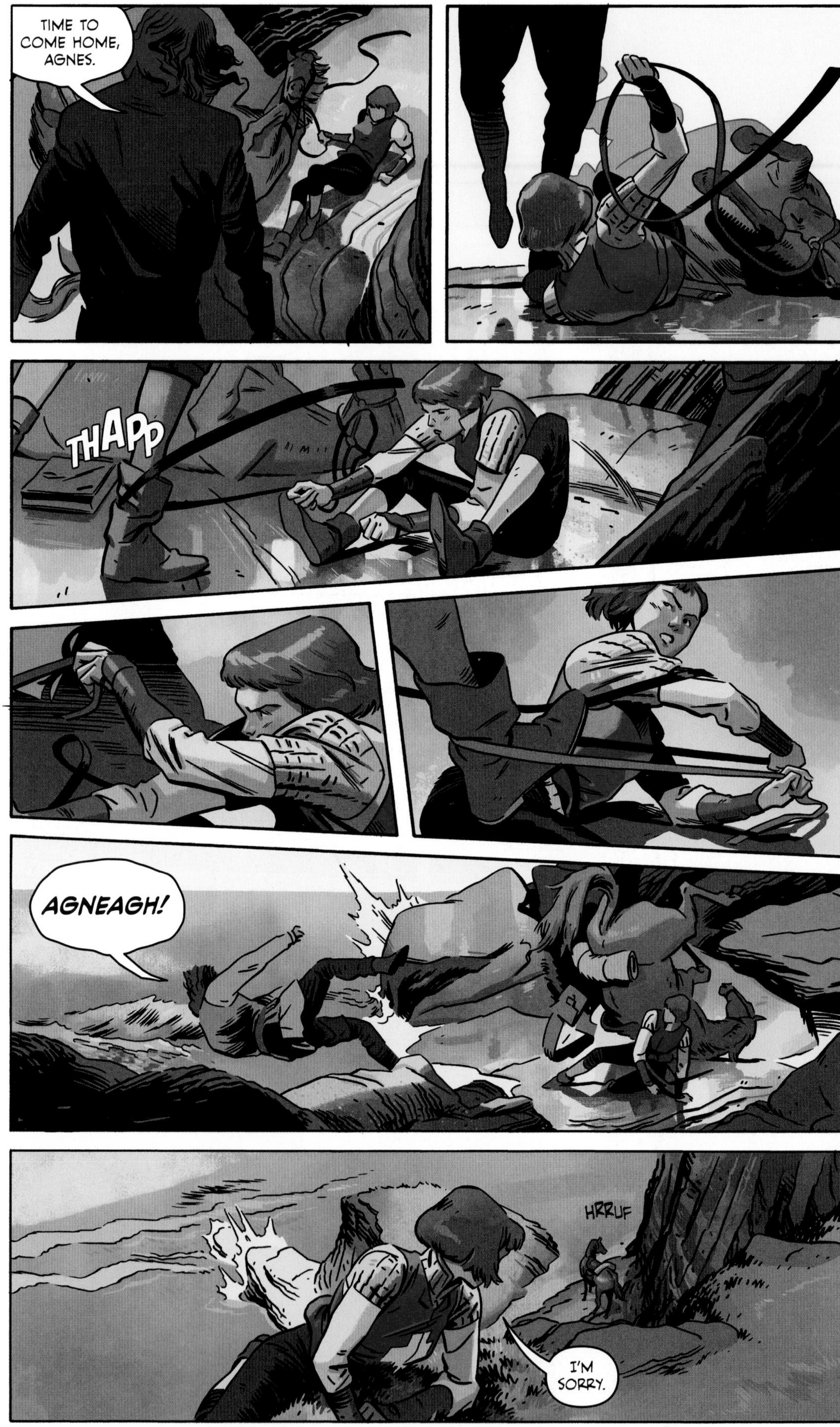
TIME TO COME HOME, AGNES.
THAPP
AGNEAGH!
HRRUF
I'M SORRY.

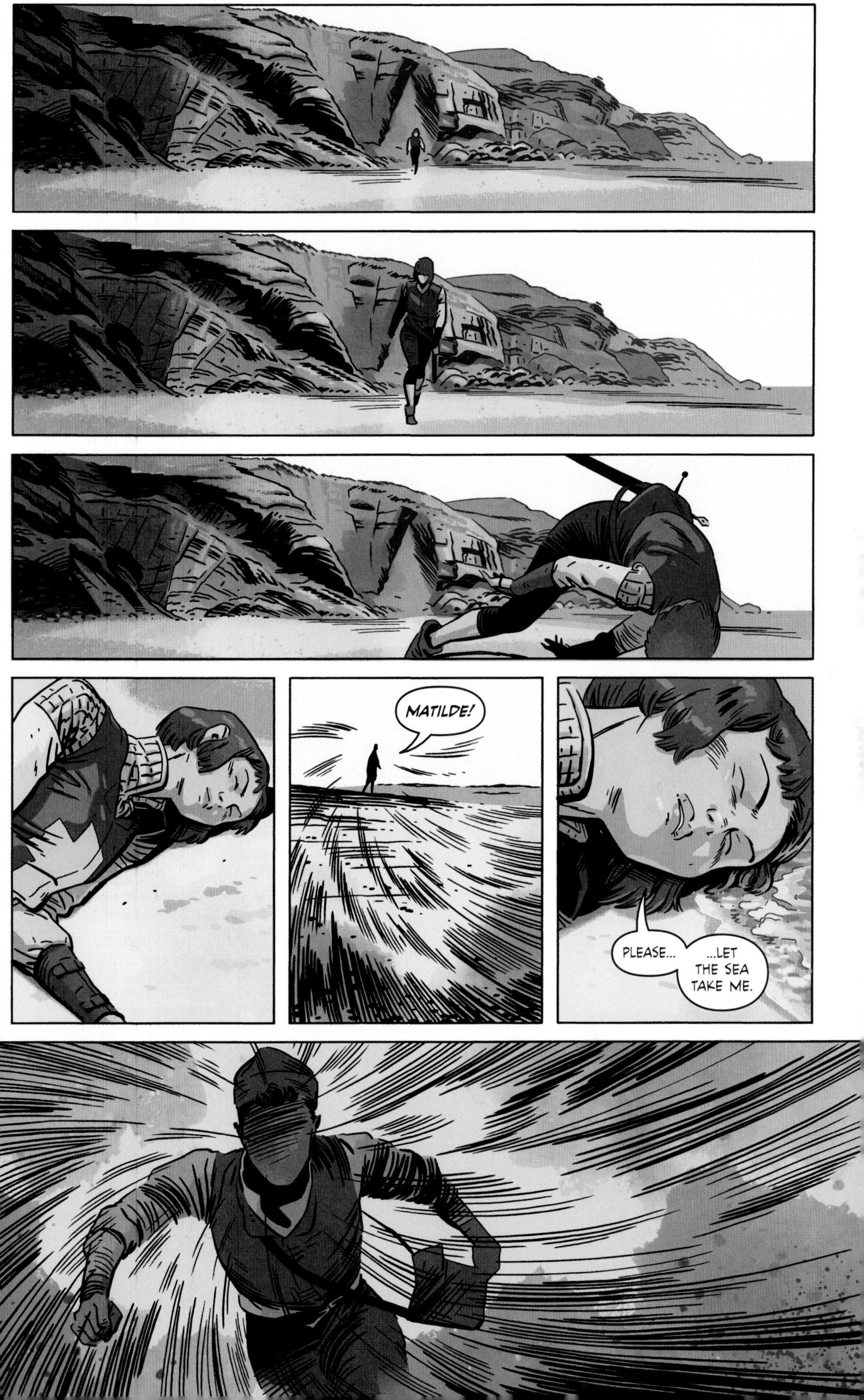
MATILDE!
PLEASE...
...LET THE SEA TAKE ME.

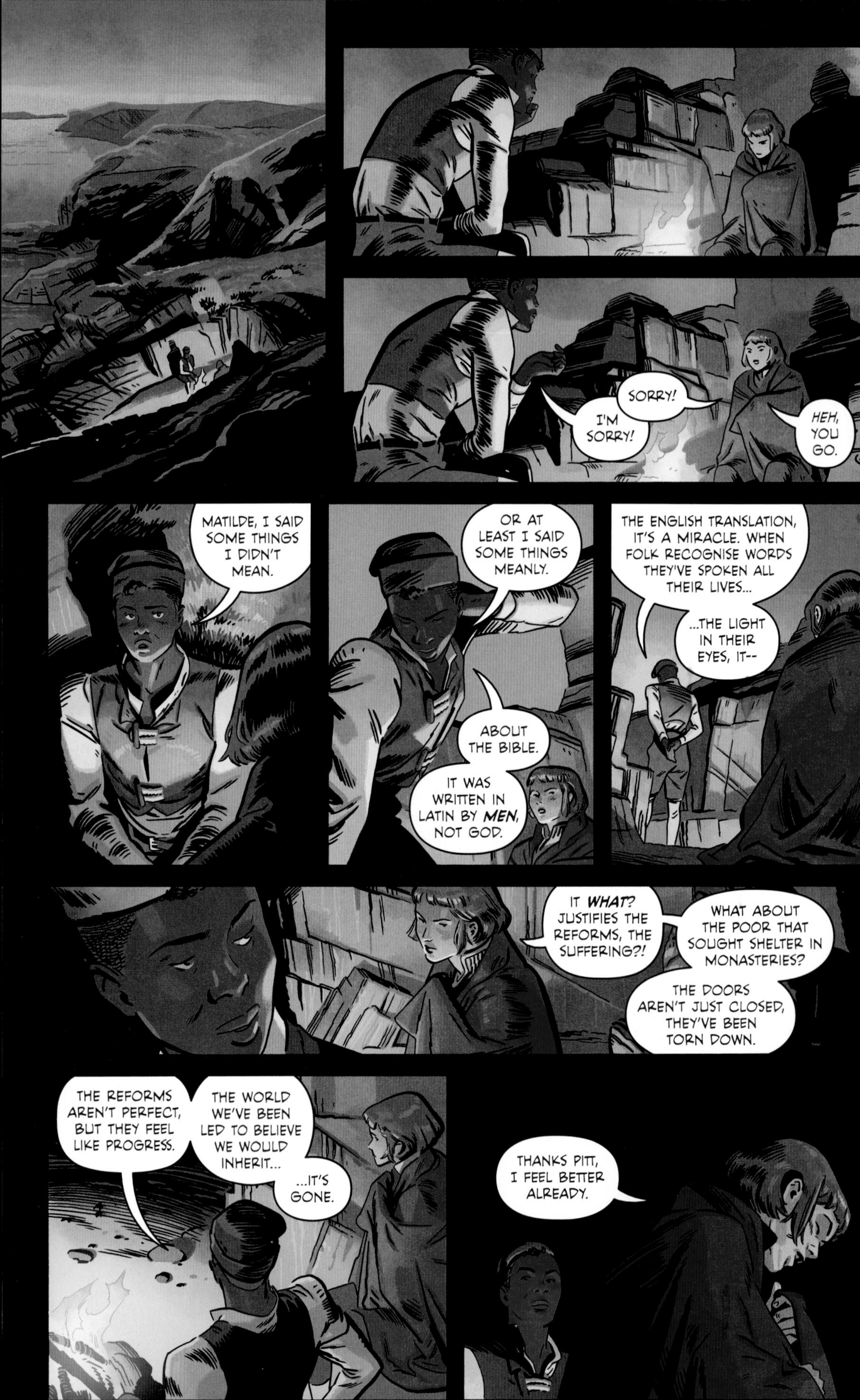
SORRY!
I'M SORRY!
HEH, YOU GO.
MATILDE, I SAID SOME THINGS I DIDN'T MEAN.
OR AT LEAST I SAID SOME THINGS MEANLY.
ABOUT THE BIBLE.
IT WAS WRITTEN IN LATIN BY MEN, NOT GOD.
THE ENGLISH TRANSLATION, IT'S A MIRACLE. WHEN FOLK RECOGNISE WORDS THEY'VE SPOKEN ALL THEIR LIVES...
...THE LIGHT IN THEIR EYES, IT--
IT WHAT? JUSTIFIES THE REFORMS, THE SUFFERING?!
WHAT ABOUT THE POOR THAT SOUGHT SHELTER IN MONASTERIES?
THE DOORS AREN'T JUST CLOSED, THEY'VE BEEN TORN DOWN.
THE REFORMS AREN'T PERFECT, BUT THEY FEEL LIKE PROGRESS.
THE WORLD WE'VE BEEN LED TO BELIEVE WE WOULD INHERIT...
...IT'S GONE.
THANKS PITT, I FEEL BETTER ALREADY.

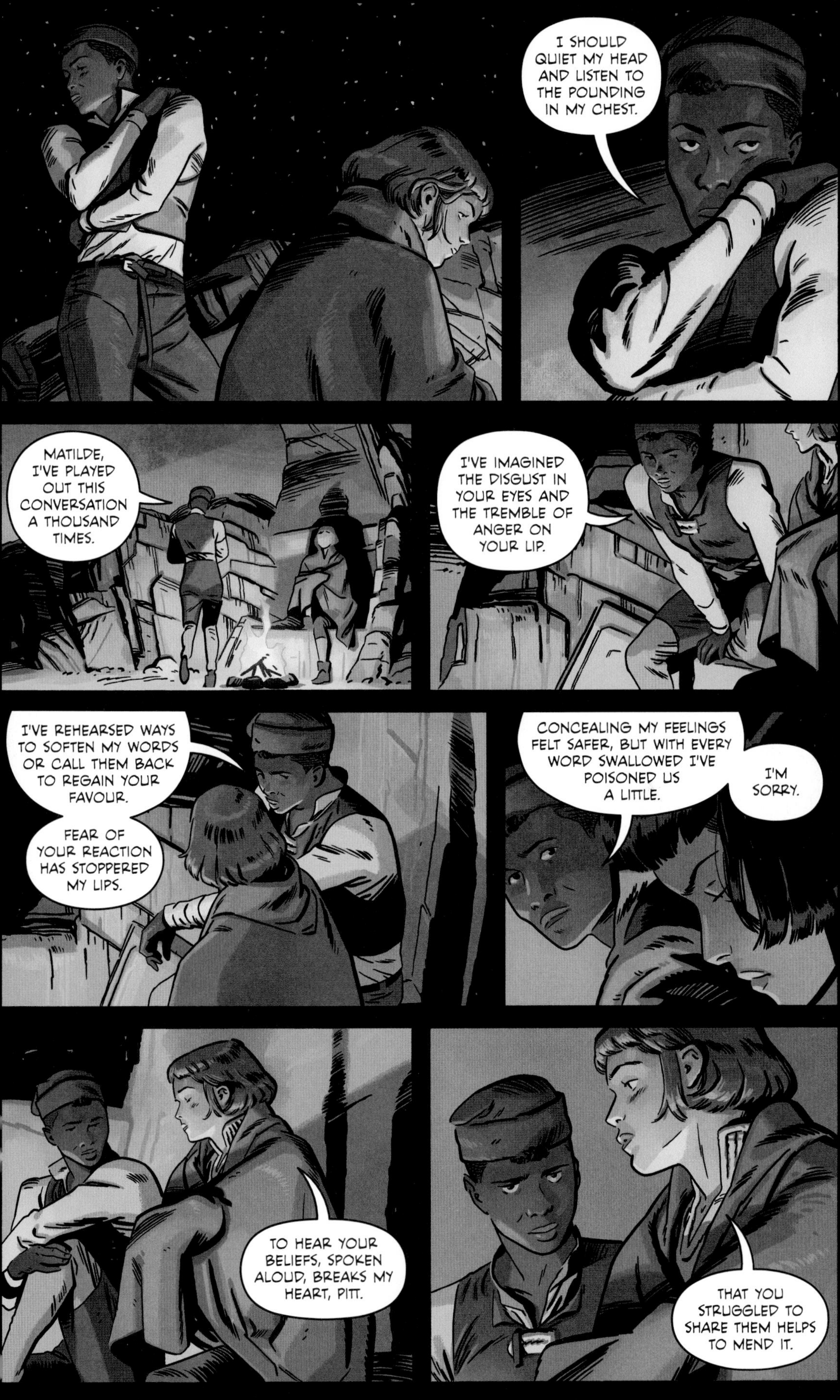
I SHOULD QUIET MY HEAD AND LISTEN TO THE POUNDING IN MY CHEST.
MATILDE, I'VE PLAYED OUT THIS CONVERSATION A THOUSAND TIMES.
I'VE IMAGINED THE DISGUST IN YOUR EYES AND THE TREMBLE OF ANGER ON YOUR LIP.
I'VE REHEARSED WAYS TO SOFTEN MY WORDS OR CALL THEM BACK TO REGAIN YOUR FAVOUR.
FEAR OF YOUR REACTION HAS STOPPERED MY LIPS.
CONCEALING MY FEELINGS FELT SAFER, BUT WITH EVERY WORD SWALLOWED I'VE POISONED US A LITTLE.
I'M SORRY.
TO HEAR YOUR BELIEFS, SPOKEN ALOUD, BREAKS MY HEART, PITT.
THAT YOU STRUGGLED TO SHARE THEM HELPS TO MEND IT.

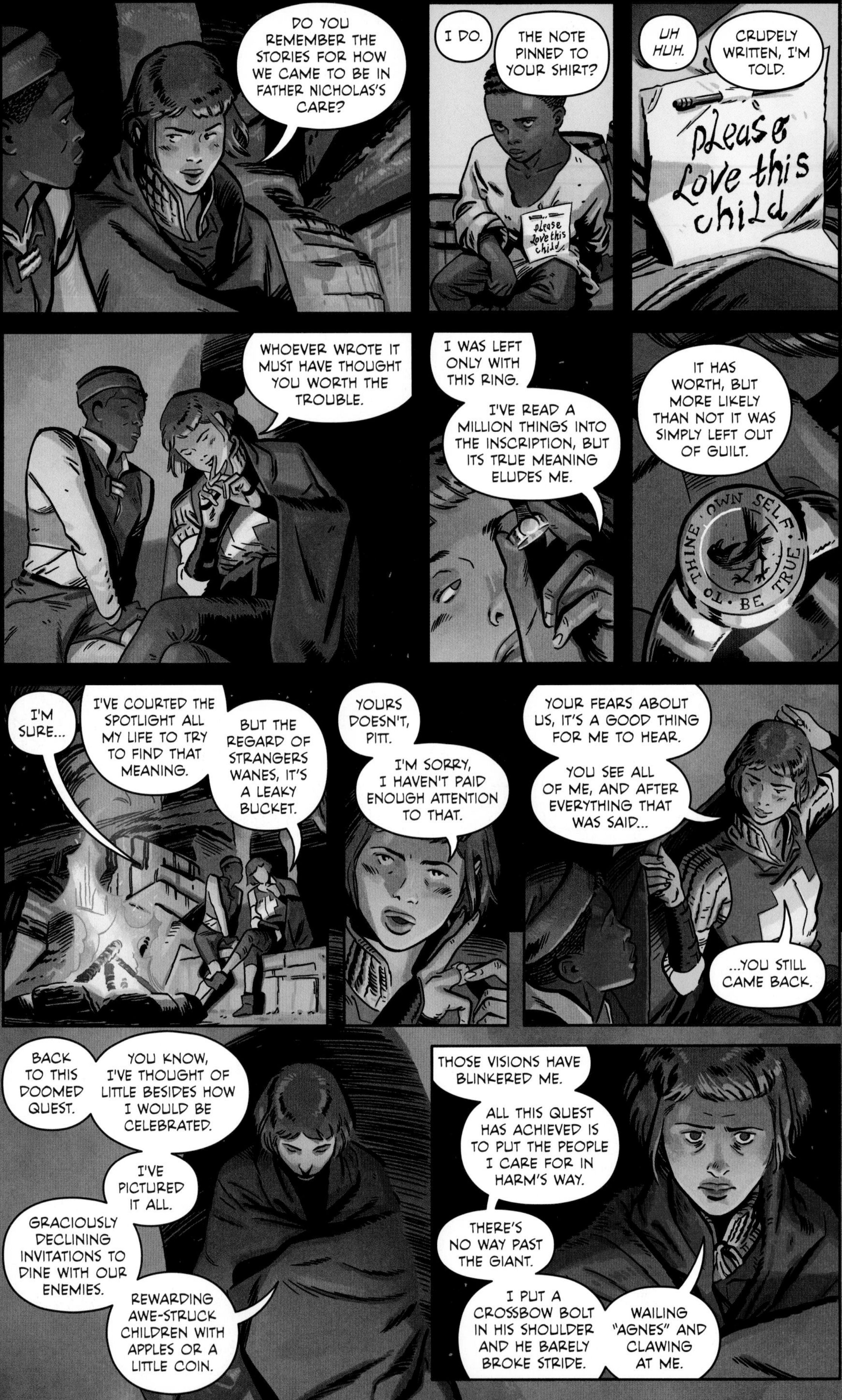
DO YOU REMEMBER THE STORIES FOR HOW WE CAME TO BE IN FATHER NICHOLAS'S CARE?
I DO.
THE NOTE PINNED TO YOUR SHIRT?
please Love this child
UH HUH.
CRUDELY WRITTEN, I'M TOLD.
please Love this child
WHOEVER WROTE IT MUST HAVE THOUGHT YOU WORTH THE TROUBLE.
I WAS LEFT ONLY WITH THIS RING.
I'VE READ A MILLION THINGS INTO THE INSCRIPTION, BUT ITS TRUE MEANING ELUDES ME.
IT HAS WORTH, BUT MORE LIKELY THAN NOT IT WAS SIMPLY LEFT OUT OF GUILT.
TO THINE OWN SELF BE TRUE
I'M SURE...
I'VE COURTED THE SPOTLIGHT ALL MY LIFE TO TRY TO FIND THAT MEANING.
BUT THE REGARD OF STRANGERS WANES, IT'S A LEAKY BUCKET.
YOURS DOESN'T, PITT.
I'M SORRY, I HAVEN'T PAID ENOUGH ATTENTION TO THAT.
YOUR FEARS ABOUT US, IT'S A GOOD THING FOR ME TO HEAR.
YOU SEE ALL OF ME, AND AFTER EVERYTHING THAT WAS SAID...
...YOU STILL CAME BACK.
BACK TO THIS DOOMED QUEST.
YOU KNOW, I'VE THOUGHT OF LITTLE BESIDES HOW I WOULD BE CELEBRATED.
I'VE PICTURED IT ALL.
GRACIOUSLY DECLINING INVITATIONS TO DINE WITH OUR ENEMIES.
REWARDING AWE-STRUCK CHILDREN WITH APPLES OR A LITTLE COIN.
THOSE VISIONS HAVE BLINKERED ME.
ALL THIS QUEST HAS ACHIEVED IS TO PUT THE PEOPLE I CARE FOR IN HARM'S WAY.
THERE'S NO WAY PAST THE GIANT.
I PUT A CROSSBOW BOLT IN HIS SHOULDER AND HE BARELY BROKE STRIDE.
WAILING "AGNES" AND CLAWING AT ME.

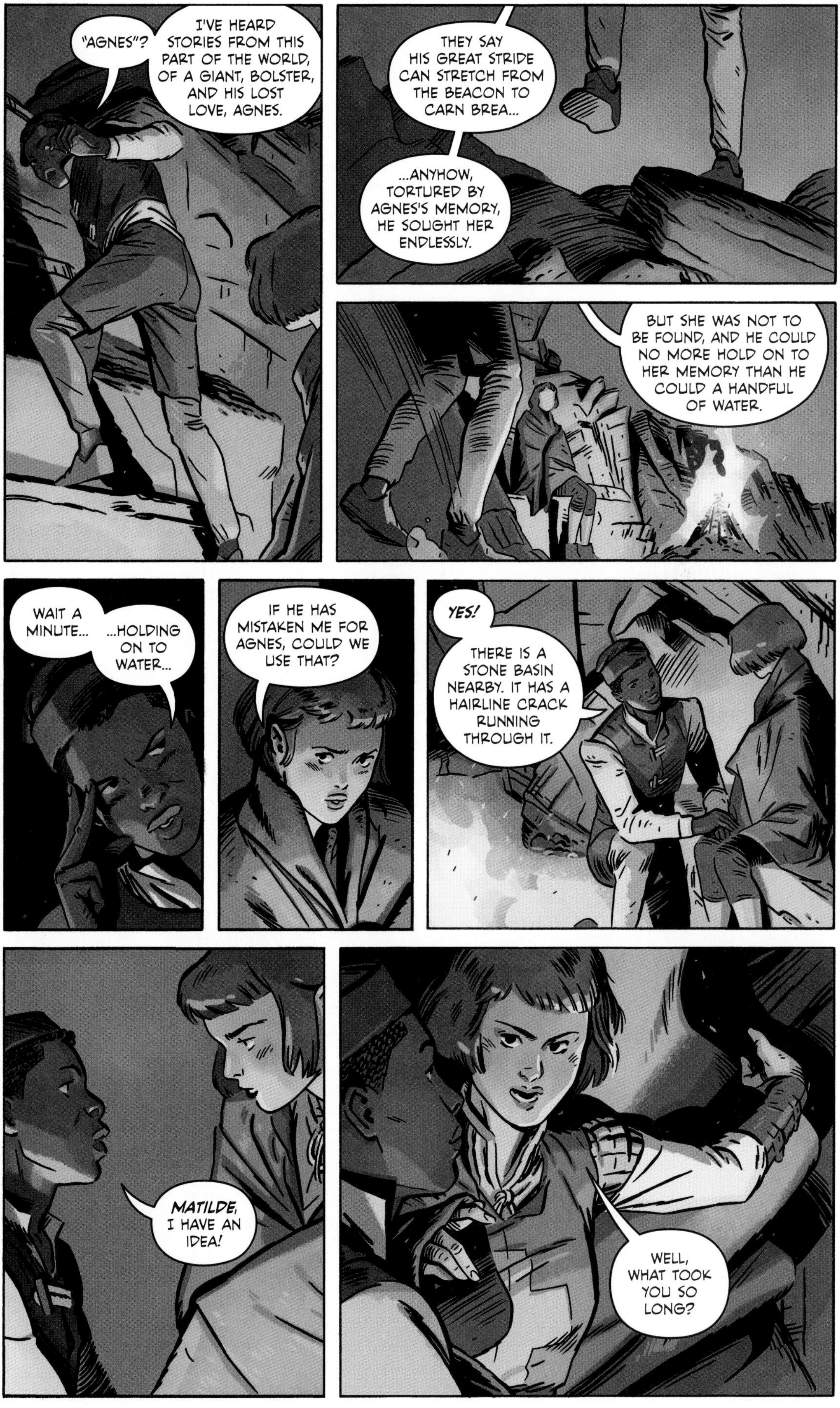
"AGNES"?
I'VE HEARD STORIES FROM THIS PART OF THE WORLD, OF A GIANT, BOLSTER, AND HIS LOST LOVE, AGNES.
THEY SAY HIS GREAT STRIDE CAN STRETCH FROM THE BEACON TO CARN BREA...
...ANYHOW, TORTURED BY AGNES'S MEMORY, HE SOUGHT HER ENDLESSLY.
BUT SHE WAS NOT TO BE FOUND, AND HE COULD NO MORE HOLD ON TO HER MEMORY THAN HE COULD A HANDFUL OF WATER.
WAIT A MINUTE...
...HOLDING ON TO WATER...
IF HE HAS MISTAKEN ME FOR AGNES, COULD WE USE THAT?
YES!
THERE IS A STONE BASIN NEARBY. IT HAS A HAIRLINE CRACK RUNNING THROUGH IT.
MATILDE, I HAVE AN IDEA!
WELL, WHAT TOOK YOU SO LONG?

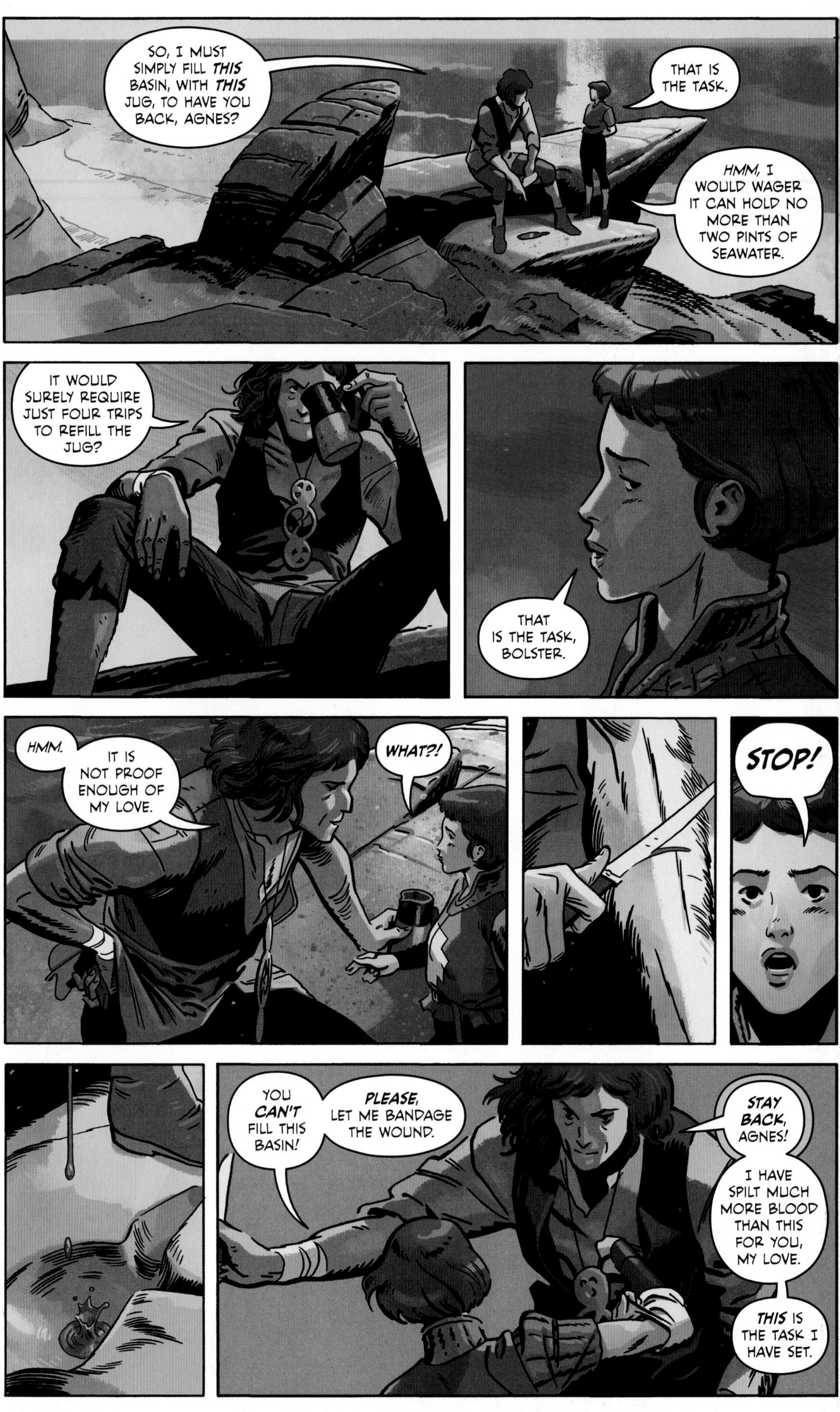
SO, I MUST SIMPLY FILL THIS BASIN, WITH THIS JUG, TO HAVE YOU BACK, AGNES?
THAT IS THE TASK.
HMM, I WOULD WAGER IT CAN HOLD NO MORE THAN TWO PINTS OF SEAWATER.
IT WOULD SURELY REQUIRE JUST FOUR TRIPS TO REFILL THE JUG?
THAT IS THE TASK, BOLSTER.
HMM.
IT IS NOT PROOF ENOUGH OF MY LOVE.
WHAT?!
STOP!
YOU CAN'T FILL THIS BASIN!
PLEASE, LET ME BANDAGE THE WOUND.
STAY BACK, AGNES!
I HAVE SPILT MUCH MORE BLOOD THAN THIS FOR YOU, MY LOVE.
THIS IS THE TASK I HAVE SET.

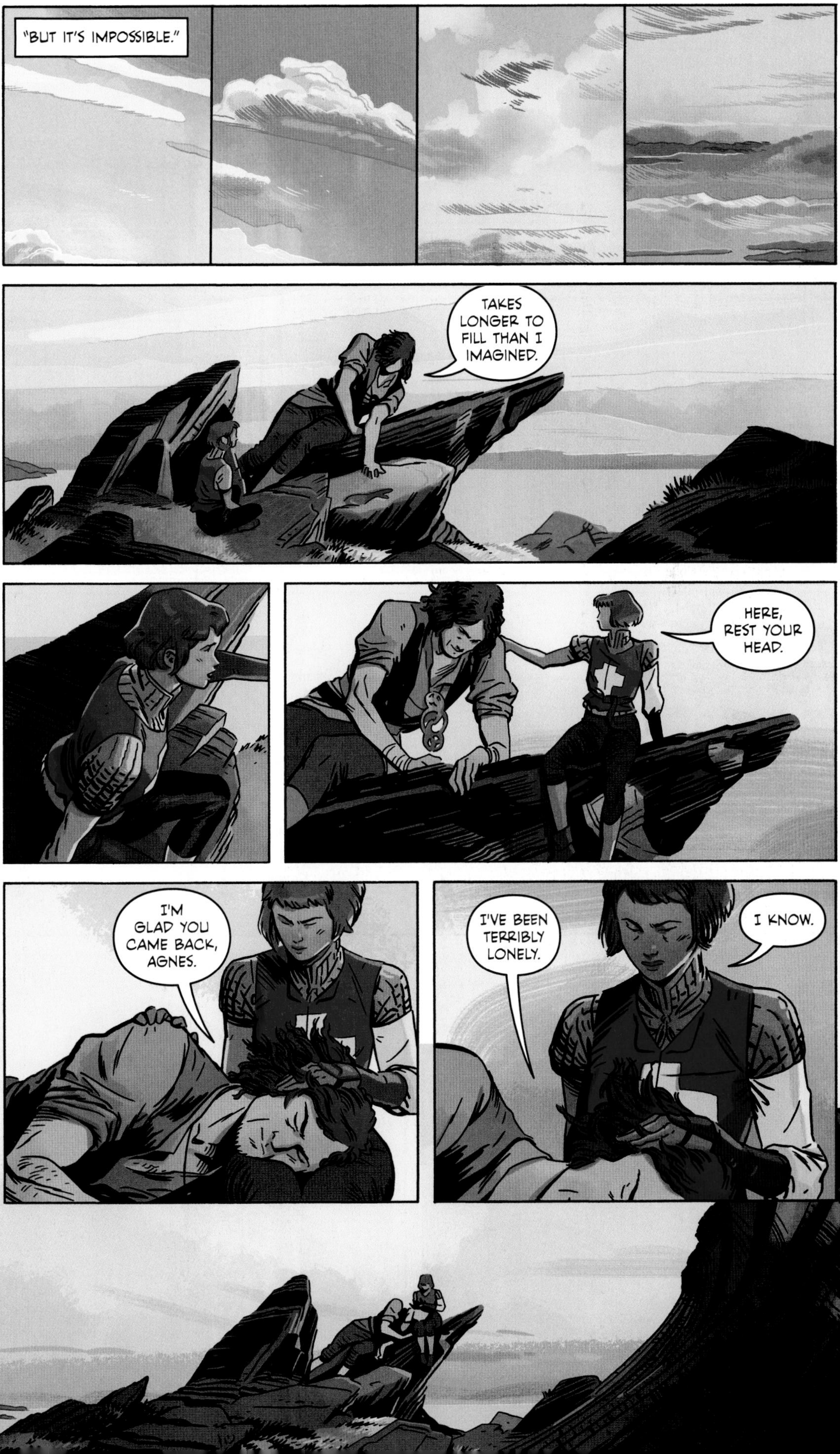
"BUT IT'S IMPOSSIBLE."
TAKES LONGER TO FILL THAN I IMAGINED.
HERE, REST YOUR HEAD.
I'M GLAD YOU CAME BACK, AGNES.
I'VE BEEN TERRIBLY LONELY.
I KNOW.

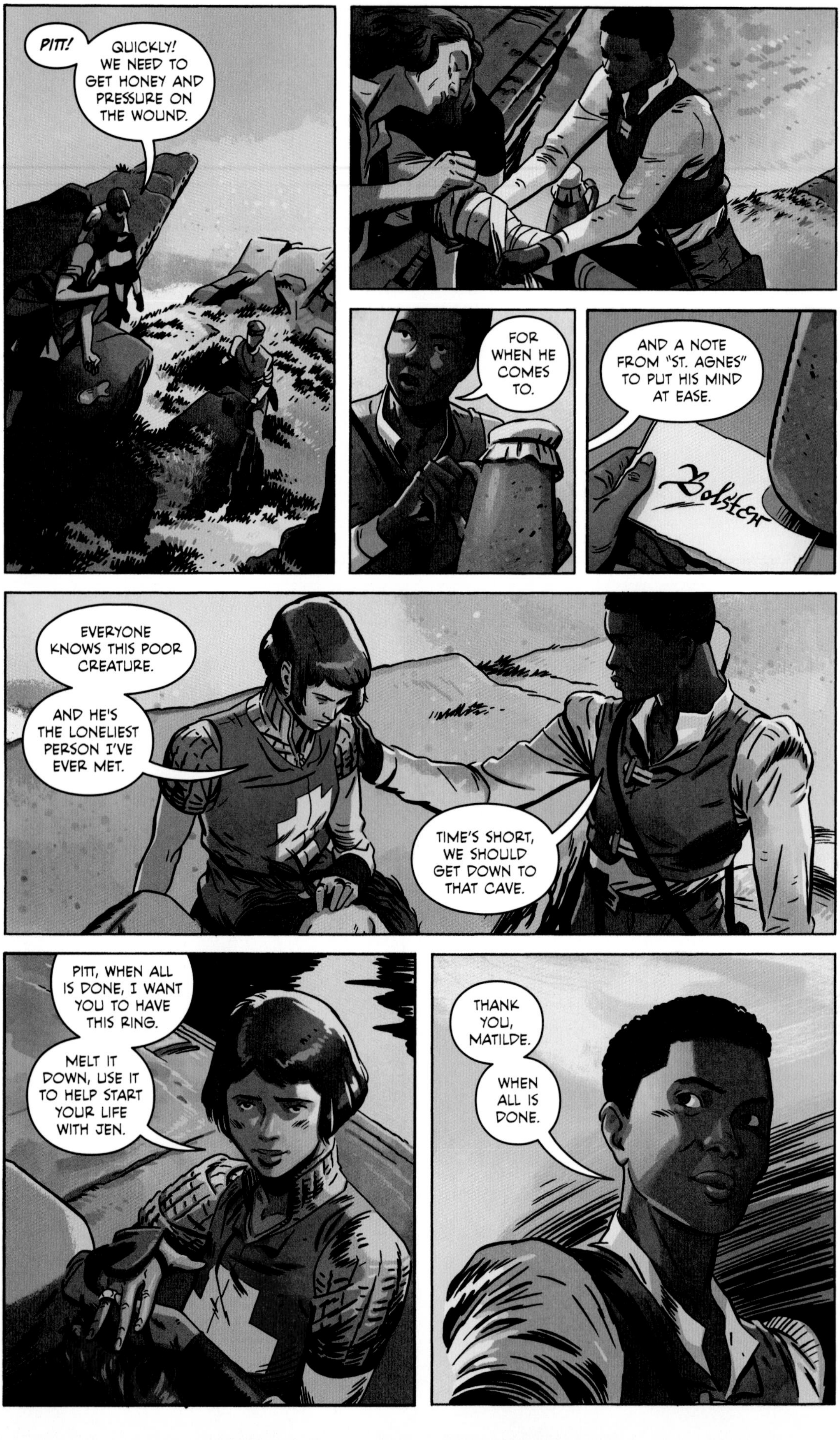
PITT!
QUICKLY! WE NEED TO GET HONEY AND PRESSURE ON THE WOUND.
FOR WHEN HE COMES TO.
AND A NOTE FROM "ST. AGNES" TO PUT HIS MIND AT EASE.
Bolster
EVERYONE KNOWS THIS POOR CREATURE.
AND HE'S THE LONELIEST PERSON I'VE EVER MET.
TIME'S SHORT, WE SHOULD GET DOWN TO THAT CAVE.
PITT, WHEN ALL IS DONE, I WANT YOU TO HAVE THIS RING.
MELT IT DOWN, USE IT TO HELP START YOUR LIFE WITH JEN.
THANK YOU, MATILDE.
WHEN ALL IS DONE.

Chapter 5

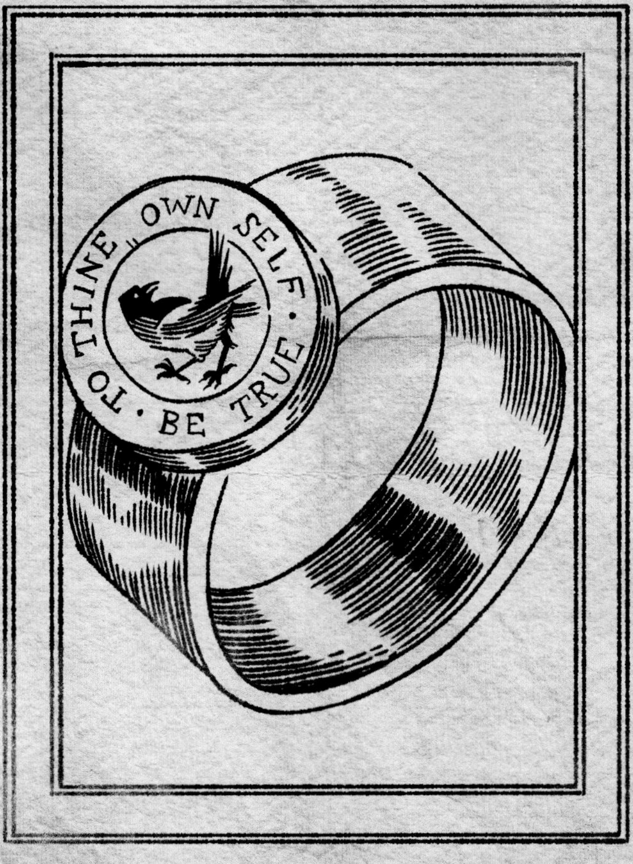
TO THINE OWN SELF · BE TRUE ·

Two days until the devil's deadline

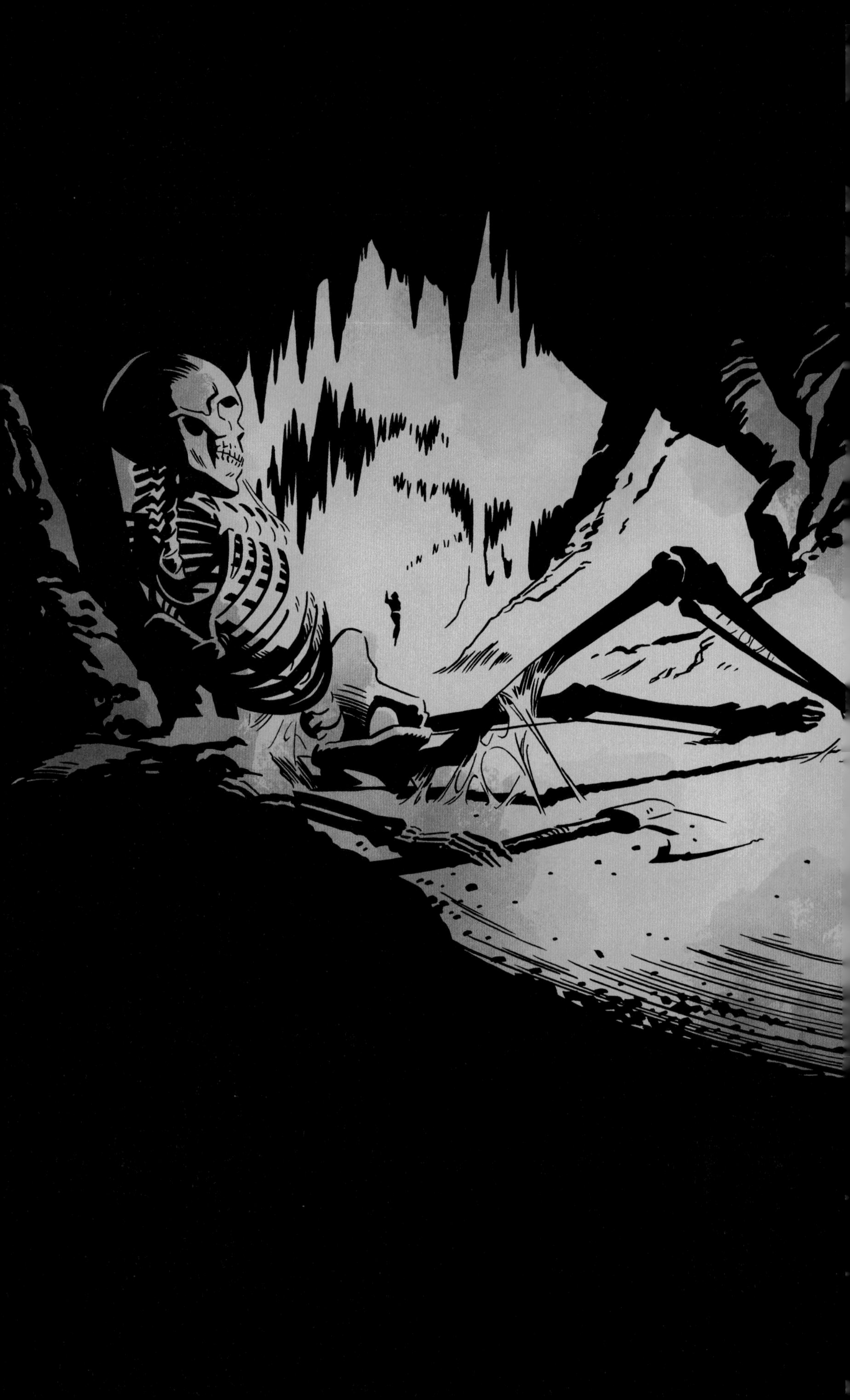

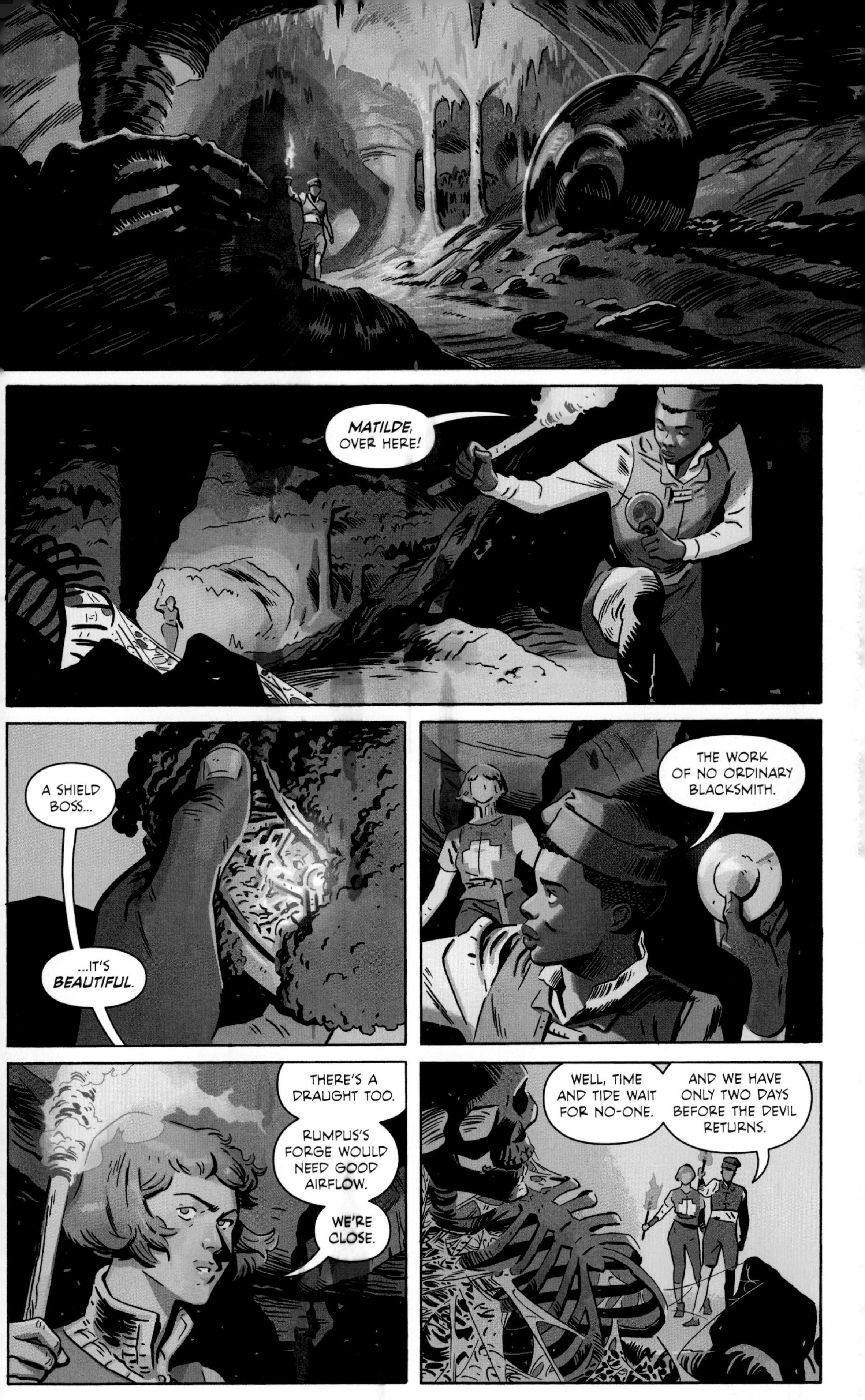
MATILDE, OVER HERE!
A SHIELD BOSS...
...IT'S BEAUTIFUL.
THE WORK OF NO ORDINARY BLACKSMITH.
THERE'S A DRAUGHT TOO.
RUMPUS'S FORGE WOULD NEED GOOD AIRFLOW.
WE'RE CLOSE.
WELL, TIME AND TIDE WAIT FOR NO-ONE.
AND WE HAVE ONLY TWO DAYS BEFORE THE DEVIL RETURNS.

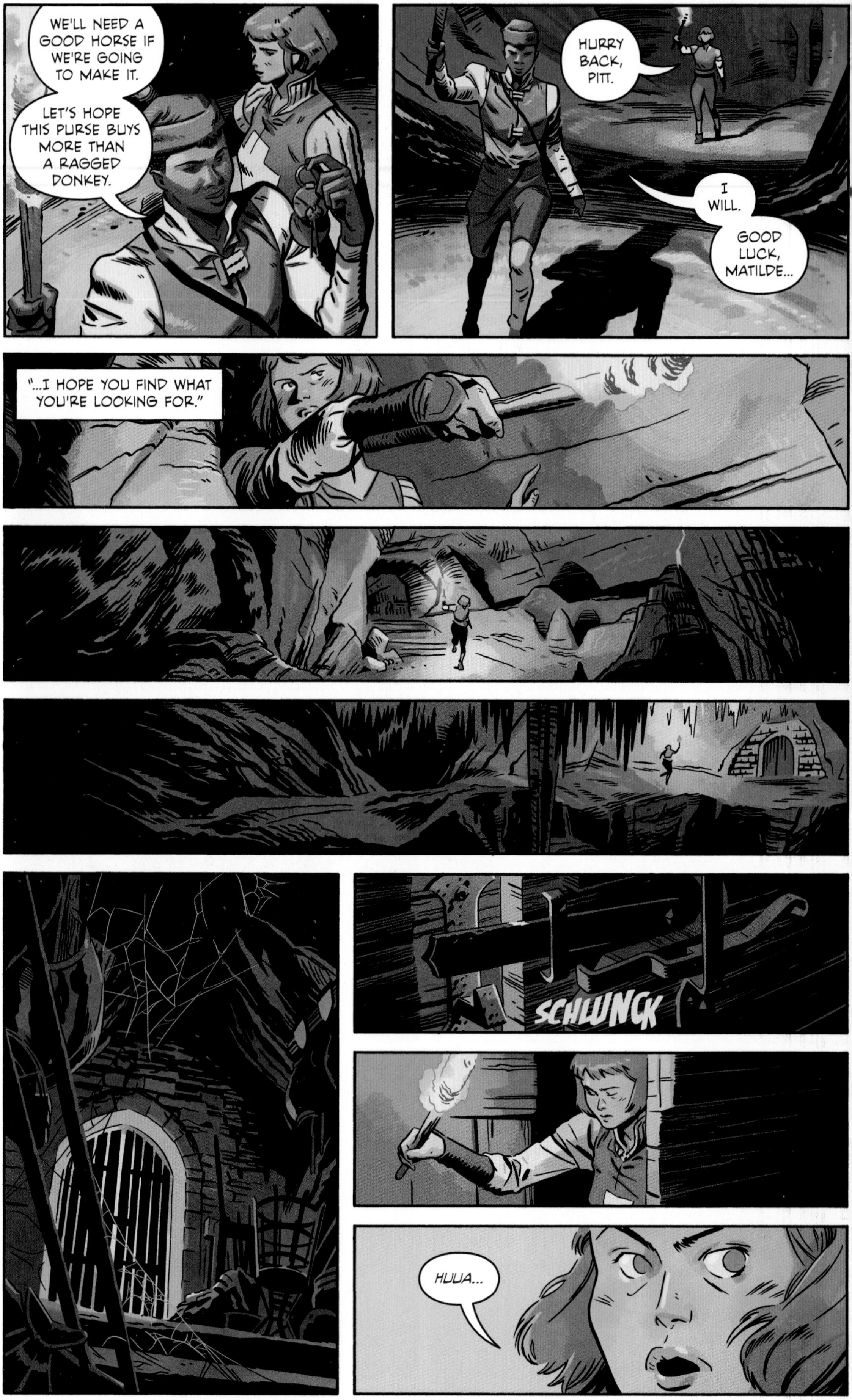
WE'LL NEED A GOOD HORSE IF WE'RE GOING TO MAKE IT.
LET'S HOPE THIS PURSE BUYS MORE THAN A RAGGED DONKEY.
HURRY BACK, PITT.
I WILL.
GOOD LUCK, MATILDE...
"...I HOPE YOU FIND WHAT YOU'RE LOOKING FOR."
SCHLUNCK
HUUA...

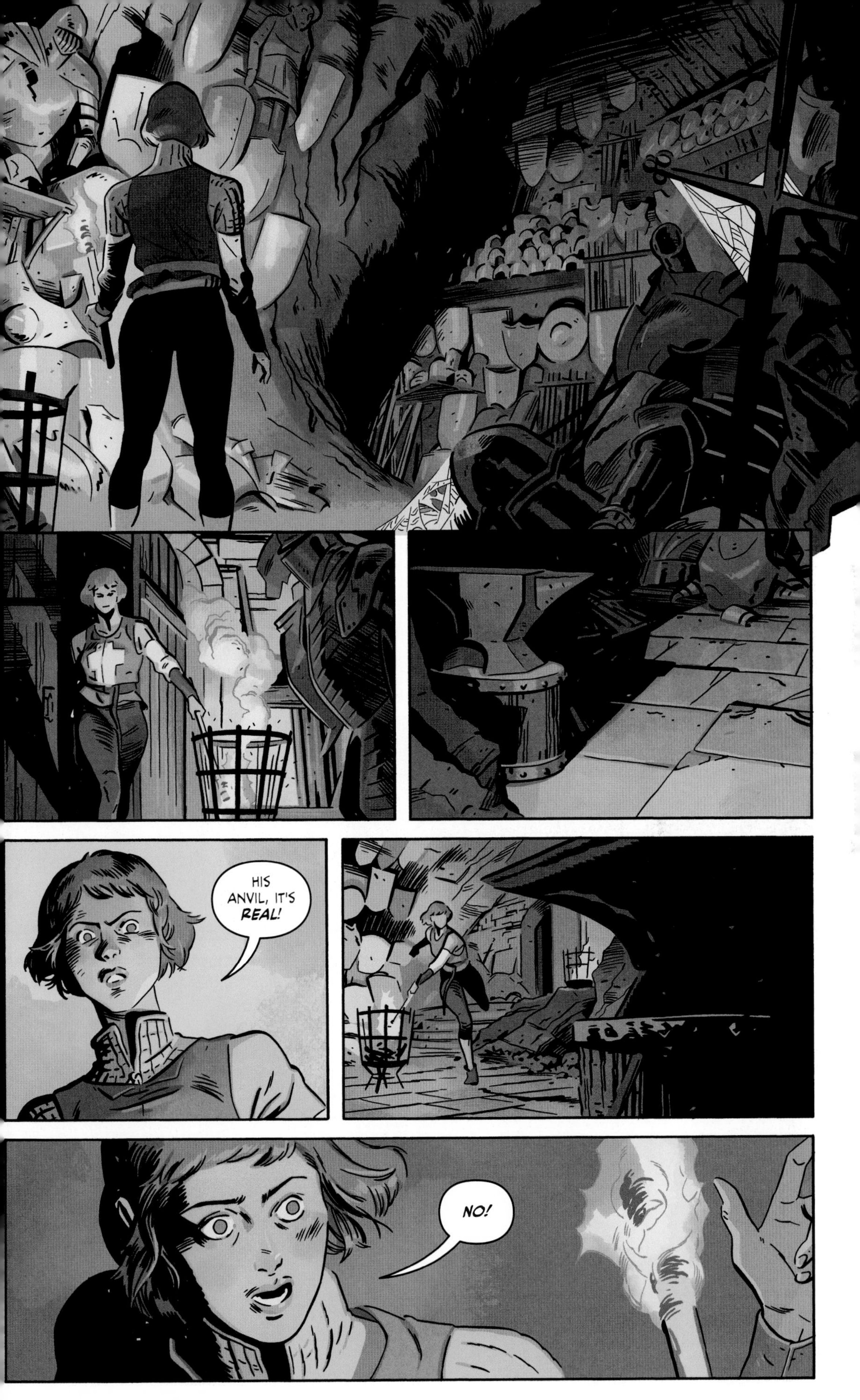
HIS ANVIL, IT'S REAL!
NO!

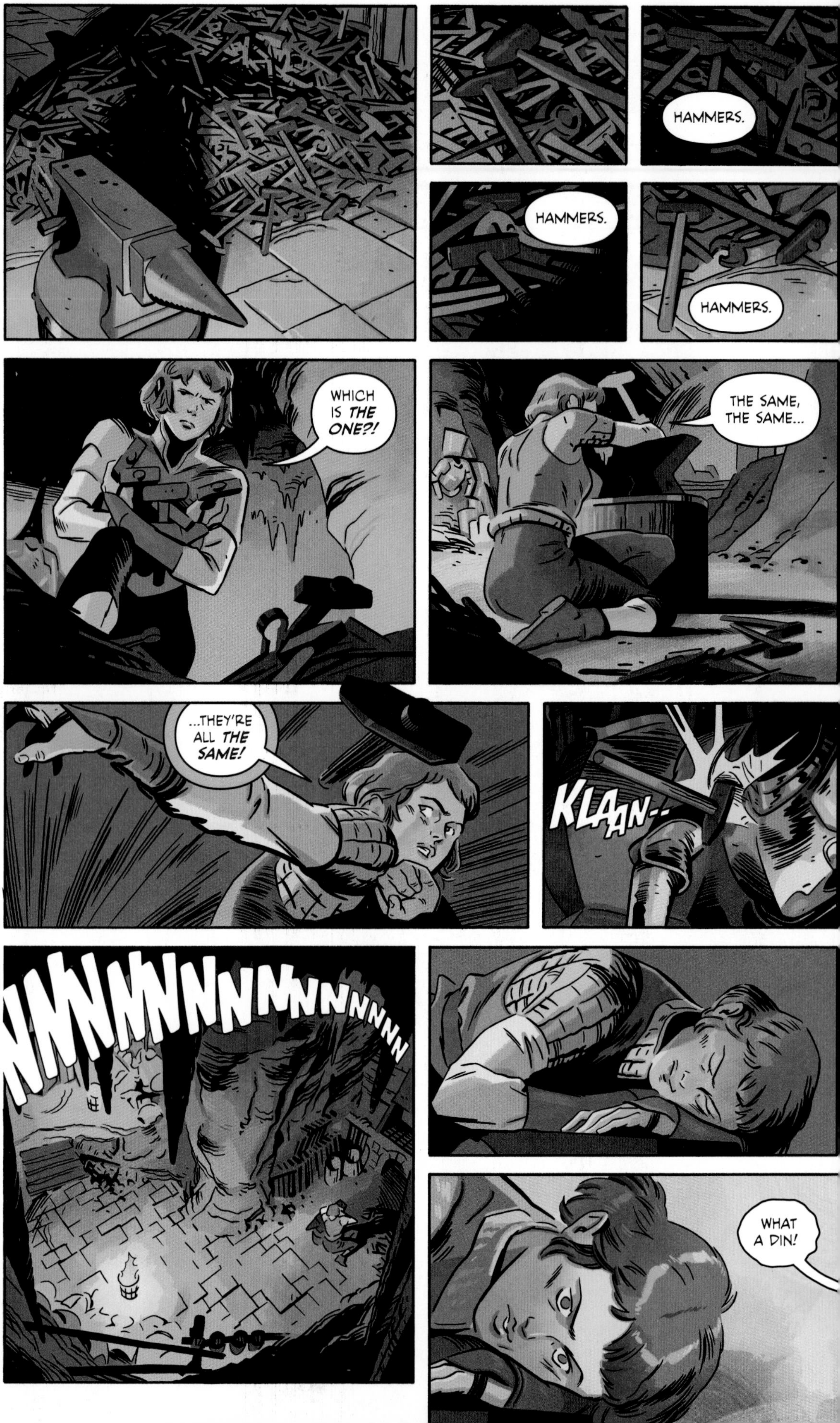
HAMMERS.
HAMMERS.
HAMMERS.
WHICH IS THE ONE?!
THE SAME, THE SAME...
...THEY'RE ALL THE SAME!
KLAAN--
NNNNNNNNNNNNNNNN
WHAT A DIN!

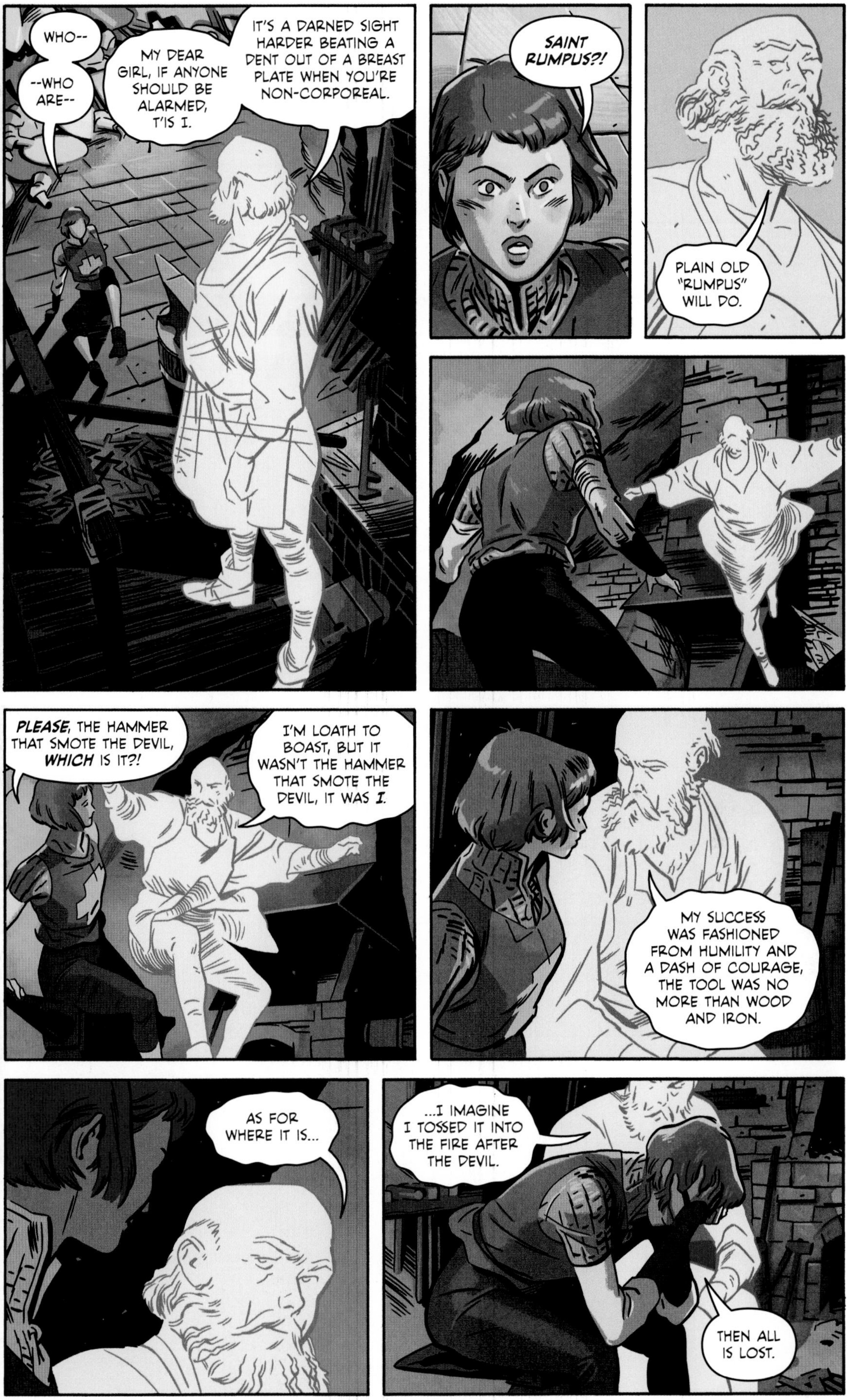
WHO--
--WHO ARE--
MY DEAR GIRL, IF ANYONE SHOULD BE ALARMED, T'IS I.
IT'S A DARNED SIGHT HARDER BEATING A DENT OUT OF A BREAST PLATE WHEN YOU'RE NON-CORPOREAL.
SAINT RUMPUS?!
PLAIN OLD "RUMPUS" WILL DO.
PLEASE, THE HAMMER THAT SMOTE THE DEVIL, WHICH IS IT?!
I'M LOATH TO BOAST, BUT IT WASN'T THE HAMMER THAT SMOTE THE DEVIL, IT WAS I.
MY SUCCESS WAS FASHIONED FROM HUMILITY AND A DASH OF COURAGE, THE TOOL WAS NO MORE THAN WOOD AND IRON.
AS FOR WHERE IT IS...
...I IMAGINE I TOSSED IT INTO THE FIRE AFTER THE DEVIL.
THEN ALL IS LOST.

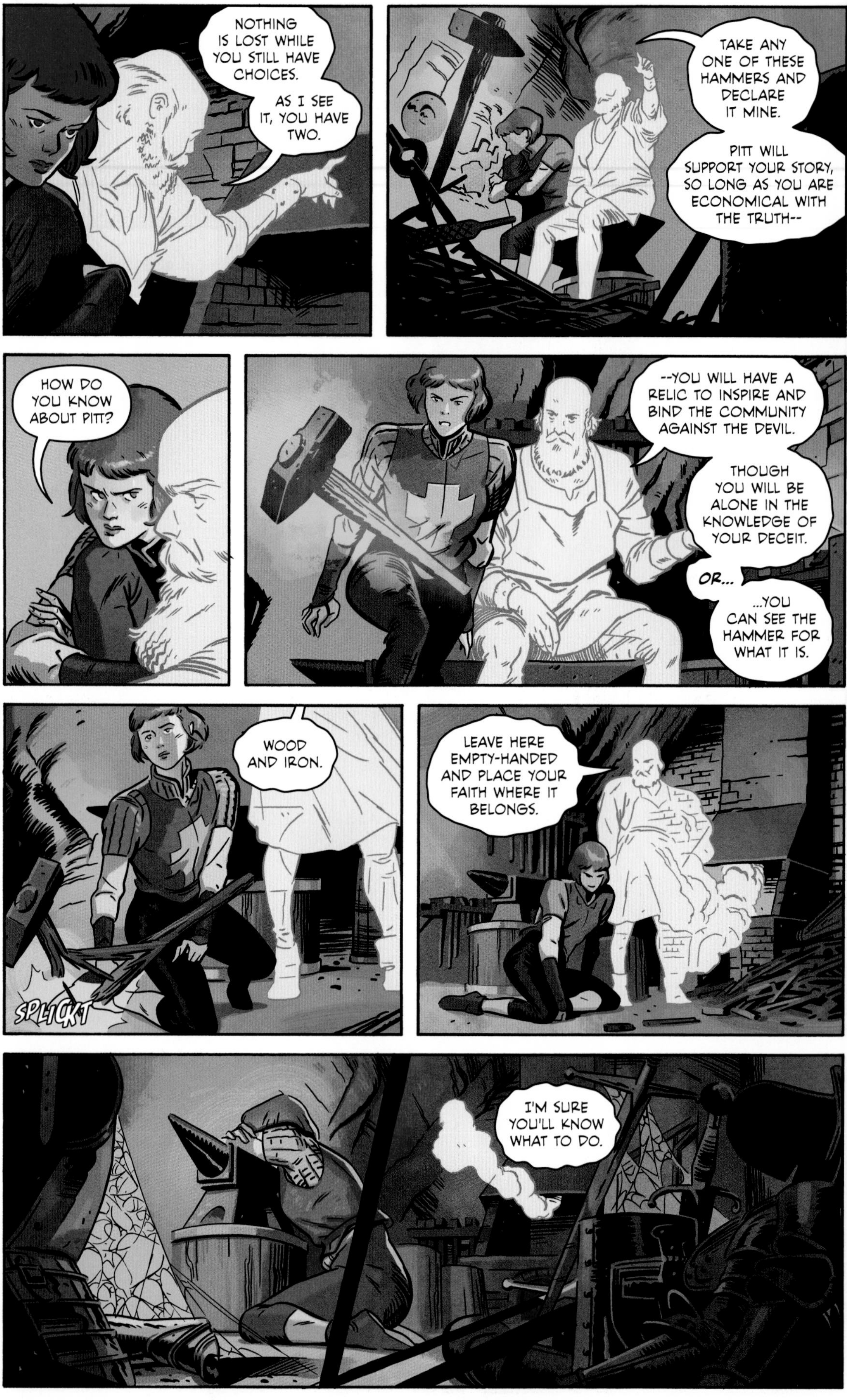
NOTHING IS LOST WHILE YOU STILL HAVE CHOICES.
AS I SEE IT, YOU HAVE TWO.
TAKE ANY ONE OF THESE HAMMERS AND DECLARE IT MINE.
PITT WILL SUPPORT YOUR STORY, SO LONG AS YOU ARE ECONOMICAL WITH THE TRUTH--
HOW DO YOU KNOW ABOUT PITT?
--YOU WILL HAVE A RELIC TO INSPIRE AND BIND THE COMMUNITY AGAINST THE DEVIL.
THOUGH YOU WILL BE ALONE IN THE KNOWLEDGE OF YOUR DECEIT.
OR...
...YOU CAN SEE THE HAMMER FOR WHAT IT IS.
WOOD AND IRON.
SPLICKT
LEAVE HERE EMPTY-HANDED AND PLACE YOUR FAITH WHERE IT BELONGS.
I'M SURE YOU'LL KNOW WHAT TO DO.

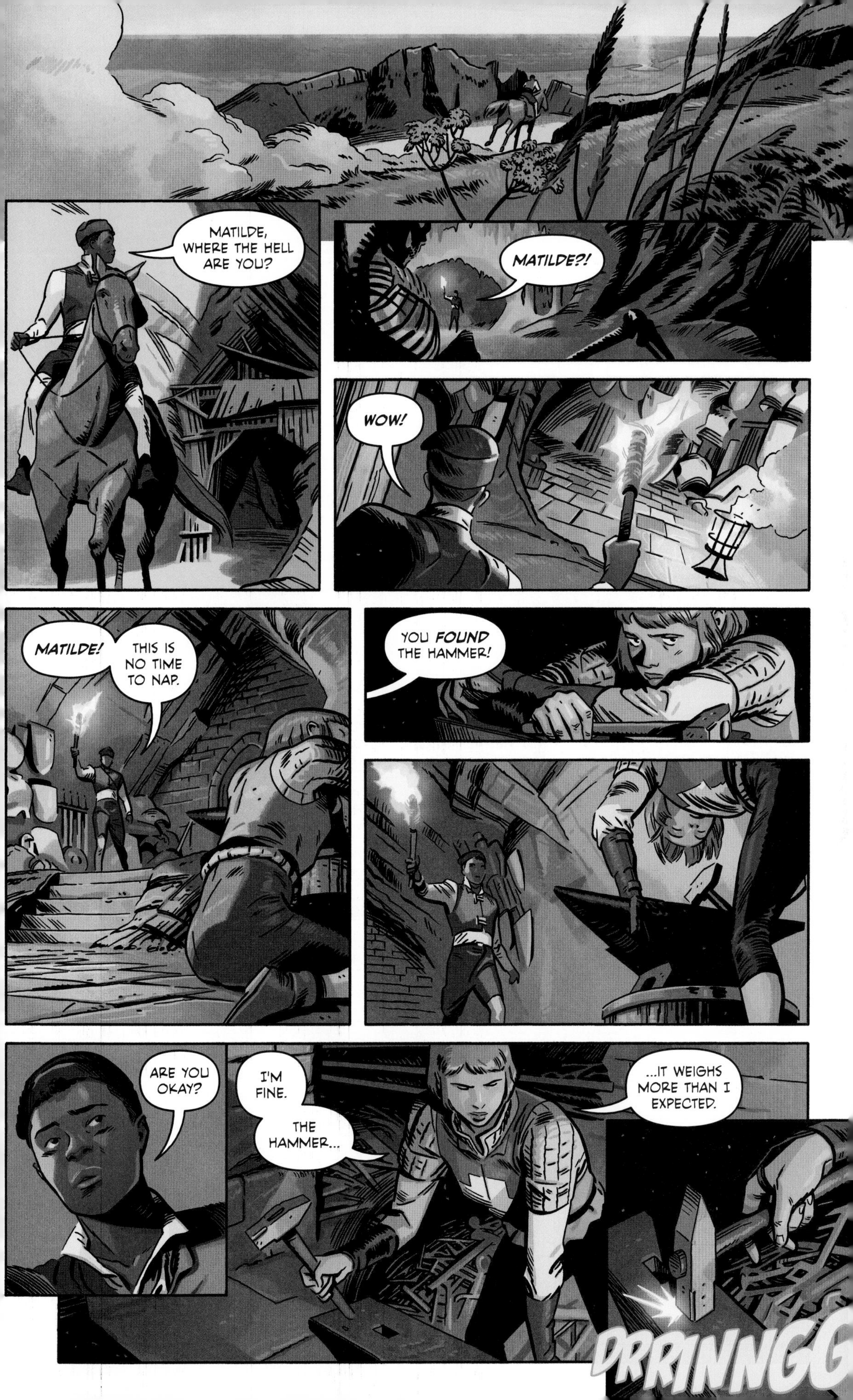
MATILDE, WHERE THE HELL ARE YOU?
MATILDE?!
WOW!
MATILDE!
THIS IS NO TIME TO NAP.
YOU FOUND THE HAMMER!
ARE YOU OKAY?
I'M FINE.
THE HAMMER...
...IT WEIGHS MORE THAN I EXPECTED.
DRRINNGG

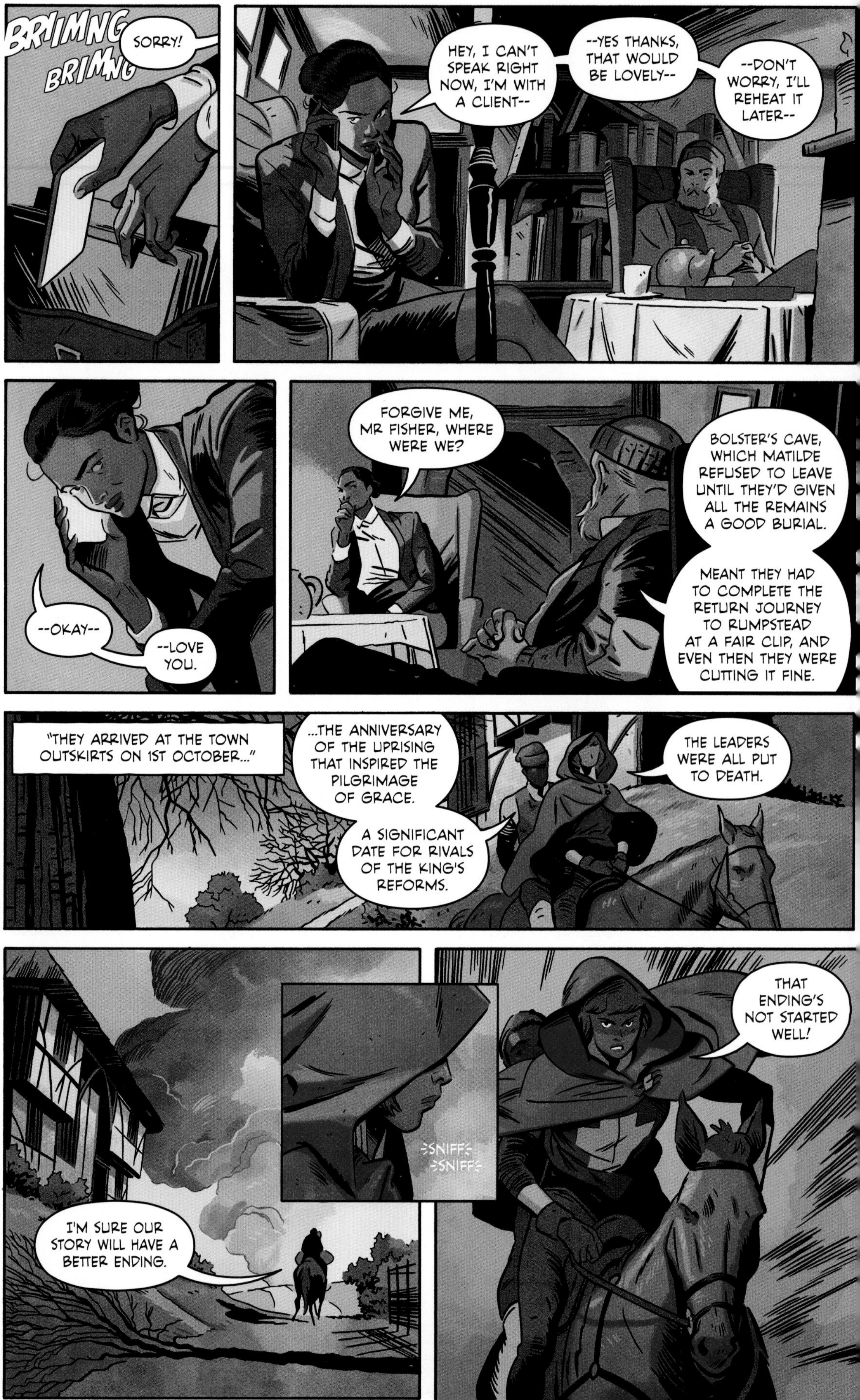
BRIMNG BRIMNG
SORRY!
HEY, I CAN'T SPEAK RIGHT NOW, I'M WITH A CLIENT--
--YES THANKS, THAT WOULD BE LOVELY--
--DON'T WORRY, I'LL REHEAT IT LATER--
--OKAY--
--LOVE YOU.
FORGIVE ME, MR FISHER, WHERE WERE WE?
BOLSTER'S CAVE, WHICH MATILDE REFUSED TO LEAVE UNTIL THEY'D GIVEN ALL THE REMAINS A GOOD BURIAL.
MEANT THEY HAD TO COMPLETE THE RETURN JOURNEY TO RUMPSTEAD AT A FAIR CLIP, AND EVEN THEN THEY WERE CUTTING IT FINE.
"THEY ARRIVED AT THE TOWN OUTSKIRTS ON 1ST OCTOBER..."
...THE ANNIVERSARY OF THE UPRISING THAT INSPIRED THE PILGRIMAGE OF GRACE.
A SIGNIFICANT DATE FOR RIVALS OF THE KING'S REFORMS.
THE LEADERS WERE ALL PUT TO DEATH.
I'M SURE OUR STORY WILL HAVE A BETTER ENDING.
SNIFF SNIFF
THAT ENDING'S NOT STARTED WELL!

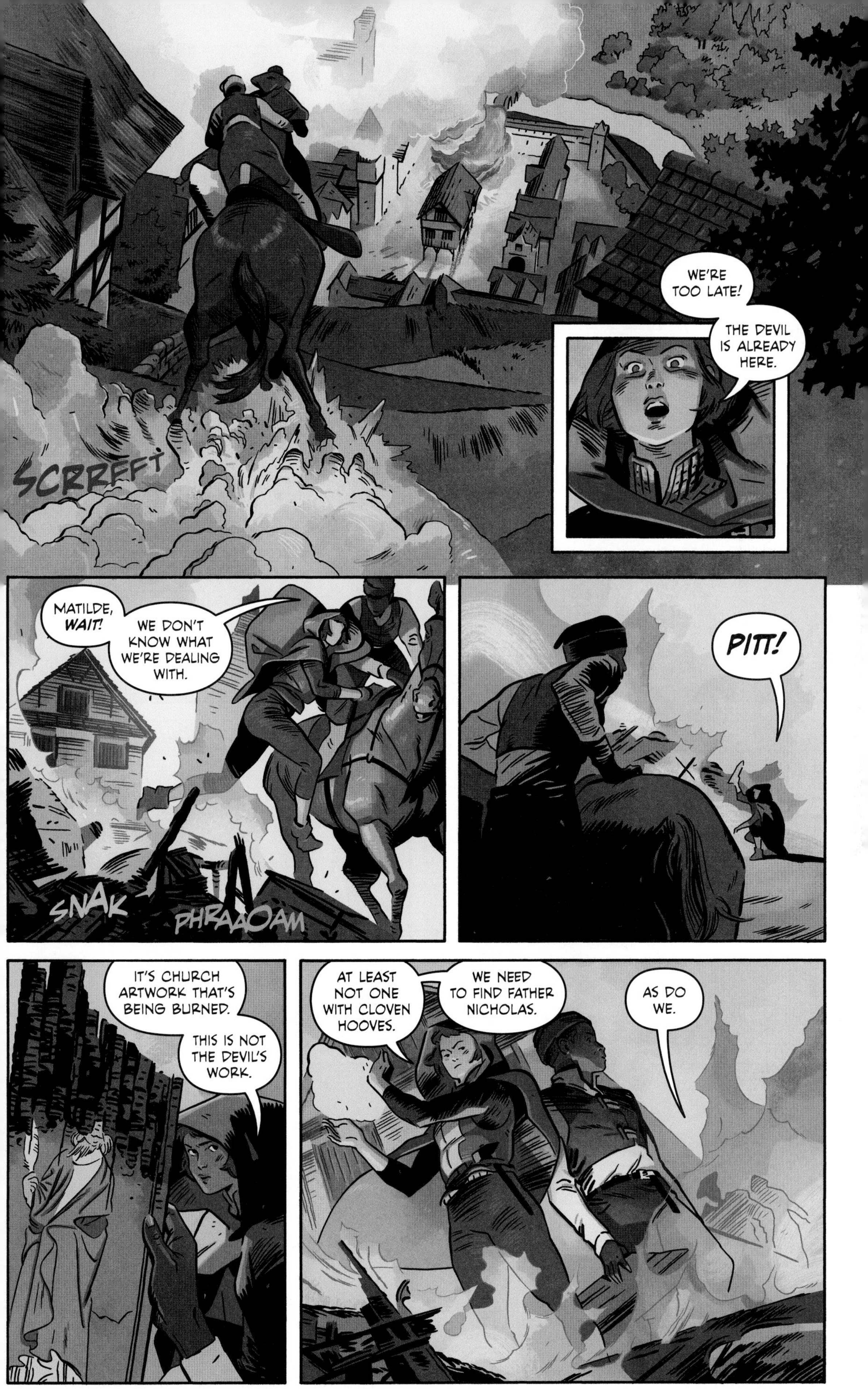
SCRRFFT
WE'RE TOO LATE!
THE DEVIL IS ALREADY HERE.
MATILDE, WAIT!
WE DON'T KNOW WHAT WE'RE DEALING WITH.
SNAK
PHRAAOAM
PITT!
IT'S CHURCH ARTWORK THAT'S BEING BURNED.
THIS IS NOT THE DEVIL'S WORK.
AT LEAST NOT ONE WITH CLOVEN HOOVES.
WE NEED TO FIND FATHER NICHOLAS.
AS DO WE.

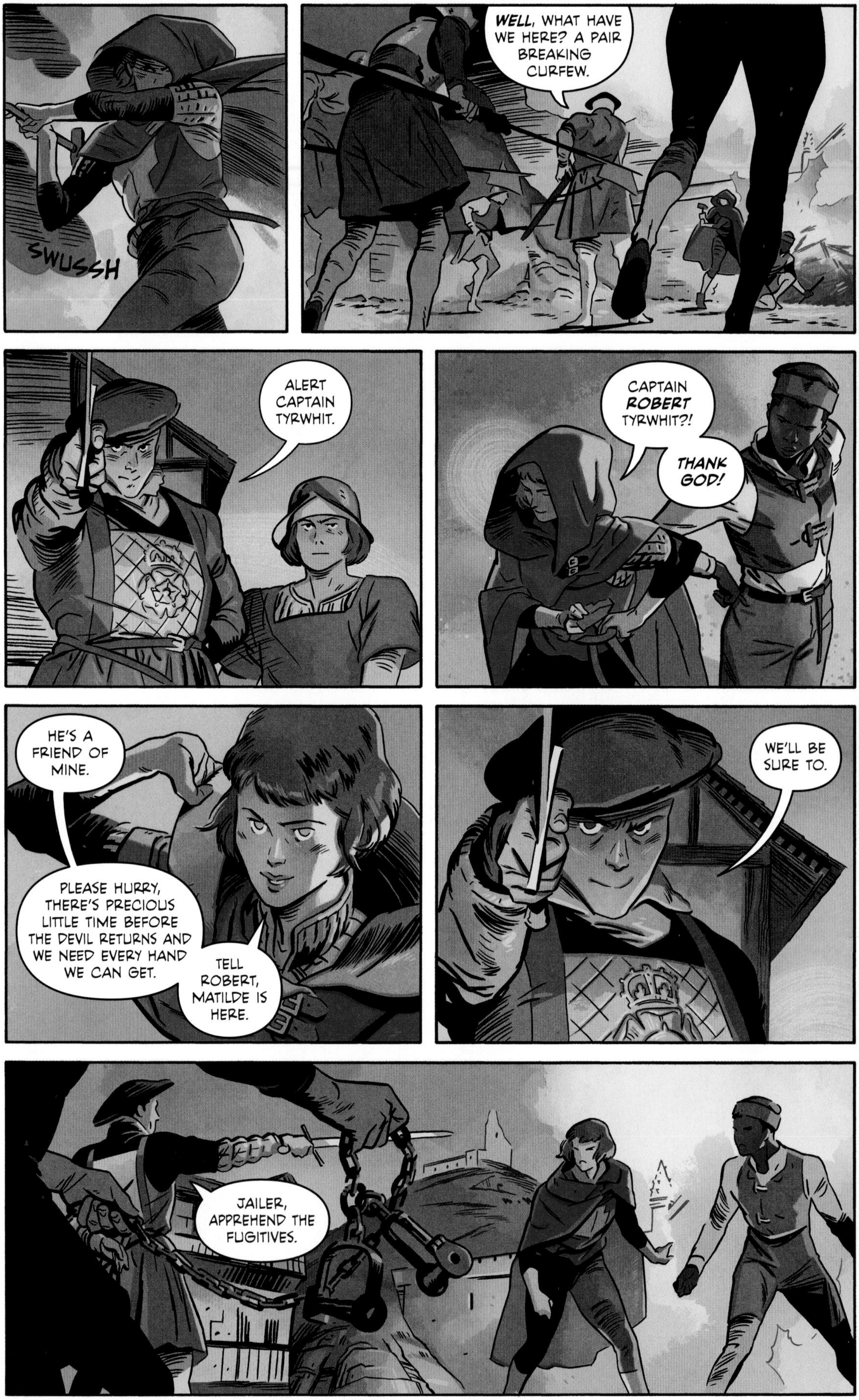
SWUSSH
WELL, WHAT HAVE WE HERE? A PAIR BREAKING CURFEW.
ALERT CAPTAIN TYRWHIT.
CAPTAIN ROBERT TYRWHIT?!
THANK GOD!
HE'S A FRIEND OF MINE.
PLEASE HURRY, THERE'S PRECIOUS LITTLE TIME BEFORE THE DEVIL RETURNS AND WE NEED EVERY HAND WE CAN GET.
TELL ROBERT, MATILDE IS HERE.
WE'LL BE SURE TO.
JAILER, APPREHEND THE FUGITIVES.

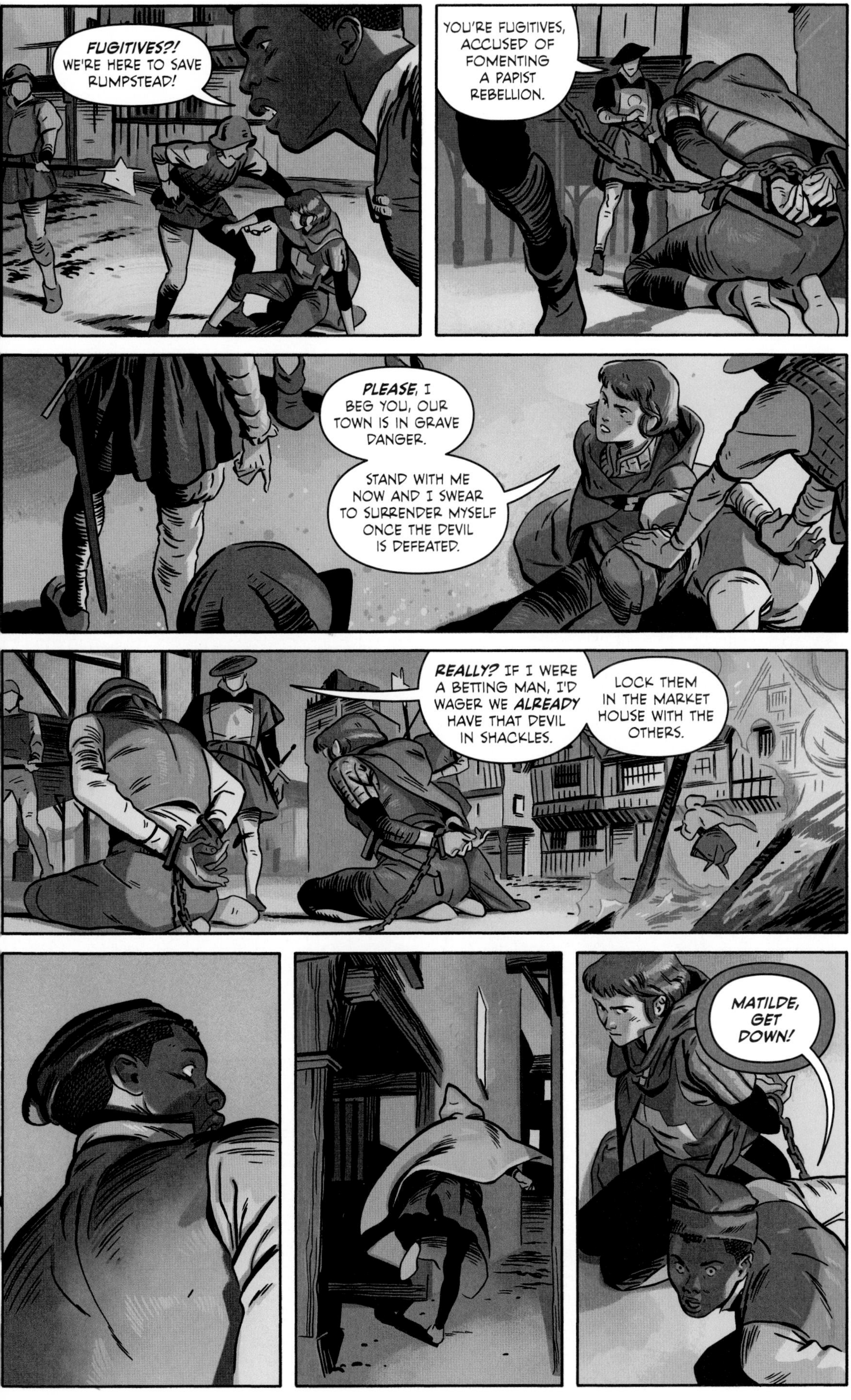
FUGITIVES?! WE'RE HERE TO SAVE RUMPSTEAD!
YOU'RE FUGITIVES, ACCUSED OF FOMENTING A PAPIST REBELLION.
PLEASE, I BEG YOU, OUR TOWN IS IN GRAVE DANGER.
STAND WITH ME NOW AND I SWEAR TO SURRENDER MYSELF ONCE THE DEVIL IS DEFEATED.
REALLY? IF I WERE A BETTING MAN, I'D WAGER WE ALREADY HAVE THAT DEVIL IN SHACKLES.
LOCK THEM IN THE MARKET HOUSE WITH THE OTHERS.
MATILDE, GET DOWN!

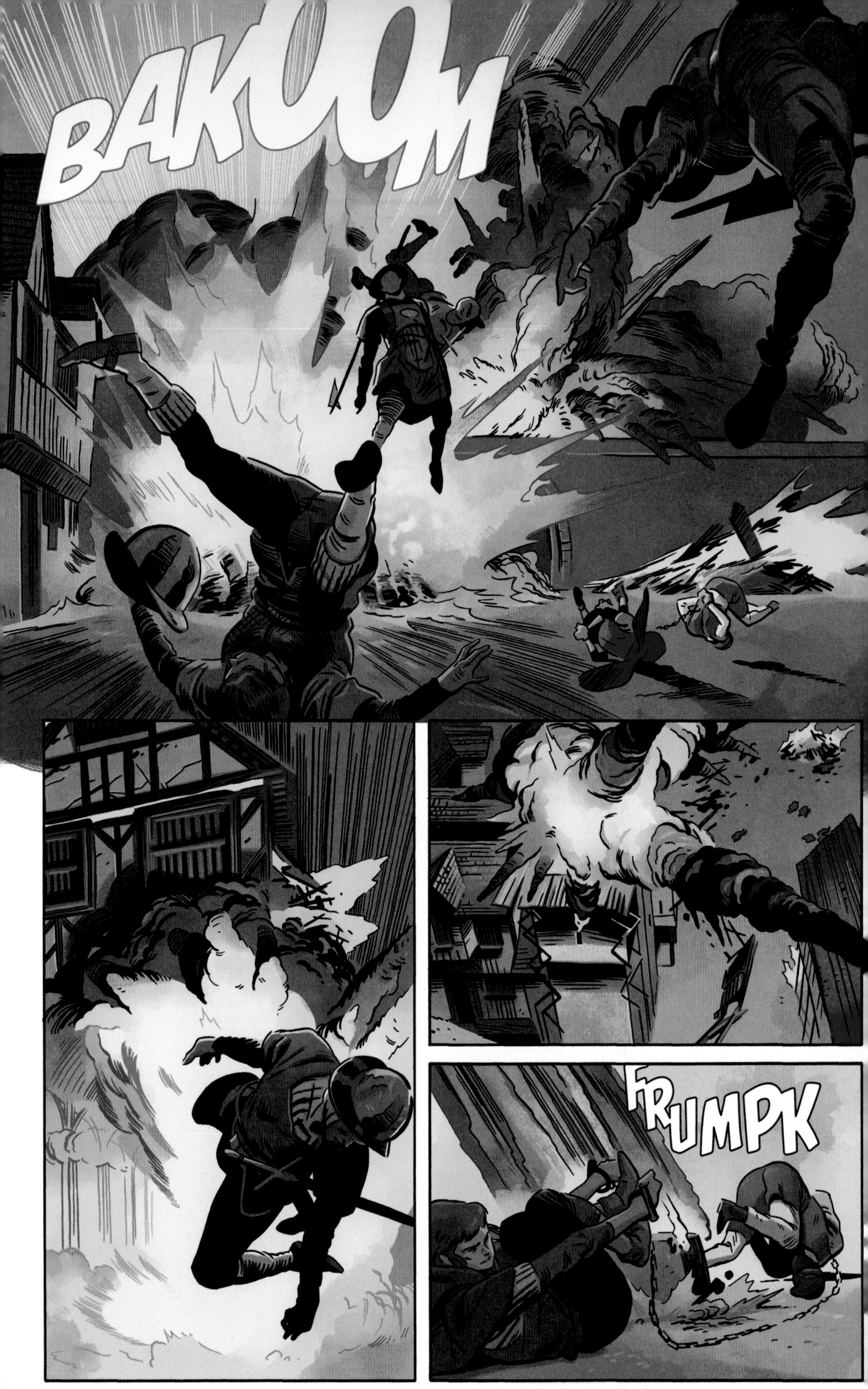
BAKOOM
FRUMPK

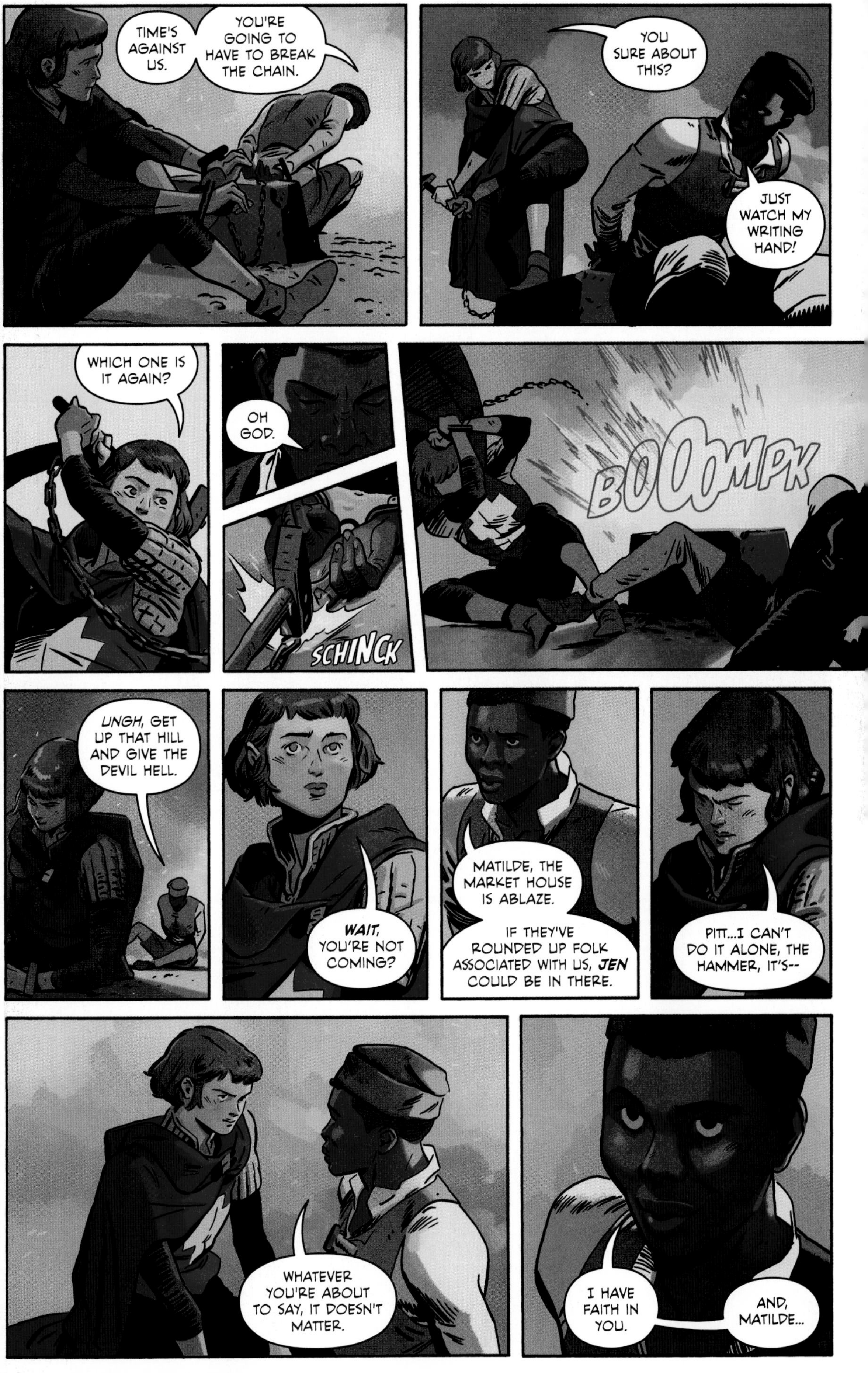
TIME'S AGAINST US.
YOU'RE GOING TO HAVE TO BREAK THE CHAIN.
YOU SURE ABOUT THIS?
JUST WATCH MY WRITING HAND!
WHICH ONE IS IT AGAIN?
OH GOD.
SCHINCK
BOOOMPK
UNGH, GET UP THAT HILL AND GIVE THE DEVIL HELL.
WAIT, YOU'RE NOT COMING?
MATILDE, THE MARKET HOUSE IS ABLAZE.
IF THEY'VE ROUNDED UP FOLK ASSOCIATED WITH US, JEN COULD BE IN THERE.
PITT...I CAN'T DO IT ALONE, THE HAMMER, IT'S--
WHATEVER YOU'RE ABOUT TO SAY, IT DOESN'T MATTER.
AND, MATILDE...
I HAVE FAITH IN YOU.

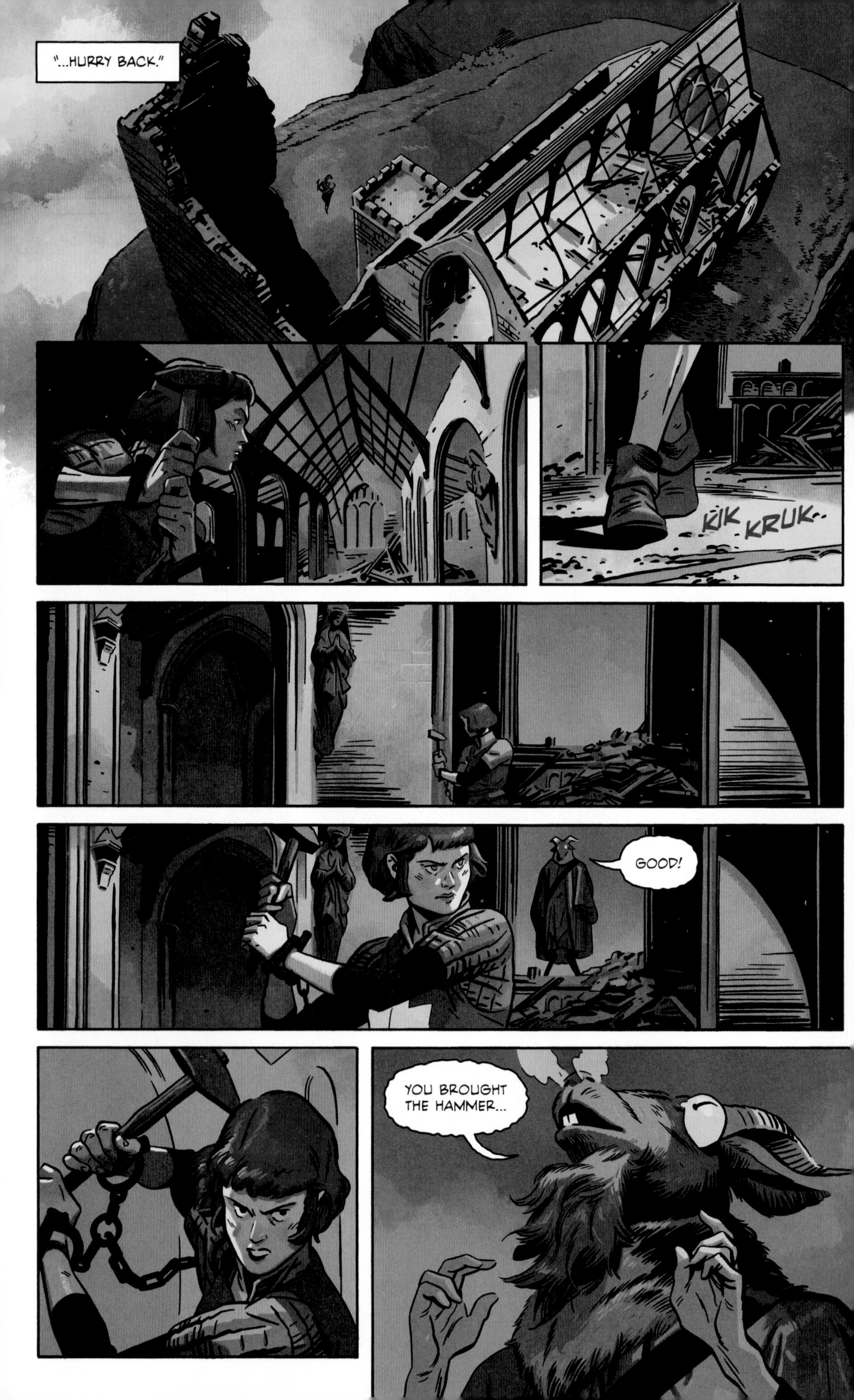
"...HURRY BACK."
KIK KRUK
GOOD!
YOU BROUGHT THE HAMMER...

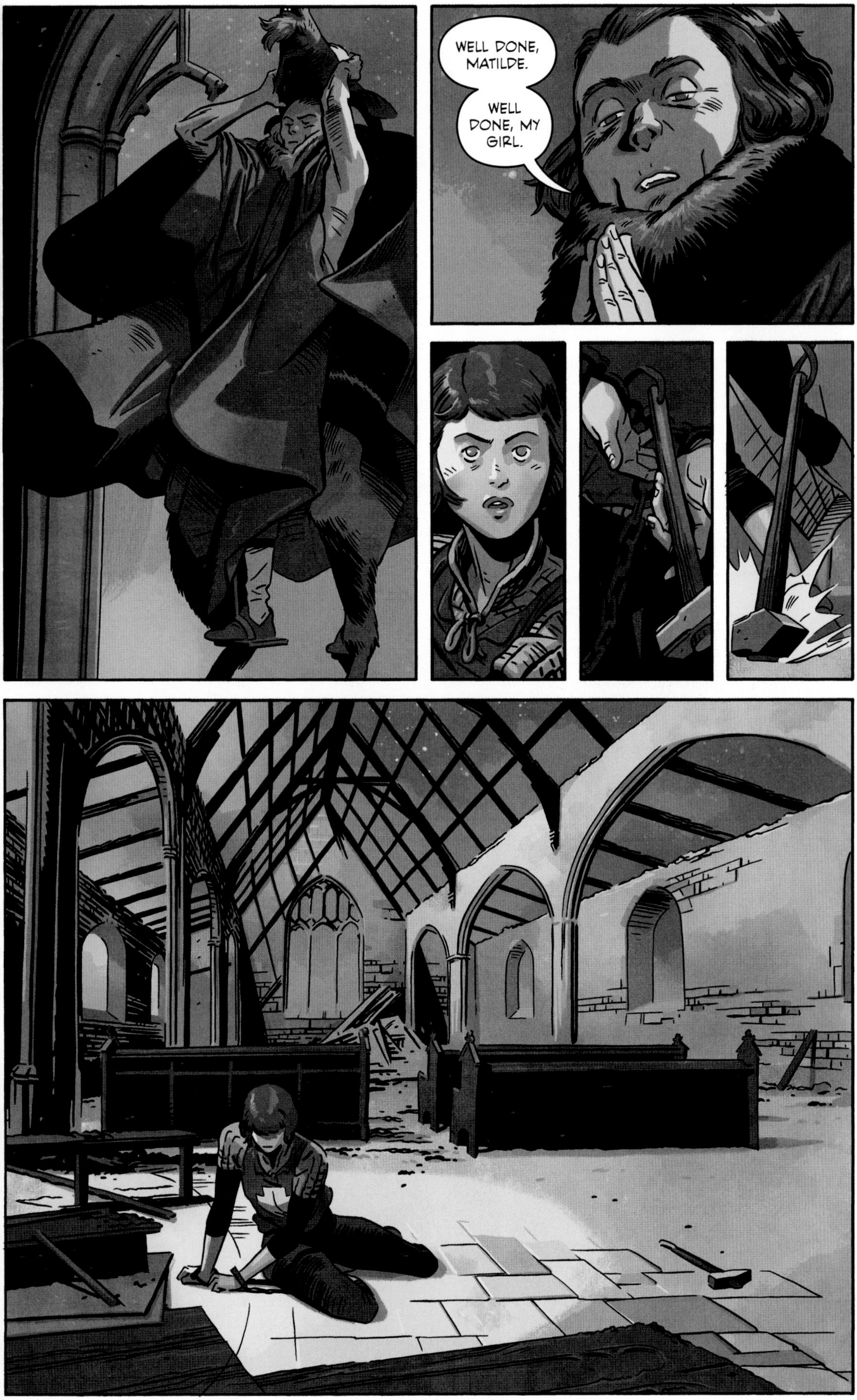
WELL DONE, MATILDE.
WELL DONE, MY GIRL.

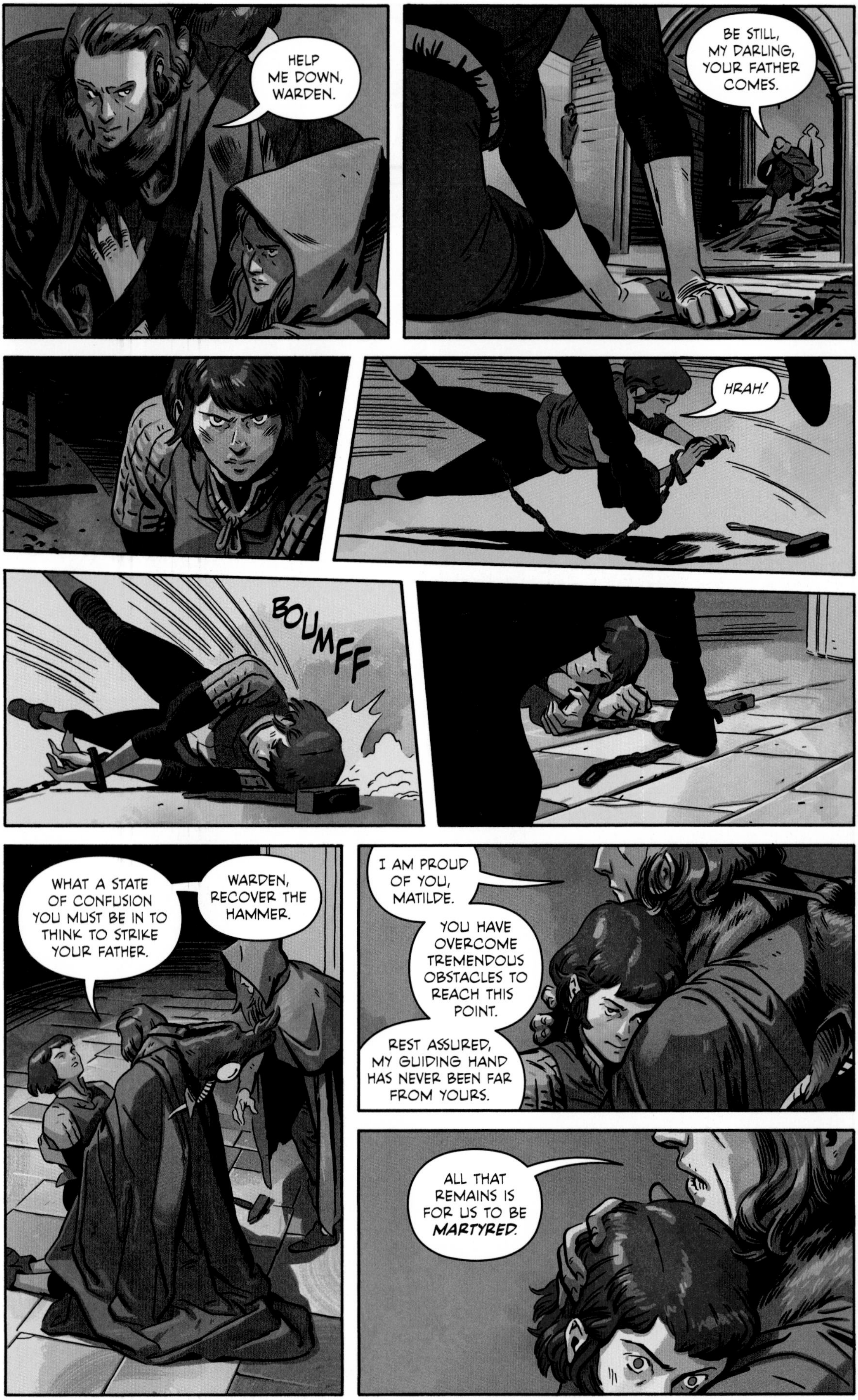
HELP ME DOWN, WARDEN.
BE STILL, MY DARLING, YOUR FATHER COMES.
HRAH!
BOUMFF
WHAT A STATE OF CONFUSION YOU MUST BE IN TO THINK TO STRIKE YOUR FATHER.
WARDEN, RECOVER THE HAMMER.
I AM PROUD OF YOU, MATILDE.
YOU HAVE OVERCOME TREMENDOUS OBSTACLES TO REACH THIS POINT.
REST ASSURED, MY GUIDING HAND HAS NEVER BEEN FAR FROM YOURS.
ALL THAT REMAINS IS FOR US TO BE MARTYRED.

MARTYRED?! YES, MATILDE.

NO!

ON MY WORD, WARDEN GORDON WILL LIGHT THE FUSE ON WHAT REMAINS OF THE GUNPOWDER SURROUNDING THIS CHURCH.

IT WILL BE A GLORIOUS DISPLAY.

FATHER, PLEASE!

THE FAITHFUL ARE IMPRISONED IN THE MARKET HOUSE, THEY BURN WITH EVERY MOMENT WE SPEND UP HERE.

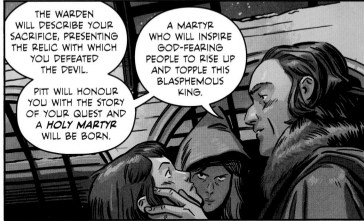

LIFE, MY DEAR, LIFE IS THE PRISON FOR THE FAITHFUL.

TONIGHT THEY WILL BE FREE.

FOR THE THOUSANDS LESS FORTUNATE, OUR GREATEST ACT OF COMPASSION IS TO PRESERVE THE FAITH, SO THAT THEY TOO MAY KNOW PARADISE.

FATH--

MATILDE, OUR MARTYRDOM MAY BE THE LAST HOPE TO RESTORE THE CHURCH.

THE WARDEN WILL DESCRIBE YOUR SACRIFICE, PRESENTING THE RELIC WITH WHICH YOU DEFEATED THE DEVIL.

PITT WILL HONOUR YOU WITH THE STORY OF YOUR QUEST AND A HOLY MARTYR WILL BE BORN.

A MARTYR WHO WILL INSPIRE GOD-FEARING PEOPLE TO RISE UP AND TOPPLE THIS BLASPHEMOUS KING.

OH PITT, YOU SHOULD NOT BE PART OF THIS.

FORGIVE ME.

CLINK

CLINK

TO THINE OWN SELF BE TRUE

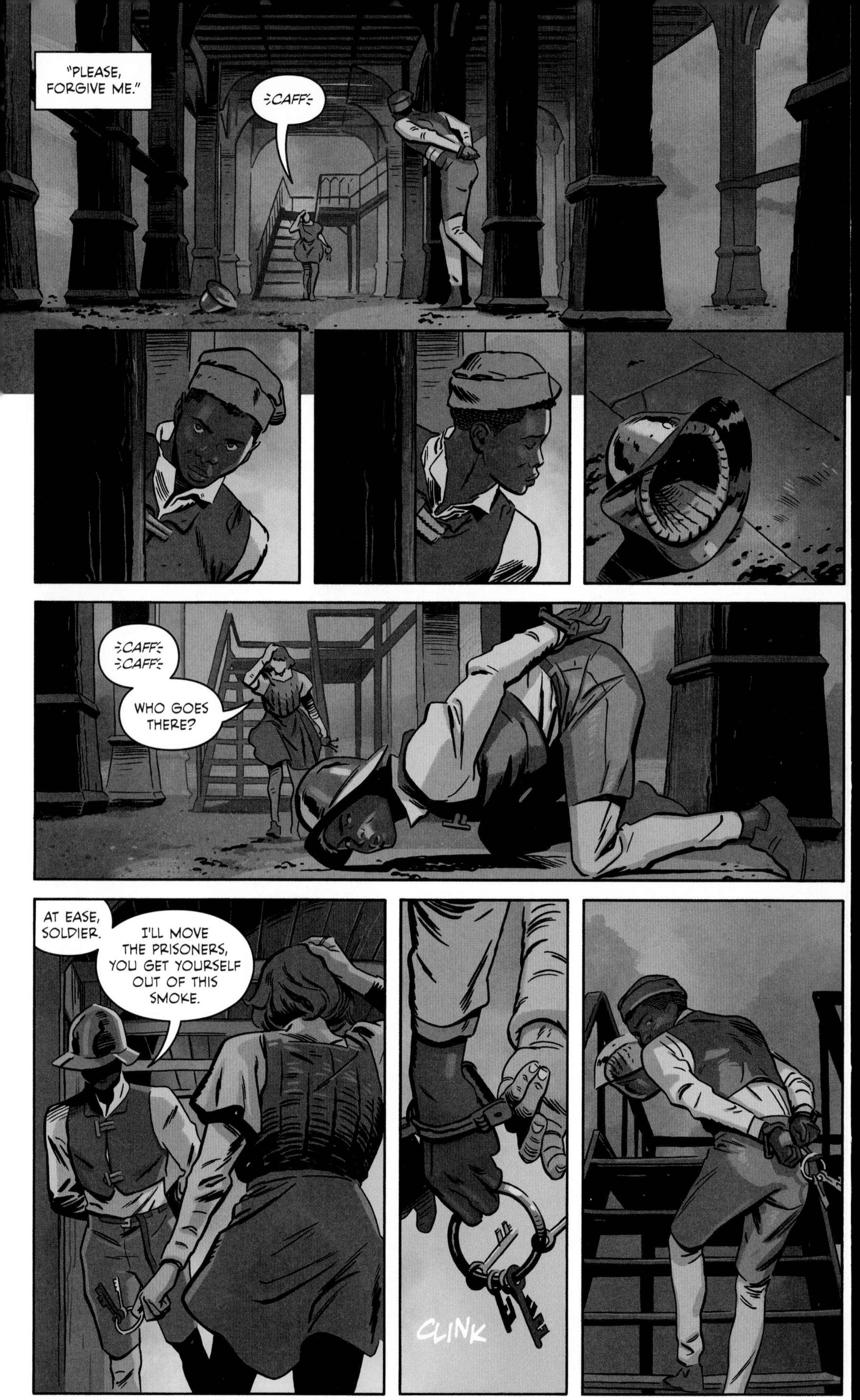
"PLEASE, FORGIVE ME."
CAFF
CAFF
CAFF
WHO GOES THERE?
AT EASE, SOLDIER.
I'LL MOVE THE PRISONERS, YOU GET YOURSELF OUT OF THIS SMOKE.
CLINK

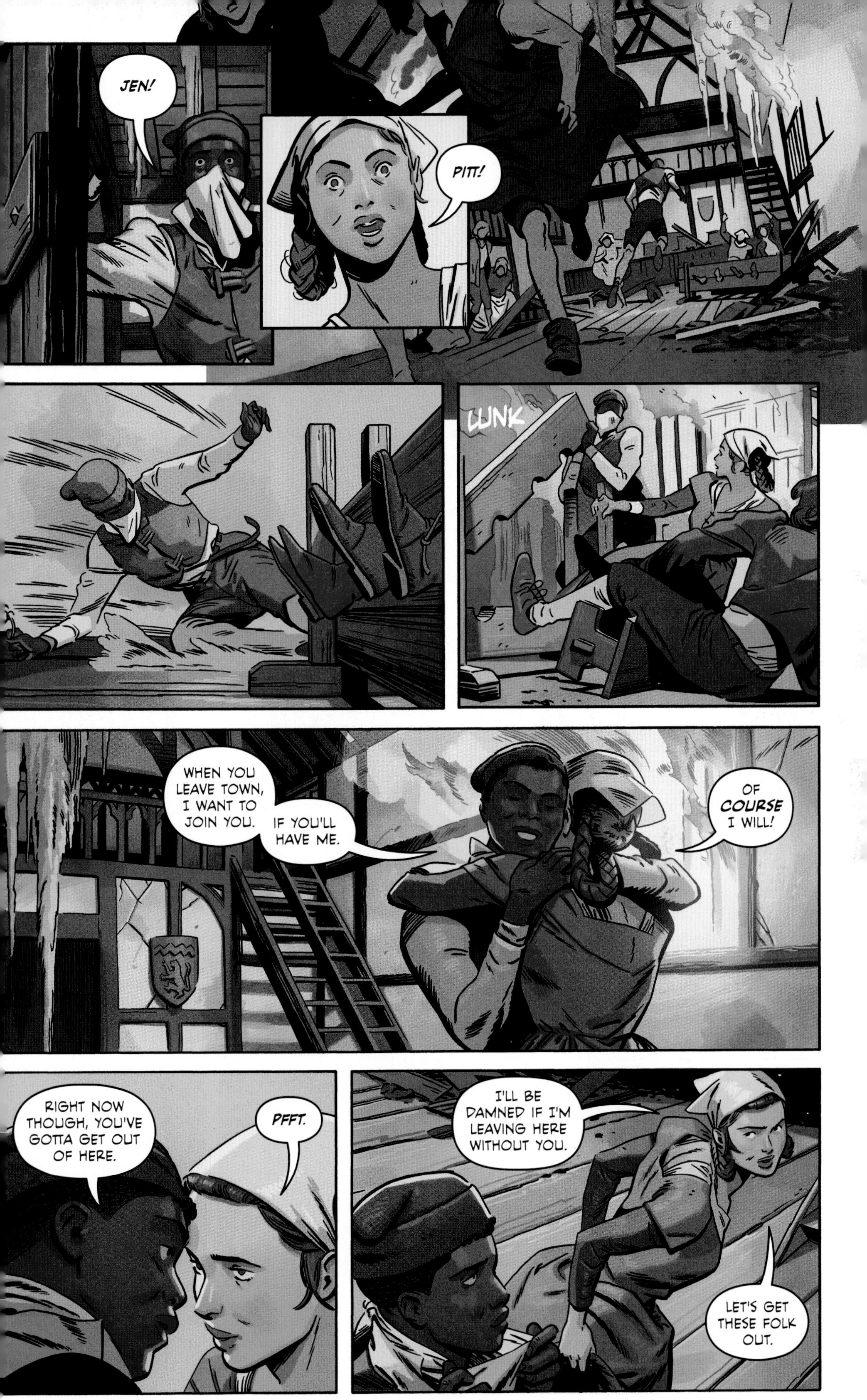
JEN!
PITT!
LUNK
WHEN YOU LEAVE TOWN, I WANT TO JOIN YOU.
IF YOU'LL HAVE ME.
OF COURSE I WILL!
RIGHT NOW THOUGH, YOU'VE GOTTA GET OUT OF HERE.
PFFT.
I'LL BE DAMNED IF I'M LEAVING HERE WITHOUT YOU.
LET'S GET THESE FOLK OUT.

YOU NEEDN'T FRET ABOUT PITT, HISTORY WILL SMOOTH ANY WRINKLES IN SERVICE TO THE GREATER GOOD.

IS THERE NO OTHER WAY?

HEAVEN KNOWS I'VE TRIED, CHILD.

FROM THE PULPIT I'VE EXTOLLED THE VIRTUES OF CHARITY AND DEVOTION, PROMISED PARADISE AND THREATENED DAMNATION.

YOU WERE ALWAYS WISER.

FROM AN EARLY AGE, YOU INTUITED THAT DULL MINDS REQUIRE SIMPLE STORIES AND SPECTACLE TO COMPREHEND.

THE CREDIT FOR ALL THIS IS YOURS.

YOU TOOK INSPIRATION FROM ME?

MORE THAN INSPIRATION, MY LOVE.

THOMAS GIPPING CONFESSED YOUR PLAN TO INVENT A DEVIL AT THIS VERY CHURCH. ALL I HAVE ADDED ARE MY RESOURCES.

YOU ARE THE MASTER MASON, I AM YOUR HUMBLE LABOURER.

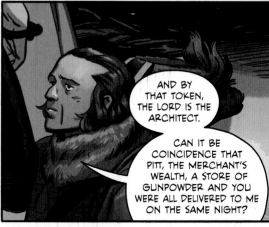
AND BY THAT TOKEN, THE LORD IS THE ARCHITECT.

CAN IT BE COINCIDENCE THAT PITT, THE MERCHANT'S WEALTH, A STORE OF GUNPOWDER AND YOU WERE ALL DELIVERED TO ME ON THE SAME NIGHT?

NO, FATHER.

BUT TO BECOME A MARTYR...

...WILL IT HURT?

WHEN PARADISE STRETCHES BEFORE YOU AND THOUSANDS OF SOULS CHEER YOUR NAME, DO YOU IMAGINE DWELLING ON THE BRIEFEST MOMENT OF SUFFERING?

YOU WILL BE CARRIED ON THE WINGS OF PRAISE TO THE HIGHEST TOWERS OF THE HEAVENLY KINGDOM.

REALLY?

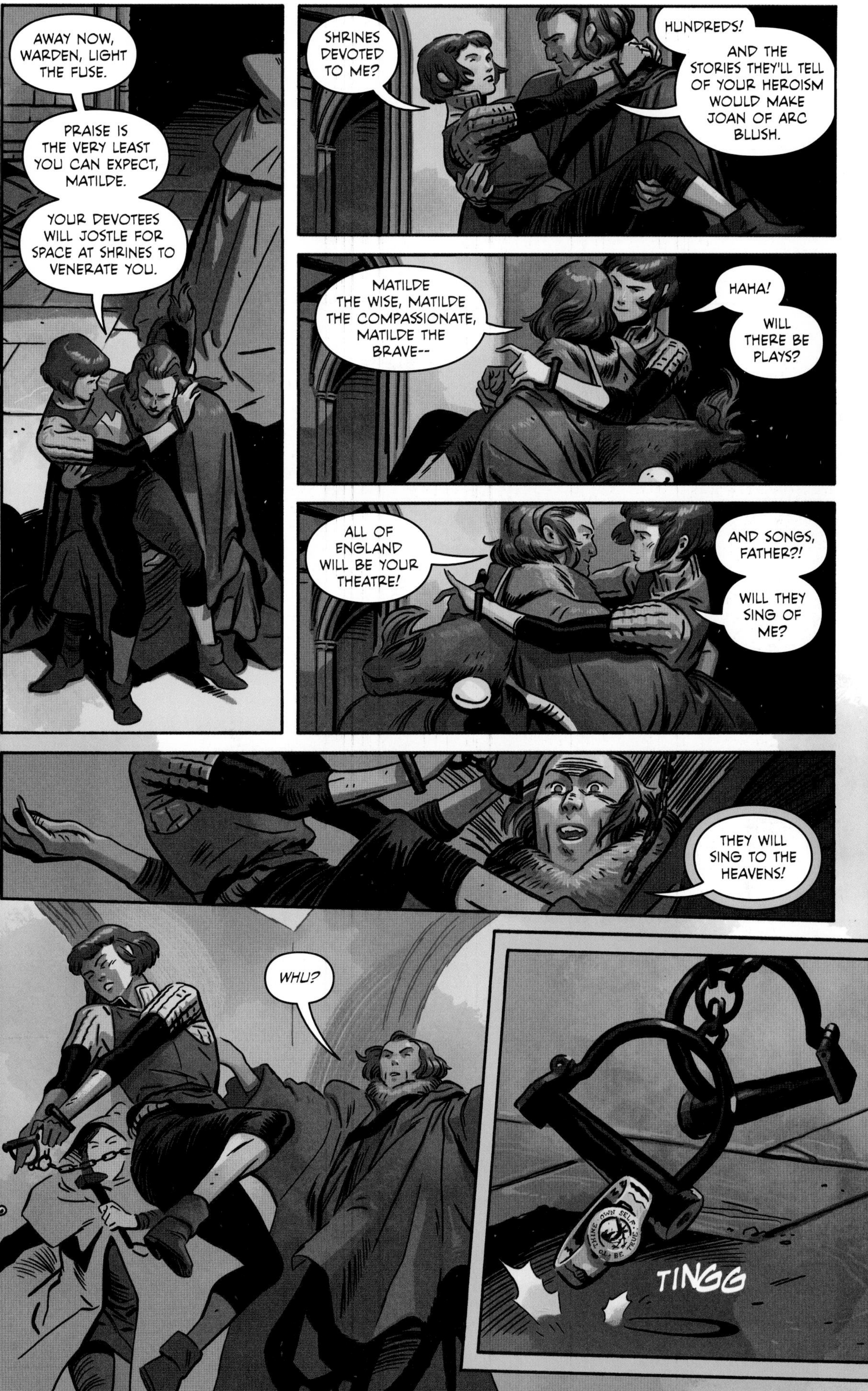
AWAY NOW, WARDEN, LIGHT THE FUSE.
PRAISE IS THE VERY LEAST YOU CAN EXPECT, MATILDE.
YOUR DEVOTEES WILL JOSTLE FOR SPACE AT SHRINES TO VENERATE YOU.
SHRINES DEVOTED TO ME?
HUNDREDS!
AND THE STORIES THEY'LL TELL OF YOUR HEROISM WOULD MAKE JOAN OF ARC BLUSH.
MATILDE THE WISE, MATILDE THE COMPASSIONATE, MATILDE THE BRAVE--
HAHA!
WILL THERE BE PLAYS?
ALL OF ENGLAND WILL BE YOUR THEATRE!
AND SONGS, FATHER?!
WILL THEY SING OF ME?
THEY WILL SING TO THE HEAVENS!
WHU?
TINGG

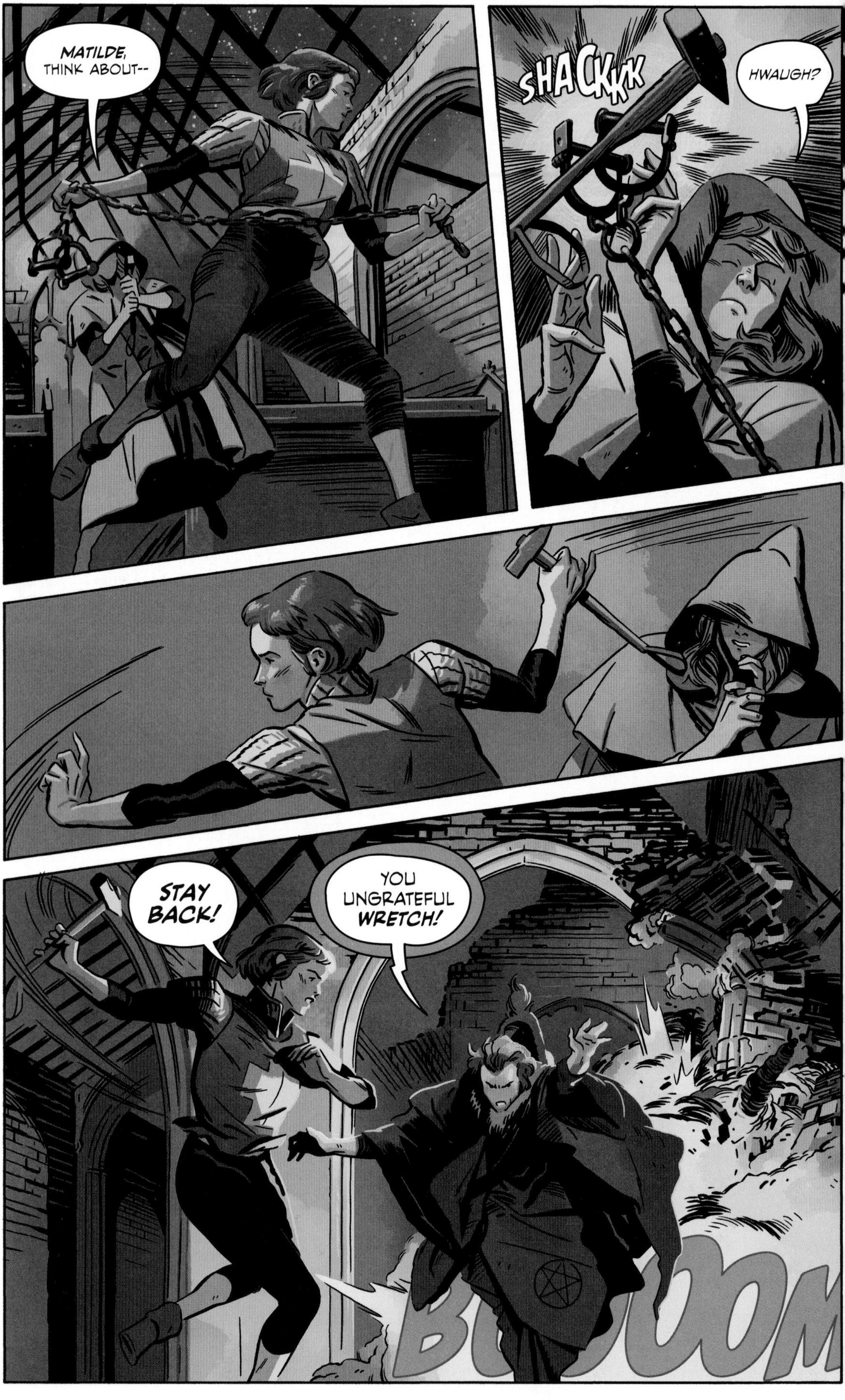
MATILDE, THINK ABOUT--
SHACKKK
HWAUGH?
STAY BACK!
YOU UNGRATEFUL WRETCH!
BOOOOM

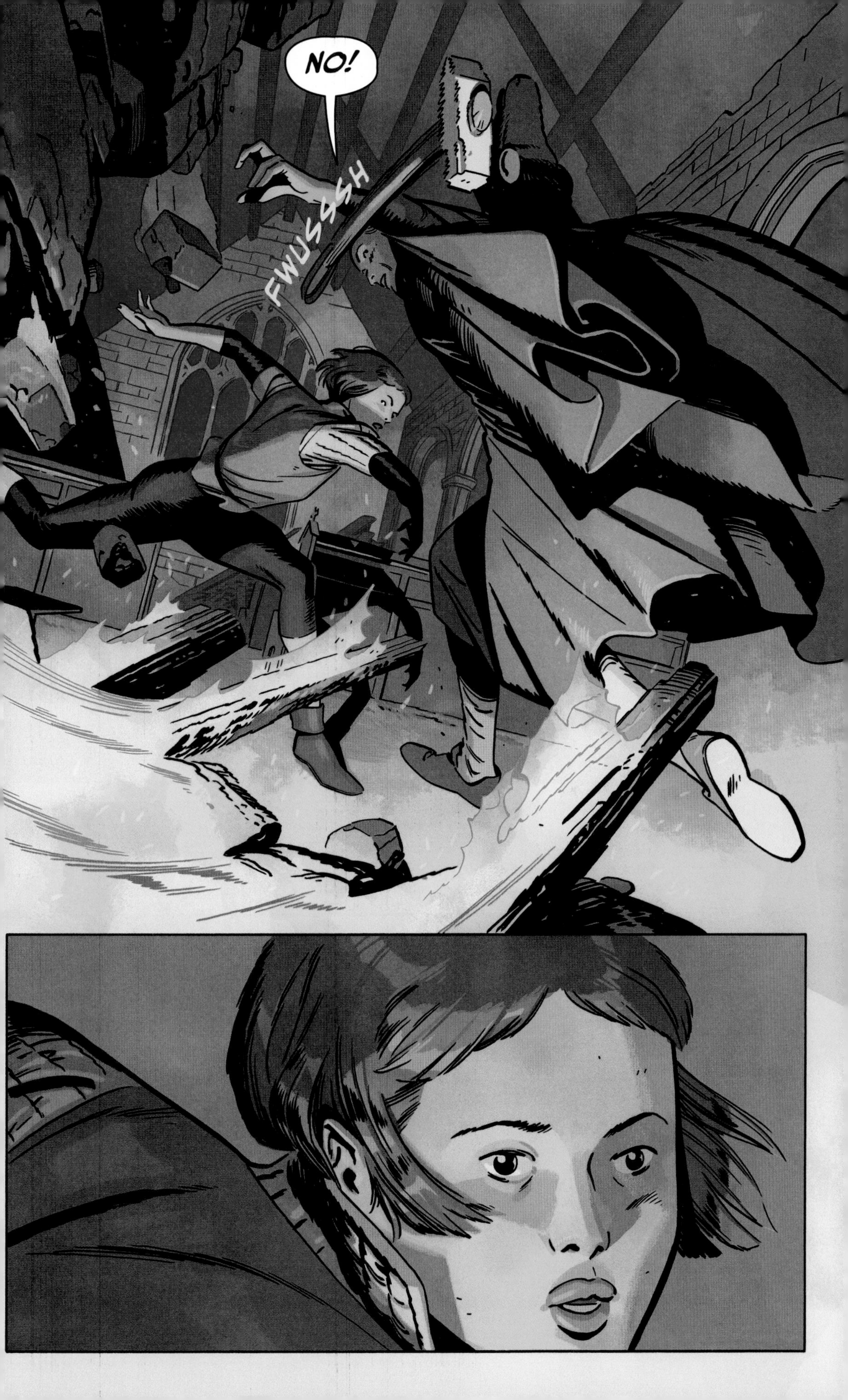
NO!
FWUSSSH

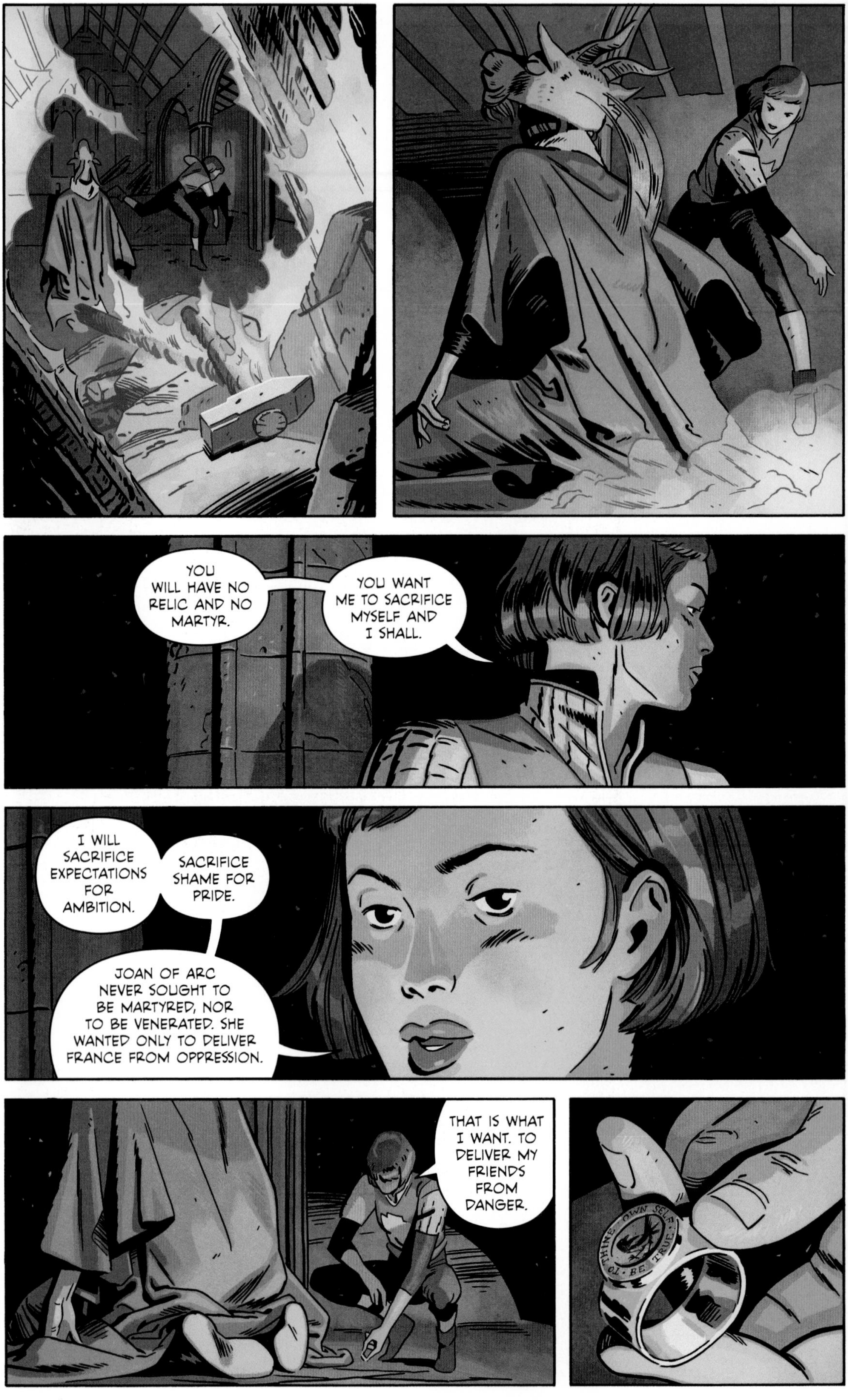
YOU WILL HAVE NO RELIC AND NO MARTYR.
YOU WANT ME TO SACRIFICE MYSELF AND I SHALL.
I WILL SACRIFICE EXPECTATIONS FOR AMBITION.
SACRIFICE SHAME FOR PRIDE.
JOAN OF ARC NEVER SOUGHT TO BE MARTYRED, NOR TO BE VENERATED. SHE WANTED ONLY TO DELIVER FRANCE FROM OPPRESSION.
THAT IS WHAT I WANT. TO DELIVER MY FRIENDS FROM DANGER.
TO THINE OWN SELF BE TRUE

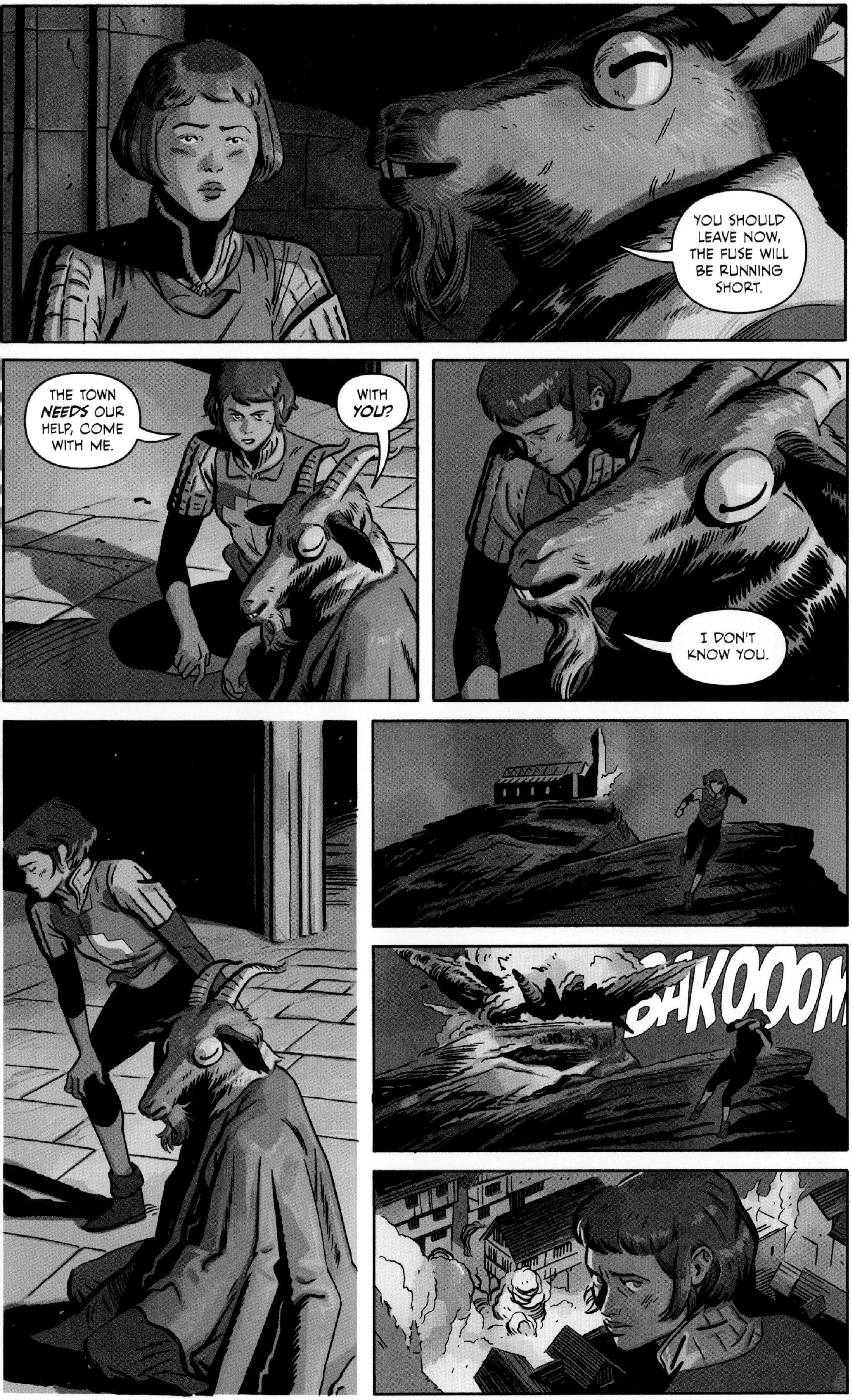
YOU SHOULD LEAVE NOW, THE FUSE WILL BE RUNNING SHORT.
THE TOWN *NEEDS* OUR HELP, COME WITH ME.
WITH *YOU?*
I DON'T KNOW YOU.
BAKOOOM

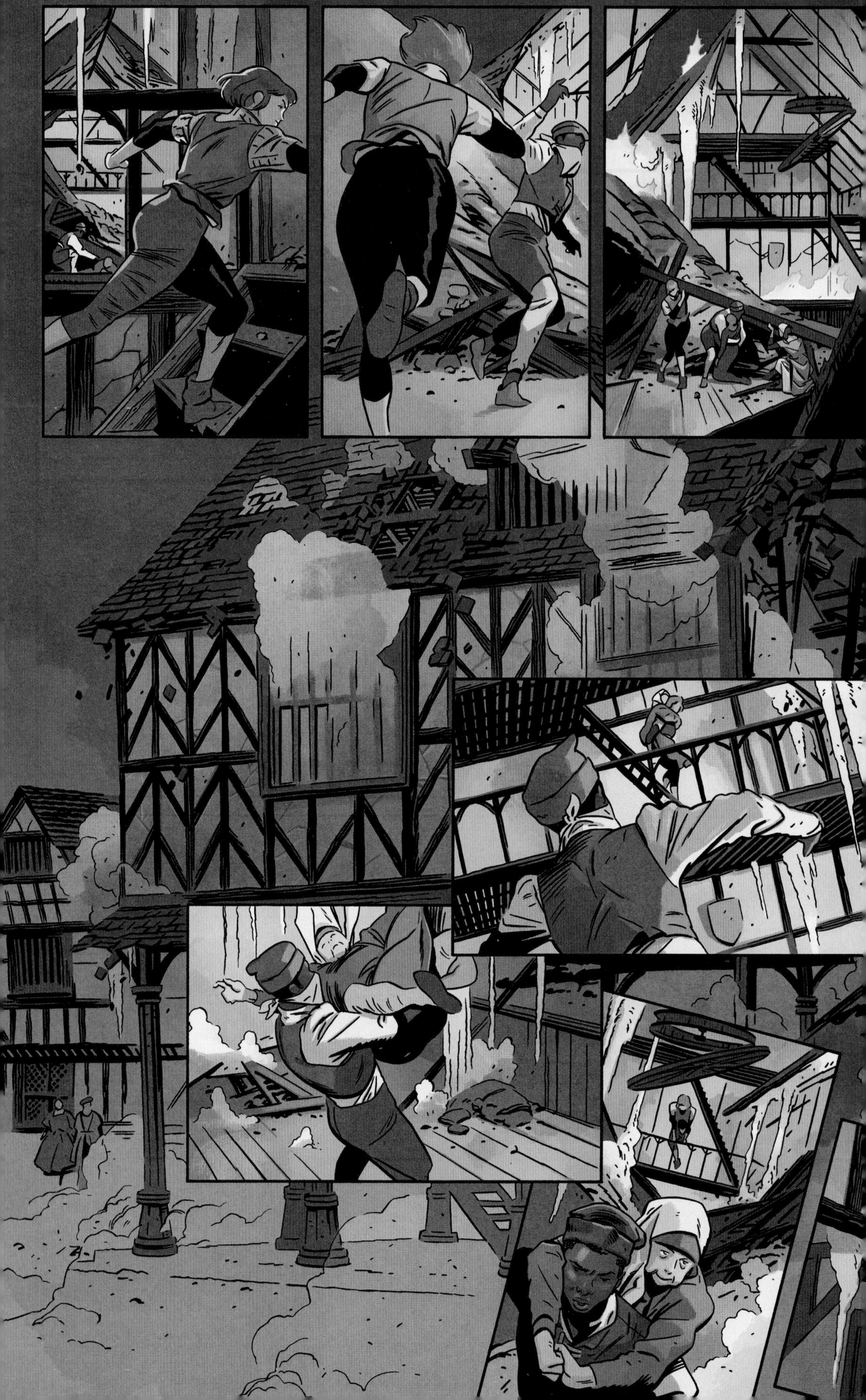

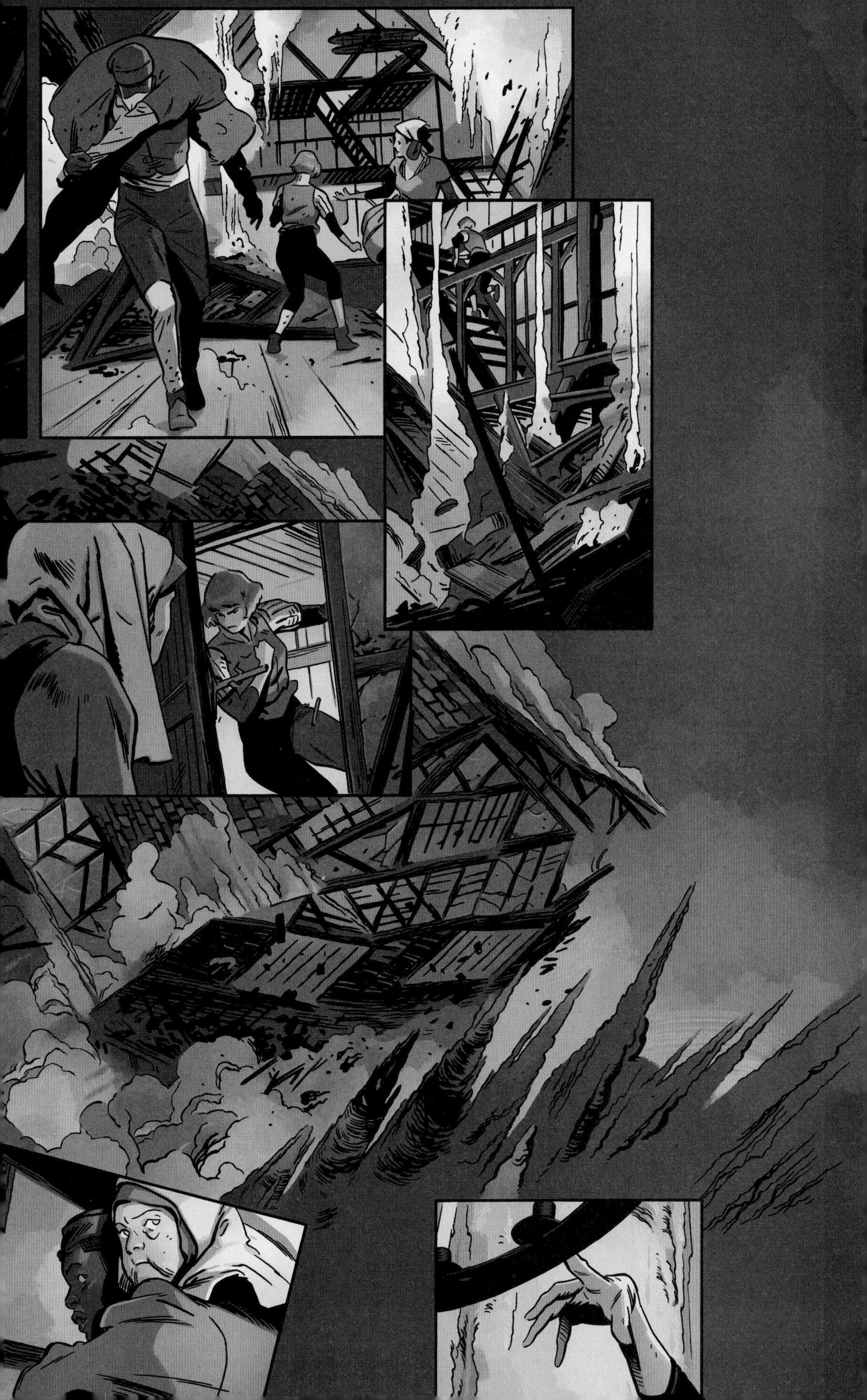

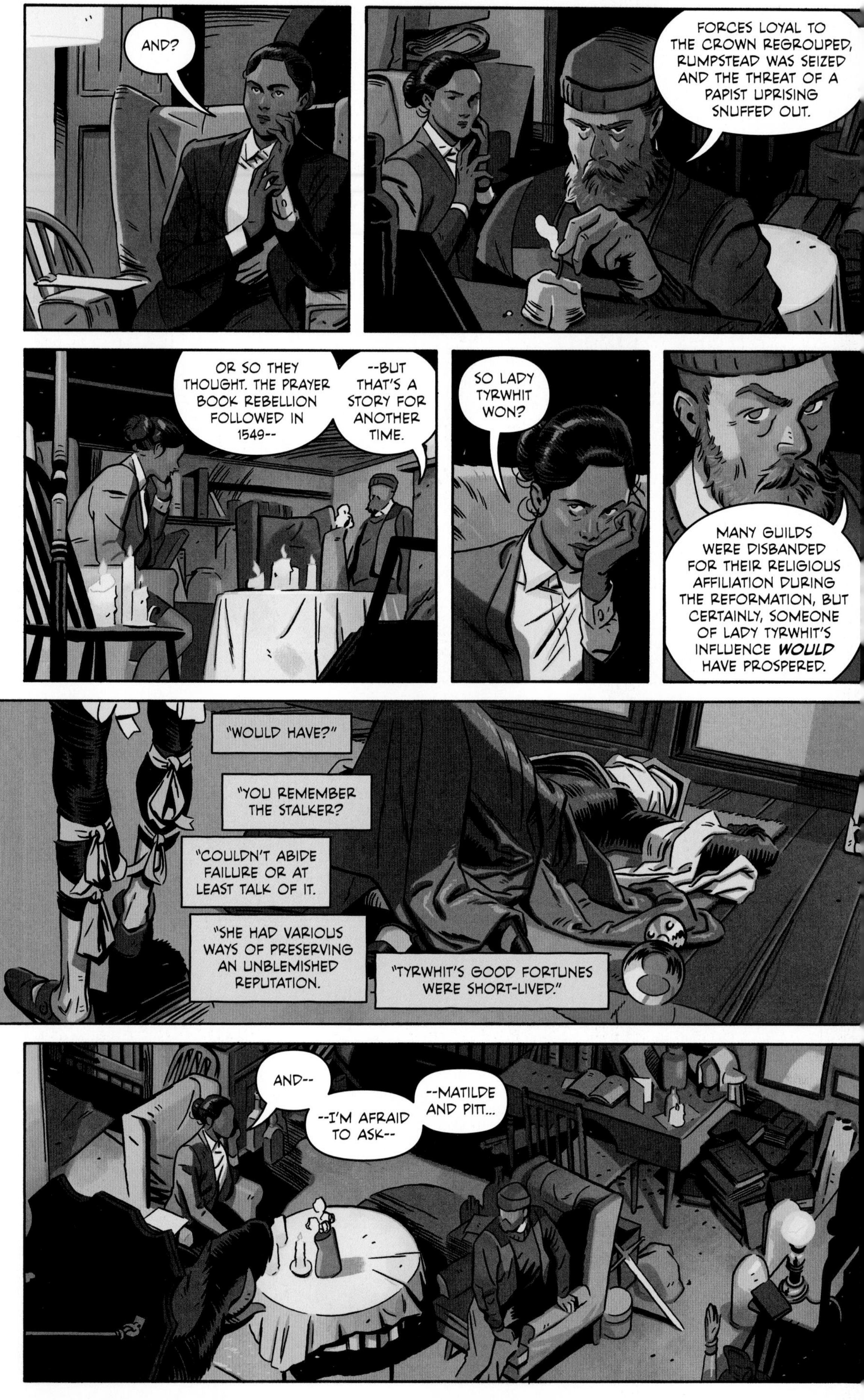
AND?
FORCES LOYAL TO THE CROWN REGROUPED, RUMPSTEAD WAS SEIZED AND THE THREAT OF A PAPIST UPRISING SNUFFED OUT.
OR SO THEY THOUGHT. THE PRAYER BOOK REBELLION FOLLOWED IN 1549--
--BUT THAT'S A STORY FOR ANOTHER TIME.
SO LADY TYRWHIT WON?
MANY GUILDS WERE DISBANDED FOR THEIR RELIGIOUS AFFILIATION DURING THE REFORMATION, BUT CERTAINLY, SOMEONE OF LADY TYRWHIT'S INFLUENCE ***WOULD*** HAVE PROSPERED.
"WOULD HAVE?"
"YOU REMEMBER THE STALKER?
"COULDN'T ABIDE FAILURE OR AT LEAST TALK OF IT.
"SHE HAD VARIOUS WAYS OF PRESERVING AN UNBLEMISHED REPUTATION.
"TYRWHIT'S GOOD FORTUNES WERE SHORT-LIVED."
AND--
--I'M AFRAID TO ASK--
--MATILDE AND PITT...

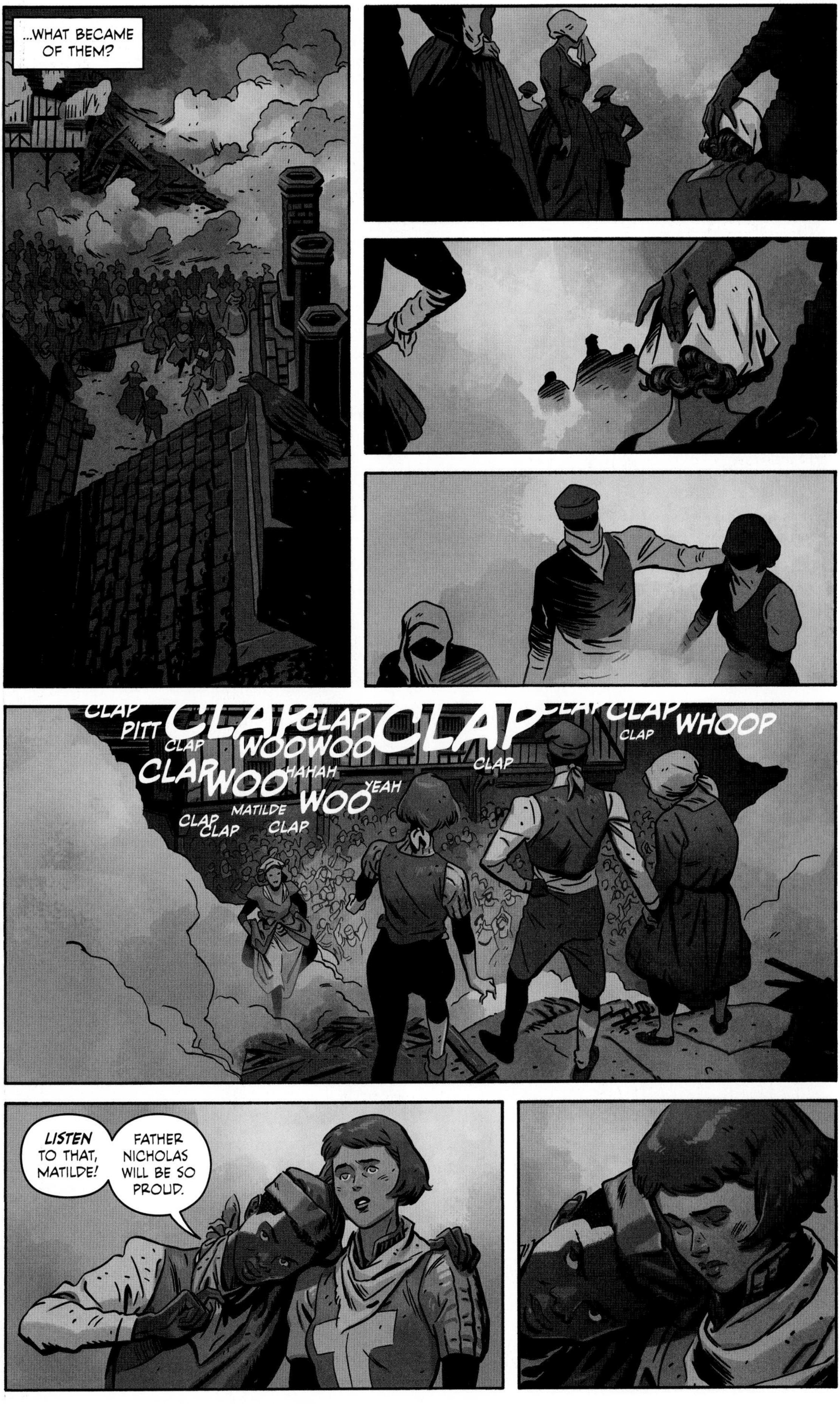
...WHAT BECAME OF THEM?
CLAP
PITT
CLAP
CLAP
CLAP
CLAP
CLAP
WHOOP
CLAP
WOOWOO
CLAP
CLAP
CLAR
WOO
HAHAH
YEAH
WOO
MATILDE
CLAP
CLAP
CLAP
LISTEN TO THAT, MATILDE!
FATHER NICHOLAS WILL BE SO PROUD.

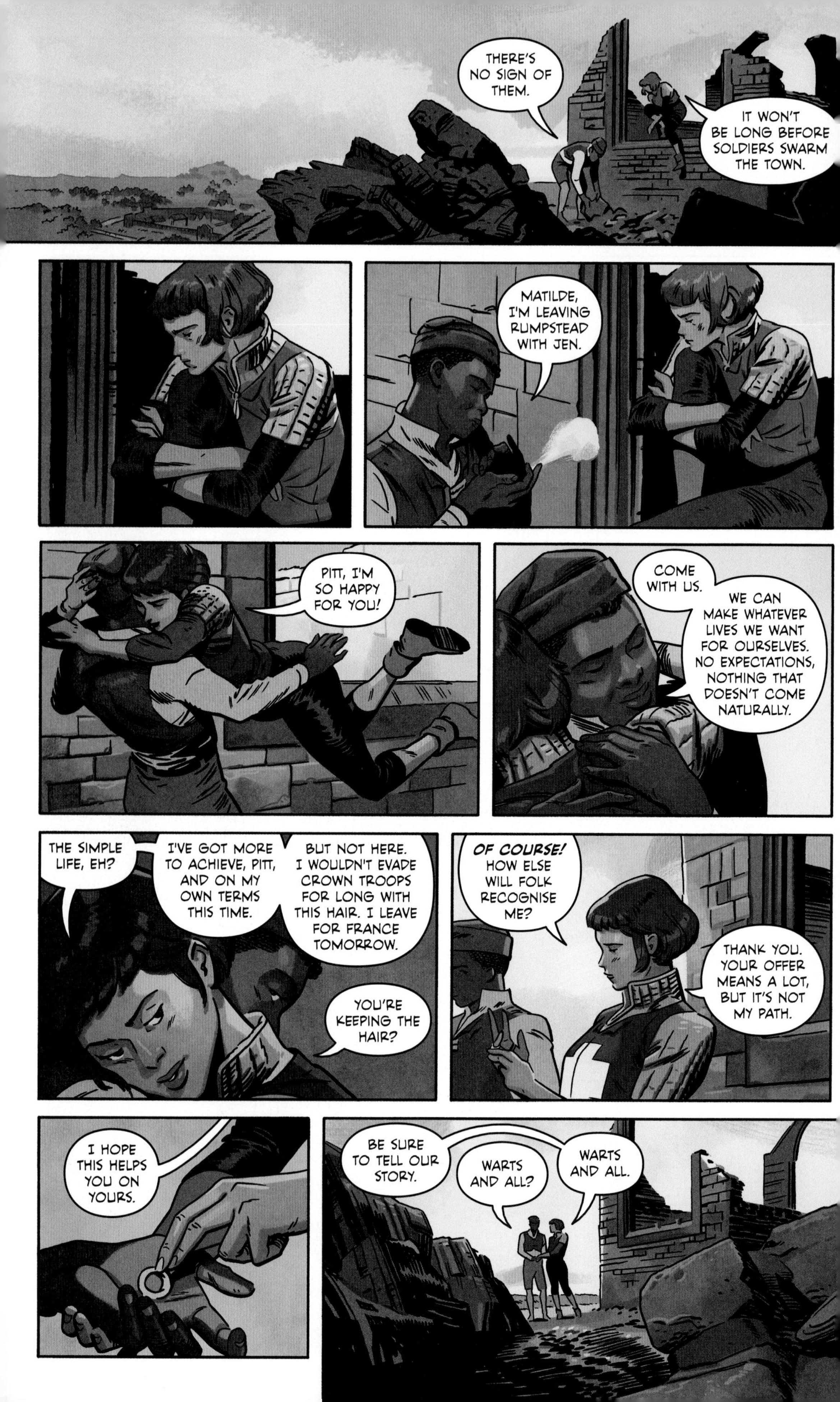
THERE'S NO SIGN OF THEM.
IT WON'T BE LONG BEFORE SOLDIERS SWARM THE TOWN.
MATILDE, I'M LEAVING RUMPSTEAD WITH JEN.
PITT, I'M SO HAPPY FOR YOU!
COME WITH US.
WE CAN MAKE WHATEVER LIVES WE WANT FOR OURSELVES. NO EXPECTATIONS, NOTHING THAT DOESN'T COME NATURALLY.
THE SIMPLE LIFE, EH?
I'VE GOT MORE TO ACHIEVE, PITT, AND ON MY OWN TERMS THIS TIME.
BUT NOT HERE. I WOULDN'T EVADE CROWN TROOPS FOR LONG WITH THIS HAIR. I LEAVE FOR FRANCE TOMORROW.
YOU'RE KEEPING THE HAIR?
OF COURSE! HOW ELSE WILL FOLK RECOGNISE ME?
THANK YOU. YOUR OFFER MEANS A LOT, BUT IT'S NOT MY PATH.
I HOPE THIS HELPS YOU ON YOURS.
BE SURE TO TELL OUR STORY.
WARTS AND ALL?
WARTS AND ALL.

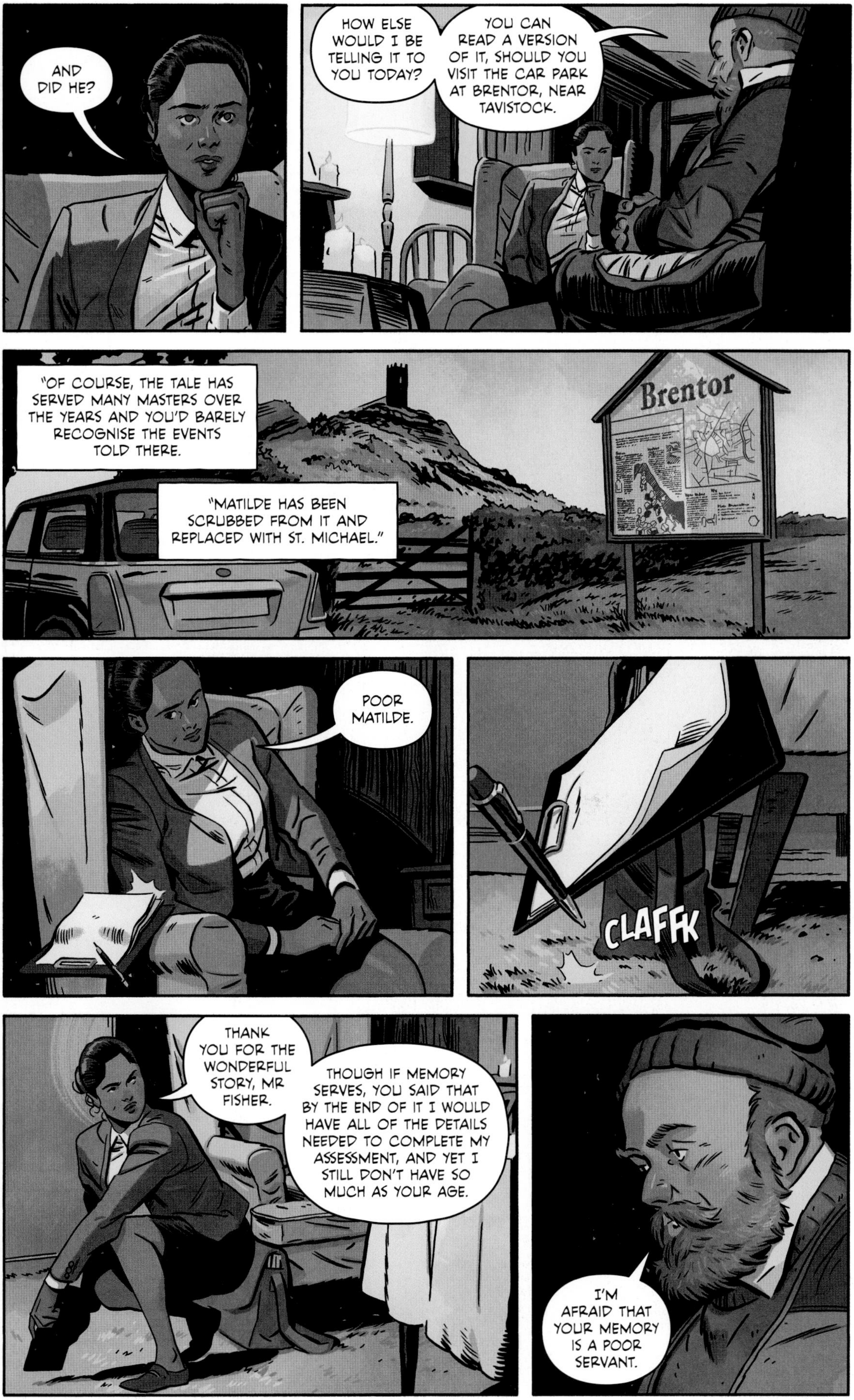
AND DID HE?
HOW ELSE WOULD I BE TELLING IT TO YOU TODAY?
YOU CAN READ A VERSION OF IT, SHOULD YOU VISIT THE CAR PARK AT BRENTOR, NEAR TAVISTOCK.
"OF COURSE, THE TALE HAS SERVED MANY MASTERS OVER THE YEARS AND YOU'D BARELY RECOGNISE THE EVENTS TOLD THERE.
Brentor
"MATILDE HAS BEEN SCRUBBED FROM IT AND REPLACED WITH ST. MICHAEL."
POOR MATILDE.
CLAFFK
THANK YOU FOR THE WONDERFUL STORY, MR FISHER.
THOUGH IF MEMORY SERVES, YOU SAID THAT BY THE END OF IT I WOULD HAVE ALL OF THE DETAILS NEEDED TO COMPLETE MY ASSESSMENT, AND YET I STILL DON'T HAVE SO MUCH AS YOUR AGE.
I'M AFRAID THAT YOUR MEMORY IS A POOR SERVANT.

HMM?

I SAID THE STORY WILL TELL YOU EVERYTHING YOU NEED TO KNOW.

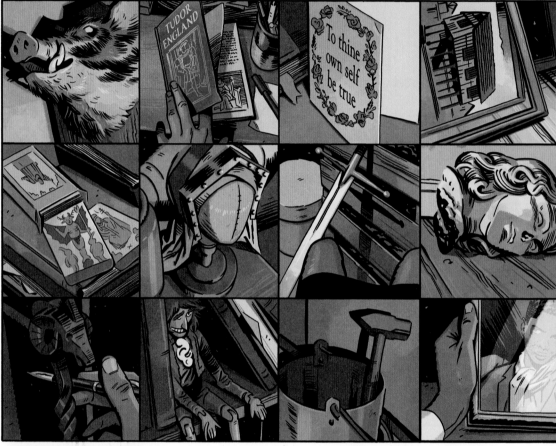

TUDOR ENGLAND

To thine own self be true

THANK YOU, MR FISHER.

I THINK I NOW UNDERSTAND WHAT THIS PLACE MEANS TO YOU.

I'LL BE SURE TO CHECK IN ON YOU SOON.

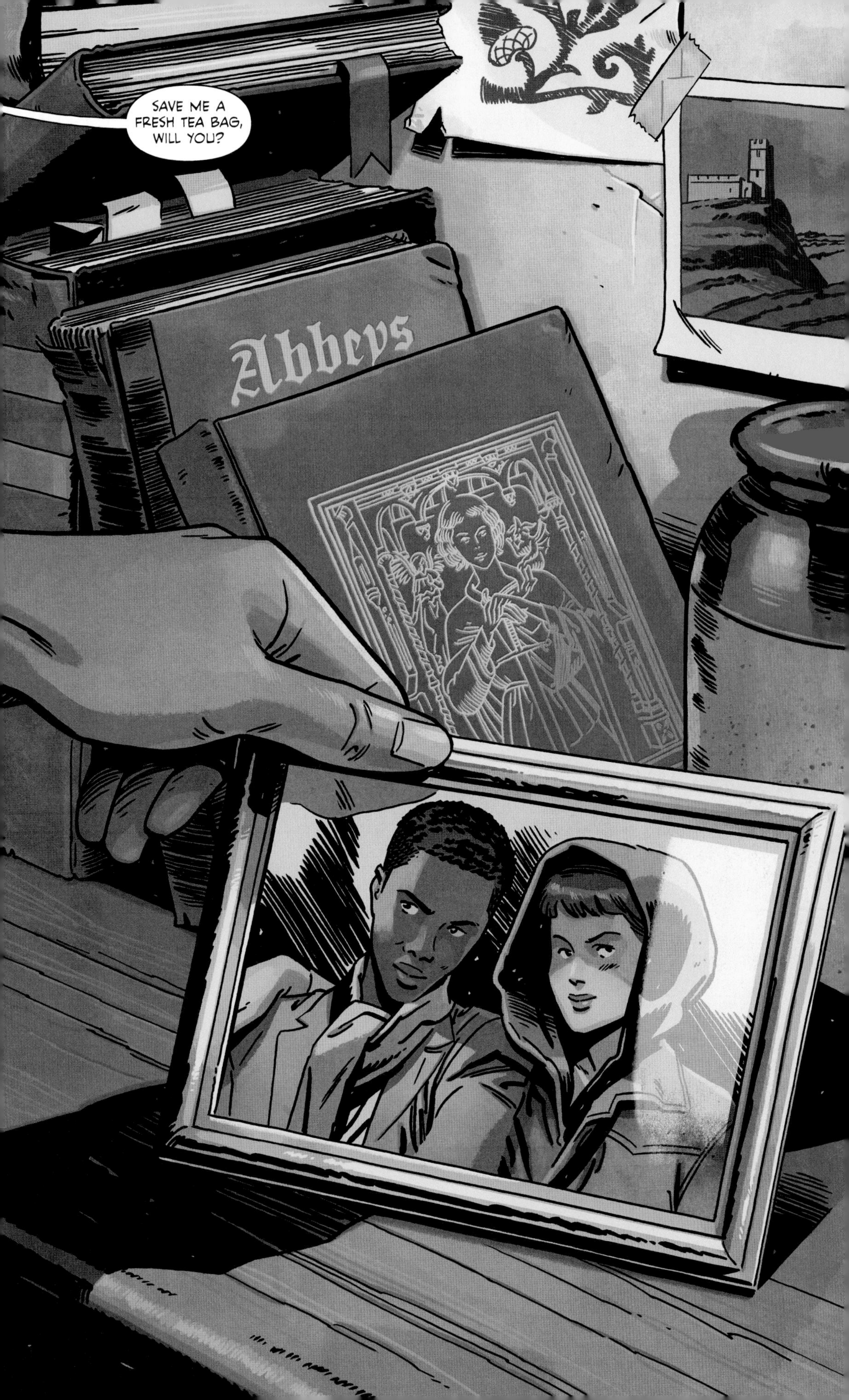
SAVE ME A FRESH TEA BAG, WILL YOU?
Abbeys

Gospel artefacts

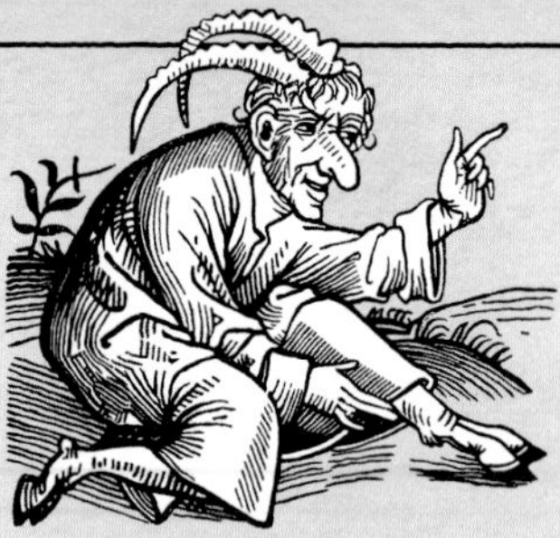

Inspired by my favourite visual guides, these pages include a handful of the ingredients that went into making *Gospel*. The impish fellow to the left is from *Treasury of Medieval Illustrations*, published by Dover Publications. A collection of royalty-free images, it is one of many books and online resources I turned to, to help *Gospel's* world feel alive.

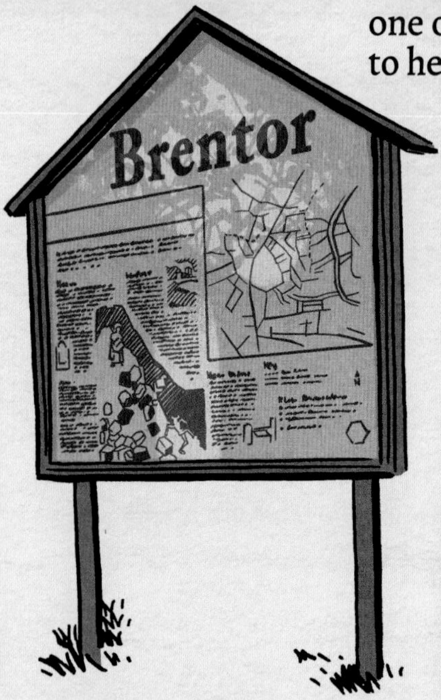
Brentor

Information board *left*
Found at the base of Brentor in Devon. The folk tale it told of St. Michael's conflict with the devil was the spark for *Gospel's* story.

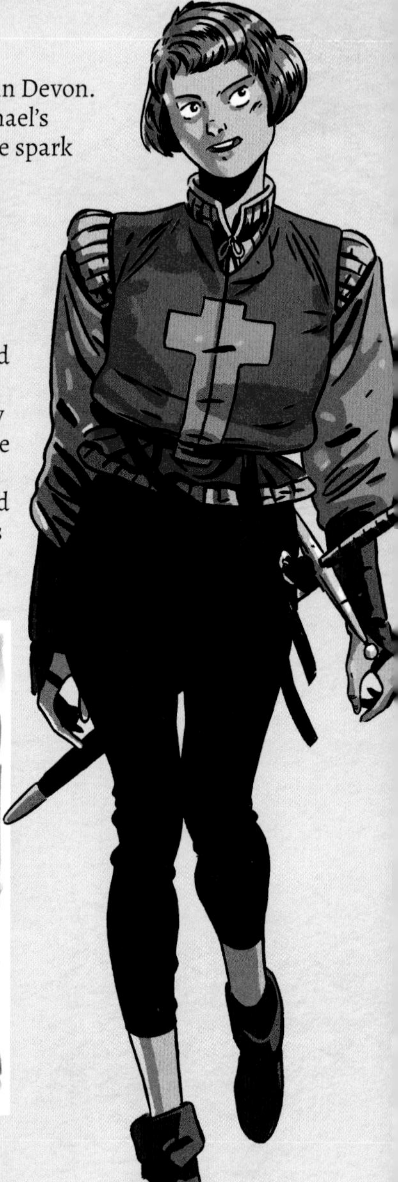

Character designs *right*
These are the first designs for Matilde and Pitt that really illustrated their individual spirits. With a boxy shape and shock of green hair, Matilde wants to project an air of easy confidence and live long in the memory. Dressed in more muted layers, Pitt is grounded and cares only that his stories do the talking.

Cover thumbnail *right*
Ver's covers captured *Gospel's* story with extraordinary beauty. The fluttering manuscript pages, which tell Matilde's stories, are a lovely narrative detail across the covers. As the story progresses those pages burn to ashes. Ver's comics and illustrations are crammed full of the richest storytelling imaginable.

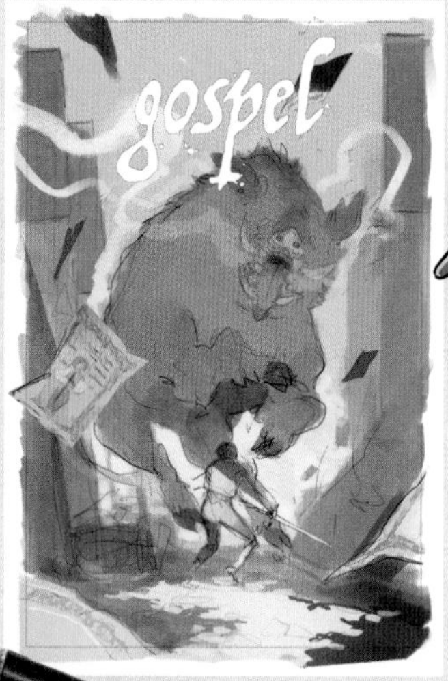
gospel

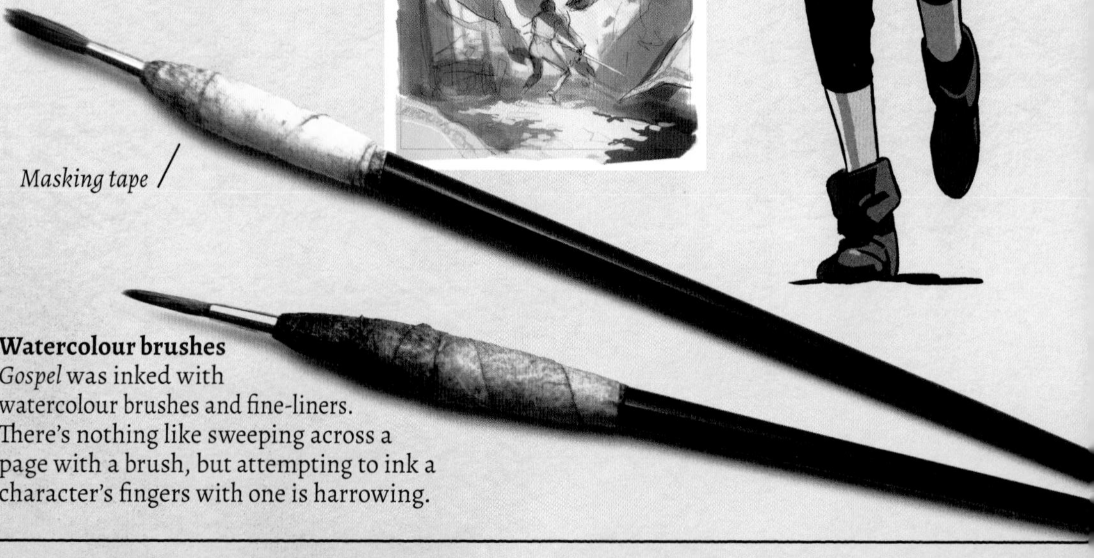

Masking tape

Watercolour brushes
Gospel was inked with watercolour brushes and fine-liners. There's nothing like sweeping across a page with a brush, but attempting to ink a character's fingers with one is harrowing.

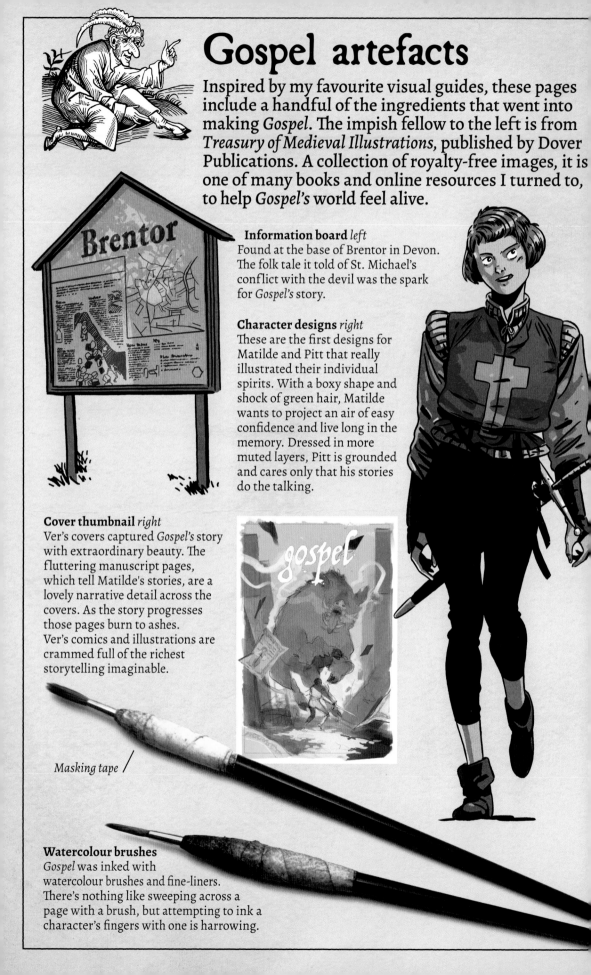

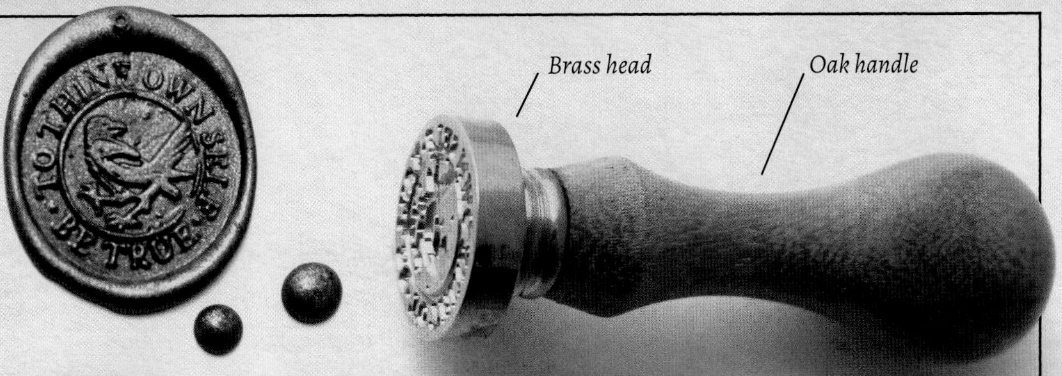
TO THINE OWN SELF BE TRUE
Brass head
Oak handle

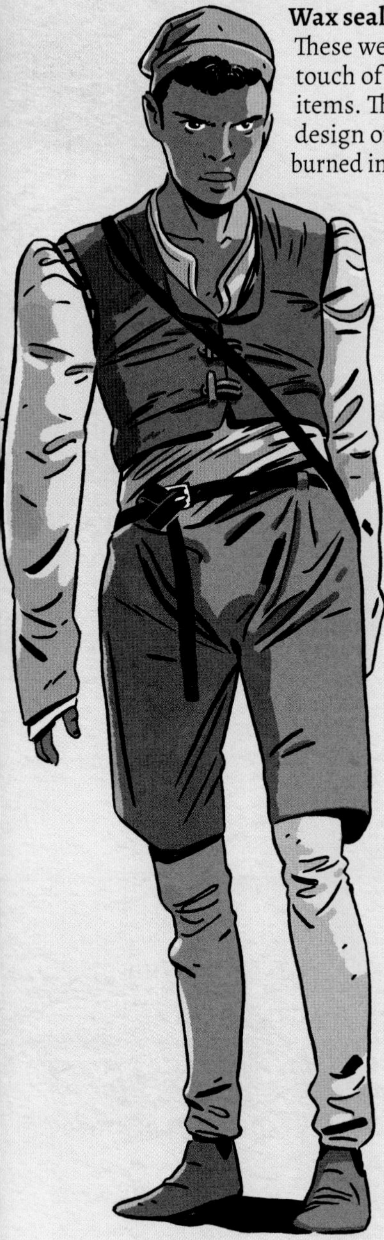

Wax seal and stamp *Above*
These were produced to help lend a touch of "authenticity" to promotional items. The stamp design replicates the design on Matilde's ring. Fingers were burned in the production of these seals!

Issue 3, page 1 - script *below*
The script was written with as much detail as I could muster. Pushing myself to visualise the specifics of the scene is a good first step in the drawing process.

PAGE 1

PANEL 1

A sun-dappled woodland path. A horse and rider trot towards the reader, their reflection rippling in a series of puddles. The rider is a rotund merchant swathed in plump, comfortable robes. He hums contently to himself.

MERCHANT
...Tiddle iddle um tum...

PANEL 2

Further along the woodland path. In the foreground, nestled in bracken, is a wiry man, swamped in layers of ochre rags. A seasoned brigand, the man masquerades as an injured traveller. He pitifully massages an ankle as the merchant approaches.

MERCHANT
...Dee di dee dum...

PANEL 3

With his free hand, the brigand reaches towards the merchant.

BRIGAND
Kind sir, help a poor man down on 'is luck.

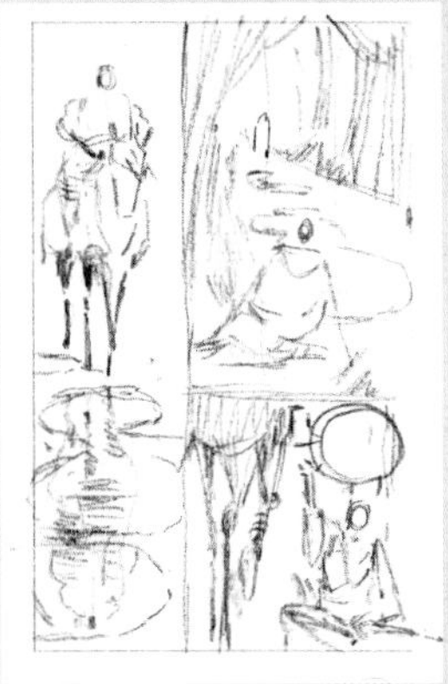

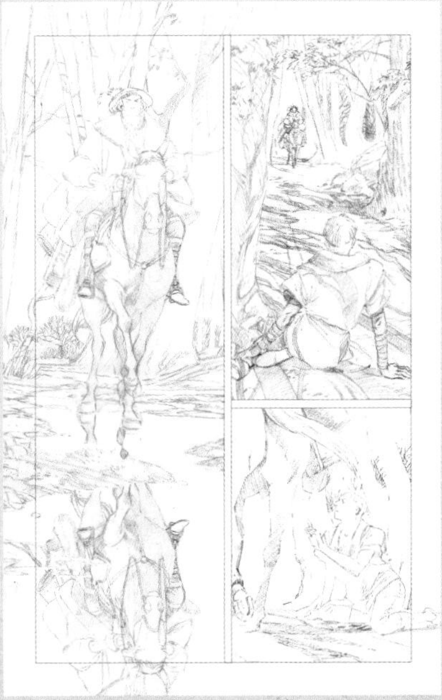

Issue 3, page 1 - thumbnail layout and pencils
I usually scrawl possible panel layouts in the margins of the script or on loose scraps of pages and then figure out the shapes of the compositions. The pencils were drawn traditionally. I use different colours to help distinguish elements of the panel - all those lines can get very busy!

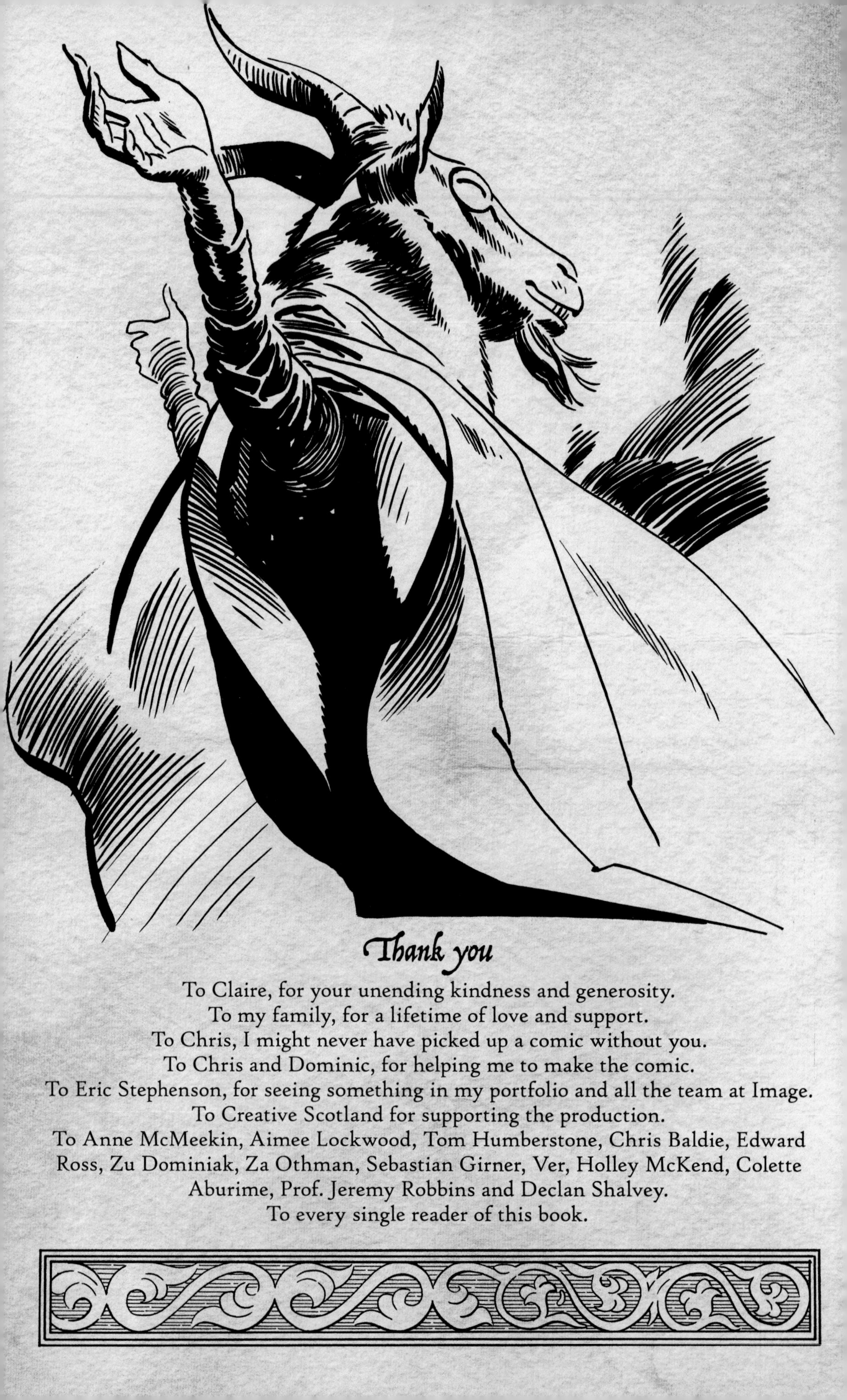

Thank you

To Claire, for your unending kindness and generosity.
To my family, for a lifetime of love and support.
To Chris, I might never have picked up a comic without you.
To Chris and Dominic, for helping me to make the comic.
To Eric Stephenson, for seeing something in my portfolio and all the team at Image.
To Creative Scotland for supporting the production.
To Anne McMeekin, Aimee Lockwood, Tom Humberstone, Chris Baldie, Edward Ross, Zu Dominiak, Za Othman, Sebastian Girner, Ver, Holley McKend, Colette Aburime, Prof. Jeremy Robbins and Declan Shalvey.
To every single reader of this book.